Amar
Akbar
Anthony

Amar
Akbar
Anthony

•

BOLLYWOOD, BROTHERHOOD, AND THE NATION

•

William Elison
Christian Lee Novetzke
Andy Rotman

▮▮▮

Harvard University Press

Cambridge, Massachusetts
London, England
2016

Film stills reproduced from *Amar Akbar Anthony* (1977), directed and produced by
Manmohan Desai. Hirawat Jain & Co. / MKD Films / Manmohan Films.

Promotional posters in the Introduction and Appendix for Manmohan Desai's
Amar Akbar Anthony (1977). Hirawat Jain & Co. / MKD Films / Manmohan Films.
Reproduced from the collection of Andy Rotman.

Library of Congress Cataloging-in-Publication Data
is available from the Library of Congress.

ISBN 978-0-674-50448-6 (hardcover)

To Amar, Akbar, and Anthony
Long live their brotherhood

Contents

Introduction: Outright Hokum *1*

1. Amar: Straight Shooter *36*

2. Akbar: *Parda* and Parody *74*

3. Anthony: Amar Akbar Irony *115*

4. *Maa—!* *150*

Conclusion: Excuse Me, Please *199*

Appendix: Film Synopsis *207*

Notes *253*

Bibliography *301*

Acknowledgments *315*

Index *319*

Amar
Akbar
Anthony

Introduction

OUTRIGHT HOKUM

. . . .

T HE YEAR 1977 was a tumultuous one in India. The state of emergency that Prime Minister Indira Gandhi had declared in 1975, allowing her to rule by decree, at last came to an end. During those twenty-one months of autocratic rule, the government's attempts to enforce order led to many excesses: political opponents were imprisoned, the press was censored, and civil liberties were curtailed. When Mrs. Gandhi finally called for elections, the political opposition joined forces to mount a campaign on the theme of "democracy versus dictatorship." The elections delivered Mrs. Gandhi a resounding loss and brought in the first non–Congress Party government since Independence. The mood of the times was mixed. There was a renewed feeling of hope, but also pent-up frustration and resentment.

Going to the movies gave the nation a way to escape from this troubled reality. Or did it? A bumper crop of films that year dealt with themes of alienation and integration: families broke apart and were reunited, highlighting the plight of the disenfranchised as well as the possibility of the nation coming together as a kind of happy family. These twin experiences were present not only in the content of films but also in the experience of watching them. Movie theaters, like the world outside them, were stratified, with the more moneyed customers—the "classes"— up in the balcony and the "masses" close to the screen, so that the former literally looked down and past those in the cheaper seats. Yet moviegoing was also a bonding experience, with most viewers watching films with family or friends. Even a solitary viewer was likely to connect with others, singing along with a hit song or chatting over a snack during intermission.[1] It was a moment for feelings of estrangement and belonging. And there was no place better to find both than in Manmohan Desai's hit film the biggest blockbuster of the year.

Amar Akbar Anthony was the year's top-grossing film (Figure 1), but its box office success was only the beginning. It became the talk of the town—and the village. It won awards, catapulted careers, and quickly became a classic. The film introduced India to three brothers from a rough neighborhood of Bombay, separated as children from their parents and one another and adopted into different religious communities: Hindu, Muslim, and Christian. The tale of how they discover their kinship and rally against the forces of discord to redeem their long-lost parents took viewers on a madcap, musical romp. At the same time, the story's course ran along a cultural topography strewn with anxieties about religious pluralism, gender, and modernity. And something about this hot mix hit the sweet spot, back then and so on to this day. *Amar Akbar Anthony* perfected the formula known as *masala,* a blend of generic elements combining music, comedy, melodrama, and morality play. Many of its songs, star-images, and sequences have come to circulate as icons for Bollywood as a whole. There was, in a sense, nothing original about the film; Manmohan Desai, its director and producer, publicly disavowed any interest in originality. Instead, Desai and his team borrowed merrily and promiscuously from sources in the literatures, religions, and folk traditions of South Asia, and from cinemas both Indian and Western. And in a phenomenon comparable to the recycling of mythological tropes in epic traditions the world over, *Amar Akbar Anthony* has come into its own as a sort of supertext. It may not be the *Mahabharata* but it has taken its place at the center of India's popular imaginary.[2]

Since its release—to near-unanimous critical despair, as we'll discuss shortly—*Amar Akbar Anthony* has become recognized in its importance by industry professionals, Bollywood fans, music lovers, pop culture mavens, and at least some academics.[3] Its broad and enduring appeal across the subcontinent and beyond has cemented its place as a cinematic milestone and a cultural touchstone.[4] Richly symbolic, the film can be read

FIGURE 1. Poster for *Amar Akbar Anthony*

as a multivalent allegory encompassing the nation, the state, civil society, and the feel-good ideology of pluralist "secularism"—and simultaneously enjoyed as three hours of sheer entertainment.

Ambiguity and critical dispute are evident in the academic writing on the film, in which we find a multiplicity of interpretations of its message. Vijay Mishra describes the film as one that "confirms the resilience of the secular nation-state [of India]."[5] Jyotika Virdi reads the film as "a testimonial . . . to the limits of Nehruvian secular nationalism" because, in her account, the brothers remain with women "of their own community," and this becomes a model in Indian cinema for a kind of "communal fraternizing."[6] Rachel Dwyer understands *Amar Akbar Anthony* as "a film about a Partition separation" that "is now a byword in religious plurality."[7] And Philip Lutgendorf describes how the film signals "(in properly descending demographic order) the Hindu, Muslim, and Christian communities['] . . . essential unity and harmony—within the copious bosom of a (visibly Hindu) Mother India."[8] What to do with such a multivalent text?

In this book we will argue that *Amar Akbar Anthony*—too easily discounted as a cheesy and cumbersome 1970s artifact—has risen to a stature well above its movie peers, and indeed now transcends its history, in large part because it serves as a multivalent metaphor. It is metonymic of religious pluralism, the nuclear family, the slum neighborhood, the state's ambiguous commitment to the principle of secularism, and so on, all the while inviting critique of these aspects of Indian society. While *Amar Akbar Anthony* is conventionally read in India as a film about national integration—and we don't altogether controvert this position—our argument will make room for the opposite reading as well. This is a comedy built of tragic elements: the venality and irresponsibility of the political class, the perceived backwardness of the masses, the compromised character of civil society, the limited compass of the state, and the vexed implications of secularism.

Amar Akbar Anthony is filled with contestation and even confusion, in which the logical and the illogical are in harmony. The film's three eponymous brothers find plenty to butt heads over, challenging one another at numerous points as they assert their identities. Yet in the end they find unity in their diversity and become, as one brother says late in the movie, "three in one." Our book takes this as inspiration and employs a methodology of sibling rivalry, offering differing and competing perspectives to create a kind of oneness—or three-in-oneness. For a cinematic corollary, think of Akira Kurosawa's *Rashomon* (1950), in which various characters offer self-serving and contradictory accounts of the same event, showing that reality is made up of multiple realities. One story is never the full story.

Chapters 1, 2, and 3 each present the perspective of one brother, and this perspectival approach defines the whole chapter's analytic focus.

As with their celluloid counterparts, these brothers of the printed page do not agree. Between and among our chapters the reader will find naked contradiction. An argument in Chapter 1 may be met with an antithetical argument in Chapters 2 and 3. Indeed, each is argued on the premise that the brother named at the chapter's beginning is the hero of the whole movie; each chapter, as such, is a hero's tale. Chapter 4, on Bharati, lets the three would-be victors offer competing perspectives on their mother, and then gives Maa herself the final say. We have made no effort to declare a winner or to mediate these multiple positions. This is not a book with a single cohesive argument; it is, we hope, a book with many cohesive arguments that also happen to be contradictory.

Some readers may find this lack of a central authoritative perspective vexing. To help understand our approach, consider the oft-told Indian fable of the blind men and the elephant. Imagine that three blind men (scholars, in fact) happen to encounter an elephant. One of the men feels the elephant's trunk and says it is a snake; another feels its legs and says it is a tree; a third feels its belly and says it is a wall. "Snake!" "Tree!" "Wall!" each exclaims, certain of what he perceives. The men talk, listen, and argue, and eventually figure out that they are all describing an elephant. What we like about this allegory is not that the blind men finally figure out they have encountered an elephant. What we like is that they find the elephant also to be a snake, a tree, and a wall.[9] They come to know they have an elephant before them, but they also have a deeper appreciation of the nature of the elephant, of its parts and the whole and the tensions among them. Blindness can lead to forms of insight, even if it precludes the possibility of a unified vision. Maa exemplifies this path to insight in the film; we try to do the same in our analysis.

We three authors approach *Amar Akbar Anthony* wearing selective blinders of our own, examining bits, pieces, and structure from one perspective and then another. Our goal is not to see the whole elephant—that is, to provide a cohesive, noncontradictory, synthetic analysis—but to see what happens when this elephantine opus is perceived through its parts. The reader, therefore, should expect contention and dissent. It's all in our script. Our aim is for the reader to finish this book with the feeling that the elephant is also a tree. And why not? If all elephants were always and only *just elephants,* what kind of fun would that be?

To make this book's multiple arguments more accessible, we have provided a detailed synopsis of the movie in the Appendix. We encourage
those of you who have never seen the film or who would enjoy a refresher
course in its plots, subplots, and counterplots to read the synopsis before
engaging with the body of the book. And we invite all our readers—
newbies and diehard fans alike—to check the back of the book each time
you come across something knotty or loopy in our arguments that could
use some straightening out. Think of the synopsis as a kind of guide—a
blind person's cane or perhaps an *ankus,* an elephant driver's hook.

The Unoriginal, Unreasonable, Unrealistic Blockbuster

When *Amar Akbar Anthony* was released, film critics mostly hated it, bemoaning its regurgitated plot points and loose logic. Following the usual
review style of the period, reviewers would summarize the film and then
recount particularly good or goofy portions in more detail, such as the
extended prologue, Anthony's drunken scene, and the Sai Baba miracle.

Film World was unimpressed by *Amar Akbar Anthony* and called the
film a "blow to prestige," suggesting that the film degraded the reputation of all those involved, Desai most of all. The magazine savaged the
film, saying that Desai's work was "stale . . . his film is a conglomeration of hackneyed situations, cliché-ridden dialogue and stereotyped
performances. . . . All that one has seen in mediocre films of the past
nauseatingly reappear." It awarded the film its lowest rating, a "poor"
for the hapless brothers.[10] The *Times of India,* referring to the Sai Baba
miracle scene, suggested that "the story needed more than a minor miracle by a saint to be retrieved from the utter shambles it was in right
after the opening sequences."[11] The *Deccan Herald* was a bit gentler,
calling the film "a hilarious entertainer packed with volatile characters
indulging in heroics bordering at times on horseplay"; nevertheless, it is
"woven with implausible situations and unrealistic characters who with
their superhuman behavior hurt the viewers' credibility rather than appeal to their human sentiments."[12]

In her review in *Filmfare,* titled, in a quirky mix of metaphors, "Amar
Akbar Anthony: Birds of the Same Blood Group," Shalini Pradhan assesses the story as "banal as ever."[13] After describing a few choice scenes,

she concludes that "such absurdities make *Amar Akbar Anthony* look like one of those movies which intends to be funny and fools you into believing it has succeeded in being so." How a film can *fool* one into thinking it is funny without actually being funny is a feat that Pradhan doesn't explain; in any case, she gave the film one lonely star out of five. *Dream Star* begins its review with the same disdainful tone—"*Amar Akbar Anthony* is an old wine presented in a new bottle!"—and likewise remarks that "the story is quite similar to *Dharam Veer, Chacha Bhatija*"—two of Desai's other films also released in 1977—"plus hundreds of previously screened films."[14] It then piles on the complaints by noting that "the three leading ladies . . . are completely wasted in the film." The review nevertheless goes on to praise the film—"the songs of the film are good and the picturisation is very good"—and then gives the film its highest rating, an "excellent."

Filmfare and *Dream Star* offer reviews that have nearly identical content, bemoaning the same hackneyed plots and tropes, yet the ratings they give the film are exact opposites: a "one star" and an "excellent." The crux of the difference between the reviews is a question of genre. *Filmfare* judges the film within the constraints of a kind of rarified "cinema" and hence is annoyed at "the inanities in the script" and "the usual twists to stretch the film to its prescribed length." But *Dream Star* evaluates the film as a "commercial entertainer," recognizing this as a category with its own rules and aesthetics, and that within those constraints it excels. It is an "out and out commercial entertainer with no hold barred," which for other films would have been no praise at all. The contrast reveals a cultural bifurcation: critics were confronted with a new beast and weren't sure what to make of it.[15]

Pradhan's review of *Amar Akbar Anthony* in *Filmfare* was an ironic harbinger of its reception at the annual *Filmfare* awards. Despite being panned in *Filmfare* itself, the film earned seven nominations and went on to bag three awards, for Best Actor (Bachchan), Best Music Director (Laxmikant and Pyarelal), and Best Editing (Karkhanis),[16] the latter of whom (more irony here) Pradhan had impeached by stating that the film didn't look as if it had "ever [been] sent to the editing table." The film would also go on to win other accolades, earning a silver jubilee in nine theaters in Bombay, the first film ever to do so, and then earning golden and platinum jubilees as well.[17] It was also the first full-length color film from India to be shown on British television, with a BBC broadcast in October 1980.[18] Whatever misgivings the critics might have had, *Amar Akbar Anthony* was a certified blockbuster.

The critical opprobrium shown *Amar Akbar Anthony* was leavened with some relief at its commercial success. There had been a sharp decline in India's economic growth rate in the mid-1970s,[19] and critics joined filmmakers in bemoaning the slump that the Bombay film industry had likewise fallen into. But Desai's films, and *Amar Akbar Anthony* in particular, promised what seemed to some to be a panacea. *Blitz* makes the point boldly: "With three bumper hits in a row, Manmohan Desai is being hailed as a messiah who saved the industry from financial debacle."[20] The *Goa Herald* concurs that "with the release of *Amar Akbar Anthony,* Manmohan Desai is considered to be the man with the Midas touch, [who] has scored a hat-trick."[21] There seemed, however, to be an inverse relationship between the film's blockbuster status and its critical reception. *Film World,* for example, addresses questions of prestige: "With this film, Desai's pockets may jingle with the sound of coins but his prestige will not be enhanced."[22] *Filmfare* likewise concludes that the story is padded with "comedy, fights, song and dance situations [so] the director is able to provide to make it a paying proposition."[23]

Still, the reviewers seem to have reserved a special ire for the film's uncouth and unrealistic sensibilities, which gestured to the fact that this was not a film for English-speaking metropolitan India, or its English-medium film critics. It was for another audience entirely. The distinction is clear in the review in the *Goa Herald,* which explains that *Amar Akbar Anthony* is "predominantly escapist fare for the masses" and that it is "heaped with all the ingredients that whet the appetite of the masses . . . a huge star cast, action which will make even the superheroes look like pygmies, and the usual quota of film songs, which go under the name of music."[24] As if the writer had not made this point strongly enough, the review concludes that the film "is a giant-sized escapist fare which the masses may find a lot to rave about." These "masses" apparently enjoy the hackneyed, absurd, and superhuman, set to a mediocre soundtrack.

Some sense of *Amar Akbar Anthony*'s appeal to the so-called masses can be discerned from a curious newspaper article that recounts the findings of a team of middle-class student researchers who, at the prompting of their professor of mass communications in Bombay, interviewed "peons" and other representatives of the subordinate classes to gain the "experience of talking to people [that they would not normally encounter] about issues they don't know."[25] The professor does not explain why he or she sent those students out to ask about *Amar Akbar Anthony,* but the previously cited reviews give some notion that *Amar Akbar Anthony* was the film that the masses massed around that year. When asked if the "scenarios" of the film were "unrealistic," the subjects would almost unanimously dissent. "It wasn't at all unrealistic that such things could happen. They were God-fearing people, they said, and God could do anything."

One student brought her questions to a village in Maharashtra to solicit rural opinion. A Hindu milkman was asked if the mother could regain her vision in real life, to which this particular representative of the masses answered yes, citing the power of deities in his own life. The milkman was also asked if he could do as Amar did and marry a "girl of bad reputation." He responded that he could not. The mass communications student persisted, asking if the milkman "sympathized with Salma or Tayyab Ali," a question he evaded rather cleverly by saying he sided with Akbar, who was, after all, "the hero." When asked, "Would you in your personal life then allow your sister or daughter to marry the man she loved?" the milkman appeared horrified at the very thought, exclaiming, "Certainly not! Girls have no right to choose their husbands." Thus the masses and their proclivities are neatly telegraphed: apparently, they are blindly religious and dogmatically sexist!

The primary audience of *Amar Akbar Anthony* is characterized as a superstitious swath of lumpen humanity, suggesting that the film itself is a crass example of market capitalism, aimed at exploiting average Indians and their unrefined tastes. Bikram Singh, in one of the first reviews of *Amar Akbar Anthony,* describes the film as "absurd but funny. . . . Logic is on leave and the story is not really intended to be taken seriously. . . . Outright hokum is what the film is."[26] The question of what constitutes filmic logic, or how to evaluate its rules of textual organization, is not raised. It appears we are simply to assume that *Amar Akbar Anthony* is at fault for not complying, for being "outright hokum."[27] Still, Singh understands that although there is a lack of logic in its realistic mode, there remains a kind of logic of absurdity. After describing the opening sequence depicting a collective blood transfusion, Singh notes that "you can't find irony of such poignant proportions anywhere—except of course in Hindi films."[28] What the critical reception suggests is that there are two logics in operation: one level is there to engage the savvy critic—a logic of irony—and the other level is there for the God-fearing masses—a logic of morality.

Critical Mass: The Maturing of the *Masala* Film

Sorting through the debates that surrounded *Amar Akbar Anthony,* one can chart the genesis of a new genre. At the time, however, critics were unaware that they were witnessing something new in Indian film, focusing as they did on the movie's collection of tropes and not on the creative way they were deployed. They tended to place the film in relation to three established categories: (1) the "multi-starrer," a kind of production associated largely with Manmohan Desai himself, in which more than one star or hero-heroine combination heads up the cast; (2) the "lost and found," a narrative theme in which children are separated at birth and reunited, usually coming together to defeat a common foe who is often also the cause of their original separation; and (3) the "social," a broad category of film that before the 1960s had stood in contrast to other genres, such as the mythological, but by the 1970s had come to refer to the bulk of popular Hindi cinema—stories organized around some contemporary social issue.[29]

As a "multi-starrer," *Amar Akbar Anthony* was loaded with talent (Figure 2). A film stuffed with three brothers necessitated three heroines, and the addition to this sextet of Nirupa Roy, Pran, and Jeevan in key supporting roles populated the film with nine prominent actors. The rationale for the multi-starrer is simple: maximize the loyalty of a large number of fans by offering a large ensemble of popular heroes and heroines. In "Future of Multi-Starrers: Amar-Akbar-Anthony—A Test Case!" Harish Kumar Mehra lays out an etiology of the form: "There was a time when stars were part of a story. And then came the time when stars became a substitute for a story. This craze culminated in a craze for multi-starrers. *Sholay* and *Dharam Veer* set the pattern for multi-starrers in

FIGURE 2. Poster with ensemble cast

recent times and the biggest of them [all is] *Amar Akbar Anthony*."[30] So why is the film a success? Mehra tells us: "The reason is simple: three of India's top leading men and their leading ladies make three adorable couples." As the three brothers sing in the last song in the film, "Better than one is two . . . better than two is three." And better still is nine!

The "lost and found" theme was a hallmark of Desai's films, especially of his 1977 releases. *Dream Star* notes that "the story is the usual separation of the father, mother and the three sons."[31] Shalini Pradhan in *Filmfare* makes the point more fiercely: "*Amar Akbar Anthony* coming so close on the heels of *Dharam Veer* and *Chacha Bhatija* makes it look like director Manmohan Desai has purchased the sole right to all stories concerning brothers who get separated from each other and their parents in childhood."[32] Another review notes that the film "carries the long lost brother story up its logical ladder of development. . . . Instead of . . . two brothers . . . this film has three youngsters finding their relations again," but this review also notes the "twist" that "the three have been reared by people of different faiths."[33] By 1977, it was news to nobody that the basic storyline was a cliché. But as his string of hits that year indicated, behind Desai's apparent fixation there was a method at work.

When it came to evaluating *Amar Akbar Anthony* as a "social" film, the reviewers were largely dismissive. They identified the social impetus of the film to be some combination of communal harmony, national integration, and secularism, although in this regard they found the film ambiguous if not opaque. As one critic explained, "It appears that in his own subtle way, filmmaker Manmohan Desai is teaching a desired lesson in communal harmony. A very laudable purpose."[34] But possibly Desai was being a little too subtle, or maybe his purpose just remained unfulfilled. In a review entitled "Cinema: Of Saints and Sinners," the *Times of India* suggested that "the film apparently seeks to promote national integration," although it fails at the task, "but we won't take up that because it is the least of the problems in the film which seems to go on forever."[35] The *Indian Express,* in a review entitled " 'The Three Musketeers' with a Planned Destiny," claims that the film "has little to do with national integration," for everything in the film happens "as usual," such that "their destiny is . . . planned."[36] An exasperated man from Bombay reiterated this sentiment in a letter to the editor: "One expects to see mutual coexistence of different religious communities and a sense of oneness contributing to national integration. But one finds nothing of this in the film."[37] This concerned citizen then goes on to offer a familiar critique: "These films are far from reality. A dominant section of the youth, who form more than 60% of the total population and rural people"—the masses, we think he means—"fall easy prey to these films and they try to imitate the 'filmi duniya' [film world] in their real lives."[38]

Only one review surveys the film on the basis of its national integration theme. In a "Tailpiece" section of the *Indian Express,* we find a review entitled "Secularism—'Filmi' Style," which concludes by suggesting that the film seeks to assuage the feelings of Muslims without upsetting the sentiments of the Hindu majority: "Muslims . . . form a major section of Hindi film audiences, script and song-writers . . . so they have to be kept happy . . . which is the only reason why movies like . . . *Amar Akbar Anthony* are made."[39] Yet the reviewer is also aware that because "the only 'normal' person is the Hindu cop," the film's stereotypes of Christians and Muslims may still cause offense. Indeed, the reviewer appears unsure by the end of the review if the film isn't actually meant to be anti-secular. Trapped by the twists and turns of the plot (and one can be forgiven for being so trapped), the reviewer resolves that "the only good thing about movies like *Amar Akbar Anthony* . . . is that they have brought down the debate on secularism from the intellectual ivory towers to the paan shop."[40] In the end, why *Amar Akbar Anthony* worked as a movie, and what message or politics it promoted, seemed more than a little mysterious to critics. But at least no one was excluded from the conversation. (And to be sure, the film was, and is, an excellent conversation starter—another one of the reasons we like it so much.)

In fact, read together from the vantage of the present, *Amar Akbar Anthony*'s reviews tell a remarkably coherent story. At a time when the Bombay film industry was in a shambles, Manmohan Desai was serving up what seemed to be more of the same, with the emphasis on *more*—he took old tropes and genre elements and piled them higher and deeper. But to the critics' disbelief, his films turned out to be blockbusters. The plots were recycled from other stories or films, the logic that connected the plot points was fuzzy, the scenarios were unrealistic, stars and spectacles took precedence over narrative cohesion, and sentimentality and low humor reigned, and yet there was something special about this mélange—something thrilling and, yes, social—that appealed to the masses.

Desai had found a way to cater a crowd-pleasing spread with prepackaged ingredients. To draw on an image that was just coming into its own in the Bombay industry of the 1970s, he had emerged as a man for all seasonings, an expert in "'blending the *masalas* in proper proportions' . . . to achieve an overall balance of 'flavours.'"[41] Indeed, the *masala* metaphor came up frequently in the film's reviews. The *Goa Herald* called it "heaped with ingredients."[42] Abbreviating the director's name tabloid-style, *Blitz* described the film as "Man's Master-Blend." The director "salts and peppers the narrative and Manmohan has blended it with the right dose of emotion, sentiments, fights, romance, songs, comedy and what not. . . . The entire drama . . . is . . . taken with a pinch of salt."[43] *Film World* referred to the film as a "pot-boiler [made] without omitting any of the formulas, recipes and *masalas*."[44]

For several years prior to the release of *Amar Akbar Anthony,* the film industry had been using the term *masala* to describe an approach to filmmaking that mixed together various flavors (be they moods, issues, tropes, or spectacles). The goal of these experiments was to create a film that would be comforting yet diverting—spiced to perfection—and thus appeal to the widest possible audience. With *Amar Akbar Anthony,* the critics' moans of "stale," "hackneyed," "cliché-ridden," and so on, were an indication that the medley of *masalas* had turned into a blend—a successful formula for filmmaking. Just as with *garam masala,* that other spicy mixture that at one time had been prepared individually and eclectically to taste,[45] the *masala* film was becoming stabilized into a named and all but trademarked commodity—the *masala* film™. While some may argue that the very concept of the *masala* film is based on the negation of genre by mixture, our position is that *Amar Akbar Anthony* catalyzes *masala* as formula: it is not a genre-breaking film but a genre-*making* film.

Manmohan Desai was the man who mastered the formula. And *Amar Akbar Anthony*—the first film he produced as well as directed and the most successful of his quartet of 1977 hits—was the "master blend" that branded the mix: Manmohan Desai's *masala* film®. M. K. Raghavendra, in *50 Indian Film Classics,* explains that *"Amar Akbar Anthony* has been described as the ultimate 'formula' film, but if it is based on a ready-made recipe, its creator never came near to repeating its success."[46] But more to the point, if it is based on a ready-made recipe, how is it that the film, to quote the same author, "uses elements from a multitude of familiar stories and puts them together in a bizarre and seemingly arbitrary way"?[47] Recipes aren't bizarre and arbitrary; they're conventional and ordered.

To the extent that the *masala* film represents a spicy yet stable amalgam of previously established codes and conventions, it can be thought of as a sort of supergenre. Films like *Amar Akbar Anthony* mark not so much a break with the Hindi cinema of the preceding decades—the so-called Golden Age—as a wholesale takeover and consolidation of genres that had become exhausted (or, in film-industry terms, "bankrupt"). Critical opinion, as we have seen, decried the new style for its vulgarity and incoherence. But it is the *masala* movie that propelled the revival of the Bombay film industry, and it is the *masala* movie that led to the birth of Bollywood, today's global media behemoth. Could it be said, then, that *Amar Akbar Anthony* is the first Bollywood film?

We tackle this question at our peril, since we would have to establish what is meant by *Bollywood* in the first place, and if there is one thing about the term that can be said for certain it's that it marks the site of intense debate. Is it (for example) a placeholder, an ahistorical and essentializing designation, a culture industry distinct from cinema, or a moment of transformation in the Hindi film industry?[48] Whatever it is, we wouldn't want to essentialize and reduce it to the *masala* genre; *masala* and Bollywood are not one and the same, although one sometimes finds that kind of reductionism.[49] Nevertheless, considering that no one has yet identified the first sighting of this cinematic creature, or perhaps cinematic chimera, we think *Amar Akbar Anthony* makes an excellent contender.

The term *Bollywood*—that portmanteau of *Bombay* and *Hollywood*—has its own mythic history, with some claiming a pedigree that stretches back to the 1930s,[50] but the first citations of the term coincide, in fact, with the making of *Amar Akbar Anthony*. The *Oxford English Dictionary* attributes the first use of the term in print to H. R. F. Keating, an English crime writer, citing a passage from his novel *Filmi, Filmi, Inspector Ghote,* first published in 1976. While investigating a murder at a film studio, Ghote interviews Bombay's premier gossip columnist, Miss Pilloo Officewala, who explains that her revelation about a certain starlet "was the greatest sensation ever to come out of Bollywood." When Ghote expresses bewilderment at the term, Miss Officewala is "totally scandalized" at his ignorance. " 'Do you not read at all, Inspector?' she demanded. 'The Bombay film set-up is called Bollywood in simply every film magazine. I had thought that Crime Branch C.I.D. were at least educated.' "[51]

Keating, in response to a query on his website, offered this genealogy of the term:

> I certainly do not think I invented the term Bollywood: I would not have dared. When I came to write *Filmi, Filmi, Inspector Ghote* . . . it was after I had been treated most generously by the Indian film industry, touring the studios and meeting the people involved there, but the industry was already saddled with the, opprobrious if you like, but possibly affectionate, name, Bollywood. Possibly emanating from the Bombay, as they were then, gossip journalists. Bevinda Collaco says she invented it in 1976/77 [when she was a gossip columnist for *Cineblitz*] but to fit my writing of the book and its publication date she may have had to coin it before that date. I may have helped to perpetuate the name but I make no claim to its invention.[52]

The film scholar Tejaswani Ganti offers a similar assessment: "The way 'Bollywood' appears in [Keating's] novel references my more common understandings of the origin of the term: that it was coined by the English-language film magazines and fanzines like *Stardust* to refer to the Hindi film world in a tongue-in-cheek manner."[53] *Bollywood*, it seems, was a witticism for the kind of film drama, on and off the screen, that inspired gossipmongers like Miss Officewala and Miss Collaco. Could it be that the term finally left the realm of English-language tabloids and entered the mainstream lexicon when the right film made it stick? Could it be that *Amar Akbar Anthony* was that film, with its potent mix of stars and starlets, passion and intrigue, fun and fantasy, which the press in Bombay loved to hate but which put the term on everyone's lips? Our answer: Well, maybe.

Amar Akbar Anthony certainly has many of the hallmarks of a Bollywood film. For however much disagreement there is over what those hallmarks are, and however much they may have changed over the decades, we can still plot some coordinates. Bollywood films are almost always made in Hindi—generally in a simplified idiom to facilitate understanding, but spiced as needed with dashes of specialized argots, such as Bombay street Hindi and Lucknowi Urdu. They are examples of popular cinema as opposed to avant-garde or "parallel" cinema—commercial products first and artistic statements second. They are set within the cultural domain of the Bombay film industry—a global nexus of symbolic and libidinal power that stands in rivalry to Hollywood. They integrate musical numbers within plots that appear to combine elements of different genres—action, drama, thriller, comedy. They are often animated by the struggle to reconcile "traditional" norms with "modern" aspirations. They are star driven, with the "multi-starrer" a typical format. They contain love stories fueled by heroic journeys laden with metaphor,[54] and the allegorical terrain of these quests is often (as many scholars concur) "the nation."[55] And they tend to last about three hours, with a complex matrix of subplots, digressions, and even "interruptions,"[56] creating a particular form of melodrama with an emphasis on formulaic plots and heightened emotion.[57] All these features are assembled in such a way as to make parts of the whole transposable to other media, such as cassettes, radio, and poster art, as well as the more recent websites, ringtones, screen savers, and so on. And a final item for a list that could easily go on and on: in its open citation of Hollywood films, its embrace of formula, and its prodigious cinematic reprocessing, no matter what it is that *Bollywood* connotes it is apparently always derivative of something else. As M. Madhava Prasad ponders, "Is this a name that incorporates a criticism?"[58]

In fact, it seems that Bollywood films have always been subject to ridicule. And just as with the exemplary *Amar Akbar Anthony,* it seems normal to find scholars offering a range of conflicting opinions as to just what constitutes the genus. Bollywood films are made for the masses, an Indian public that is primarily poor, rural, and often low caste, but they're also made for the upper middle class of the Indian diaspora,[59] even though they represent the yearnings of lower-middle-class and slum-dwelling Indians.[60] They reflect the diversity of the Indian nation,[61] but they also homogenize that diversity, creating "a receptacle, like a wax mold."[62] They are situated within late-modern transnational "media assemblages,"[63] but they also replicate ancient Hindu mythologies and aesthetics.[64] They are "global," but they're also highly local, particularly with relation to Bombay;[65] and they feature heroes that are as likely to be a local, smart-talking *tapori,* a hapless nonresident Indian, or an equally hapless *deshi* in Brooklyn or New Jersey.[66] Bollywood, in short, is something like what Benedict Anderson famously called the nation—an "imagined community."[67] It must be conceptualized into existence, and this imaginative ontology means that it can and will change according to the powers of those who imagine it. *Amar Akbar Anthony* provides just such a feast for the imagination. The critics imagined it as one thing, the masses imagined it as something else, and we see it as a massively multivalent masterpiece. (It is at once an elephant and also a snake, tree, and wall.)

So *Amar Akbar Anthony* epitomizes the *masala* film; it could even be the first Bollywood film. To these speculations, we'd like to consider one more possible "first." *Amar Akbar Anthony* is self-consciously mimetic. It replicates and recycles plots, characters, and scenarios such that it functions simultaneously as story, metaphor, and allegory, although irony is ever present to undermine any single reading. Literary critics have pointed out that such irony and play are the defining characteristics of the postmodern literary form.[68] The *jouissance* of Roland Barthes's literary theory likewise invokes the way that irony invites play and pleasure, and is definitive of the postmodern text.[69] M. K. Raghavendra argues for something similar in his review of *Amar Akbar Anthony,* which he titles "Quotation Marks" and explains as such: "The film plays shamelessly with every popular convention and tends to overdo everything so thoroughly that it places itself within quotation marks."[70] In introducing these quotation marks, these fingerposts of irony, *Amar Akbar Anthony* can be thought to have inaugurated a late-modern aesthetic in Indian cinema. Could it be that *Amar Akbar Anthony* is also the first postmodern Indian film, one that consciously and ironically questions its own being? Or is it the strictures of a narrowly defined Western modernity that Bollywood cinema, and *Amar Akbar Anthony,* seek to exit, showing their viewers the way out? And if so, toward what?

The Social Message of Escapism: Travels in an Idealized Moral World

Sounding much like one of the film critics cited previously, Shyam Benegal, the great New Cinema director, offered this explanation of Desai's films: "I think Manmohan Desai is totally uninterested in social messages; everything happens by miracle on screen. People leave the cinema without taking any messages, but they have been entertained."[71] We disagree. Desai's films are far more than miracle tales. What's more, Desai was interested in social messages, and these social messages do have political implications. In fact, we believe that Desai's success depended in large part on the social and political content of his films—even though this content, especially in the case of *Amar Akbar Anthony*, opens itself up to multiple readings.

First of all, Desai wasn't interested in making realist films but in making escapist films with realistic characters. Unlike Satyajit Ray, from whom he repeatedly distinguished himself,[72] he didn't make films that chronicled life's difficulties; he made films that helped us forget them. As Desai explained: "There are a lot of problems on this earth, like where the next meal is coming from, but the man who spends even four rupees on a movie has every right to my esteem. . . . The person who comes to the movies should be happy to see whatever he's seeing."[73]

But this happiness was also tempered. Desai offered his audiences only a temporary respite from their troubles—a catharsis, not a lasting utopian vision. Reflecting on *Coolie* (1983) and the suffering railway porters it depicts, Desai explains:

> I'm not encouraging revolution. I say let them let their steam off. Don't oppress them all the time so that they can never rebel, so they can't speak their mind or express themselves. Let them speak out. Let them also feel for a change, "All right, we are somebody." Why do you want to make them suffer, to grind them to dust all the time. They (art directors)—[including, no doubt, Satyajit Ray]—are trying to grind their characters deeper and deeper into the ground. Let the steam be vented.[74]

And in just this way, the coolies of the film are allowed to be victorious for one day, and then the status quo returns. As Amitabh Bachchan's character Iqbal shouts, *Kal tumhara, aaj hamara!* (Yesterday was yours. Today is ours!) But since *kal* can mean both "yesterday" and "tomorrow" in Hindi, perhaps we can think of this as saying, "Yesterday was yours, and tomorrow will be again . . . but today is ours!" Here the "revolution" lasts a single day, much like the carnivalesque Hindu festival of Holi, with its suspension of rules and riot of colors.[75]

Desai, in short, offers a tempered fantasy—a temporary though fantastic reprieve from daily drudgery. The key is to create a mesmerizing vision, compelling in the way it mobilizes emotions, so that one loses track of one's own worries. As Desai explains,

My only interest is to see that I present something fantastic there on the screen, something that will make the audience focus all their attention on the screen. My only concern is their everyday problems. My constant efforts are to take people into a world of fantasy where there is no worry, no serious thinking, just fun and entertainment all the way. Who wants to see realism?[76]

Yet Desai's world of fantasy doesn't fit neatly in the fantasy genre, for it is created more by narrative leaps than by imaginative spectacles. Instead of Jedi masters, hobbits, and faraway worlds—per the likes of *Star Wars* (George Lucas, 1977) and *The Lord of the Rings* (Peter Jackson, 2001)—Desai offers us clichés, coincidences, and Bombay backdrops, transgressing ordinary laws of storytelling rather than those of nature or physics. This isn't science fiction, creating a fantasy of possible worlds or futures, but something closer to its converse. It's a kind of disordered naturalism: Bombay in the funhouse mirror, where fantasy meets melodrama.

According to scriptwriter Anjum Rajabali, "Manmohan Desai had a pact with his audiences. You can have either logic or emotions, but not both. It was manipulative, but the audience knew that and as long as it was being entertained, it accepted those leaps of logic."[77] Such "leaps of logic," in fact, were key to Desai's filmic fantasies, for some kind of "illogic," whether magical or supernatural, diegetic or extradiegetic, is necessary for fantasy.[78] Desai's particular brand of illogic, however, was aimed at creating *emotional* fantasies[79]—what Shabana Azmi described as Desai's "unabashed love for all things illogical but with a strong emotional content."[80]

Desai may have been illogical with his stories but not with his characters, and this is key to his films' appeal. The filmmaker states, "My plots are not realistic. My characters are realistic. You see, if I make the stories real, they're not interested in seeing them. But put those characters on a trip to fantasy!"[81] He grew up in Khetwadi, a crowded "townie" neighborhood in the old southern part of Bombay, and his films feature characters from that milieu. As Desai notes, "I know their frustrations. I know their likes. I know their dislikes. I know what makes them beat. Small things that make them happy. You see, all my characters are from the lower middle class, characters who are down-to-earth, who have seen life in the raw. If I had been born an aristocrat, I could never have made it."[82]

Perhaps it is this trick of creating down-to-earth characters with whom his viewers could identify, such that they feel "hailed" or "interpellated," to use a term from Marxist theory,[83] that helps make Desai's twisted logic so captivating.[84] His characters are so likable that one almost forgets this is a work of fantasy. Maybe this is why the "masses" in Maharashtra, according to those previously mentioned student researchers, didn't find the scenarios of *Amar Akbar Anthony* "unrealistic." In other words, he succeeds in his attempt "to make the impossible possible"— to quote the climactic song from the film—and to make the unbelievable believable.

Another difficulty in reading Desai's films is deciding how to make sense of his narrative recycling. As remarked before, the plots of his films are often derived from other films—frequently his own—or from the epics, the *Ramayana* and the *Mahabharata*. *Amar Akbar Anthony*, for example, is a lot like the blockbuster *Waqt* (Yash Chopra, 1965), which also features three brothers separated from one another, as does *Yaadon Ki Baaraat* (Nasir Husain, 1973). This "lost and found" theme found its way into all four of the films Desai directed in 1977, and they also shared many of the same actors, themes, tropes, and plot points. Desai's films are best thought of as variations on a few themes rather than wholly new works. And this was by design; he didn't want to be original. As Desai explained, "People seem to like the same thing again and again, so I repeat it . . . but you always have to give them something different too. . . . There can be no such thing as a 'formula film'—if there were, everybody would be making nothing but hits."[85]

Naseeb (1981) is a wonderful example of this recycling, being as it is a kind of "*Amar Akbar Anthony* lite."[86] Amitabh Bachchan plays a waiter with the hybrid name John Jani Janaradan, signifying the same religions that the names Amar, Akbar, and Anthony signal, although encompassed in one person. It also features a cinematic climax that is strongly reminiscent of *Amar Akbar Anthony*: three heroes and their love interests enter the villain's lavish home, unrecognized despite their outrageous disguises—a matador, a Cossack, Charlie Chaplin, and so on—and then break into song and dance, which turns into a fight scene. The film was hugely successful with the public but pilloried by the press as a spectacular though stale reworking of an already stale story:

Want to make *Naseeb?* Don't bother about a story or screenplay. You can do without both. Instead rope in almost the entire industry. . . . Throw in the entire works: revolving restaurant, London locales, and outfits which even a five year old would be embarrassed to wear to a fancy dress competition. Now, sit back, relax, and watch the cash pour in.[87]

There is, however, artistry in Desai's reworking of ideas, and this is a crucial feature of the successful *masala* film. As *Naseeb*'s screenwriter K. K. Shukla explained: "It's much more difficult to write a screenplay for *Naseeb* than for a Western or 'art' film, where you have a straight storyline. A commercial Hindi film has to have sub-plots and gags, and keep its audience involved with no story or logic."[88] Rosie Thomas offers this helpful gloss:

> What is meant by "no story" is, first, that the storyline will be almost totally predictable to the Indian audience, being a repetition, or rather, an unmistakable transformation, of many other Hindi films, and second, that it will be recognized by them as a "ridiculous" pretext for spectacle and emotion.[89]

The pleasure of the film is in the ways that the film will be *almost* totally predictable, but not quite. While Desai was a master at "blending the *masalas*" of tropes and clichés in a predictably unpredictable way, he was equally adept at setting these against a wide range of moods such that the audience would cycle through love, laughter, anger, compassion, disgust, heroism, and wonder on an emotional roller-coaster ride that was thrilling and, by design, ridiculous.[90] The key was to generate the right mood at the right time and in the right amount. This meant judiciously serving up a balance of drama, melodrama, comedy, parody, fights, romance, and more, with the hope that the mix of stories and moods would come together to create cohesive and "emotional" entertainment.

Getting the mix right, however, was never a given even for Desai. The wildly manic *Mard* (1985), for example, again features the "lost and found" theme, Amitabh Bachchan righting wrongs, and Nirupa Roy as Maa (although here she loses her voice, not her sight, and regains it at a Durga temple protected by a lion, not at a Sai Baba shrine protected by a cobra).

There is even a villain named Zabisko! The film offers an overt parody of *Amar Akbar Anthony* in a party sequence. Amitabh Bachchan emerges from a cake—not an egg this time—in character as the padre he impersonated in *Amar Akbar Anthony,* wearing the same costume, playing the same tune on the violin, and is met with immediate recognition from his on-screen love interest, who calls out, "Father Anthony!" *Mard* was a hit. But *Gangaa Jamunaa Saraswathi* (1988), Desai's last film as a director, which was envisioned as a sequel of sorts to *Amar Akbar Anthony,* had all the hallmarks of a blockbuster—the "lost and found" theme, Amitabh Bachchan righting wrongs, Nirupa Roy as Maa, as well as love, betrayal, revenge, memory loss, and a Michael Jackson–style single silver glove—and it was a flop. Desai was a master at spectacle, emotion, and "self-plagiarism,"[91] but here the *masalas* didn't blend together. It was, perhaps, one recycling too many—the spice had gone stale.[92]

One component of Desai's films that was "totally predictable" and crucial to their success was an affirmation of an idealized moral order. For all their use of comedy and embrace of the ridiculous, Desai's fantasies always affirmed a moral universe in which good triumphs over evil, villainy is vanquished, patriotism is enshrined, and the laws of family duty are affirmed. Thomas's insights here are apt:

> The Hindi film [of the late 1970s and early 1980s] can be regarded as a moral fable that involves its audience largely through the puzzle of resolving some (apparently irresolvable) disorder in the ideal moral universe. . . . It is important to stress the ideal moral universe is not necessarily believed by anyone: it is a construct of the filmmakers, with the connivance of their audience.[93]

In this regard, Indian viewing audiences can be said to be discriminating, for there is a "firm belief that the audience will simply boycott a film that is 'immoral' or clumsily transgresses the moral code,"[94] and they are complicit not only in maintaining the current moral order but in creating a better one. In *Mard,* for example, the audience can indulge in an outrageous postcolonial fantasy that reenvisions the past and the present, and imposes an idealized moral code on both. In the film, an archvillain named General Dyer—after the notorious officer who perpetrated the

1919 Jallianwala Bagh massacre[95]—with his sadistic son, British cronies, and Indian toadies, torment an Indian population, gunning them down, enslaving them in labor camps, draining their blood (for wounded British soldiers in Burma), and razing their shanties. The film mocks the British for their callousness and rapaciousness, although in the end they get their due when Bachchan's character, with the help of the father with whom he had just been reunited, slays the evil General Dyer and then his malicious minions. Yet as Philip Lutgendorf notes,

> Given the fantasy framework, chronological and locational ambiguity, and the fact that . . . the arch villains are all played by Indian actors, one may propose that the ridiculously evil *firangis* may as easily be read as stand-ins for the "brown sahibs"—the Indian elite of the long-running Congress Raj—who succeeded the colonial masters only to become associated with home-grown corruption and oppression. Their arrogant ways and brutal policies—speaking Hindi studded with English phrases . . . amassing hoards of untaxed "black money," and promoting "urban beautification" through the bulldozing of shanty towns—are pointedly pilloried here, yet any overt critique of the ruling regime is deflected to the red-faced *rakshasas* of the recent past. Raju [Amitabh] at one point mocks Indira Gandhi's onetime election slogan (*Garibi hatao*, "Remove poverty") by asking [the immoral Anglo-Indian mayor] Sir Harry (apropos of his program of slum demolition), "Do you want to remove poverty or just the poor?"[96]

Here, again, the audience is beckoned to comply with the filmmaker, urged to fantasize about a different world, especially as Bachchan's character chastises India's heartless rulers in the song "Buri Nazar Wale" (Evil Eye Giver), calling them out as wealthy overlords with blood on their hands.

All this is to say that, Shyam Benegal to the contrary, Desai's films do have a "social message," even if he isn't calling for revolution, and this message is political. It offers a generalized politics of "escape" from poverty, from oppressive governments, and from the drudgery of reality, but also from the constraints of cinematic form itself. Although Desai's films offer a dizzying recycling of clichés and parody upon parody, his films are invariably morality plays. And this orientation provides the compass for differentiating heroes from villains, reality from fantasy, justice from injustice, and drama from melodrama. Moreover, these idealized morality plays allow the audience to enter a kind of liminal fantasy world, more equitable and joyous than our own, and to leave with a new vision—of an idyllic world somehow closer at hand.

To the extent that Desai's films offer an idealized vision and yet are somehow "almost totally predictable," they tell us quite a lot about the expectations of his original audience. Or to phrase it another way, since the goal of a Desai film is to mix together a variety of ingredients—characters, logic, mood, and denouement—to produce something tasty yet satisfyingly familiar, the familiarity of the concoction tells us a lot about the tastes of the time. In this way, *Amar Akbar Anthony* offers a glimpse into the imaginary of a viewing public, a kind of bellwether for the public mood, a joint effort between filmmaker and viewer to salvage the dream of an idealized nation in post-Emergency India.

Bombay as Allegory: The Geography of Time

"*Amar Akbar Anthony* is a resolutely Mumbai film and couldn't have been located anywhere else,"[97] says one chronicler of the movie, and we certainly agree. But a tour of the places that Manmohan Desai shows us in the film unearths something surprising at the basis of his idealized moral world: his picture of the metropolis is distinctly un-urban. Absent from *Amar Akbar Anthony* are Bombay's crowds and its trademark structures— Victoria Terminus, Flora Fountain,[98] the Gateway of India, the Hajji Ali *dargah*. Indeed, Bombay proper—the "island city," whose official boundaries as the Mumbai City District are drawn on three sides by shoreline and to the north by Mahim Creek—is almost entirely external to this film's diegesis and production. *Amar Akbar Anthony*'s Bombay is not, strictly speaking, the city at all. It is the suburbs, and one suburb in particular.

In what follows, we will take a close look at how the Bombay of the film has been assembled and deployed as a way to ground the film's moral vision. The film, we argue, maps India's history onto Bombay's geography, and the account of history it narrates follows a telos of modernization. Development into a modern society is accomplished by purging antinational elements and embracing national minorities within a morally grounded, familial order. Some spaces are those of the past; some belong to the liberating future; and the balance, which provide the staging grounds for most of the film's misrecognitions and disguise-based antics, are spaces of the problematically modern present. To put it boldly: space, in *Amar Akbar Anthony,* signifies time.[99]

But set aside any expectation of a realistic representation of the Bombay of 1977. Some scenes were shot at real locations that have been renamed to suit the diegesis. Others were fabricated as sets and named after real places they imperfectly resemble. Nowhere in the film, in fact, can we find a matchup of a real location shot with a real name, although it is hard to be sure.[100] The various locations represented in the film will be identified with reference to the events that they emplace in the narrative, so readers unfamiliar with the story of *Amar Akbar Anthony*—or those whose memory could use some refreshing—are once again invited to skip ahead to the synopsis provided in the Appendix before starting the tour.

The name *Bombay* (Hindi *Bambai,* Marathi *Mumbai*) is never actually spoken in the movie. What we do hear are names of discrete neighborhoods located in the suburban district: Bandra, primarily, and also Borivali.[101] Visually we are given a picture of a city bounded on one side by the sea (in the west) and on another by a wooded wilderness (in the north). This corresponds with Greater Bombay's spatial coordinates in real life. But the fit is more snug if we isolate the northern half—the Suburban District—of which Bandra and Borivali signify, respectively, the southernmost and northernmost neighborhoods.[102]

Both of these frontiers are encoded in the film with symbolic values that have roots in Indian mythology and other forms of cultural expression. The sea is the source of marvelous bounty—wealth in the form of smuggled gold, for example. The people who act as the conduit for this adulteration of the national economy are themselves only marginally national; they are outlaws, members of gangs headed by the Anglophile Christian Robert and his Hindu but even more overtly colonial mimic man, Kishanlal. The sea's association with the wealth and exotic culture of the West is also cited in the shots of the waterfront and beach that host the romantic frolics of the Christian couple, Anthony and Jenny, in the song "Hamko Tumse Ho Gaya Hai Pyar Kya Karein."

The forest and associated wilderness areas function as a zone of transformation. This is where Bharati, running through the dark woods on that fateful Fifteenth of August, is blinded when a lightning bolt fells a tree branch. Around the same time and in the general vicinity, Kishanlal wrecks his getaway car on top of her and discovers its load of contraband gold, which marks his own transformation into a crook. The forest is identified in dialogue as Borivali Park, which in real life is a large nature preserve also known as the Sanjay Gandhi National Park, more than a hundred square kilometers in area. Additional wooded tracts flank the park to the present day; in 1977, when the development of the outer suburbs was just starting up in earnest, the impression must have been powerful indeed that the city's frontier was a jungle.

In this connection we call attention to the barren, unfinished look of the locations of the film's numerous car chases. Building sites dot the landscape, offering a picture of suburban settlements under construction. And the highway that figures in the film's major chase sequence—the four-car spectacle involving dueling station wagons—runs through a rural landscape whose main feature is a sugarcane field. This terrain can be identified as yet-underdeveloped tracts bordering the national forest, or—better—as the land that has been carved out of the wilderness to be settled as suburbs-to-be. It appears that Robert and Ranjeet's later terror ride with Bharati also runs along the same highway. When they crash their car (Robert's second wipeout of the day), Bharati stumbles out and flees from the desertlike roadside into the wooded environs of her sanctuary, the Sai Baba shrine. Here Bharati will attain redemption, the forest again hosting transformation.

The traversal of rural spaces by traffic originating in the city comes to make sense once we locate the roadway scenes in the outskirts of the forest reserve. These are portions of the suburbs of the future. The only built-up site to be identified as part of Borivali is the little plaza with the Gandhi statue where Kishanlal entrusts his children. This spot is named in dialogue as the entrance to Borivali Park (which it doesn't resemble, although the real park does contain a modest Mahatma Gandhi Memorial), and the Catholic church that fronts one side of the plaza is the fictional Borivali Church. The set of the Sai Baba shrine was actually built on a patch of vacant land in the real Borivali, and our logic here places it in the diegetic Borivali as well.

Heading south through the actual suburbs we come to where the beach scenes were shot for "Hamko Tumse Ho Gaya Hai Pyar Kya Karein": Aksa Beach, which can be lumped in with Borivali as a generically outer-suburb location. Silver Beach, the location of Kishanlal's seaside bungalow, implies an address in Juhu, a neighborhood whose fancier sections are associated with film stars and other high-flying types, perhaps including underworld dons. Jenny's entrance into the story takes place nearby at Santa Cruz Airport. And to Juhu's south is Bandra—bastion of Catholic culture, the celebrated "Queen of the Bombay Suburbs"—which is the center of the film's action.

With the exception of the locations noted above, virtually all the movie's scenes take place in a network of proximate sites that can be grouped together as a diegetic Bandra. It is here, for example, that we find Nanavati Hospital (although in the real world it is located up by the airport).[103] A single ward of the hospital hosts most of the movie's medical drama: the blood-transfusion sequence over which the credits roll, the scene in which the bedridden Akbar affirms his vow of nonviolence, and the missed-connection scene where Bharati enters the room immediately after Kishanlal has been removed from it.[104] This is the ward where the beds are lined up against a wall with three windows. Reiterating the order in which the three brothers are lined up to give blood, the first window opens on a temple, the second on a mosque, and the third on a church. These views are keyed to the background of the big neighborhood set we are calling the Muslim Quarter, where the street to the left leads to the church, the street to the right leads to the temple, and the middle position marks where the mosque would go.[105]

Just as the hospital is next to the Muslim Quarter, the Muslim Quarter is next to the rough-and-tumble area known as Anthonyville. Anthony, the local strongman, arrives swiftly from his base of operations to straighten out Salma's father, Tayyab Ali, after his hirelings have beaten Akbar. In their general atmosphere and architectural style, both Anthonyville—with its extralegal "country bar"—and Tayyab Ali's timber-bazaar neighborhood resemble actual Bandra locales. Haider Ali's tailor shop, in the back of which he lives with his foster son, is likewise located in a bazaar district, possibly the same as Tayyab Ali's; it too is evidently located close by Anthonyville, since Akbar feels free to saunter over dressed in his *lungi* wrap (a degree of informality that lands, in an American context, somewhere between going out in your sweatpants and going out in your pajamas).

And close to Anthonyville is St. Thomas's Church, where the Padre raised Anthony to manhood.[106] The church's interior is that of Don Bosco in Matunga, in the city proper, but the exterior is easily recognizable as Mount Mary—among the most famous Catholic sites in South Asia, and undoubtedly Bandra's most prominent landmark. And with this piece of the puzzle in place, two other locations can also be fitted in. The Christian social club, or "gymkhana," is up the road to the right of the so-called St. Thomas's, as signaled by Anthony's gesture when he asks Jenny to the Easter dance. Amar's bungalow, with its garden where Lakshmi hangs the washing, would also seem to be in the vicinity, since Lakshmi happens upon Jenny's kidnapping at the church when she is walking along the road with a shopping bag in hand.

Next is Bandra's Koliwada—an area *(wada)* originally settled by Koli people (local fishermen) that has become absorbed as a neighborhood within the city.[107] This is the site of the ancestral home of Kishanlal, Bharati, and their family. The depiction of the Koliwada collapses two iconic sorts of Hindi film spaces: the village and the slum. The first mansion Robert inhabits is lavish and colonial-looking, all the grander by juxtaposition with the Koliwada, but the two spaces seem to be within walking distance from each other, judging by Kishanlal's swift arrival there in the opening sequence. And the Koliwada, St. Thomas's Church, and the hospital would appear to fall together in a sector under the jurisdiction of Amar's police station, which must also be in Bandra. Finally, the tree-lined residential streets on which Kishanlal's men abduct Anthony from the police wagon thus become yet another Bandra location.

This leaves just a handful of sites to place. The theater where Akbar gives his first *qawwali* performance, "Parda Hai Parda," is actually "played" by a real theater, the Birla Krida Kendra, located in South Bombay. And the rendezvous spot where Robert tells his agent Pedro to send the priest and one-man band he has hired is also marked by a reference to a real South Bombay institution—Café Naaz on swank Malabar

Hill—although the site is not actually pictured.[108] We may infer that Pedro's garage is located not far off, albeit surely in a lower-rent part of downtown.[109]

We end the tour with the first place shown in the movie: the Central Jail. If this obvious set has a real-life referent it is the Arthur Road Jail, located well south of Bandra in Mahalaxmi, which was officially renamed Mumbai Central Prison in 1994.

Our reading of the city's spaces as symbolic of time coheres around the identification of the three boys' family as the nation-state. We track the movements of the family's members from one space to another as a passage through stages or conditions of history. The story of the brothers' coming of age and joining of forces thus symbolizes the unification of India's diverse communities in a mature civil society. As children of the humble Bharati and her volatile, flawed husband Kishanlal, the brothers share an origin in the Koliwada, which can be read as the space of India's impoverished past under feudalism and colonialism. And as Amar and his father discover when they find themselves back home near the movie's end, nothing has changed in the Koliwada across a span of twenty-two years. The old neighborhood stands as a reiteration of the Indian stereotype of the "eternal village"—and a rebuke to the promise of Independence. We explore the Koliwada in Chapters 1 and 4.

One of the other main components of the diegetic Bandra is also a space of the past. This is the set we call the Muslim Quarter,[110] which is associated almost exclusively with Akbar and those involved in his romance subplot: his sweetheart, Salma; her father, Tayyab Ali; and the courtesan Bijli. In Chapter 2 we argue that the Muslim Quarter is configured as a space of desuetude and nostalgia not only with reference to the history of Islam in India but also as a cipher of an obsolete cinematic genre, the "Muslim social." For someone like Akbar to move on from a condition of minority "backwardness" into responsible citizenship means to leave the Muslim Quarter fully behind.

We group together most of the film's other spaces in a montage of the present moment—that is to say, 1977. This is the background against which the film's comic melodrama unfolds. On closer examination, however, fun hardly seems to be the mark of the majority of sites that make up the modern city. Both within the film's Bandra and beyond, when we see a road we can anticipate the worst: a car wreck, an abduction, or that double whammy that epitomizes the modern condition, a hit-and-run—a hazard at once anonymous and mechanized. The hospital is likewise a site of anonymity, functioning as a sort of clearinghouse of misrecognitions and near reunions.[111] This is a world of mean streets, where people no longer recognize each other properly. And note the city's many spaces that are reserved for purposes of confinement, punishment, or even torture: the Central Jail, the police-station lockup, with its subterranean dungeon, and Zabisko's secret chamber. It is this modern environment of disorientation and alienation that we theorize in Chapters 2 and 4 as the City of Illusion. And this is the amoral backdrop to the film's moral drama.

Finally, if space is to be understood as time, we must ask, Where will the members of our reconstituted national family embrace the future? The answer would surprise few, either in 1970s India or in 1970s America. Our movie looks to the suburbs. To be precise, it looks to Bombay's outer suburbs-to-be—to the spaces under construction in the zone the film vaguely designates as "Borivali." This is virgin territory, cleared for settlement out of the traditional space of transformation: the forest. In the film's final scene, the three brothers and their brides drive together along the highway and through a wooded field. Here is the landscape where the impossible will be made possible and their parents' legacy redeemed. It is a moral world realized. The other side of the sunset—the utopian horizon just a car ride away—is a fresh start in a space beyond history.

Methodology: Sugar Coated, Homeopathic . . . or Bullshit?

It was Desai's belief about *Amar Akbar Anthony* that he had created a film with a positive message about secularism, national integration, and communal harmony. But he had purposely given it an oblique method of delivery:

> Had I stood on a platform preaching "Hindu-Christian *bhai-bhai* (brother-brother)," they would have said, "We don't want to hear that bullshit from you." So I said, best give it in a very palatable, say, homeopathic pill. We gave a sugar-coated pill; they took it. They liked it. So we had communal harmony in it.[112]

We find inspiration for our own project in Desai's words, for some parts of *Amar Akbar Anthony* do seem to be sugar coated—sweetened to be made palatable—and other parts homeopathic—not "illogical," as many of his critics would contend, but counterintuitive. In homeopathy, a patient is treated for a disease with a dose of a substance that brings up the disease's symptoms; in reacting against this stimulus, the patient develops immunity to the illness. The homeopath, in other words, carefully irritates the patient and, in triggering resistance, summons a cure. We propose that something similar is at work in *Amar Akbar Anthony*. There are feel-good parts of his message that come coated in sugar and troublesome bits that we encounter as homeopathy—irritating disjunctures and discrepancies designed to provoke critique and reflection.

To pursue the medical metaphor, both these alternative therapies face the charge of quackery, particularly from someone accustomed to allopathic medicine, with its prescription of aggressive, even invasive therapies. In cinematic terms, such pills would be the "realistic" and overtly didactic films that Desai insisted he never wanted to make but that the critics kept wishing he did. This might help explain the argument in "Secularism—'Filmi' Style," an article discussed previously that appeared just after *Amar Akbar Anthony*'s initial success. It begins with this assessment:

> If you've done undergrad History then surely you know about the logic that history is supposed to have, and about how nothing happens unless the time is ripe for it, and about how each significant event has a host of lesser events leading to it in logical succession. Now I'm not saying that the success of *Amar Akbar Anthony* is a significant event: but it does show something, and is the logical culmination of the Hindu Muslim Sikh Isaai [Christian] *Sab ko mera salaam* [I salute them all] sort of formula . . . not because of any genuine feeling of secularism [or] communal amity.[113]

The reviewer is referencing the film *Chhalia* (1960), Desai's directorial debut (to be discussed in greater depth in Chapter 1), in which an aptly named con man with a heart of gold introduces himself with the song "Chhalia Mera Naam" (Fraud Is My Name) and explains how he offers respect to Hindus, Muslims, Sikhs, and Christians alike. The reviewer then argues that this platitudinous sentiment reaches a kind of apotheosis in *Amar Akbar Anthony*, and that what appears to be an argument for "secularism or communal amity" is nothing more than a placebo—a pill that is presented as medicine but contains no intrinsic virtue. In other words, Desai is a quack or, worse, a "fraud," like his eponymous hero. It isn't an issue of Desai being prosodic, ironic, metaphoric, parodic, or postmodern, though we believe him to have been all these things. The reviewer is just saying that he "doesn't want to hear that bullshit."

In what follows, we are not concerned with Desai's personal integrity nor with the ideological purity or intellectual lucidity of his film—but we are concerned with the film's message. The three of us are scholars of Indian religion, history, literature, society, and popular culture, and in *Amar Akbar Anthony* we recognize a wealth of material to ponder: ideas about religion and secularism, the city and the state, the village and the slum, gods and goddesses, gender and politics, communalism and nationalism, and much more. With careful attention to the film's details, contexts, and ideological constructions, we unpack how its arguments and images exert their power. For the most part, we analyze these processes outside of authorial intent, and yet it's Desai's own assertion we are building on as we argue for the multiplicity, the trickiness, and even the mutually contradictory character of his film's modes of address. As such, we are just as interested in how *Amar Akbar Anthony* delivers its message as in what that message—or messages—might be.

Our book thus offers a playful and wide-ranging engagement with the film's logic and ideas. And paralleling the film's eclecticism and complexity, our own interpretations are multiple, tricky, and yes—at points they contradict each other. We seek to open up meanings, not shut them down. The solution, as we discussed earlier in this Introduction, has been to structure our book around a sibling rivalry. Which of the three brothers is the real hero? Is it Amar, scion of an implicitly Hindu-dominated state, or Akbar, the romantic Muslim as model minority, or Anthony, the good-hearted Christian hooch peddler? Or is the movie's true hero their long-suffering mother? And which of us three authors—each championing in turn his favorite brother—has gotten it right?

Each of the four chapters that make up the core of this book is centered on one of the main characters—Amar, Akbar, Anthony, and Maa—with the argument being that the film's true protagonist is him (or her). Each argument is further defined by a distinct thematic and methodological approach to analyzing the film as a whole. Chapter 1, on the Hindu police officer Amar, assesses the way the Indian state is indexed to a corporeal ethic of "muscular Hinduism," and its analytic approach is textually grounded. "Amar: Straight Shooter" pursues a close-grained reading of the film's message, decoding its secularist ideology to reveal Hindu majoritarian assumptions and implications. Chapter 2, on the Muslim singer Akbar, is intertextual. "Akbar: *Parda* and Parody" diverts Amar's ideologized reading by making two turns: tracing the narrative's repurposing of dated Golden Age tropes through parody, and theorizing the songs on the film's famous soundtrack as ruptures in the narrative. Chapter 3, on the Christian outlaw Anthony, advances the analysis of Desai's tricky delivery system one level further—into metatextual irony. "Anthony: Amar Akbar Irony" projects the convergence of the star-body of Amitabh Bachchan, perceptions about Christians in Indian society, and the social-psychological theory of the "intimate enemy" in a kind of postcolonial catharsis. Finally, Chapter 4, on Bharati, the mother of the three brothers, allows each of the characters to comment on the film's invocation of the nationalist symbol of Mother India. *"Maa—!"* situates Bharati variously as a figuration of failure, alienation, penitence, nature, divinity, and ultimate triumph.

This book owes a great deal to the field of film studies, but its methodology originates largely outside the discipline. We have not rejected such tools as structural analysis, psychoanalysis, and the concept of the auteur, but we have engaged them selectively. We are committed to the practice of close reading and have, in the main, approached the film as a text—but a text whose exegesis best takes a variety of complex routes. Our partnership brings together discrete research methods, most notably philology, history, and ethnography. And the range of contexts in which we have found it necessary to situate our analyses reflects this threefold orientation. It includes Hinduism, Islam, and Christianity as formulated textually, observed historically, and practiced in contemporary India; the field of modern Indian visual culture, specifically Indian cinema, and yet more specifically Hindi-language popular cinema; norms of gender and sexuality as represented and practiced historically and in the present day; and ideological formations such as contemporary Indian nationalism and its intimate associates—Gandhism and secularism. Finally, our multiple inquiries originate in a shared proposition: *Amar Akbar Anthony,* the tale of three representatives of different faiths who discover their brotherhood, is a powerful allegory of the nation.

It remains here to offer a few words about choices we three have made as writers. We have chosen to call the city *Bombay,* which was the only name used in English through the period of the film's production and up to 1995, when the name was changed to *Mumbai,* making official the Marathi pronunciation. When converting Hindi and Urdu into Roman letters, we have opted to eschew diacritics in favor of an unsystematic style of transliteration that follows the norms of mainstream English-language Indian publications. Thus *sindoor,* not *sindūr.* We feel this is truer to the demotic spirit of the film and the flavor of its dialogues. Where we quote Sanskrit, on the other hand, we follow scholarly convention in transliterating words with full diacritics, except in cases in which the Sanskrit words have been assimilated within English.

All personal names belonging to actors and others listed in the film's credits have been spelled as in the credits, even when the individual's name is better known under a different spelling. Thus, for example, Mohamed Rafi, not Mohammed or Muhammad Rafi (except when we are citing someone else's text). We have identified all the major roles in the film with the characters' names, but where the text contains no name, we have dubbed the character with a name based on his or her role. Thus the Padre and the Grandmother. When citing titles of Hindi films, we have reproduced the original orthography under which they appeared in public. And all translations from Hindi, Urdu, and Sanskrit that appear in this book are our own, unless otherwise noted.

So *bas,* as they say in Hindi, *bahut ho gaya*—"we've had enough" (alternatively, "we've had too much"). Let's get on with the movie!

1

Amar

STRAIGHT SHOOTER

. . . .

Lovers of a country don't die . . . they become *amar* [immortal].

—from *Desh Premee* (Manmohan Desai, 1982)

A s ONE can't help but notice, *Amar Akbar Anthony* is a commentary on the formation of the Indian nation. Three children are separated from their parents and one another sometime in the 1950s on the Fifteenth of August—Independence Day. The film chronicles how they recover from this loss, highlighting the roles played by religion and love, family and surrogates, the city and the state. But this is also a story about Partition and the Emergency, the wounds they caused and their legacy, and the importance of an unmarked but muscular form of Hinduism as a balm for healing. This configuration of Hinduism sidelines Gandhi and embraces violence, and it promotes a domestic form of love and police action for rehabilitating fallen women, families, and ultimately the state. The catalyst for this process is a new dharma, which echoes and inverts the logic found in the stories of the gods Rama and Shiva, and which allows the state to be embodied—through a kind of sexual and somatic discipline—in Amar himself. What follows is an Amar-centric view of the film to explain why it is that big brother is a Hindu with a gun that he never uses, and what role he has to play in creating an idealized moral world to offset the parody and irony of Akbar and Anthony.

Here's a Story of a Man Named Kishanlal, Who Was Busy with Three Boys of His Own

In order to make sense of Amar and his view of the world, we first need to understand how the three brothers became separated from their parents and one another, the role of fathers in the formation of the boys' identities, and why Amar is so afraid that guns might end up in the wrong hands (and whose hands those might be). Much of this backstory takes place in the film's prologue sequence, which lasts nearly twenty-five minutes and helps explain Amar's perspective on India's ills and why violence in the hands of the state is, to his mind, the remedy.

In the film, Kishanlal, the father of the family, is a driver for an underworld leader named Robert. After Robert hits and kills a man with his car, Kishanlal agrees to confess to the crime and then serves the latter's prison sentence. Although Robert promises Kishanlal that he will pay his family double his monthly wages while Kishanlal is in prison serving Robert's sentence, he ultimately gives them nothing. Kishanlal's three children suffer in poverty, as does his wife, Bharati, who contracts tuberculosis. When Kishanlal is released from prison and returns home, he sees the pitiful condition of his family and learns they have received no payments. Infuriated at this double cross, Kishanlal goes to Robert's lair, where the latter is lavishly celebrating his daughter's first birthday. He beseeches his boss for the money but is rebuffed, then taunted and degraded. Filled with anger and shame, Kishanlal shoots Robert three times, but only hits the chain-mail vest protecting his chest.

Kishanlal then jumps out a window and escapes in one of Robert's cars, which contains a crate of smuggled gold bars. He eludes Robert's goons and drives home. Bharati, however, has already left. In her place is a letter explaining that she is going to end her life so that Kishanlal can use whatever he earns to provide for their children, not treat her illness. Kishanlal hustles the boys into the car and drives off. With Robert's men giving chase, he understands the danger he's in, so he stops his car at a park and rushes the boys inside, leaving them underneath a statue of Gandhi, the Father of the Nation. Inscribed on the side of the statue is *ahiṃsā paramo dharmaḥ* (Nonviolence is the supreme law), acknowledging the safety that

Gandhi provides, as well as the difference in Gandhi's and Kishanlal's ideologies. Like Gandhi, Kishanlal and his family are Hindus, but Gandhi, unlike Kishanlal, never shot a man. Kishanlal has already transgressed the ethics hewn beneath the Mahatma's statue.

Before Kishanlal can return to fetch his children, each is taken in by a replacement father. The youngest child is abandoned not only by his father but also by his two older brothers. The oldest runs after his father and is struck unconscious by the gangsters' car, and the middle child runs off to find food to calm his younger brother, who is in tears. Multiply abandoned, the youngest is seen by a Muslim tailor who has stopped his car and is praying on the side of the road. Finding the boy all alone, the man decides to adopt him, and the camera nicely juxtaposes him with the Gandhi statue, signaling the similarities between the two men (Figure 3). The boy will be raised as Akbar, a *qawwali* singer with a big heart, who is the only brother to espouse the Gandhian ideal of nonviolence.

The middle brother eventually passes out on the steps of a Catholic church abutting the park. The head priest finds Bharati's suicide note in the boy's pocket and, concluding that the boy's father must have likewise abandoned him out of poverty, brings him inside. The boy will be raised as Anthony, and the Padre will be the boy's guardian and de facto father. But Anthony will never embrace the Padre's Catholic vision. Nor will he join Akbar in adopting Gandhian nonviolence or sign on with the police, like Amar. Instead, Anthony will take over a neighborhood bar and become a local big man, beating people up to get his way, and the area around the bar will be known as Anthonyville—a testament to his popularity and the power that he wields. Like the Padre, Anthony imagines that he is doing God's work, but his dispensation involves illegal activities (like harboring the fugitive Robert and his crate of gold from the police), which he believes are sanctioned by a higher authority (Jesus), to whom he gives half of his earnings.

Unlike his brothers, Amar, the oldest child, is not found at a place of refuge, like a Gandhi statue or a church, and is not found by an overtly religious man. Instead, he is found on the street by a police inspector, who then raises him as his own. Although Amar keeps his given name, he takes on his new father's family name—Khanna[1]—and, also unlike his brothers, his new father's profession. Later in the film we see Police Sub-Inspector

FIGURE 3. Haider Ali and Gandhi

Amar Khanna reporting to his father, who is now Inspector Khanna. Much like Anthony, Amar protects and provides for his community, but he does so officially, as an instrument of the state. Also like Anthony, he beats up people to get his way.

Kishanlal just misses intercepting the police officer as the latter drives away with his son. After having left his children at the Gandhi park, Kishanlal crashes Robert's car on a forest hillside and, in the process, discovers the crate of gold hidden inside. Now on foot, he approaches the park, but when he sees the police car he turns away, shielding himself and the gold as he pretends to urinate. With this act, however, he turns his back on Amar, who is taken away by the policeman. Once in the park he yells only for Amar, acknowledging the special connection he has with his oldest son. But it's too late. He's traded his children for a box of gold.

What is the faith of Inspector Khanna? Unlike the adoptive fathers of Anthony and Akbar, the inspector isn't overtly religious. Judging by his name and manner, he is a secular Hindu, privy to the power and privilege of India's dominant religion but more concerned with the rules of state than those of Hindu orthodoxy. Amar appears to be the same. He is never seen in prayer or in temple, his home has no shrine, and he wears

FIGURE 4. Amar buries the gun

no identifying religious insignia.[2] Amar's religiosity is seemingly unmarked, especially in comparison to that of his brothers, but it is certainly not indistinct.

Kishanlal tells Amar to stay under the Gandhi statue with his brothers,
but Amar runs away from Gandhi, literally and figuratively. For Amar,
nonviolence is *not* the supreme law. Amar uses violence repeatedly to
uphold the authority of the state. Amar beats up a gang of extortionists;
he beats up Anthony; and he beats up Robert's men twice, once in jail
and once at their hideout.[3] In this way, Amar is the progeny of both Inspector Khanna, his adoptive father, and Kishanlal, his biological father.
Like the former, he upholds the law, and like the latter, he doesn't eschew
violence, even if it's reckless. Amar is a personification of Max Weber's
famous definition of a state: he claims a monopoly on the legitimate use
of violence.[4]

Amar does avoid guns, however, at least one in particular—which we'll
revisit later in the chapter—and this is crucial for making sense of his character. When Kishanlal is released from prison and returns home, he
finds the middle brother fighting with Amar and the youngest crying, and
he tries to appease them all with gifts: a toy cricket bat for the youngest,

a cart for the middle brother, and a pistol for Amar, which is presumably a toy but looks quite realistic.[5] Amar, however, never plays with the gun, for the middle brother immediately tries to claim it as his own: "Brother Amar, don't take the gun! Leave my gun alone!" Amar then runs out of the kitchen with the gun, and as Kishanlal leaves the house to confront Robert, he sees Amar burying it in the ground outside their home. Questioned, Amar explains, "I'm hiding it. If my little brother sees it, he'll want it for himself" (Figure 4). The gun is in his hands, quite literally, yet his concern is that the gun might end up in the hands of his middle brother, the future Anthony. This concern, as we'll see, is central to Amar's identity—and to the moral world of the movie.

Guns in the film are certainly dangerous, albeit for Amar's fathers, not his brothers. Three times Amar is almost orphaned because guns end up in the wrong hands. Kishanlal grabs a gun from one of Robert's henchmen and then fires at Robert, setting in motion the events that lead Kishanlal to abandon his family. Later Robert grabs a gun from one of Kishanlal's henchmen and fires at Kishanlal, and later still he grabs another gun and fires at Inspector Khanna. Kishanlal is saved because he's wearing a chainmail vest—taking after Robert but shrewdly using it to cover his back—but Inspector Khanna is less fortunate. He is hospitalized in critical condition, frightening Amar that he might be orphaned once again, but the inspector soon recovers. As a police officer, Amar is justified in wanting to prevent guns from falling into the wrong hands—and he uses his own hands, balled into fists, to do so (Figure 5).

Adoptive Fathers and Lovely Ladies

What drives the plot of the film, however, is how everyone—both the crooks (Kishanlal and Robert) and the brothers—tries to reconstitute broken families. The fracturing of the family and the trauma that ensues is a common theme in Indian film and literature, often gesturing back to the partitioning of Britain's Indian empire, when millions of households were displaced, decimated, and forced to move and reconfigure.[6] Within the film, the brokenness of families can indeed be read against Partition. Yet the film itself seems to gesture more directly toward the previous years of Emergency Rule, when civil liberties were radically curtailed and civil

FIGURE 5. Amar's fist

life fundamentally transfigured. There are, of course, myriad other causes and conditions that lead to family dysfunction (micro and macro, social and political, and so on), but the film's diagnosis of this dysfunction and the cure that it offers—particularly as exemplified by Amar's character—places it in direct conversation with the state as a social actor, much as it was in the 1970s.

Reminiscent of Amar is Saleem Sinai, the main character in Salman Rushdie's *Midnight's Children,* which was published in 1981, four years after the release of *Amar Akbar Anthony.* Saleem is sterilized during Emergency Rule, and then, following this traumatic event, severs ties with the past and re-creates himself, even finding new parents. "Giving birth to parents," he explains, "has always been one of my stranger talents."[7] This untethering of biology in the formation of identity, breaking down the traditional lineage of fathers and sons, appears in a negative formula on the novel's last page: "My son . . . is not my son, and his son . . . will not be his, and his . . . will not be his."[8] Yet Saleem does have a patrimony, which is enjoyed by all the midnight's children, whose birth coincided with the birth of the new nation: "All over the new India, the dream we all shared, children were being born who were only partially the offspring of their parents—the children of midnight were also the children of the time: fathered, you understand, by history."[9]

This formulation of paternity and "elective filiation" reproduces the logic in *Amar Akbar Anthony,* which is similarly "fathered by history."[10] Amar, Akbar, and Anthony are reborn on Independence Day as a kind of midnight's children—and Gandhi's children too—and although their new fathers choose them and not the converse, both the book and the film share a sense of betrayal by India's progenitors. In the book, the betrayer is an infanticidal Mother India—the Widow, a fictionalized version of Prime Minister Indira Gandhi—whereas the movie's Mother India figure, Bharati, is among the betrayed. Another point of divergence between these two national allegories is that *Amar Akbar Anthony*'s hero is not one son but an entire family, and the key issue is how the family, after its great fall, can—like Humpty Dumpty—be put back together again.

Kishanlal, for one, tries to make up for the loss of his children by trading identities with Robert, his betrayer and nemesis (although Kishanlal is less cruel).[11] After losing his children beneath the Gandhi statue, Kishanlal next appears in the film twenty-two years later looking just like Robert, and Robert appears looking just like Kishanlal did when he was Robert's servant. Kishanlal has used the box of Robert's gold with which he absconded to hire Robert's men and re-create his smuggling operation, and he now wears the identical clothes that Robert wore when Kishanlal begged him for money—chalk-striped suit, red vest, red tie, chain-mail vest—and speaks Hindi with the same thick British-sahib accent. Robert likewise wears the identical worker's white suit that had been Kishanlal's uniform. Robert's fortunes have fallen as his foe's have risen.

When Robert sees Kishanlal, he immediately begins to plead, "Where is my daughter? My daughter, where is she!" for on the very day that Kishanlal lost his children he went to Robert's house, in his dirty white uniform, and kidnapped Robert's only child, Jenny.[12] Although Kishanlal has traded places with Robert and raised Jenny as his own—educating her abroad, far away from Robert—his replacement life, and the misery it generates in Robert, offers him only partial solace. Kishanlal plays the role of Robert, degrading the latter as the latter had degraded him, but what Kishanlal has lost cannot be replaced by a new child or making Robert suffer a parallel fate.[13] Indeed, Robert is traumatized at the loss of his child. Before Jenny's kidnapping, Robert apparently raised her as a single parent, for there is no sign or mention of Robert having a wife,[14] and although we later learn that he has a twin brother, the two are deeply estranged.[15] Losing his young daughter on her birthday was a terrible present for Robert—the loss of the most important woman in his life—and Robert spends the rest of the film trying to get Jenny back.

Kishanlal and Robert grieve at the loss of their biological children, but these children don't seem to take much comfort in their biological fathers (although everyone seeks comfort in the film's sole mother, Maa, a point we'll discuss in Chapter 4). Biological fathers are largely reprehensible, re-placeable, and quickly forgotten. Kishanlal first abandons his children for the promise of a pay raise—and to help keep his criminal boss from serving deserved jail time—and then he abandons them again for ven-geance and gold. His children, in turn, have completely forgotten him. None of them ever discuss him or his disappearance, and even when Amar and Anthony meet him, neither recognizes him.

Akbar too has little interest in Kishanlal, even when it is revealed that the latter is his biological father. One night Salma tells Akbar that the missing husband of the old flower seller that he considers his mother was admitted that day to the hospital. Earlier that day, Akbar had discovered that the flower-selling surrogate was actually his biological mother. This could only mean that the man in the hospital is his biological father! Yet Akbar says nothing to Salma about these discoveries.[16]

We next see Akbar arriving at his mother's home and telling her that the small box he has in hand will fill her with happiness: it contains *sindoor,* the powder worn by married Hindu women. According to the logic of the film—on which Hindu and Muslim characters appear to be in accord—a woman's pleasure is to be found in a husband, and now Bharati too can be happy. The discovery, however, does not seem to bring Akbar some previously unknown happiness. Akbar is already happy; he has a close relationship with his adoptive father, and he shows no interest in getting to know Kishanlal. In fact, the two don't meet again until the final scene in the movie, when Kishanlal emerges from behind bars to hug his three children. Akbar has an adoptive father who, quite literally, made him forget everything about his biological one. What more could he want?

The three would-be brides for the brothers also have contentious rela-tionships with their biological fathers. Jenny treats Robert, her apparent biological father,[17] not as a parent but as a kidnapper, if not a murderer. Salma grudgingly obeys her father, Tayyab Ali, although she doesn't hold him in high esteem. He hires thugs to beat up Akbar, the man she wants to marry, because Akbar hints at the truth about her father's long-standing relationship with a prostitute. Lakshmi's biological father is never named, but the plot suggests his incompetence: after his wife's premature death, he chose a terrible woman to remarry and died shortly thereafter, leaving an orphaned Lakshmi to contend with a tyrannical stepmother.

Adoptive fathers, however, are held in high regard, trumping their biological counterparts, even when their worthiness is in question. Kishanlal kidnaps Jenny from Robert as an infant and then tries to keep her ignorant of the fact that he stole her. Jenny loves Kishanlal, her kidnapper-cum-foster father, and despises Robert, her doting biological father. To the extent we are shown Robert together with Jenny, he appears to be a loving parent—she gets a movie at her birthday party as well as a fancy cake, and at night he sleeps protectively by her side. We even see a swing outside their bedroom, suggesting that Robert plays with her. Kishanlal likewise treats Jenny well after her kidnapping, sending her to Europe for her education and—judging by her clothes and demeanor—rearing her with care, although from a distance.

Nevertheless, when Jenny returns to India, Kishanlal greets her with lies and deception. After sending another woman as a decoy to come forward as "Jenny" and be kidnapped from the airport by Robert, Kishanlal explains that the performance was staged to ensure her safety. The kidnapper, he tells her inaccurately, was her father's murderer, who was also planning to kidnap her. It is unclear, however, what danger Robert actually poses at this point to Jenny, for Robert doted on her in the past and has certainly been tormented by her absence. Robert, moreover, is her father, not her father's murderer, so it's unclear as to who the real kidnapper is. While the performance does keep Jenny from Robert, it also allows Jenny's double to be taken in so that she can attempt to kidnap Robert at gunpoint. When Robert is later reunited with Jenny, it is through another kidnapping, with Robert reprising Kishanlal's earlier role as kidnapper.[18] Robert claims his paternity, but Jenny refuses to believe him. He implores, "You must believe me, darling. I'm your father!" but to no avail. Jenny, in fact, never recognizes Robert's claim, for biological fathers are not to be trusted; surrogates serve fatherhood best.

Although biological parents show themselves to be lesser parents than their adoptive counterparts, parental punishment for abandoning one's biological family is nevertheless quick and severe. After leaving his three children at the Gandhi park, Kishanlal soon enough crashes his car, lucky to escape with his life, although he will now be separated from his family for what will turn out to be decades. Kishanlal's wife, Bharati, is likewise punished for her decision to leave her family behind. Fleeing through the woods on what appears to be a clear day, a lone bolt of lightning fells a tree branch, which pins her to the ground. When she is later found and roused by Akbar's adoptive father, she finds she has lost her eyesight—punished by God, as she herself concludes.

The three brothers, although abandoned by *both* their parents, find great solace in their relationships with their adoptive fathers. These men are their only family, as no new mother or siblings ever emerge to replace their biological ones.[19] Each of these adoptive fathers is single, unencumbered with a biological family of his own, and ready to be a father. Helpful here is the classical Hindu idea of the *trivarga*—that the "trinity" of *dharma, artha,* and *kama* (that is, "duty," "profit," and "pleasure") are the three "aims of human life" *(purushartha).* The adoptive fathers, one could say, are more concerned with duty than with profit or pleasure, and they perform their respective duties in exemplary fashion. They are proverbial do-gooders, well intentioned and well mannered but perhaps a bit naive about the ways of the world and how to change them. The brothers have enormous respect for their adoptive fathers, but they each end up following a slightly different conception of duty, in terms of both work and family. Their work is more theatrical and less genteel, and while their adoptive fathers take comfort in finding sons, the brothers, it seems, would rather produce them. The older men find children; the younger men find wives.

The three brothers, however, pursue wives for different reasons. Whereas Robert and Kishanlal are enticed by profit, Akbar and Anthony are enticed by pleasure, although mindful of paternal advice. The two brothers pursue love and love-marriages, barely able to control themselves or their emotions. Akbar fakes ailments to see the doctor Salma, the woman he loves, lamenting the psychosomatic pain his love for her produces, making his whole body ache. In "Parda Hai Parda" (There Is a

Veil), the song he performs on stage before Salma, five other veiled family members, and her father, he declares his intention to remove the veil of her modesty and ruin her name if she doesn't comply. Comply she does, damaging her reputation and exhibiting her own love in the process, but her father still won't consent to their marriage. Akbar then tries to coerce his acceptance by hiring a group of transgender performers, or *hijras,* to join him in singing "Tayyab Ali Pyar Ka Dushman" (Tayyab Ali Is the Enemy of Love), but her father doesn't succumb to this emotional blackmail. Only after Akbar heroically saves Salma and her father from their burning home does Akbar earn her father's respect and thus Salma's hand.

Anthony agrees with his adoptive father when the latter asks him if he'll obey his wishes and do what he says, but when he then instructs Anthony to get married immediately, the young man protests. He doesn't want to marry unless he meets a woman who makes him hear bells and steals his heart, which is just what happens when he sees Jenny on Easter Sunday. Anthony is lovestruck. The church bells ring in his ears, and the world literally begins to spin. Driven by desire, Anthony chases after Jenny as she is leaving Mass. Looking for a pretext to meet her, he picks up someone else's purse on the way so that he can ask Jenny if it's hers. Jenny declines, of course, but later that day when they share a dance at the Christian "gymkhana," she accepts his love. Anthony lies and steals to win Jenny over, yet as Easter is a day for resurrection, Anthony embarks on a new path of love and family, vowing to quit all of his illicit activities on his wedding day, which will come soon enough.

Amar, however, the oldest brother—the only one with a full-time job, the only one to dutifully follow his new father's career, and the only one to remain a Hindu—follows a more dharmic model of love and marriage, which offers a powerful vision of the role to be played by the state and secular Hinduism in family politics. Amar is called into Inspector Khanna's office and told about a series of crimes in which a woman hitches a ride, and then she and her friends rob the driver. Amar then dresses in a stylish suit and, driving an unmarked car, tracks down the woman. She wears high-waisted yellow pants and a floral blouse, and comes on to him as a prostitute, suggesting they go somewhere discreet for some action. At an abandoned construction site, the woman screams that Amar has tried to rape her. Her cohorts then appear, led by her sleazy stepbrother Ranjeet, and try to extort money from him. Amar reveals that he is a police officer and beats them up, although Ranjeet escapes before more police arrive.

The woman, however, whose name is Lakshmi, doesn't fight or flee. She implores Amar to arrest her, for a life in jail would be better than what she has now. What can she do? She is an orphan, all alone except for her grandmother, living with a stepmother and stepbrother who force her to perform this work, and beat her if she doesn't. Lakshmi, like her grandmother, has no father, husband, or son to protect her, and her stepmother has only Ranjeet, a gangster and extortionist. After his deputies arrive and arrest Ranjeet's gang, Amar takes Lakshmi back to her house and arrests her stepmother. Lakshmi and her grandmother are thankful, but since the lease for the house is in the stepmother's name, they now have no place to live. Amar immediately invites them to move in with him, offering Lakshmi his own home, instead of the jail cell she requested, for her rehabilitation.

The film tells us nothing more about the relationship between Amar and Lakshmi until, forty minutes later in the film, we come to a song that begins by showing the courtship of Anthony and Jenny. Singing their love for each other, they frolic on a boat and then on a horse-drawn cart. Then suddenly we cut to Lakshmi, now dressed demurely in a sari, clutching a picture of Amar to her heart and wearing a *mangalsutra* necklace, signifying her matrimony and embrace of Hindu custom. The two have apparently skipped a courtship and married straightaway. She sings the same song, and then walks outside to check on the laundry while Amar, dressed in a white *kurta pajama* instead of his usual khaki uniform, lounges peacefully in a hammock reading a book (Figure 6). Theirs appears to be a thoroughly restrained and domestic existence. Unlike Anthony and Jenny, there is no sensual caressing and no adventures outside the home. They barely meet each other's gaze. As if to underscore this difference, the film cuts to Akbar and Salma, who are on a tourist train and, much like Anthony and Jenny, are courting, flirting, and even hugging. When we cut back to Amar and Lakshmi, they are singing the same words as the other couples but exhibiting their love much less demonstrably. Although behind them fall monsoon rains, which by convention indicate passion, they sit back to back, fully restrained.

FIGURE 6. Amar and Lakshmi

Akbar and Anthony fall in love with women, then court them and marry them. By contrast, the ever-dutiful Amar rehabilitates his woman of choice and only later enjoys her love—and even then, dispassionately. Amar shepherds a wayward woman away from a life of crime and into his home, creating a happy Hindu family. The wayward woman, in this case, is multiply saved. She is saved from a world of extortion, and perhaps even prostitution, and she is saved from a fractured, unwholesome family, with a stepmother who forces her into crime and a stepbrother who commits those crimes with her. The stepbrother, Ranjeet, manhandles and lasciviously threatens her later in the film, showing not just the dysfunction but also the depravity of her family life. In addition, she is saved from her life as an orphan, for now Amar can play the paternalistic role of male guardian and protector—much the same role that Inspector Khanna played for him.

Unlike his brothers, Amar is inspired by dharma when he courts his wife, and also unlike his brothers, he is the only one whose marriage abides by the constraints of dharma according to classical Hindu law. Akbar and Anthony have arrangements that are *pratiloma*—"against the grain" of the law—in that they seek to marry "up." They are seduced by pleasure, but they also find profit in these alliances, which is inappropriate for bridegrooms.[20] Amar's arrangement with Lakshmi, however, is *anuloma*—"with the grain" of the law—for he is of a higher station than she is.

Yet Amar's dharma is hardly normative; his marriage, as well as his way of reconstituting self and family, follows a dharma of his own making. This is made very clear in the newspaper article, cited in the introduction, in which the "masses" are interviewed about their reactions to the film. When a student researcher asks a milkman in rural Maharashtra if he would follow Amar's "dharma," his answer is a kind of disgust mixed with incredulity:

> *Gulnar:* Amar loves a girl of bad reputation. After seeing this movie, did
>   you feel that you could ever accept a girl of that kind if you loved her?
> *Naresh* (looking at [Gulnar] with horror): Bibiji, you should not ask such
>   questions. I am a poor man but I come from a respectable family. I would
>   never dream of even looking at such a girl let alone marrying her.[21]

Whereas Amar's father tries to heal his fractured life through thievery, and Amar's two brothers try to do so though love—although all three use deception and coercion to achieve their goals—Amar's healing process involves practices of dharma and duty that are classical in some ways but also revisionist, even activist. Finding an adoptive father and a suitable bride are part of his recovery, and his brothers' as well, but Amar's role as the true hero and rehabilitator of the film requires something more.

Rehabilitating Fallen Women with Love and Fraud

The novelty of Amar's sense of dharma and duty can perhaps best be seen through a comparison with Manmohan Desai's directorial debut, *Chhalia* (1960),[22] which shares similar story lines and themes with *Amar Akbar Anthony* but offers a different solution to the problems of familial disintegration and societal dysfunction. In that film, which takes place in affluent Lahore, a young Hindu beauty named Shanti ("Peace") marries the handsome Kewal ("Alone"), but their wedding night is interrupted by the flames of Partition violence, and they are separated.[23] Kewal and his family flee to Delhi, but Shanti is left behind. Stumbling through the streets to escape on her own, Shanti is saved from a mob by a powerful Pathan named Abdul Rehman Khan, who shelters her honorably for five years, never even gazing at her face, in the hope that his own sister, Sakina ("Peace"), who has been left behind in India, will be shown the same kindness by Hindus and Sikhs. As Shanti later explains, he behaved toward her "exactly like Lakshman"—Lord Rama's brother—and that if "God *(Bhagvan)* has incarnated Himself in this terrible age *(kali yug),* He is in the form of Abdul Rehman."

When Shanti finally returns to India, she arrives in a refugee camp only to be multiply rejected, first by her natal family, then by her in-laws, and finally by her husband. Reading of her arrival in the newspaper, her father wants nothing to do with her, claiming that he is "helpless," for the family has maintained its honor the past five years only by proclaiming that she is dead. To appease her mother, however, the natal family goes to get a glimpse of her, but they refuse to recognize her. Her father twice tells her, "I am not your father"; her brother tells her, "My sister is dead"; and her mother, traumatized by these acts of nonrecognition, collapses into a form of blindness such that she can't recognize anyone. They leave, and then her husband Kewal arrives. He has rebuffed his own parents in coming to her, but when he learns that she has a five-year-old son with the Islamic name Anwar ("Luminous"), he doubts the boy's parentage and her fidelity, even though she insists that he is the father, and drives off.[24] Shanti then writes a suicide note and leaves to kill herself, but soon realizes that Anwar is dependent on her and returns, only to find that he too has gone. Now she is truly alone.

Enter Chhalia ("Fraud"), a lovable con man played by Raj Kapoor, who finds Shanti's suicide note and then offers her refuge, which she accepts, in his hovel atop a crumbling city wall. As Chhalia tells his friends, he was born a "saint" *(sadhu sant),* unlike those others who become saints, yet like them he too makes no distinction between classes, castes, and creeds. He is a saint, he continues, because he doesn't know who he is, whether he is Hindu, Muslim, or Christian. In song, he explains his name and, as it were, his game: "Fraud is my name / Fraud is my game / Hindu, Muslim, Sikh, or Christian / I salute them all!"[25]

Chhalia soon falls in love with Shanti, who reveals nothing of her past, although he is too shy to tell her his feelings and too honorable to act on them. Later he discovers that she is a wife and a mother, although separated

from both her husband and her child. Chhalia relinquishes his love for
her so that he can reunite Anwar with Kewal—who teaches his son at a
school for orphan boys but still won't acknowledge his parentage—and
then reunite Shanti with both of them, and even with her family and
in-laws.

This final reunification happens during Delhi's Ramlila, the annual
reenactment of the story of Rama and Sita, under the shadow of a tow-
ering effigy of Ravana, the story's villain, who will eventually be destroyed.
Here the film also invokes another part of the Rama and Sita story, "known
to all Indians and already implicit in *Chhalia:* not that of Sita's abduction and retrieval, but rather that of Rama's later rejection of his pregnant
wife because of suspicion that she may have been unfaithful to him during
her captivity, and that the child she bears may not be his."[26] Chhalia then
makes this symbolism explicit through a song, "Gali Gali Sita" (A Sita in
Every Street), which "Sita-fies" the plight of abducted and repatriated
women, and admonishes everyone, particularly family members, to trust
and accept them. The Ravana effigy is set ablaze, and as everyone watches
it burn, the young Anwar wanders dangerously close, lost and alone.
Shanti, hearing his cries, comes and embraces him. Although they are finally reunited, both have now been placed in danger. As the scorched
Ravana begins to topple, Kewal—prodded by Chhalia—rushes in and
rescues Shanti and Anwar, then tells them with a smile: "Let's go home.
Along with this Ravana, the Ravana of my suspicions has burned up."
Shanti's natal family then comes forward to reclaim her as well, and all de-
part together, leaving behind Chhalia to walk over Ravana's ashes.

The film offers a vision of an unjust world spawned by Partition, where
"men have become monsters," to quote Shanti, and corrupted versions
of propriety and righteousness rule. Both Abdul Rehman and Chhalia
repeatedly say that they're "not very good men," setting themselves
against the norms of justice. But in a monstrous world where justice is
unjust, these two nonetheless manage to be virtuous, and the film places
this virtue in an explicitly Hindu framework. Abdul Rehman is "exactly
like Lakshman" and also an avatar for the Kali Yuga, setting him up as a
Rama for the degenerate modern age.[27] Chhalia is likewise a saint by
birth, one who sees beyond human differences to set the world straight,
but his method is fraud—he is a pickpocket[28]—not chivalry, and it is far

more effective.[29] Chhalia's "play" *(lila)* is the real story at the film's Ram-lila, with the "Hanuman-like Chhalia-Kapoor [functioning] as India's latter-day conscience," leading to a reunion that "*improves* on the Rama narrative by subverting its rigid patriarchal dharma (albeit within a patriarchy-friendly framework of guaranteed female chastity)."[30] In this misguided age, when women are maligned and neither the state nor the family can help them, the old dispensation needs improvement. It needs to defeat the proverbial Ravana—in this case, a patriarchal intimate enemy, not a for-eign foe—and it needs a new ethics. In a word, it needs a little fraud.

The film's account of Shanti functions as a critique of the efforts made by the Indian state to help those women who had been abducted or sepa-rated from their families in the chaos of Partition. The Indian state mounted the Central Recovery Operation from 1948 to 1956 in order to locate, recover, and rehabilitate such women by returning them to their families, forcibly if necessary, although many of the families wanted "nothing further to do with their 'dishonored' sisters, wives, daughters, and daughters-in-law."[31] This idea of "dishonor," which is closely con-nected with ideas about "shame" *(sharm, lajja)*, is what gets burned to ashes at the end of the film.

Conspicuous by its absence from the film, however, is the role of the state in this recovery project. We see no government officials help Shanti return to India or Sakina return to Pakistan. Shanti and the other "re-turnees" must fend for themselves, even in an overcrowded refugee center when they are rejected by their families. There is certainly no rehabilita-tion. Sakina is likewise offered no official help or services. She is escorted on the train by her Sikh guardian, but he then beseeches a total stranger for help in repatriating her to Pakistan, for there are no representatives of the state to offer help or answer questions.

Here the state is damned by its absence, although the film could have followed many other critics and made a much stronger claim of state mal-feasance: that the state was, in a word, *chhalia*.[32] There were many cases of the Indian government repatriating women even when they were re-luctant to be recovered,[33] and "women who ostensibly professed reluc-tance to be sent back to their original fold were . . . segregated in special camps and there exposed to a process of resolute persuasion."[34] All this further stripped women of their dignity and agency, making them pawns in the state's game of legitimation. Urvashi Butalia argues that these re-patriations allowed the Indian state to play Rama, creating a Ravana out of Pakistan and casting its new nation as the perfect state, the veritable *ram rajya* of the epic.[35] Rama's goal is to get Sita back, in the epic and here too, yet Sita's recovery is more for Rama's honor than for Sita's benefit.[36] The state emerges heroic, the family honorable, and Sita bereft. The epic also sets a mythic precedent for families to ultimately reject their repatriated Sitas. And in the epic, a rejected Sita commits suicide, setting another precedent, which Shanti tries to follow but Chhalia prevents. These Sitas have been repatriated only to be rebuffed and left for dead. The state hasn't "rehabilitated" these Sitas; the state has used these Sitas to rehabilitate itself.

Rehabilitating the State in the Bedroom

Amar Akbar Anthony certainly bears many similarities with *Chhalia,* as Amar and Chhalia both provide for a "fallen" woman who has been be-trayed by her family, yet this is more than a simple narrative recycling. Amar, like Chhalia, is the moral center of the film, a veritable avatar for ushering in a new ethical order. He is by name an "immortal one" *(amar),* both "divine" and "deathless," and following the traditional protocol of avatars, he has as his consort an incarnation of Lakshmi, the goddess of wealth. But even if he isn't an avatar, only an aptly named superhero, Amar nevertheless plays a crucial role in the film in constructing an idealized moral order. And this, as we mentioned in the introduction, is an essen-tial component of all Desai's films. Amar offers the viewer drama rather than melodrama, verisimilitude rather than illusion—and, in so doing, he provides a provocative affirmation, contra *Chhalia,* of the state as moral exemplar.

One noticeable characteristic of Amar, and one that marks him as very different from his brothers, is the collapse of distinctions between public and private, as well as work and play. Amar really is all work and no play, and he doesn't seem to have a private life separate from his role as state functionary. He was raised by his police officer father to be a police officer, and he fully inhabits that role, never ceasing to be an embodi-ment of the power of the state and never resisting or questioning its rule.

For Amar, there is no extrajudicial action, for all his actions are within the purview of the law as he sees it, even when he's helping Anthony steal the clothes from a priest and a musician so that the two can impersonate them.

If the Amar avatar indeed represents a new rule of law—for according to classical doctrine every avatar inaugurates a reworking of dharma—how do we then define that reworking? One way to start is to think of it as a form of Protestant Hinduism, with a work ethic that corresponds to Weber's famous formulation. Like his Protestant counterparts, Amar engages in work in the secular world with a religious zeal, with little evidence of other religious endeavors, and the accrued capital can be seen as instrumental in the development of a larger political order. Here, however, that order is as much "capitolism" as capitalism, for his efforts lead not only to a reification and rehabilitation of the state but also to a reformation of the police, casting them as unmarked Hindu adepts.[37]

Consider, for example, the scene where Amar comes to Anthonyville in search of Robert, who has absconded after shooting Inspector Khanna, and then comes to blows with Anthony because he won't disclose Robert's whereabouts. Anthony offers smart-aleck replies to Amar's inquiries, and Amar twice rebuffs Anthony's offer of a handshake. Then, in a show of power, the policeman throws Anthony to the ground. Anthony explains that he always offers respect to lawmen, but this new officer doesn't show him respect in kind, and that if it weren't for his uniform he would have already beaten him up and sent him to the hospital. Amar takes the bait. He hands his shirt and gun to one of the four constables who arrived with him, and then he challenges the local kingpin to a fight. Anthony comes forward and again offers his hand, which this time Amar grasps but then uses to throw him to the ground and begin their battle.

The scene takes place in Anthonyville, where Anthony as the local *dada* is a kind of officer in his own right, although Amar doesn't recognize the latter's jurisdiction. It's Amar who is the law, not some neighborhood big shot who thinks he's doing God's work, and the state must inevitably triumph over the shadow state. Moreover, Amar is the law with or without his uniform. After Anthony first throws Amar to the ground, two constables come and seize Anthony, giving the lie to the idea that his opponent is somehow no longer a policeman without his uniform.

Anthony then explains with a sly smile that he won't hit the police because they are his *maai-baap*—his "parents," namely his patrons or masters—but this too is a lie. Amar is the police, whether dressed as an officer or a civilian, and Anthony will give him a good fight, but he will lose. And he does.

Likewise crucial for understanding Amar and his new dispensation is the way the state operates through bodies in a very literal form of the body politic. While the state can insinuate itself through various mechanisms—for example, the surveillance state, the bureaucratic state, the military state—with Amar the state acts in a more direct and intimate way. It isn't just that Amar is always a police officer, with no discernible difference between public and private personas; police work is also *embodied* in the police, such that even the files Amar writes and the punches he throws are performances of statecraft. And when Amar offers his blood to the woman who has been hit by a car—a woman who unbeknownst to him is his own mother—he does so not as a dutiful citizen or fellow human being but as a state representative. All his actions in the film are acts of state, whether dressed as an officer or dressed as a civilian, whether being honest or being deceptive. Amar, like Rama, is "dharma incarnate."[38] Put another way, Amar doesn't need to take the law into his hands, for the law is his hands. This is the police state incorporated.

This form of body politics is most apparent in the episode when Amar first encounters Lakshmi. After posing as a prostitute and trying to extort money from Amar, Lakshmi begs him to arrest her so that she can be released from the misery that has been forced on her. Instead, Amar takes Lakshmi back to her stepmother's house, and Lakshmi lies, quite convincingly, telling her stepmother that the police have arrested her son, Ranjeet. The stepmother is furious, slapping Lakshmi across the face and insisting that she bail him out of jail. When Lakshmi laments that she doesn't have the money, the enraged woman tries to seize the gold jewelry worn by Lakshmi's grandmother. At this point, Amar enters with two constables, personally handcuffs Lakshmi's stepmother—although the crime she has committed isn't named—and has his men take her away to the police station. The grandmother expresses fear that Ranjeet will return for revenge after his release, at which point Amar tells her the truth—that he is still at large—but promises to provide the house with round-the-clock protection. Lakshmi and her grandmother lament that the house belongs to their step-relatives and the rent is so far overdue that the landlord has given them notice. "Fine, then," Amar says. "Why don't you both come with me?" And then he clarifies, with a little smile, "To my home."

Amar offers Lakshmi his home rather than a police cell—where he has just sent her stepmother—in another instance of what might be thought of as an extrajudicial rendering of the law. If only Amar made such distinctions! Instead of following the standard procedure and bringing Lakshmi directly to the police station, Amar creates his own protocol: he brings her to her home, has her lie to her stepmother to somehow ascertain the truthfulness of her story about being coerced into a life of crime, and—when he finds out that she's on the verge of either being attacked by her vengeful stepbrother or getting evicted along with her elderly grandmother—asks her if she would like to come to his home. The other, unstated options are jail or homelessness. She agrees, demurely and with downcast eyes. But does she really have a choice? The next time we see her, the two are clearly married. Has Lakshmi merely traded one sphere of bondage for another?

One compelling way to read this is to step for a moment outside of the film and encounter the two characters, in the manner of many Bollywood fans, primarily as stand-ins for the stars who play them. Vinod Khanna, the actor behind Amar, is literally a child of Partition—his family emigrated from Peshawar to Amritsar—and for many decades he was a star of mainstream Hindi cinema, playing tough yet sensitive males. In 1997 he joined the Hindu nationalist Bharatiya Janata Party (BJP), and the following year he was elected to the Lok Sabha, the lower house of the Indian Parliament. In 2002 he became union minister for culture and tourism and then a Minister of State. Like the Amar character, he too is a modern Hindu, although his political agenda is more explicitly Hindutva.

Conversely, Shabana Azmi, who appears as Lakshmi, is a child of Partition more figuratively. When *Amar Akbar Anthony* was released in 1977, she was already famous for her work in the social reformist "parallel cinema," winning a National Film Award for Best Actress for her debut in *Ankur* (Shyam Benegal, 1974). And she had become infamous for having played the mute and pathetic Janta ("Public") in a scathing satire of Indira Gandhi's government, *Kissa Kursi Ka* (Amrit Nahata, 1975; finally released in 1977), which so enraged Indira's first son and enforcer figure, Sanjay, that he had all available prints of the film burned.[39] Shabana was also widely known by the successes of her parents—the progressive poet Kaifi Azmi and the theater actress Shaukat Azmi—most prominent of which was an award-winning film they both worked on, *Garam Hawa* (M. S. Sathyu, 1973), about the difficult plight of Muslims in post-Partition India.[40] She has won many acting awards in the decades since. And she has become an outspoken social activist for the Left, emerging as a forceful critic of religious extremism after the Bombay riots in 1993, winning the Rajiv Gandhi Award (named after Indira's second son) for Excellence in Secularism in 1994, and joining the Rajya Sabha—the Indian Parliament's upper house—in 1997.

If Amar's rehabilitation of Lakshmi is also Vinod Khanna's rehabilitation of Shabana Azmi—in the past and, as the film's success continues, into the present—*Amar Akbar Anthony* can be seen to enact a conservative agenda on multiple counts. It brings a Muslim woman into a Hindu family, an icon of leftist parallel cinema into mainstream Bollywood entertainment, a social activist into a proto-Hindutva world, and an advocate for women's rights into a situation in which women must be saved by men.

Back within the film, Amar's intervention seems no less patriarchal. His actions here offer a rejoinder to Pierre Trudeau's famous remark, uttered in 1967 when he was Canada's minister of justice, that "there is no place for the state in the bedrooms of the nation." Here rehabilitation occurs courtesy of the state and in the state's own bedroom, and this is presented as a natural extension of Amar's duty. During the Central Recovery Operation it is said that "in many instances the police themselves were the abductors of women,"[41] yet there is no sense here (or anywhere else in the movie) that Amar has acted improperly or immorally. And although we never again see Lakshmi's grandmother, leaving the viewer to wonder whether she too made it to Amar's home or suffered some alternate fate, we are not invited to question Amar's motives or methods. The decades following the release of *Amar Akbar Anthony* were filled with movies about "family values" and how the nuclear family could (and should) be a model for the nation,[42] but what we find here is the opposite. The family needs the state, for the family and its values are in disarray.

This kind of government involvement in the family and in family planning, and the way the state insinuates itself into the bedrooms of the nation, is perhaps best understood with reference to the Emergency. During those years, in what might be thought of as a state-sponsored eugenics movement, the government focused its efforts at birth control with a campaign to encourage small families, "Hum Do, Hamare Do" (We Two, Our Two), and with sterilizations, many of which were coerced to fill political quotas.[43] Sterilizations, in particular, became commoditized within the logic of the state: the procedure yielded sterilization certificates, and the certificates became a precious commodity in a variety of illicit markets. This created a system that fostered coercion and corruption, eliciting in the population a combination of forced opportunism, pragmatism, and complicity. Most notably, Emma Tarlo notes, "sterilization had become a medium through which people could negotiate their housing rights."[44]

In *Amar Akbar Anthony,* Lakshmi finds herself in a bizarre inversion of this formulation. At first Lakshmi isn't a prostitute but must pose as one because she is coerced to do so. Yet in taking up with Amar, who can put her in prison if he isn't pleased with her "rehabilitation," she is in a situation not far removed from prostitution. She has given her body to the state to avoid a prison cell, turning her sexuality into a medium for negotiation, for a happy Hindu family needs Hindu children. But, as we said before, does she really have a choice? It is this relationship with the state—one of codependence, intimacy, and complicity, all with the veneer of respectability and propriety—that gestures to the Emergency. One young man, reflecting on Emergency-era sterilizations, put it succinctly: "The pressure was everywhere."[45] Whereas in *Chhalia,* with its allusions to Partition, the state was absent and useless for any form of family planning, here the state is eerily present—in public spaces, private spaces, and even in bedrooms—and it is a moral force and exemplar. In this way, as Amar rehabilitates Lakshmi he likewise rehabilitates the state. It is the state embodied in Amar—certainly not "fraud" as embodied in Chhalia—that is the basis for the idealized moral order.

The Buried Gun: Disciplined Celibacy
and Muscular Hinduism

If we've established that Amar's sexuality, unlike that of his brothers, is controlled and dispassionate, and if this sexuality has been mobilized in the service of the state, then the next step is to think about the particulars of Amar's sexual restraint as a way of understanding the politics they help engender. One of the most suggestive moments that cites this restraint occurs early in the film, when Amar buries the gun that his father has given him. When his father questions him, Amar explains that he wants to keep the gun away from his middle brother, the proto-Anthony. Later in the film, when he digs up the gun and is once again questioned by his father, he offers the same response. Such talk of a father giving his oldest son a gun—and the son not wanting another to have it, then burying it, forgetting it, and later retrieving it—certainly invites some form of symbolic reading, whether psychoanalytic or allegorical. Sometimes a gun is just a gun, and sometimes it's something else. In this case, we think it's both.

To the extent that the gun Amar puts aside is phallic, both weapon and male sexual metonym, Amar comes to look strangely like his apparent opposite: Gandhi. As a child, Amar ran away from Gandhi—literally and figuratively, as previously mentioned—but he didn't distance himself from Gandhi's idea that one's "gun" mustn't be touched or fired, and that one's biology and morality are closely tethered and must be cultivated in tandem. To this end, Gandhi engaged in rigorous sexual, dietary, and behavioral constraints, with the idea that this "biomorality" was necessary for cultivating both self and nation. As he explained in a letter to Shankarlal Banker in 1918:

> It is easier to conquer the entire world than to subdue the enemies in our body. And, therefore, for the man who succeeds in this conquest, the former will be easy enough. The self-government which you, I and all others have to attain is in fact this. Need I say more? The point of it all is that you can serve the country only with this body.[46]

Crucial to Gandhi's biomoral regimen was the practice of celibacy, as he was a firm believer in the power of semen retention to provide life-giving power: biologically, morally, and politically.[47] Celibacy and semen retention have long been practiced in the subcontinent following a similar logic, often as the key to both physical and moral health.[48] As Joseph Alter notes, "Many Hindu men were able to fully appreciate the logic of celibacy as a means to psychological security, self-improvement, and national reform," and this was crucial to Gandhi's mass appeal.[49] This merging together of bodily discipline, personal conviction, and political ideology to create a new kind of citizen and citizenry can be thought of, following Alter, as a form of "somatic nationalism."[50]

Compared with Gandhi, however, Amar enacts a much more muscular version of somatic nationalism, akin to the practice of North Indian wrestlers, who also follow a program involving sexual restraint, somatic discipline for a higher purpose, and mastery of grappling moves. Amar certainly looks like a wrestler when he beats up Anthony,[51] yet he also acts like a wrestler by adhering—as best the viewer can tell—to the code of restraint and disciplined celibacy known as *brahmacarya*.[52] The modern version of this code of conduct is "absolutely imperative" for a wrestler to follow,[53] for doing so produces vigor, powerful semen to engender powerful male offspring, and overall "a citizen who embodies the essence of national integration and strength."[54] In addition to sexual abstinence and rigorous exercise, a wrestler—like Amar—is to display "absolute devotion to one's guru, respect for one's elders, a serious attitude toward learning and knowledge, [and] devotion to God, and keep company with like-minded youth."[55]

But the code of *brahmacarya* also dictates that the young wrestler "be protected from the seduction of modern life where consumption, sensuality, and lust threaten to undermine discipline"—which means, in fact, that he should not go to cinema halls and watch films.[56] As Alter explains, "Popular cinema, which is saturated with romantic themes and suggestively lurid images, is unanimously regarded [in the literature on *brahmacarya*] as the most debauched aspect of modern life."[57] As a form of entertainment, writes K. J. Shastri, "cinema is a great enemy of modern society. It is full of obscene, erotic, and indecent images which enter the sub-conscious, lie dormant, and then result in night-emission."[58]

This aspect of *brahmacarya* gestures toward an irony of Amar's character, for while Amar is a veritable exemplar of the *brahmacarya* ideal, this idealized moral order is not particularly cinematic. Put another way, Amar isn't *filmi*. Akbar and Anthony take center stage, quite literally, singing and dancing, but Amar has no song-and-dance numbers of his own. He is nearly always workmanlike, exemplifying the ideal, popularized by Gandhi, that "work is worship." Amar exhibits little of the playfulness and sentimentality that mark his brothers—commendable restraint for a policeman but perhaps not for a film star. In this way, Amar is the anti-Anthony (or perhaps Vinod Khanna is the anti–Amitabh Bachchan). Those who would recognize themselves in Amar would likely not be film devotees; they'd be responsible workers, whether strict followers of *brahmacarya* or not.

What Amar exemplifies is a form of muscular Hinduism, the subcontinent's answer to muscular Christianity, "which was a broad cultural movement concerned with the moral training of young men through exercise and organized sport from the late 1850s through the end of the first World War."[59] Muscular Christianity made great inroads in England and the United States, shaping ideas of masculinity, sportsmanship, and imperialism,[60] and it also helped form corresponding ideas in India.[61] In these places, "the connection between masculine potency and social and economic power seem[s] to have been alive in the minds of most marginalized men,"[62] as well as in the minds of elites and politicians, such that efforts to masculinize man and country came from both directions. The "somatic nationalism" involved in these projects is apparent. As one British author wrote in 1901: "If asked what our muscular Christianity has done, we point to the British Empire. Our nation would never have been built up by a nation of idealists and logicians."[63]

Seminal Statecraft: Shiva and Rama

Talk of burying one's gun in the ground also brings to mind images of castration, a desideratum for many Indian ascetics,[64] and this gestures to another divinity and another story. The most striking parallel here is Lord Shiva's self-castration—a voluntary act like Amar's—which helps account for the world's creation as well as its flaws. There are numerous versions of this story, but the account in the *Mahabharata* (10.17) is perhaps the most instructive and iconic.[65]

In the beginning, we are told, when the universe was just a single ocean, Brahma asks Shiva to create living beings, and although Shiva agrees, he then plunges into the water, where he remains in meditative austerity. After a long wait, Brahma finally engenders another creator, Daksha, who quickly creates the entire world. This world—which is our own—is beset by hunger and violence, and although Brahma creates food, the strong still consume the weak and beings multiply sexually. In time, Shiva rises out of the water, and seeing this imperfect creation, he is enraged and cuts off his penis *(linga)*. The world has been created by someone else, so what use does he have for his penis? Shiva's detached penis falls to earth, where it remains, worshipped by Daksha's flawed creation. Shiva himself abides as an ascetic, angry and withdrawn but also compassionate, creative, even seductive. And this antierotic withdrawal and discipline, which is a model for the *brahmacarya* code, provides Shiva with great sexual potency, which from time to time he will put to use.

The story creates an opposition between two types of creation, as David Shulman observes, "one a deathless, perfect creation mentally conceived but never physically achieved, the other a real, external, but hopelessly limited and muddled world."[66] The latter creation, we might say, is the world of Robert, Kishanlal, and their gangs. It is beset with hunger, desire, and struggles for power. It is a world dominated by violence, and it is definitely real—all the more so during the two years of Emergency Rule that preceded the film, with police detentions, slum razings, and forced sterilizations (which bear a painful reminder of Shiva's self-castration).

The *Mahabharata* itself has a lot to say about our "hopelessly limited and muddled world," and it goes into great detail about how it is governed by the gun's predecessor, the Rod *(danda)*—which can mean "stick" or "club," "force" or "assault," as well as "punishment" or "penis." The Rod, according to the text, is the true ruler and it is worthy of veneration as dharma, the true law: "The Rod rules all subjects and it alone protects them. The Rod stays awake while they sleep. The wise know that the Rod is dharma itself. The Rod protects dharma, O prince, and likewise protects profit *(artha)* and pleasure *(kama)*. The Rod, it is said, is the sum of the three aims of human life *(trivarga)*."[67] Arjuna, in the *Mahabharata*, as well as Manu, in the *Manusmriti*—his famous treatise on dharma—agree that the Rod "is a sort of king who pre-exists the king and which controls absolutely everything on earth."[68]

The gun is today's Rod, a veritable law unto itself—and, like Shiva's *linga,* an object of veneration. And that's a good reason to bury it and to keep it away from one's brothers, in the hope of bringing about a different world. The inhabitants of Daksha's creation are led by their allegiance to violence as well as to sex—two of the four major addictions described in Sanskrit texts, along with gambling and drinking—and both allegiances are closely allied and extremely common. The violence of ecstasy and the ecstasy of violence are staples of life and art, especially in Sanskrit literature and Hindi film.[69]

The other world is that of Amar—"deathless" *(amar)* by name—whose perfect creation is an idealized moral order. This is a cinematic conceit, not a tangible reality, yet to the extent that this world is "physically achieved," it is done through the physical comportment of Amar himself. Amar can be likened to Shiva, who casts off his penis in disgust at the state of the world and then engages in a somatic discipline of his own creation for its benefit, first as an ascetic and then as householder.[70] And, like Shiva, Amar's goals in these pursuits are less sexual than social; both are trying to make the world a little less muddled. But questions linger for Amar's Shiva-self: "If Shiva no longer needs his *linga,* the world can certainly use it—indeed will worship it, as we know. But how, exactly, are we to understand this human exploitation of the *linga?* What functions does it serve? And what is the effect of this 'loss' upon the god? Are his anger or his depression ever really assuaged?"[71] And is his rage, unleashed for a moment on Robert's men after his adopted father is shot, appeased by his marriage, by Robert's imprisonment, or by his family's reunification?

The human exploitation of Amar's *linga*—in this case, the gun—provides its devotees with a form of empowerment, but it is not a divine instrument. This form of "human exploitation"—shooting people or holding them at gunpoint—simply leads to more humans being exploited and being forced to act against their will. It is an instrument of Daksha's dispensation, not Shiva's. So how does its "loss" affect Amar? Here is the answer: the loss becomes Amar's gain. Amar disciplines his body to become an instrument of the state, a tool for social betterment, and this seems to assuage his anger. And to the extent that he is "depressed," domesticating and rehabilitating Lakshmi seems to lift his spirits. But just as Shiva casts away his *linga* yet remains connected to it, and responsible for it, Amar cannot make the gun go away, for it is ultimately his responsibility. His rage at our imperfect world dissipates with his triumphs, but it is sure to return. Guns don't stay buried for long in Daksha's world.

Nevertheless, Amar still looks a lot like a version of Lord Rama, for unlike Shiva his personality is defined by his relationships to his brothers and his father, and this might help explain his continuing appeal (particularly in paternalistic and patriarchal states). Amar shares Rama's archetypal relationship with his younger brothers. In both cases, there is an indissoluble bond between younger siblings and oldest brother; and in both cases, the former recognize the latter's authority as paramount, willingly subordinating themselves to his vision of the law. Furthermore, like Rama, Amar is provisionally a team player but in the final analysis, a solo act. As eldest brothers, Amar and Rama act as effective heads of family, nurturing and directing their younger brothers according to their own sense of propriety, and yet they also envision themselves as solitary and self-contained.

At the end of *Amar Akbar Anthony,* Amar and Anthony steal the clothes from a musician and a priest who are on their way to meet Robert, and then Amar, dressed as the musician and disguised with a beard, arrives first at Robert's home. With a crash of his cymbals and a salute, he announces himself: "The Amar Lal and Brothers Band reporting, sir!" When Robert asks about his brothers, Amar says incredulously, "Mine?" And then, "Oh, sir! I'm three-in-one. Everybody here is my"—catching sight of Akbar—"brother." He goes and embraces Akbar, thus completing the fraternal reunification, and affirms, "Hindu, Muslim, Sikh, Christian—all of us are brothers." Robert continues to express his doubts about Amar's abilities, and Amar replies, "By the Lord's blessing, I'm the equal of twenty men. Just give me the opportunity—I'll play a whole band's worth all by myself."

Amar's reply begins with a mock show of service and then bewilderment, for why would Amar need the assistance of brothers? He is truly a one-man band, armed with bongos, cymbals, accordion, trumpet, and penny whistle. But more than that, he is somehow all of his brothers in one, and perhaps because he embodies their respective faiths as well, everyone present is his brother. Here he prefigures Amitabh Bachchan's character John Jani Janaradan in *Naseeb* (Manmohan Desai, 1981), who likewise encompassed Hinduism, Christianity, and Islam in one person, and he echoes Chhalia, that earlier avatar of Manmohan Desai's creation who had sung, "Hindu, Muslim, Sikh, or Christian, I salute them all!" But unlike Chhalia, who saw no distinction between religions, Amar sees them as brothers—with big brother, apparently, subsuming and eclipsing his siblings. Fraternity here does not imply equality. Amar is a conglomeration of faiths that places Christianity and Islam inside the domain of (an unmarked) Hinduism, relegating the former to somehow latent status within the latter.

Such religious readings become explicit in what follows, for Akbar and Anthony are flamboyantly disguised as hypermarked religious figures—a Muslim tailor and a Christian priest. Amar remains unmarked by religion until the final song, when the three brothers sing, "To make the impossible possible / The possible impossible. / Together in one place, we three united: / Amar Akbar Anthony!" As each brother sings his name, he performs the iconic gesture associated with his religion: namaste, salaam, the sign of the cross. And although they sing that "two is better than one, and three is better than two," as Philip Lutgendorf observes, "Amar does so, tellingly, as an empty signifier of 'All-India' encompassment: a *one-man band* to whose tune the junior brothers dance, as (from a certain hegemonic perspective) minorities invariably and properly do."[72] Also tellingly, and also during the final song, Amar takes his penny whistle and, looking like the proverbial pied piper, plays a tune at triple time and darts around the room so miraculously fast that no one can follow him. Amar is the leader, for sure, and it's only by his choice that his brothers can even keep up. He is, after all—much like Lord Rama—"the equal of twenty men."

Yet Amar stands in stark contrast to Rama when it comes to his relationship with his father, his patrimony, and his conception of the law. Rama offers complete fidelity to his father's honor and never asserts himself against parental authority. As he explains, "There is no greater act of righteousness *(dharma)* than this: obedience to one's father and doing as he bids."[73] Moreover, this version of patriarchal law becomes the basis for state law, such that Rama's idealized form of government is family law writ large.

Amar, however, has no fidelity to his own father's honor, whatever little of it there is, and directly disobeys him. For example, when Kishanlal deposits his three children under the Gandhi statue, he says, "Amar, my son, don't any of you leave here. I'm coming right back." But before Kishanal has even made it back to his car, a defiant Amar starts chasing after him, running out of the park and down the street, screaming for him to stop, as his father drives away. Kishanlal had abandoned his children previously, to go to prison and then to confront Robert, and each time his family suffered. Why would Amar expect anything different this time, without even a mother to care for them? As Amar chases after his father's car, however, he gets run over by Robert's men who are chasing it as well. Kishanlal—only a few car lengths ahead and thus sure to have heard his son's screams and likely to have seen the accident—doesn't circle back to pick him up. But this is fortunate, for it allows Amar, unconscious on the side of the road, to be rescued by Inspector Khanna and begin a new life with a new father whom he can trust.

It is perhaps this recognition of the inadequacy of his father as a provider and protector that leads Amar as an adult to invert Rama's logic—*Amar*, after all, is *Rama* backwards—and make state law the basis for family law. Even Kishanlal seems to concur. In the film's penultimate scene, Robert is thrown into the police lockup and falls before Kishanlal, clutching his feet in the familiar gesture that signals another's authority and one's own subservience. But Kishanlal's authority isn't final. Kishanlal approaches the bars, on the other side of which stand Bharati, her sons, and their partners, and says, "Inspector Sahib, just once, I would like to grasp my three sons to my breast." Inspector Khanna nods in consent, unlocks the cell, and father and sons share a hug. Here Kishanlal recognizes that Inspector Khanna, Amar's adoptive father, literally holds the key to his family's reunification. Amar may have two fathers, but the biological one is the lesser—and everybody knows it. Even Kishanlal's request to hug his three sons "just once" hints at the possibility that this has never happened before. This is a family union made possible by a surrogate and brought about both in and by the penal state. The film has been a kind of state-sponsored family therapy session, and it concludes with a family that has actually improved as a site of love and support—and with justice served.

The Gun Unburied: Amar, Kishanlal, and Manmohan

Amar is separated from both his father and the gun he buried for twenty-two years until a fortuitous set of circumstances leads to a happy reunion. But the unearthing of the gun also raises questions about what precisely Amar lost on the fateful day the gun was interred and what he can now regain. What meaning do we ascribe to the unburying of the gun? What exactly is being reclaimed?

After Akbar discovers that Kishanlal is Bharati's husband as well as his own father, and that he is missing, he goes to the police station and asks Amar for help. He provides the name of the missing person and the only address Akbar knows—the Koliwada, the old family home. Remarking that the name and place seem strangely familiar, Amar sets off in search. Kishanlal now lives in a tonier part of town, but he has come back to the old neighborhood to smack down one of his underlings, who has failed to pass on the funds allotted to one of the area's impoverished families. Kishanlal personally distributes the money, and promises to return every month to do the same. He then reflects aloud on how the neighborhood looks exactly the same as it did two decades ago. Although he has changed, becoming richer, he'd give it all up to be reunited, just once, with his lost children. Wandering into his old house, which stands with the front door open, he muses, "Bhagvan, everything You've sent my way since—take it all away. But once—just once—bring me back together with my lost children."

Just then he sees Amar approaching and, fearful of the police, hides behind the doorway. There he watches as Amar, in an evident daze, walks over to the rock wall across from their home. In a flashback, Amar sees himself crouched there as a young boy, with his father's gift of a gun in his hand, digging a hole in the dirt. Amar finds the spot and digs frantically until he unearths the gun. "Amar, my son," gasps Kishanlal, then approaches him to ask how he knew about the gun. "Twenty-two years ago, on the Fifteenth of August, my father gave me this pistol, and to hide it from my brother I buried it here. . . . But why are you asking me this?" Kishanal, with tears in his eyes, replies, "You remember the pistol your father gave you, yet you don't remember the father who gives you his heart?" Then the two embrace, reunited at last.

FIGURE 7. Amar, gun, and Kishanlal reunited

Although Amar has a glimmer of recognition at the name "Kishanlal,"[74] it is seeing his childhood home that brings back a vision of childhood, which otherwise appears to have been totally forgotten. Even when he sees his father he doesn't recognize him, just as he didn't recognize his mother or brothers. Amar's childhood is connected more closely with place than with parent or sibling. But now, as Amar is drawn to the wall outside his childhood home—like the rest of the neighborhood unchanged by the intervening years—he sees himself and the moment when he buried his father's gift. Suddenly he is desperate to recover it. After scrabbling at the rocky earth to find the gun, he then holds it tenderly, clutching it to his chest, just as Kishanlal comes forward and touches him on the shoulder (Figure 7). Father, son, and gun are reunited simultaneously.

Amar is now ready to accept the proverbial Rod, with its various meanings. Growing up in poverty, with a father in jail and a mother with tuberculosis, and then moving in with a new father who was childless, one can imagine that Amar might have been anxious about fathering children himself.[75] (The follower of *brahmacarya* would know that the practice produces potent semen for creating progeny but that ejaculation enervates the system.) But reconciled with his father, he is now ready to become a father himself. Furthermore, Amar is now ready to wield the Rod in a more personal and punishing fashion, for soon he will jail his father. And Kishanlal seems to recognize this inevitability. As a smuggler and racketeer, he stands on the wrong side of the law. Simply daydreaming in a doorway, breaking no laws, he is scared of the police. And yet he is pleased that his son has joined their ranks. When the two are finally reunited, and the tears flow for both, Kishanlal says, "All the earnings that Bhagvan took twenty years ago He has returned to me today with interest. My son has become a police officer!" As the film nears its end, Kishanlal accepts his imprisonment with calm resignation, even urging his wife, whom he has neither seen nor touched in more than two decades, to be happy in his absence. "Bharati," Kishanlal says cheerfully. "Why are you crying? Today you should be happy. You had lost three sons, hadn't you? But today, along with your three sons, Bhagvan has given you three daughters-in-law." Amar likewise remains dispassionate, for this meting out of justice is just, perhaps even God given.[76]

Yet the gun could have other meanings, especially for Amar or Kishanlal. One possibility is that the gun, as a toy, represents childhood: more specifically, a childhood in Bombay's poor and ramshackle neighborhoods. In the film, the neighborhood in question is an area of Bandra identified as a Koliwada, a hybrid village and slum.[77] In this way, Amar is successful in keeping "the gun" away from his brothers, and Independence Day in the movie is truly an independence day for all the siblings—they move out of the neighborhood and into better areas. In Amar's flashback, the neighborhood looks exactly as it did twenty-two years ago, and the past and the present merge seamlessly in his vision. Kishanlal concurs. "Not a thing back here has changed," he reflects. And this includes the difficulty of scraping by.[78] Kishanlal is providing for a mother and two children, and they are, as he makes clear to his errant flunky, literally dying of hunger. Even after Kishanlal has given the woman a wad of money, she stands in her doorway lifeless and disengaged. They're in the same desperate situation that Bharati and the boys faced when Kishanlal was in prison. It is a world in which survival likely depends on a benefactor or on corruption, or even on both, as when Kishanlal worked for Robert, a known thief.[79] Knowing this, Kishanlal promises personally to deliver the funds to the family each month, for if not, someone in the neighborhood is likely to pocket the money, just as before. But how can one get such a benefactor without doing

something corrupt? One wonders what the family did to "earn" Kishanlal's kindness. Can an honest person survive in this rough neighborhood?

But life in the old neighborhood also has its pleasures. As Kishanlal
reflects, "Yesterday's Kishanlal—how happy he was in this neighborhood,
together with his family!" Kishanlal now lives in a fancy bungalow by the
ocean, and it's not that he's ready to move back, but life in the old neighborhood fills him with a warm nostalgia.[80] Amar's relationship with the
Koliwada is more fraught, especially considering the traumatic years he
suffered there in his father's absence. His final departure afflicted him
with a severe case of amnesia. After what otherwise might have been a very
memorable Independence Day, Amar remembers only his first name and
almost nothing else. Still, seeing his old home triggers memories of his
childhood and that fateful day, and it brings out new emotions: Amar embraces the recovered gun lovingly, much the way Kishanlal holds his
three boys at the end of the film. Amar buried the gun to keep it from Anthony, but he is certainly happy to have it back. Reconnected with the
gun, Amar is soon singing, dancing, and roughhousing with his brothers
as they defeat the bad guys, as though the gun's retrieval brought back
the playfulness of youth. It is, after all, a *toy* gun. As such, one could argue,
the gun represents his childhood in the old neighborhood—a time and
place filled with difficulties, and an existence one wouldn't wish for one's
brothers but that can be looked upon with nostalgia and even joy.

Kishanlal's account has echoes of Desai's own story. Desai's father had
been a successful film director, and the family lived in a big bungalow in
Versova, an upscale neighborhood in the western Bombay suburbs, but
when his father died suddenly at the age of thirty-nine, his mother was
left with large debts and three small children. Manmohan, the youngest,
was only a toddler. His mother sold off the bungalow and much of their
property, and the family moved to a cramped *chawl*, a Bombay-style ten-
ement building, in the bustling South Bombay neighborhood of Khetwadi.
The area remained a touchstone for Desai, a place where he kept an office even after he moved to a more stylish part of town, where he would
come on Sundays to play cricket, and where he found the characters who
populated his films. Like Kishanlal, he felt at home in the old neighborhood, and the street in Khetwadi that housed Desai's office, even in 1984,
"looked not unlike Kishanlal's in *Amar Akbar Anthony*."[81] And when

Desai spoke about Khetwadi, he sounded like Kishanlal reflecting on the Koliwada: "Khetwadi may not be the centre of the world, but from here I can see the joys and sorrows of the middle class."[82] Although Kishanlal's neighborhood might have been yet humbler than Desai's, both looked back on their old stomping grounds with wistfulness, happy to remember the good times and inclined to forget the bad ones.

Like Kishanlal, Desai also experienced real suffering in his place of origin, and of a similar kind. In 1962, Desai's wife contracted a form of tuberculosis, and with no job and a young son to care for, he didn't have enough money to treat her. Unable to scrape by, he needed the help of a benefactor. Fortunately, he found someone better than Robert. As Desai explains,

> I swear upon God, I didn't have money to treat [my wife]. I remember how I scrounged for money, how Mr. Shammi Kapoor [who starred in Desai's flop *Bluff Master* (1963) and] who is now my son's father-in-law—we have been friends since then—came to know of my plight. He gave me Rs. 2000, and I felt very embarrassed. I paid him back within 25 days. I didn't want to take it. He put it in my pocket, you know.[83]

Again like Kishanlal, Desai responded to this period of hardship by focusing his efforts on making money, becoming more the high roller than the family man, dressing as a playboy, and developing his own version of a prosperity gospel. In Desai's words,

> I would like to have lots and lots and lots of money because I know when I had no money what it was like. . . . Money can't give you happiness, but money can bring you everything else, everything but happiness. Without money you can't do anything in this world. . . . I need money. You go in a crowd of 200 people. Without money nobody speaks to you; with money you're a big man.[84]

Here too Desai sounds like Kishanlal, or even Robert. All of them share a passion for making money and the belief that money is the only capital with real currency in the world. Likewise, they all take pleasure in being big men, reveling more in foppish pleasures than in Amar's world of law and order. All of them, the classic texts might say, think that by accruing enough "profit" *(artha)* and relishing the resultant "pleasure" *(kama)*, they can somehow bypass the more quotidian world of "duty" *(dharma)*, and in this way leverage the three aims of human life for their future happiness. But Daksha's flawed world is fickle (and cruel), and just as Kishanlal and Robert ended up in jail, so too did Desai fall on more difficult times.

After a string of blockbusters culminating in *Mard* (1985), Desai's career fizzled. *Gangaa Jamunaa Saraswathi* (1988), the last film that Desai directed, was a flop, even though it was a veritable sequel to *Amar Akbar Anthony.* As Sidharth Bhatia notes, "It must have been a blow for a man who had continuously directed hits. Smart man that he was, he would have realized that the connection he had with the audience had broken. Perhaps it was time for a newer, younger generation to take over."[85] Then came *Toofan* (1989), which he produced and let his son direct, but that flopped as well. Desai was despondent and never made another film. During these final years, Desai moved back to Khetwadi, where he suffered doubly—no longer able to make films and crippled with chronic back pain. On the first day of March in 1991, Desai jumped (or fell) off the building that housed his home and office in Khetwadi. Whether intentional or accidental, his death seems to confirm Thomas Wolfe's famous reflection:

> You can't go back home to your family, back home to your childhood, back home to romantic love, back home to a young man's dreams of glory and of fame . . . back home to the father you have lost and have been looking for, back home to someone who can help you, save you, ease the burden for you, back home to the old forms and systems of things which once seemed everlasting but which are changing all the time—back home to the escapes of Time and Memory.[86]

Desai lived a life full of passion, mirroring various aspects of the characters he created, particularly in *Amar Akbar Anthony,* and living up to the legacy of his divine namesake. According to Desai, "Manmohan is one of the names of Krishna. My father and mother must have given me the name because they knew I'd turn out a womanizer; they gave me the correct name."[87] Yet Desai had little love for the god, kinship with Krishna aside, perhaps seeing a little too much of himself in the latter's exploits: "Krishna! He's no god! He left Rukmani for Radha. Why glorify a man who has a mistress, who was a womanizer with all those gopis! And he won the whole Mahabharata war by cheating, by deceit, treachery. I have no respect for Krishna. He makes my blood boil."[88] Desai needed someone else to be the center of the moral universe, and he chose Amar.

2

Akbar

PARDA AND PARODY

. . . .

> Enthralled by the charms of all religions,
> I dance in the mosque to the call of the bells.
> Brahman! I'll call every river my mother—
> Unconfined to the Ganga or Narmada.
>
> —Akbar Ilahabadi, "Aata hai wajd mujhko
> har deen ki ada par"

AKBAR, the film's exemplary Muslim, is named in the middle of the title. The position gives him neither the honor of precedence nor the satisfaction of the last word. Is this the place to decry the plight of the middle brother, sandwiched between straight edge Amar and bad boy Anthony?

Inshallah, this chapter will establish something very different. Our argument opens with a proposition: Akbar's association with poetry situates him within Indian film tradition as a well-established type of romantic hero. We will make an intertextual move to survey a well-loved but also well-worn genre of the previous decade: the "Muslim social." We will then rewind to the start of *Amar Akbar Anthony* and explore the narrative stratum our Muslim brother dominates—a sort of ghettoized subplot—as a parodic appropriation of that genre. On the way, we will explore his role as a poet, focusing on the song "Parda Hai Parda," and we will press on with some ideas about his role as a spiritual adept, concluding with some thoughts about another song, "Shirdi Wale Sai Baba."

This argument will build on the interpretive scheme laid out in our introduction, in which we read the urban geography the film constructs as symbolic of India's history. And it seems useful to define two more of this chapter's building blocks up front. First, the Muslim social: a genre of Bombay film whose fortunes peaked in the 1960s. Its features include the use of literary Urdu in dialogue and song and an urban, North Indian milieu in which stock figures—Muslim aristocrats, courtesans, and poets—come together in an evocation of a feudal past. A double nostalgia clings to these works: the nostalgia toward bygone days the films themselves purvey is compounded by the attitude with which filmgoers would have greeted them, as early as 1977, as relics of an obsolete genre.

Second, the Muslim subplot, by which we mean the strand of *Amar Akbar Anthony*'s narrative that is dominated by Akbar in isolation from his two brothers. It hinges on his courtship of the feisty doctor, Salma, against the wishes of her rich and conservative father, Tayyab Ali. What connects the Muslim subplot of our *masala* movie to the Muslim socials of the previous generation is a relation of parody. Through its parody of the older genre, we argue, *Amar Akbar Anthony* assimilates and neutralizes potentially volatile aspects of Indian Muslim identity as represented through cinema.

But the Muslim hero who emerges from our text is not a passive or disempowered figure. In fact, the character we are going to introduce here has an extraordinary power, for while his face presents one message to the world, his voice transmits another. The actor who plays Akbar moves him along through the story in a playful and agreeable way, but when the narrative reaches certain points of crisis, the singer takes over and enacts interventions through music. This multidimensionality is the key to the character. At the narrative level, Akbar is a lover, not a fighter. But the task he assumes in the film's musical numbers is worthy of any hero, for his singing voice—to drop another cliché—speaks truth to power. And however disparate they may seem in style and content, considered as speech acts, his songs are aimed at the same sort of radical effect. They dissolve barriers—illusory or ideological curtains—that prevent people from connecting with one another. By this chapter's end, it will turn out that the middle brother is indeed the central brother. And as the bearer of this musical gift, he is nothing less than the movie's beating heart (Figure 8).

FIGURE 8. Akbar's big green heart

From Emo to Hero (via Urdu)

Diegetically speaking, to be sure, of the three brothers Akbar is the baby.
But his juniormost position in the triad is more than a simple reflection
of the chronological order of the three religions the brothers represent.
We have argued in the preceding chapter that Amar's senior rank comes
with a portfolio of responsibilities, privileges, and expectations. Akbar's
status is similarly loaded. The character's emotional openness and vul-
nerability relative to his brothers—along with an indication of his vocal
talents—are established definitively with his appearance in the film's
opening sequence. Raju, the not-yet-Akbar, is a squalling toddler. And
as played (or, to use the more precise Indian English term, as "picturised")
as a man in his early twenties by Rishi Kapoor, he is a different sort of
hero, more winsome and cuddly than the two-fisted model represented
by Vinod Khanna and Amitabh Bachchan.

Rishi Kapoor is the son of Raj Kapoor (1924–1988), "India's showman,"
a giant of the post-Independence Golden Age of Hindi cinema and one
of its premier directors into the 1980s. Rishi's debut in his father's *Mera
Naam Joker* (1971) and the cementing of his stardom two years later in

another family production, *Bobby* (1973), were thus heralded by a certain characterization of him as the crown prince, the heir apparent.[1] In addition to the physical resemblance, Rishi's screen persona follows the precedent of Raj in a certain affective similarity, but in the son the father's insouciance is transmuted into something more fresh faced and ingenuous. At the time of *Amar Akbar Anthony*'s release, Rishi was twenty-four.

Boyish, rounded where his brothers' edges are hard, possibly even somewhat coddled and spoiled—what kind of hero is this? The ready answer: As a profile, this is actually not far removed from a classic sort of Indian film protagonist. Rishi's cuteness indexes the recuperation (in a playful 1970s spirit) of a trope the previous decade had just about worn out. This is the sensitive soul with whom the spectator is invited to identify through vicarious struggle with his torments, a type discussed by Ashis Nandy in his essay on the "Terribly Effeminate, Maudlin, Self-Destructive Heroes of Indian Cinema."[2] The definitive role here is the tragic Devdas, the scion of Bengali gentry trapped between his feudal inheritance and colonial modernity, in the story of the same name. Devdas's great interpreter was Dilip Kumar, who played the doomed romantic in the 1955 version; other stars who were cast in a similar mold included Guru Dutt, Rajendra Kumar, and, to some extent, Raj Kapoor himself.[3] Devdas was a Hindu, but the persona has important antecedents in Indo-Islamic literature, and some of its more endearing cinematic incarnations are to be found within the genre of the Muslim social.

So the question, What is a hero like this doing in *Amar Akbar Anthony*? now becomes, Why does our film's example of a pretty-boy hero just happen to be Muslim? There is a correspondence to be drawn between the emo-like Devdas, trapped between the feudal realm of his past and the anomie of the modern present, and the effete aristocrats who populate Muslim socials. And it is those older movies that supply the specific details that encode Akbar as a Muslim. Like the films it parodies, *Amar Akbar Anthony*'s Muslim subplot turns out to be structured by a conflict between the historical past and the modern present; of the three brothers, Akbar is the one for whom history is the weightiest burden. Now, to be sure, our roly-poly hero—the adopted son of the neighborhood tailor—is far from being an aristocrat. And yet enclosed within the parody are the marks of a lineage of distinction. However modern and down-to-earth he may seem, per generic precedent Akbar is nevertheless defined in his cultural particularity by a heritage of courtly manners and letters.

Let's begin with the character's name. *Akbar* is derived from Arabic. Along with *Allahu Akbar,* the phrase "God is great"—the most recognizable portion of the call to prayer and thus synecdochic of the Islamic presence in India and other societies—the word's primary referent is a historical one: the sixteenth-century emperor Jalaluddin Akbar. Akbar is generally recognized as the greatest of the Great Mughals, a model ruler in his ethical rectitude as well as his political effectiveness. More than anything else, Akbar has been elevated as a precursor to the postcolonial Indian state on the basis of his vaunted "tolerance," or ecumenical generosity. Recall that the birth name of the film's Akbar is Raju, a common nickname among Hindu boys that combines a reference to kingship with a diminutive—something like "LeRoy"—and there is a resonance here not only with the monarch and with the actor's father, Raj Kapoor, but also with an august figure who encompasses both. The Emperor Akbar's definitive screen appearance is in the epic *Mughal-e-Azam* (K. Asif, 1960)—"The Great Mughal"—in which the role was played with aplomb by Prithviraj Kapoor, father of Raj and grandfather of Rishi.

Now let's take up the question of language. Alone of the three brothers—and in distinction from all the non-Muslim characters in the film—Akbar knows Urdu (the sister language of Hindi) whose more technical and literary registers are supplied by Persian and Arabic (as opposed to Sanskrit) derivatives. At a narrative level, facility with the Perso-Arabic *nastaliq* script in which Urdu is written gives Akbar the means at the story's climax to encode a secret message to his foster father and ladylove and thus help save the day. But our hero's mastery of Urdu goes well beyond a mere plot device.

Each of the three brothers speaks in a distinctive register that expresses individual personality traits but also plots important coordinates on a map of Indian society. It could be said with only slight exaggeration that each brother has a different dialect. Amar's clean, grammatical Hindi, which incorporates a good amount of English vocabulary, connotes uprightness and education, and perhaps offers a sort of baseline norm of Hindi usage (from which the film's other characters deviate, in varying degrees).[4] By contrast, Anthony's street cred and urban attitude are conveyed through the character's stylized argot, a creative evocation of the Bombay lingua franca that serves up a mash-up of Hindi, Marathi, and English on a thin crust of Hindi grammar. Akbar's everyday speech lands somewhere between these two extremes, although he tends to use fewer English words than either. But as the occasion demands, he can switch. And the code he switches into is an elaborate Urdu of a literary sort.

Urdu of a literary sort: In the context of *Amar Akbar Anthony*'s place in Indian cinema history, this formulation is actually something of a tautology. For in this film—as established by a generation of films that precedes it—Urdu *is* poetry. As such, the Urdu stratum of the soundtrack is the medium of a certain affective register, and a character who commands Urdu words is thus endowed with a certain special power.

Fast-forward another generation: Two decades after *Amar Akbar Anthony,* the enduring conflation of the Urdu language with poetic inspiration was made plain in one of the iconic films of the 1990s, *Dil Se* (Mani Ratnam, 1998), whose hit song "Chhaiyya Chhaiyya" relies for its effect on precisely this metonymy. In the first throes of a crush that will grow into an obsession, the Hindu character played by Shah Rukh Khan channels the look and stylings of a *qalandar,* a Muslim mendicant, to sing: "That dear one who's like a fragrance/Whose words are like Urdu[5]/Who is my evening, my night, my very existence/That dear one is my beloved!"[6]

In *Amar Akbar Anthony,* unlike films of previous decades set in Muslim-dominated milieus, the use of Urdu is confined to a handful of characters, chief among them Akbar. And importantly, Akbar expresses himself in Urdu in a sustained manner—as opposed to sprinkling his speech with catchphrases and pleasantries—chiefly when he sings. The connection between poetic declamation and music is very strong in Indian performance traditions, and in the case of *Amar Akbar Anthony* it is fair to say that poetry equals song. At this stage, then, we have formulated a chain of correspondences: *Urdu → poetry → song.*

Amar Akbar Anthony's approach to integrating songs within its diegesis calls for some exposition. The musical numbers in this movie advance narrative action in linear fashion, but they do so within a privileged frame analogous to ritual time.[7] Within this frame, heightened affect prevails over social conventions and other inhibiting falsehoods to lay bare true relations and motivations. Music enables the characters to express

themselves openly. And although the same might be said of the song-
and-dance numbers in a typical Broadway musical, given the particularities of the *Amar Akbar Anthony* story this is an effect akin to a magic spell.
Within the film's narrative, powerful correctives are enacted and truths
are revealed when somebody sings—and that somebody is usually Akbar.
And if it seems that the shift from narrative prose into musical verse has
something dreamlike about it . . . well, we would agree. For in the resolutely nonnaturalistic world of *Amar Akbar Anthony,* dreams may have a
greater claim to knowledge of the true state of affairs than waking life in
the city of illusions.

But this business of dream-as-reality is as yet a digression. Let's return
to the formula *Urdu → poetry → song.* Within the film, Akbar, the tailor's
son, is a poet, but not a sentimental wordsmith of the sort that populates
the previous decade's Muslim socials. He is no declaimer of elegant cou-
plets; he is a singer of *qawwali* songs.[8] Making singing his business is a
narrative device that provides a rationale for integrating his songs within
diegesis. They are the character's performances—that's straightforward
enough.

But on another level, we argue, the move is audacious. It works not to
assimilate Indian Muslims or reduce them to junior partners but to ele-
vate Islam as the film's primary mode of religious expression. Having
established song as a privileged register for making meaning, we direct
attention to the sort of messages expressed in the lyrics. *Qawwali* shares
a vocabulary with *ghazal* and other Indo-Islamic poetic forms that claim
a Persian literary inheritance. As such, it is part of an allusive discourse
rich in mystical tropes and symbolism.[9] There is an esoteric code at
work here whose key is Islamic soteriology as interpreted by spiritual
masters whose insight derives from mystical experience: in a word, by
Sufis.

With this move, we have completed the formula: *Urdu → poetry →
song → mystical testimony.* Akbar thus becomes a medium through
whom the characters in the film—and maybe us too, the spectators in the
audience—are able to experience elevated, even revelatory moods. This
is a tall order, and if Akbar is shown to be worthy of the task, he will
surely emerge as the principal character in the film. As the following sections demonstrate, recognizing Akbar as a poet and a mystic explains a

great deal about the work the character does as a representative of Indian Islam. Akbar's poet persona also helps explain motifs as yet unaddressed, such as his renunciation of violence and his fondness for roses; furthermore, it's what allows the film privileged access to truth and the ability, all on its own, to establish it.

But let the argument that he is the true hero of the movie get started in earnest with a simple matter of math. *Amar Akbar Anthony* has seven songs in it. Of these, no fewer than four are Akbar's solos: "Parda Hai Parda," "Tayyab Ali Pyar Ka Dushman," "Shirdi Wale Sai Baba," and—it can easily be conceded—the song that accompanies the title sequence, "Yeh Sach Hai Koi Kahani Nahin." Akbar takes a prominent part in the two ensemble numbers, "Hamko Tumse Ho Gaya Hai Pyar Kya Karein" and the finale, "Anhoni Ko Honi Kar De." In fact, the only number from which his voice is absent is the one that begins, "My Name Is Anthony Gonsalves."

Akbar is not the movie's moral center. Here we will not contest that the honor goes to Amar, who steps to front and center at the inception of the tale of the brothers' separation and again at its resolution. Nor, when all is said and done (and it will be, in Chapter 3), is Akbar the narrative's protagonist. To turn again to the authority of numbers, Anthony appears in 44 percent of the movie's scenes as compared with 35 percent for Akbar. But who goes to see a movie for the plot, anyway?[10] The fortunes of a mass-market Hindi film rise or fall with the success of its songs. This is a fact of the formula—and of the industry system that supports it— universally recognized by Bombay producers.[11]

Akbar may get second place in the title and third place in terms of seniority and social hierarchy, but the balance of this chapter makes it clear that the movie really centers on him. As embodied by Rishi Kapoor, he is winning, winsome, and ebullient—everybody's favorite kid brother. But the baby-faced actor is not the only performer involved in bringing the role to life. Akbar as voiced in his musical transports by the Bombay industry's dean of male vocalists, Mohamed Rafi—that's something else again. As the big green heart that frames his logo in his first musical performance indicates, the sentimental Akbar is the movie's heart. And our argument claims yet another something else. By following up on the implications of the powerful effects he conjures through one song after another, we will demonstrate that Akbar also functions as the movie's soul.

Akbar of Allahabad

In the film's last act, the brothers infiltrate the villain's headquarters and, bringing on the denouement, unmask. Akbar's disguise consists of a false beard, a fez, and a *sherwani* frock coat: the Muslim gentleman of the old school, last year's model (Figure 9). He strips off the whiskers. "This unworthy is known as Akbar Ilahabadi," he states in Urdu, as if introducing himself at a formal function. *I am not what I seem,* he declares of the stereotypical trappings. *Here is who I really am:* Akbar Ilahabadi, "Akbar of Allahabad."

The appellation has the ring of a *takhallus,* a conventionalized Urdu nom de plume—in Urdu literature as in hip-hop, artists generally don't circulate their verses under a prosaic birth name.[12] What's more, not only does the name Akbar Ilahabadi follow the *takhallus* format, but it is an already established *takhallus* designating a historical poet of some renown. To reiterate: *Who I really am* turns out not only to be an alias but to be an alias claimed by someone else altogether—somebody outside the world of the film. What does it mean for our modern young Muslim to claim the handle—and by implication the mantle—of the real Akbar Ilahabadi, who lived from 1846 to 1921?

Let's unpack the character's self-identification at two levels: that of his historical namesake and that of the name's generic associations. The Akbar Ilahabadi of Urdu literature was born Syed Akbar Husain, not far from the city he would claim for his cognomen. Seated at the confluence of the Ganga and Jamuna rivers, Allahabad defines the eastern limit of the Doab, or "Two Waters," the North Indian heartland of Urdu culture. The Abode of Allah is also a holy city for Hindus and a landmark of some prominence in the secular mythology of Indian nationalism, in that it has functioned for generations as home base for the Nehru family.[13] It is a major urban center in the state everyone calls U.P., modern India's Uttar Pradesh, which was known in the poet's time as the United Provinces. Akbar Ilahabadi lived his whole life in areas under British colonial administration. In fact, most of his professional career was spent as a part of that administration. He studied law and secured successive appointments in the judiciary, retiring from his post as district judge of Banaras in 1903 to dedicate himself to poetry. Along the way he acquired

FIGURE 9. Hereditary tailormaster

the title of Khan Bahadur, bestowed by the British Raj upon its exemplary servants.

If a certain doubling movement defines the character Akbar's moment of truth—*I'm not that* (the sort of person you think of as a Muslim, a pretentious fellow with a beard), *I'm actually this* (a poetical soul whose talent attests to a deeper level of personal authenticity than mere appearance)—the poet Akbar's literary persona likewise gives voice to a double life. For through his verses the Khan Bahadur ventilated a thoroughgoing critique of colonial modernity in its technological and institutional manifestations. His targets included photographs, phonographs, typesetting, newspapers, and even indoor plumbing, not to mention the very legal edifice of which he was a high-ranking part.[14] Anticolonialist Akbar certainly was—in his writings—and yet it would be a distortion to describe him as a nationalist. If there is a call to action to be discerned in his words, it has nothing to do with overthrow, or even reform, of the colonial state. His program was subtler.

The historical Akbar Ilahabadi was above all a satirist. He decried the modern disruption of Indian lifeways by highlighting its absurdities and contradictions. In a thoughtful and provocative essay on the poet's oeuvre,

Shamsur Rahman Faruqi offers a bold endorsement: Akbar's only rival as a claimant to the status of India's first and greatest postcolonial writer is Muhammad Iqbal, the leading voice of Islamic modernism and the visionary of Pakistan.[15] The literary greatness of Iqbal is generally recognized, whatever may be thought these days of his social and political ideas. Akbar's poetry, by contrast, has been denied the honor it merits. Faruqi cites several reasons for this. The first is a prejudice that has prevailed across generations of Urdu literary critics against the humorous voice in poetry. The second is a lack of sympathy for opinions that have not aged well (how can anybody be against *indoor plumbing?*). The third is the imputation of hypocrisy to a public figure who liked to pose as the last honest man standing but who owed his station to his service of foreign masters.

We attribute these three charges—unseriousness, reaction, and hypocrisy—to the same basic misreading of his work, for the target of Akbar's mockery is in large measure himself. Far from betraying hypocrisy, his poetry exhibits a degree of self-knowledge on the part of a colonized subject that feels painfully acute. In taking aim at representational media like photographs, sound recordings, and newsprint—and their unreflective embrace by Indian moderns—Akbar mourns the demise of intimacy in human relations. Mass-reproduced artifacts like government licenses or legal forms, say, have become interposed between human subjects with the effect of obscuring or veiling an authentic mutual recognition. In a bureaucratic scenario like that of a colonial magistrate's court, the question of whether a supplicant's file accurately represents his case has a curious, even comic way of becoming inverted: Does the man before the bench plausibly look like his paperwork? Viewed in this light, even a water pipe can be seen as a disruptive interpolation—a veil installed between the thirsting subject and the wellspring.

Yet there is no material solution. Akbar does not call for the abolition of the courts or the waterworks department, let alone the colonial state as a whole. The system cannot be overthrown; what can be done, perhaps, is to see through it. Laughter offers a way to expose the modern order for the web of illusions that it is. In heightening modernity's contradictions, the poet Akbar's sense of the absurd opens up a fleeting rupture—and this poetic effect can be situated in parallel with the cinematic Akbar's power to cut through the vexations of narrative with song. The difference is that in the film, the rupture effected by Akbar's final solo number, "Shirdi Wale Sai Baba," extends so far as to disentangle part of the web—to enact lasting change, to borrow the idiom of political activism. But even in *Amar Akbar Anthony*'s fictive world, such a miracle, as we will see, requires the intercession of a divine agency.

It remains to note one last aspect of the poet's work before we return to cinema. Toward the end of his life, Akbar Ilahabadi became a supporter of Gandhi's political program. The Mahatma's mystique seems to have impressed even Akbar. But would he fulfill his promise as the truth-teller of the poet's ideal? A collection of poems, mock-heroically titled the *Gandhi Namah* in the style of a Persian kingly epic, was published shortly after Akbar's death. It reads at points like a vexed romance. The trademark caustic humor is not diluted but, by the same token, neither is the underlying concern for authenticity.[16] To the end of his days, Akbar seems to have searched for a beacon to guide him past the flighty winds and murky currents of the age.

Akbar Ilahabadi's career as a satirist is exemplary for showing how *Amar Akbar Anthony* puts the poet persona to work. This seems to us no accident. Although our argument has no stake in the question of authorial intent, the authors in this case—whether Anand Bakshi, the lyricist; Kader Khan, the dialogue writer; or Manmohan Desai himself—surely connected the name Akbar Ilahabadi with the historical personage. And whether well read in his oeuvre or not, they would likely have identified him as modern Urdu's premier exponent of the humorous voice in poetry. But none of that is really important. What is important, where the filmmakers are concerned, is the expectation that their audience will recognize the Muslim character's name as a citation of a particular type— a *takhallus*-format name, an Urdu poet's name. And what such a name would have invoked for many Indian filmgoers of the 1970s, as mediated through a preceding generation's worth of cinematic references, is a much-filmed realm of Urdu manners and letters. It's time to return our focus from the biographical to the geographical—from the *Akbar* to the *Ilahabadi.* For if the image of the bearded gent in a fez is a mask that our playful hero doffs at will, so too is the claimed place of origin in Allahabad something of a mask—or a veil.

Doomed Past: Lucknow

Bombay is home to a vast Muslim population made up of communities committed to diverse schools and sects of Islam. Not all of these people speak Urdu, let alone enjoy poetry in it.

Where do the old-school Muslims of Bombay movies, with their flowery speech and formal manners, come from?[17] We have alluded already to *Amar Akbar Anthony*'s sequestration of action dominated by Muslim characters and motifs in a subplot that can be retold with little reference to the main narrative. This subplot is also partitioned spatially, isolated in the main to scenes shot on a single set: the city block dominated by the timber business of Tayyab Ali. In keeping with our reading of the film as an allegory of the nation, we propose that *Amar Akbar Anthony* frames this Muslim Quarter as a space condemned to the historical past. But in order to make sense of the Muslim subplot—and its implications for the film's construction of national spaces and times—we first need to make an intertextual move to understand its past and pedigree. *Amar Akbar Anthony* is a film about Bombay, but the Muslim subplot it incorporates (and thus digests, assimilates, tames) comes from another city. More precisely, it comes from films about another city.

So again, where do movie Muslims come from—fussy, bearded men of a sort recognizable to anyone who gets that Akbar's final-act impersonation, with his fez and pretensions, is of an ethno-religious stereotype writ large?[18] In a geographical sense, *Ilahabadi* is imprecise at best. A better tell comes when the supposed tailormaster nags the villain Robert into permitting him to send back to his shop for the tools he needs to fulfill his order. Here Akbar strikes an attitude: he is no simple bazaar tailor but an aristocrat among tailors.[19] "It's a matter of lineage, sir—*Mashallah*—lineage," he says. "I have machines from the time of the British. And from the time of Wajid Ali Shah."

Wajid Ali Shah was the last of the reigning Nawabs of Awadh, or Oudh, the North Indian kingdom occupying much of the Doab, and centered on the capital of Lucknow. Famously, Awadh was taken over by the East India Company in 1856 (the outbreak of the Great Revolt, or Mutiny, of 1857 is attributable in part to resentment throughout the region of this usurpation). The British conquerors made no bones about having deposed the decadent Wajid Ali on the grounds of his unfitness to rule, as exemplified by his preference for patronage of the arts, such as poetry, over the more hardheaded aspects of statecraft. The episode, and the colonialist rationale behind it, has been made familiar to followers of a certain highbrow strand in Indian culture through Satyajit Ray's *Shatranj Ke Khilari* (*The Chess Players*, 1977), the Bengali auteur's film of a story by the Hindi writer Premchand. Both works use the image of a pair of aristocrats absorbed in a chess game to symbolize the ineffectuality of the ancien régime in the face of colonial modernity.[20]

For fans of Hindi popular cinema, however, Lucknow had become established as the locus classicus of Urdu culture in the movies of the previous decade. Indeed, the opening credits of two of the best-known Muslim socials of the 1960s, *Chaudhvin Ka Chand* and *Palki*, roll over songs dedicated to the city.[21] Here we reiterate a point made earlier: the Muslim subplot of *Amar Akbar Anthony* is a self-enclosed parody of a Muslim social. Bombay shrinks, wraps, neutralizes, and gently mocks Lucknow, even as Rishi Kapoor puts a smiley face on Devdas. But the particularities and insights of that parody necessitate a deeper look at the Muslim social. What, precisely, is our film making fun of?

Representing Lucknow as the site of cinematic cliché, then, four Muslim socials will be synopsized in what follows: *Chaudhvin Ka Chand* (Mohammed Sadiq, 1960), *Mere Mehboob* (Harnam Singh Rawail, 1963), *Palki* (Mahesh Kaul and S. U. Sunny, 1967), and *Pakeezah* (Kamal Amrohi, 1972).[22] A consideration of the basic narrative and thematic contours of each will turn up some family resemblances. In turn, these will allow us to see just how Akbar's two sides come together—the boy next door and the Voice from Above.

Chaudhvin Ka Chand ("Moon of the Fourteenth" or "Full Moon")

The film follows three young friends from the *ashraf*, or Muslim gentry, of Lucknow: the rich aristocrat Pyare Miyan (Rehman), the not-so-rich Aslam (Guru Dutt), and the representative of the ascendant professional classes Shaida (Johnny Walker), a police inspector's son. The story is set sometime before Independence, although there are no nationalist references, and Shaida's association with the police is made to signify not the oppression of colonialism but, on the contrary, the liberatory possibilities of modernity. If there is a system that oppresses the characters, it is that of custom—the code of manners, attitudes, and pretensions in which upper-class Muslims are shown to be trapped. The key visual motif here is the *parda* (veil) that marks a respectable woman even as it conceals her, and its signal mood is a fatalistic melancholy. To be well born in Lucknow on the cusp of modernity is to be cultivated but doomed; one is sophisticated enough to recognize that doom and sensitive enough, if not to write poetry about it, then to extemporize in song.

Pyare Miyan, whose old mother is busy with his marriage plans, is the tale's tragic hero. He catches a glimpse of the unveiled face of Jamila (Waheeda Rehman) and is smitten. Jamila attends his own sister's wedding party at their home and attracts much attention from the assembled ladies, who sing a mocking song about the beauty guarded by the veil and the efforts of voyeurs to see around it; among Jamila's admirers are not only her female friends but also Pyare Miyan, who peeps on the women from behind windows and screens upstairs. Identifying Jamila by a piece of veiling fabric, he makes an arrangement with Aslam: his bosom friend will marry the match intended for Pyare Miyan, thus freeing Pyare to court the object of his desire. But it develops that Jamila had swapped veils with a friend, and when Aslam's bride uncovers herself at the wedding's conclusion, the face she reveals is that of Pyare's beloved. Pyare, his heart broken, kills himself by swallowing a diamond. The inexorable logic of the script—*that which is written*—has been apparent to the audience from the moment the two friends seal their pact, if not before. But the countdown to tragedy is lightened at intervals by the comic appearances of their crony Shaida, who experiments with disguises that expand his freedom of action beyond that prescribed for his station into explorations of the byways and corners hidden behind Lucknow's façades.[23]

Mere Mehboob ("My Darling")

This is the sunniest of the four films, with Johnny Walker again hamming it up as a character who doesn't live by quite the same rules as the hide-

bound *ashraf.* And providing another counterpoint to the insular world
of Urdu mores and manners—of *andaaz-o-riwaaz*—is the inclusion of a
space on the other side of the *parda.* Indian modernity is represented in
this film by the university at Aligarh, not far from Lucknow, which was
founded by Syed Ahmad Khan (Akbar Ilahabadi's foil and interlocutor)
with the mission of grooming Muslim leaders for the modern era. At the
start of the story, Ghayal, the Johnny Walker character, and Anwar
(Rajendra Kumar) are students. Anwar is idolized by Ghayal and all
their right-thinking classmates because he is the big poet on campus.
But our hero is blocked from composing his entry for the great competition that marks the end of the school year; he is obsessed with a fellow
student whose eyes met his through her veil when they bumped into
each other and spilled their poetry books. The film loses no time in getting right to the point, as ventriloquized through Ghayal's advice:
Project your desire into the audience. Your muse will recognize herself
in the words she has inspired and seek your gaze with her own. And so it
comes to pass, although a reciprocal exchange—in poetry and prose—has
to wait until everybody has returned to Lucknow.

On the train back home, Anwar is introduced to a great Nawab of the
city (Ashok Kumar). The Nawab hires him as a poetry tutor for his sister,
who turns out to be none other than the fated beloved, Husna (Sadhana).
Along with the *parda* that is physically interposed between them during
the lessons, the lovers encounter other obstacles to their union in the form
of secrets behind the walls of both houses. In Anwar's case, it is that his
education has been bankrolled by his sister, Najma (Nimmi), who works
as a dancing girl. In Husna's case, it is that the opulent life to which she
and her brother have been accustomed has been paid for by debts that are
coming due—among the Nawab's extravagances being the protection of a
dancer, Najma herself. Ghayal too maintains pretensions, if not exactly a
secret: the name he likes to go by is a *takhallus,* his nonliterary identity
being that of the son of a philistine Hindu moneylender. If the weight of
custom is not as oppressive as it is in *Chaudhvin Ka Chand*—and the happy
ending not so surprising—it is because in place of a historical doom the
narrative substitutes a human agency: the villain, a rich rival *nawab,* is
played by *Amar Akbar Anthony*'s flawed father figure, Pran.

Palki ("The Palanquin")

This movie finds Rajendra Kumar reprising his role as the poet-hero and Waheeda Rehman hers as the veiled beloved. Naseem is an impoverished poet of Lucknow, and Mehro, his betrothed, is his lovely but no less impoverished neighbor. They communicate chastely through a hole in the wall partitioning their dwellings, shared respectively with his mother (Protima Devi, the Grandmother from *Amar Akbar Anthony*) and her brother, Sultan (Johnny Walker). At a poetry competition convened by a cultivated Nawab (Rehman), Naseem wins enough money to get respectably married but rejects it because he feels humiliated by the assembly, some of whom have mocked his poverty. Sultan recovers the money by a trick and uses it to get his sister married, but at the wedding's conclusion, when Mehro claims the right to be shown the brideprice before unveiling herself, the subterfuge is revealed. Deferring the consummation, Naseem decamps for Bombay, where he vows he will earn enough to pay back the Nawab and redeem both families' honor.

Even Johnny Walker plays it largely straight through this overheated scenario. Naseem and Mehro, though penniless, are no less bound by custom than the courtly Nawab himself. Bombay, the space of modernity, is a dynamic contrast—a place open to mercenary interest. Through the patronage of a businessman, Jaffarbhai (Nazir Hussain, the Padre from *Amar Akbar Anthony*), Naseem obtains work on the docks. When arsonists blow up part of the port, Naseem risks his life to save his employer's son, dashing into a blazing building. A false report of his death reaches Lucknow, and the shock propels Mehro into a state of fey denial. When, after a long convalescence, Naseem returns, it is to discover that his bride has been remarried to none other than the Nawab. Mehro's second marriage likewise remains unconsummated when her new groom discovers she remains pledged in her heart to another. Making things even more complicated, Naseem moves into the household as poetry tutor. To try to communicate while keeping her modesty intact, Mehro feels obliged to don a shroud and appear before her true love in the form of her own ghost. Catharsis is reached following a *qawwali* performance in which the dilemmas the three characters face are outlined in allegorical terms; of the three, the only one who can act, within the matrix of custom, is the Nawab. He relinquishes Mehro in an act of patronage as autocratic as the passing of judgment on a line of poetry.

Pakeezah ("The Pure One")

Finally, *Pakeezah* recapitulates several of *Palki*'s motifs: the image of the marital palanquin; contrived trials of sexual chastity; above all, the occultation of a woman's identity by the veil.[24] Meena Kumari plays Nargis, a Lucknow courtesan who falls in love with a Nawab, Shahabuddin (Ashok Kumar again), and dies brokenhearted after their marriage is rejected by his father, the Old Nawab (Kamal Kapoor, Inspector Khanna from *Amar Akbar Anthony*). The actress also plays the child of this ill-fated union, Sahibjaan, who is trained in the business but also imbued with the desire her mother just missed realizing—to leave the pleasure quarter in the palanquin that can deliver her to married respectability.[25]

The contrast in this movie between antique Lucknow and the world outside is as sharp as it is in *Palki*. Along with the railroad as a signifier of industrial modernity, *Pakeezah* locates the wilderness traversed by trains and boats as another space outside the confines of custom. Sahibjaan falls asleep on a rail journey, chastely covered except for her feet; their beauty is enough to inspire love in a mysterious stranger, who expresses his admiration in an Urdu note he slips between her toes. A renowned dancer, Sahibjaan narrowly escapes defloration when her rich client's pleasure barge gets in the way of an elephant stampede. She wanders through the jungle, happening on the tent of a forestry officer, Salim (Raaj Kumar), who turns out to be not only a Muslim aristocrat but also her secret admirer from the night train. Feigning amnesia, she avoids revealing her *bazaari* origins but nevertheless excites mistrust in his family (the hidebound Old Nawab, her own estranged grandfather, also turns out to be Salim's uncle). Salim chooses love over family honor and brings his mystery lady to a remote shrine to be married, giving her name as Pakeezah. But when prompted by the *shaikh* conducting the rite, the Pure One is unable to state her assent and flees down the hillside; the veil flies off her head and back up to her lover. She returns to the brothel, thence to be summoned by the embittered Salim to dance at his wedding to somebody else. By the end, when her performance over glass shards stains the sheet on the floor with the blood of her beautiful feet—at once citational of both the virgin's purity and the trials of wandering Sufis in the desert—we get the message that however purportedly happy the outcome when Salim weds her at last, she has not so much escaped the prison of custom as had a transfer approved from one cell block to another.

To summarize: The realm of the Muslim social is circumscribed not only by religion but also by class, gender, geography, and history. Its characters hail from the *ashraf*. Its musical numbers highlight the role of this class as patrons of the arts and letters, particularly those displayed in the pleasure quarter, even as its narratives center on the longing of lovers across the bounds of the *parda*—both physical and symbolic. The genre is itself now extinct. But this "feudal" milieu (to use the term in its colloquial Indian sense) was always presented in the movies as a lost or vanishing world, marked apart through lush schemes of costume and mise-en-scène. A certain self-Orientalizing tendency comes to the fore at points, particularly when the diegesis calls, jarringly, for the milieu's juxtaposition with spaces of contemporary life, demarcated (as in *Pakeezah*) by such signal elements as trains and unattractive Westernized fashions. The space of this elegiac fantasy, where poets exchange graceful compliments and frock-coated *nawabs* gamble the honor of the family name in the dancing girl's parlor, is Lucknow; and its time is always yesterday—once upon a time in North India.

When Is a Veil Not a Veil?

What does *Amar Akbar Anthony* do with this fund of received images of Muslim identity? What does it repurpose, and what does it redeem? Let's examine Akbar's stratum of the film's narrative against the conventions of the genre.

Akbar's antecedents as a romantic poet-hero have now been laid out in detail. But no sooner do we try to find the points where inexorable fate or custom sets obstacles between lover and beloved than we are already in on the joke. Akbar and his ladylove, Salma, exercise their own agency in pursuing a modern romance. This is the pivot of the film's parodic Muslim subplot. At the start of their story, the lovers' freedom of movement would appear to be curtailed by custom . . . and yet it takes no more than Akbar's first performance as a *qawwali* artist for the power of his voice to free Salma. Such conflict as remains to vex true love's progress has to do with securing Salma's father's blessing on their union. But through the subplot's whole course, the weight of custom—the honor of the noble house, the modesty of a woman of virtue—is featherlight. In fact, as Akbar states in so many words, the importance laid on parental consent is a matter of his own personal choice.[26]

To begin at the beginning—before the title even rolls—we first encounter the grown-up Akbar, in the person of Rishi Kapoor, on a visit to the hospital. Akbar is not physically ill, and even his declarations of emotional pain—befitting a poet—are delivered in a voice more farcical than lyrical. He's there because he has a crush on a pretty doctor, Salma (Kapoor's real-life girlfriend and eventual wife, Neetu Singh), whom we see covered in conformity with the modern space she occupies: professional over religious persona, white coat as opposed to black cloak. As the doctor checks him out with her stethoscope, Akbar waxes in Urdu, "*Dard-e-dil . . . dard-e-jigar,*"—"pain in my heart . . . pain in my liver"— naming the two organs that seat emotional life in South Asia. The bantering dialogue reveals that the two are no strangers. Akbar's attentions to Salma have met with her father's disfavor, and the hospital is a space that affords them license to meet. Akbar tries to get her to promise to attend his next *qawwali* performance, but Salma remonstrates that her father wouldn't permit her to go. Or if he did—even worse—he would insist on coming along.

The next step in the Muslim subplot is the *qawwali* number itself, "Parda Hai Parda," which may be translated as "A Veil Is a Veil," or perhaps "There Is a Veil." To go by the fans who throng the theater entrance and the signs decking it, Akbar Ilahabadi is already a *qawwal* of some repute; the narrative indicates that this performance occurs some time after the one Salma had felt obliged to miss. For those of us in his extradiegetic audience, however, this is Akbar's debut. And there is much to say about it.[27] It is a Clark Kent moment: a character who had to this point seemed charming enough, but was shaping up to be a sort of sidekick figure, leaps from the wings in shiny Islamic green onto a stage that has already been claimed with his logo—the Urdu letters "Akbar" splashed over a big green heart. The house is packed; his fans spill into the aisle.[28] Into his double audience, he projects this *cri de coeur:* "Behind the veil / There is a beloved / And if I don't succeed in unveiling that object of desire / Then my name isn't Akbar!"

Make that his triple audience. The poet-hero is at once appealing to (1) his diegetic audience, the community of *qawwali* lovers; (2) Salma, the individual who embodies his beloved within the diegesis; and (3) his extradiegetic audience, which is to say all of us watching the movie. Salma enters the theater accompanied not only by her father but by five other women swathed in black hijabi outfits.[29] Salma wears hijabi dress too. Understood in terms of speech-act theory, Akbar's challenge works at all three levels as a powerful, even radical utterance. Not merely performance, it approaches a performative statement, one that hinges on a gesture of reciprocal recognition: *If I can't remove the barrier between your eyes and mine, then I am not who I say I am. If I can't compel you to affirm my desire, then I don't exist.*

Each audience encounters Akbar's challenge through a distinct figuration of *parda*. What the narrative requires is for Akbar's poetical appeal, at some point, to be met by Salma's reciprocal gesture—her unveiling. And what the narrative does is to deliver this promptly. At the three-minute mark, Akbar's charisma has already proven so potent that Salma and all five of her fellow hijabis begin to lift their veils in unison, only to be swatted back down by the patriarch with his walking stick. Salma holds out for less than three more minutes, baring her face but then veiling herself again in response to the part of the *qawwali* in which the suitor accuses the beloved (per poetic convention) of cruelly toying with his heart. But all is going according to plan. Salma's response holds, as yet, too much of her own volition. Akbar's goal is not persuasion but compulsion; his words go beyond the transmission of meaning to the projection of an effect. The hypnotic beat only builds as our *qawwal* presses on into confrontational, antinomian territory. Akbar moves from stage magic–like prop work with mirrors and flowers (a red rose) to splashing liquor about and torching it to holding up a symbol of the *parda* he has vowed to conquer—a diaphanous red scarf—and then ripping it (a move as suggestive of the spilling of hymenal blood as the lacerating finale of

Pakeezah). By the eight-minute mark, the beloved has truly surrendered. She maintains just enough self-composure to get up from her seat and place a hand over her lover's lips. To expose herself thus is the lesser shame. Akbar's work would appear to be done; Salma is never to veil her face again.

How is all this supposed to work? And what are the viewers' expectations, such that we would want it to work? Here it will help to revisit, briefly, the precedents for "Parda Hai Parda" in the Muslim socials of the 1960s. A staple device of the genre, as we have seen, involves the elusiveness of the beloved, masked as she is from the male gaze by sartorial and spatial *pardas*. Given these practically daunting if fetishistically promising circumstances, how does one communicate his avowal to the curtained-off object of desire? In one Muslim social after another, what pierces the veil is Urdu poetry.

If you're Rajendra Kumar in *Mere Mehboob,* for example, you appeal to your beloved to lift her veil in a campus *mushaira,* or poetry competition, and scan the auditorium for the co-ed whose response will confirm her as your heart's true desire. This is the well-loved "Mere Mehboob" number, which closely resembles "Parda Hai Parda," both in formal structure and in its position at the start of the film. (The reason this showstopper doesn't just stop the eponymous narrative cold is that it has a bit of a backfire effect: Rajendra gets so swept up in the image his own words have evoked that he fails to pick up on Sadhana's full-frontal glance.)

What remains to be added is how the plea is delivered: in the voice of Mohamed Rafi. Likewise, the poet played by Rajendra Kumar in *Palki* performs a composition called "Chehre Se Apne Aaj To Parda Uthaiye" (This Is the Day to Lift the Veil from Your Face) before his noble patron, Rehman. But the voice that reaches behind the Nawab's curtains to his true love, Waheeda Rehman, belongs to Mohamed Rafi. And if you're Guru Dutt in *Chaudhvin Ka Chand,* serenading Waheeda as she lies sleeping in the bridal chamber, the voice that compares her bare face to the full moon—"Chaudhvin Ka Chand"—is of course that of Mohamed Rafi.[30] Finally, if you're Raaj Kumar in *Pakeezah* and you catch a glimpse in a train compartment not of your beloved's eyes but of her feet, instead of waking her by singing at her in Urdu you write her a poetical little note, so that Meena Kumari can then obsess over it for years. But when fate at last brings you together, and she has revealed the face that was the promise of those dainty feet, how do you deliver on your own promise—the one implicit in your well-penned note? Perhaps you'd join her in a duet, like "Chalo Dildar Chalo." Which playback singer do you think you'll hire?

It may be protested by those who know their *filmi* music that it's no great feat to demonstrate that five well-known Hindi movies share the same male vocalist. One of the most peculiar features of commercial film production in Bombay, especially given the centrality of songs to the format, is the limited circle of elite recording artists who get hired by music directors. Famously, in the 1960s and 1970s (and beyond), two singers sang the female parts on virtually all A-list film soundtracks: Lata Mangeshkar and Asha Bhosle, who were sisters.[31] In the earlier part of that period, Rafi could perhaps seem nearly as ubiquitous.

Nevertheless, as his domination of the most famous Muslim socials indicates, there is a case for situating Mohamed Rafi as Bollywood's premier interpreter of *qawwali,* along with related idioms that have an Islamic provenance. What is more, his work was (and is) esteemed for a certain spiritual charge it was felt to carry. In his heyday, the singer was popularly known as "God's voice"; his colleague Talat Mahmood expanded on this by saying, "The voice was a gift from God to Rafi, but what Rafi made of it was a gift to God."[32] Even less reserved was another fan whose idolatry sounds a rather Hindu note:

> I would go to hear him and then go and touch his feet. . . . I think that was the voice of God. . . . The man was so versatile! . . . My childhood idols were Lata Mangeshkar and Mohammed Rafi, and I have said that even God got jealous of his voice and wanted to hear him in person; that's why He called him up at such a young age.[33]

Quoted in the passage is none other than *Amar Akbar Anthony*'s director, Manmohan Desai. A key factor to be called out here is that in the early 1970s, the singer's career had fallen into a slump. Desai again:

> There was a time when many of the big music directors boycotted Mohammed Rafi for three or four years. . . . But when I made *Amar Akbar Anthony* . . . I told Laxmikant–Pyarelal that I wanted only

Mohammed Rafi to sing my songs and nobody else. . . . They were a little hesitant . . . and they asked me whether he would be ready to sing for them because he was almost boycotted for a couple of years. I went to Rafi Saab and I said, "Saab, this is my first film; these are the films I'm making. I'm coming up in a big way. Would you please sing for me?"

And I remember Rafi Saab telling me, "Manmohan, for your sake I am willing to sing for these people; otherwise, I would never sing for them."

. . .

After that, Rafi Saab never looked back again. Due to certain power politics he was shunned by the music directors, and when I brought him back in *Amar Akbar Anthony,* everybody flocked to Mohammed Rafi again, and rightly so.[34]

To the extent that *Amar Akbar Anthony* was the star's comeback vehicle, it was because Rafi, out of a playback roster that included his rivals Kishore Kumar and Mukesh, was best suited for the film's principal singing role.[35] How better to mediate Akbar's special power—to the movie's other characters, to the Indian moviegoing public—than through a voice on loan from God?[36]

Parody behind the *Parda*

Now to return to the task at hand: reviewing the Muslim subplot. What could there be left to tell of this story? Twenty minutes before the curtain rose on "Parda Hai Parda" the hospital scene introduced us to Akbar and Salma. At the number's close, it would appear that *miyan bibi raazi,* as they say in Urdu: boy and girl are in accord. Yet the movie has more than two hours to go.

What the film does is shelve the two lovers for a considerable stretch, long enough to allow Akbar's older but slower brothers to catch up and find their own dates. The Muslims resurface just before the Interval. The occasion is the fourth song, "Hamko Tumse Ho Gaya Hai Pyar Kya Karein" (Can't Help Falling in Love with You), an omnibus number in which each of the three couples explores the romantic possibilities of representative spaces within a suburban Bombay milieu.

The Muslim playground is the miniature train that runs through a corner of Borivali National Park. The tourist train is a real service (operative once again after having been retired for many years), and the segments in which it features were shot on location.[37] The venue works on two levels—as a modern, public space and, simultaneously, as a space of parody. It is an actual train, an established cinematic image of modernity (compare *Pakeezah*). And it is a ludic toy of a train, whose passengers hail from across Bombay's diverse communities but come together in their enjoyment of that middle-class institution: the recreational weekend. Within this space of leisure, before a public united in play, the young couple enacts modern romance through singing and dancing. Akbar plays second fiddle to Salma, who makes flirtatious moves with her *dupatta,* the long scarf that goes with her Punjabi-style outfit. The way the beat steps up when the Muslims take their turn in the song echoes the earlier *qawwali* number, even as Salma's somewhat fetishy manipulation of the scarf demonstrates how the veil has been transformed from desire's obstacle into its accessory (Figure 10).

Adding to the merriment is the stymied presence of Salma's conservative but decadent father, played by Mukri, a comic actor whose defining physical characteristic was his very short stature. Here he makes his appearance not, as before, in *nawabi* coat and hat, but in a colorful leisure-wear ensemble topped with a newsboy's cap. Tayyab Ali is a manikin in a tourist costume, a human counterpart of the toy train. Also worth noting is how both father and lover are set apart from Salma's other spectators by the mediation of their gazes—desiring and controlling—through optical devices, the recreational gear of well-off consumers. Akbar wears a shiny new camera around his neck, and Tayyab Ali sports sunglasses and a pair of binoculars. He shakes his fist as his daughter and her lover dance on a train that has gotten away from him: before his spying eyes, the train enters a tunnel and comes through the other end. If one of the takeaways of this omnibus number is that lovers from different communities follow different styles of romance, these are the impressions Akbar, Salma, and Tayyab Ali leave us with: Muslims are hot blooded and zesty, and their apparent repression is no more than curtain deep.

Our first sight when we return from the intermission is a row of crude wooden poles. Opening a gap from behind as if they're curtains, Akbar

FIGURE 10. Salma with veil

peers back at us from a dark interior. He has sneaked into Tayyab Ali's lumber business at night with his new camera, and hopes to take an auspicious inaugural snap of his girlfriend.[38] Juliet-like, Salma appears at her balcony across the way and dissuades him: her father is in the house; he's sure to interfere. But as it turns out, the old man has more urgent business. A servant approaches him in his parlor. The scene is very Lucknow, with the two attired in flowing white, as is the message the servant bears: Tayyab Ali's mistress, the courtesan Bijli, awaits him outside, on the other side of his timber warehouse. Akbar has already decided to pack up his new toy when he happens on the rendezvous. In another encounter that cites the Muslim social in its voyeurism, our young hero gazes on the sordid dealings of the older generation through a hole in the wall.[39]

As played by Madhumati, who made her name in earlier films as a dancing star, Bijli ("Lightning") is Tayyab Ali's mistress in more than one sense. She meets him at a part of the diegetic warehouse where a wire mesh comes between the two to form a distinctly down-market *parda*. Indeed, the production designer seems to have fabricated the warehouse set entirely out of surfaces like corrugated metal, which translate the silken drapes of a *nawab*'s palace into the idiom of urban grit. The negotiation

FIGURE 11. Bijli

is tense (Figure 11). In a message all the more menacing for its elegant Urdu diction, the courtesan warns her patron of dire consequences if he does not pay her what he owes. Akbar's first photo is an incriminating candid.

The next morning, Akbar paces the crossroads in front of Tayyab Ali's house and business, moodily chewing some paan. This is the set we have dubbed the Muslim Quarter, dominated as it is by the residence of the half-pint *nawab* at the center. To be sure, the designers have been at pains to show that diverse communities share the block; there are signs for businesses carrying logos in Urdu, Hindi, English, and Gujarati, and the horizon is defined, just as in the hospital-ward set, with the outlines of religious buildings. When the camera faces Tayyab Ali's, the road to the left leads to a (two-dimensional cutout of a) Christian church, and the right-hand road to a (similar cutout of a) Hindu temple; in this framing, the mosque—along with the timber warehouse—is where the camera would be.

There is a certain old-town styling to the buildings, which come together in a typical bazaar arrangement: businesses packed together cheek by jowl, residences on the upper floors. This set is the most densely urban exterior to be seen in *Amar Akbar Anthony,* and it might be identified at first glance as a bustling downtown area, perhaps Manmohan Desai's own neighborhood of Khetwadi.[40] Yet a closer look will show not the well-planted buildings of South Bombay but rather flimsy-looking two-story structures. In its physical look, the set corresponds well with the older blocks of Bandra's bazaar district. At the same time, among the set's referents on an intertextual level are the scenes of Lucknow street life in Muslim socials—specifically, exteriors in the pleasure quarter.

Bijli's presence on the scene invokes the common association of red-light districts in Indian cities with Muslim neighborhoods.[41] And reinforcing it now, coming up the road toward Akbar is a band of *hijras*, transgender "eunuchs" dressed in gaudy saris. Considered by many Indians to be a bad omen or a nuisance when encountered on the street, for our bohemian hero they are a welcome sight. He enlists their help in their capacity as street performers and also as socially marginalized persons whose very marginality places them in the position of ritually sanctioned truth-tellers. In this, *hijras* may be said to resemble poets, although the *hijra* specialty—to be put on full display here—is the calling out of shameful truths.[42] Akbar will unleash the power of his voice in another song, but his target this time is not Salma but her father. The veil he will aim to lift is the façade of the old hypocrite's piety and respectability. And in place of arousing passionate longing in his audience, he will call up scorn.

"Tayyab Ali pyar ka dushman," sings Akbar, "Tayyab Ali is the enemy of love," and his carnivalesque chorus chides, *"Haay haay!"* An amused crowd gathers. Akbar wags his finger under his chin in mockery of the old man's beard. Salma, bare faced but with a *dupatta* draped over her hair, rushes down the stairs and is chased back to her room by her irate father. Akbar's lyrics take his antagonist to task. Tayyab Ali shows the heartlessness of rich people; as a businessman, he makes his living taking advantage of people smaller (figuratively speaking) than himself. "You deal in wood / You don't understand / The yearnings of a girl," Akbar sings on, but this is where the hypocrisy comes in. The *seth,* of course, is conducting a furtive romance of his own. In a gag that reverses the relation between the lover and the veiled beloved, the poet dons sunglasses against the old roué's dyed hair and dentures. "Sixty years of age, and does anyone's face glow like that?" He holds up the photograph. "Want me to name names?" "No, no, no, *ji!*" "Want me to show pictures?" "No, no, no, *ji!*"

"I'm not one to drag family reputations through the bazaar, Sir," Akbar concedes, ruling out one of the major narrative concerns of a Muslim social. But Tayyab Ali is not mollified. Far from being shamed into granting his blessing, he pays off some rowdies to teach Akbar a lesson. They make quick work of it, finishing the job, to Salma's distress, by heaving her beau into a well-established symbol of *nawabi* decadence: a dovecote.

Hijras, hoodlums, and hoochie-coochie girls, however, are not the only inhabitants of the neighborhood, and Tayyab Ali is hardly the local boss. Breaking through the glass front of his office, Brother Anthony seizes the little man, totes him out to the street, and tosses him onto the luggage rack of a taxi; they drive off to the hospital.

Tayyab Ali enters the hospital ward on Anthony's shoulder. They are accompanied by a *qazi,* a bearded jurist out of a Muslim social. Akbar lies in bed with a bruised-up face; Salma stands by at the neighboring window, through which a church can be seen. Anthony demands that his friend get up: "Now we'll get you and Salma married. This minute!" Salma's smile implies sympathy to the scheme. But in spite of all the mockery and bullying to which he's been subjected, Tayyab Ali makes clear his opposition to the match—as does our hero to his friend's strong-arm tactics. "I could have raised a hand too, if I had wanted to. But hitting people's not my way, Brother Anthony."

This statement of principle, at the narrative level, is as central to the character's identity as the challenge voiced musically in "Parda Hai Parda." It is important here, but not hard, to lay out the logic of making the Muslim the nonviolent brother among our three heroes. Any Bollywood story involving cops and gangsters requires a good dose of what in Hindi is called *maara-maari*—fisticuffs. It's a staple ingredient of the spicy *masala* mix. At the same time, the film is a nationalist allegory, and to leave out the theme of nonviolence would be to miss the most Indian thing about the Indian nation-building myth. Now, the majority community cannot be denied the right to wield righteous violence—at some level that is what modern nationalist ideology is all about—and as the agent of state authority, Amar collapses within his person the Hindu principle of dharma onto the state's official monopoly of violence. Anthony, on the other hand, represents a community that is demographically small but nevertheless highly visible in Bombay. He shares the task of executing un-sanctioned acts of violence with the film's villain, the Christian Robert.[43]

Here Akbar is placed not in between Amar and Anthony but some-where outside the equation. The construction of the Muslim community as consisting of fierce warrior people—and its corollary, that of the Hindu community *tout court* as peaceful or passive—has been basic to the for-mulation of nationalist and other kinds of ideologies across South Asia for a long time. The decision to choose the Muslim to carry the torch of nonviolence, then, was a strategic one on the part of Desai and his team.[44] Visually the film marks Akbar as Gandhi's heir in several ways. In the prologue sequence, he is the only one of the three children to stay put at the Gandhi statue, where in place of Kishanlal, the tailor Haider Ali comes along to collect him. And Akbar's mission statement—"If I'm going to win someone over, it's through the power of love"—resonates with the Gandhian rhetoric of *conversion* over *coercion*. "Truth resides in every human heart," said Gandhi, "and one has to search for it there, and to be guided by truth as one sees it. But no one has a right to coerce others to act according to his own view of truth."[45]

Yet the politics of Indian secularism is not all there is to the move. As this chapter has argued consistently, it is in the film's musical dimension—which is to say, its poetic dimension—that Akbar comes into his own. He takes on the persona of the truth-telling poet, deploying a set of anteced-ents valorized in Indo-Islamic literary and mystical discourses—a persona that has already been disseminated at a popular level through the medium of cinema. When Akbar stands up for nonviolence, then, his position is grounded in a recognizably Muslim heritage.[46] What's more, when he puts his powers into action through the virtuosic command of words and music, he shows that nonviolence is not only halal—it's fun.

Anthony concludes the hospital scene by storming out in a huff. But not much time passes before the two friends make up. When we next see them—about midday on the same day—they're driving together some-where in the outer suburbs when they intercept a car chase. The hunters are the wicked Robert and his minions; the prey are Kishanlal, the boys' (unbeknownst-to-them) father, and Anthony's girlfriend, Jenny. Anthony rescues Jenny, and Akbar, the unconscious Kishanlal. Returning to the hospital, Akbar checks the older man into the bed he himself vacated "two hours ago." And just a short while later, the familiar hospital ward becomes the scene of more missed connections.

Robert and his men have traced Kishanlal to his hospital bed. They whisk him off to the operating theater just as Bharati enters the ward in search of Akbar, whom she wants to bless with some red flowers she has brought from a *dargah,* a Sufi shrine. In the operating theater, Robert attempts to revive his captive from his comatose state; his henchman Ranjeet coerces the aid of a doctor they have taken captive—Salma. Still seeking Akbar, Bharati calls at the door, and Robert recognizes the blind woman as Kishanlal's wife.

Here we enter the third act of the Muslim subplot. Having taken Bharati hostage, Robert races off with her on a terror ride, but Ranjeet wrecks the car and, in the commotion, Bharati flees but then trips and goes rolling down a slope.[47] Robert and Ranjeet set off in pursuit. The blind woman's tumble has delivered her from the desert of the roadside into a verdant, garden-like space. Mohamed Rafi's voice comes wailing over the soundtrack. This is the film's second *qawwali,* "Shirdi Wale Sai Baba."

When we are shown the source of the singing, we recognize a destination forecast in Bharati's allusion to the Sufi shrine she had just left. The image's cinematic antecedents are to be found in *Palki* and *Pakeezah,* among other films. A building rises before her in the wilderness, and as the camera zooms past the crude mud enclosure that screens it, we see that it is a little sanctuary styled with Islamic arches but flying the saffron flags seen on Hindu temples. The colors on the walls likewise signal an ecumenical embrace, with a wing in an Islam-friendly shade of green abutting a main structure in a pinkish tone not far removed from saffron. White accents add a third color to suggest, in combination, the national flag. The overall effect is of a secret oasis, a haven the seeker attains through successive layers— wasteland, forest, outer wall. When the lens shifts to her oppressors, getting their bearings amid the trees and bushes, red flowers offer another hint that they're trespassing on sacred turf, whence blessings flow.

The lens zooms in through the shrine's entrance to present us with the object of veneration: it is the garlanded statue of a thin, bearded man, slightly larger than life. This is Sai Baba of Shirdi, a Sufi charismatic who attracted a cross-sectarian following around the turn of the twentieth century. By 1918, the year he passed on from the phenomenal world, the solitary Sufi who based himself in a ruined mosque in a Maharashtrian village had become recognized as a saintly dispenser of divine power *(barkat)* by many Muslims and as the human incarnation of a god *(avatar)* by many Hindus. This was the case not only in rural Shirdi but also in the metropolis of Bombay, where icons reproduced from photographs transmitted his charisma among urban devotees, mostly Hindus.[48] The cult continued to spread into the 1970s, gaining adherents among the urban poor. Crucial to that development were representations of the Baba in popular cinema, including the very scene under discussion here.

One reason for the attention the film lavishes on Sai Baba—visually, narratively, musically—over other divine personalities like Jesus, Mary, and Santoshi Maa is undoubtedly the personal devotion of Manmohan Desai's wife, Jeevanprabha (who also received a story credit for the film). Desai imbibed some of her enthusiasm and, years later, would go on pilgrimages to Shirdi to mark the date of her death.[49] But another reason, very likely, is the interest taken in Sai Baba worship in this period by a powerful agency: the Maharashtra Congress Party.[50]

It is of course Akbar who leads the mixed congregation of Hindus and Muslims, men and women, in a rousing *qawwali* in the saint's praise. He has dressed for the occasion in a white frock coat that would not look out of place in Lucknow itself, but he has accessorized it with a red rose and with a kerchief on his head printed with yet more roses. The love of the nightingale for the rose is one of the most celebrated motifs of Urdu poetry and the Persian tradition from which it descends: the nightingale represents the poet-lover, and the rose is the beloved. Yet the combination of rose and Nehru coat also brings us back from Persia and even from Lucknow—back to the realm of an Akbar Ilahabadi, in the sense of a Great One from Allahabad, for the rose was the personal emblem of Indira Gandhi's father, Pandit Nehru. At the level of national allegory, the tableau at the Sai Baba shrine picturizes the secularist ideology the Congress likes to be seen to champion: Muslims and Hindus united in the observance of an authentic Indian spirituality—under the edifice of the nation-state, under the leadership of Nehru and his heirs.[51]

Akbar's *qawwali* musicians accompany him from their seats on the floor as our exemplary Muslim capers with his hand drum before the idol

FIGURE 12. "Shirdi Wale Sai Baba"

(Figure 12).[52] When the blind woman gains her sanctuary, Akbar exerts his musical powers to strip the veils from her eyes. (A thorough analysis of this feat will wait for Chapter 4.) Once sighted again, the homeless woman everybody knows as *Maa* is soon reacquainted with other dear things she had thought forever lost—for this is the miracle that sets into motion the chain of events that will conclude in a grand reunion. But before that can happen, of course, the Muslim subplot must be resolved.

Our hero began his day at the crossroads in the Muslim Quarter, and that is where he ends it (half an hour of screen time has passed). A blaze lights up the night sky: Tayyab Ali's house is on fire, and the courtesan Bijli looks on in satisfaction. "Let's go, Mother dear," she says to her madam, "our work here is done." Thus has the house of the old *seth* been brought literally to ruin by his association with a woman of ill fame. Akbar arrives on the scene after a crowd has already gathered; Salma's voice can be heard crying out for her father, but no one seems to be doing much to save them. Akbar puts his wits to work. He finds a way to a wall facing the conflagration—very likely it's part of the warehouse complex—and emerges on top of it, framed against the set's pasteboard mosque. He throws across a rope with a grappling hook and swings to the balcony

Tarzan style, calling fervently on the revered son-in-law of the Prophet, Ali, to see him through the trial.

Entering action-hero mode, Akbar rescues first his girlfriend, then her father. He climbs back on the rope (which appears to be suspended from some sort of skyhook), they climb onto him, and all three swing back together to shelter under the mosque's silhouette. Tayyab Ali makes clear his change of heart with a handsome apology. Akbar and Salma have won the elder's consent and his invocation on them of Allah's blessing. The Muslim subplot is at length concluded. And all that really needs to be added is that its concluding act, with its strenuous yet nonviolent heroics, has been lifted wholesale from *Palki,* in which the poet-hero risks his life to save his patron's son from a fire. Of course, *Palki*'s hero entered a long convalescence and was reported dead to his family back in Lucknow; Akbar, Salma, and Tayyab Ali emerge a bit blackened around the edges, as if from an explosion in a Bugs Bunny cartoon.

A mention of the finale will serve here as a coda. Playing his own part in thwarting the villainous Robert—author of the original partition of his family—Akbar infiltrates his mansion as the bearded tailor who will fit his daughter, Jenny, with her wedding gown. The arrival of his brothers—revealed as such at last!—provides the occasion for a final musical number, "Anhoni Ko Honi Kar De," whose theme is the invincibility of the three united. The hijinks develop into a climactic fight, and while the big brothers duke it out with the villains, sensitive Akbar confines himself to providing the musical accompaniment.[53] The fight presents him with one opening in which to violate his vow of nonviolence. An already battered Robert comes staggering in front of him. "O Lord, until today when I've raised my hands it's always been to pray. But today, for the first time, I ask your forgiveness. *Yah Ali—!*" Akbar's haymaker knocks Robert clean out of the scene and into the next one, where he lands in a jail cell already occupied by Kishanlal—bowed at his enemy's feet in the conventional South Asian pose of submission.

Man behind the Curtain

If there is a final statement to be made about the Muslim subplot, it revolves around the multiple meanings of the *parda,* the curtain or veil. At the start of our analysis of "Parda Hai Parda," we proposed that Akbar as singer addresses three audiences: (1) the audience in the diegetic theater; (2) Salma; and (3) us, the audience watching the film. We have examined the first two audiences in some detail. But how are we to interpret the song's address to us? What veil is there between Akbar and us that he pledges to strip away?[54]

The poet-hero's message to us is best reached through his message to the audience inside the movie—that is to say, by revisiting the mystical symbolism within which his *qawwali* lyrics are encoded. We spoke earlier of the nightingale and the rose, symbolic of the lover who expresses his desire and the beloved who inspires it. If the relation between the lover and the beloved is the central structuring principle of poesy in this tradition, the repertoire does admit a supporting cast of characters. Of these, the most pertinent to the case of *Amar Akbar Anthony* is the Shaikh, the bearded representative of Islamic dogma. His insight shallow and his attitude square, the Shaikh serves as a foil to the antinomian poet, whose words extoll the value of experience over blind adherence to rules such as the proscriptions on wine and idolatry.

Up to the end of "Parda Hai Parda," Akbar's conduct might suggest the nightingale in his narrative life. But developments quickly prove that Salma is no more thorn-hedged rose than shrinking violet. To the degree that Sufi allegory is present in the characters' own romance, it is bundled, as it were, in two obscuring layers; for as we have seen, the film's subplot is a repackaging of a Muslim social, which itself repackages the classical topos for popular consumption. As a representative of the poet persona before his diegetic audience, however, Akbar does follow the code in his language and his self-presentation. In fact, it could be said that it's precisely when Mohamed Rafi takes over from Rishi Kapoor that the character enters the matrix of Sufism. In his *qawwali* performances, he appears accessorized with roses—not a token of his love for Salma or anyone else in particular (unless it's for the Congress Party)—but because he is an exponent of the discourse of the tormented lover.

What remains to be added is that the symbolism of frustrated lovers is but one layer of an esoteric discourse that thrives on veil imagery. This is the hermeneutical layer known as *ishq-e-majazi,* or "profane love." Crucially for the theological bona fides of Sufi literature, there is also a mystical stratum of true or sublime love, *ishq-e-haqiqi,* in which the beloved stands in for the figuration of the divine, and the veil could be interpreted variously as the illusory quantity of material creation or the superficial legalism and hypocrisy of the orthodox. But in the interest of making sense of *Amar Akbar Anthony* in its historical and sociological contexts, we advance a third, avowedly heterodox interpretation. The object of desire addressed here is a certain construction of the Muslim community, and the *parda* to be stripped away—readily enough glossed as veil or curtain—is also a *screen* that reveals even as it conceals: the cinema screen.

What Akbar does is to expose on this cinematic *parda,* through generic conventions of displaying and masking, the fabrication of a domain that had become definitively identified in the previous decade as the locus of Muslim manners and narrative tropes. The Muslim social's 1960s efflorescence was followed by a decline that, in retrospect, seems in keeping with its trademark themes of nostalgia and loss. Within the subplot outlined here, it is the already dated conventions of this realm of nattering nabobs to which our optimistic young suburbanite of 1977 relates in a mode of affectionate satire or parody.

But what is at stake in this *parda*-y? We have already discussed the film's tendency to tame or make innocuous a potentially uppity national minority through diminution and humor—to smother Muslim particularity, perhaps, in a fraternal embrace. Let's wrap up this argument with a further proposition. That the parody of a Muslim social contained in *Amar Akbar Anthony,* in which the great house brought to its doom by a woman of ill repute is a neighborhood timber yard; in which the aristocratic poet is a paan-chewing tailor's son; in which his inaccessible beloved is the thoroughly modern Dr. Salma (who has examined his heart with a stethoscope before the movie has even begun); in which the rose of the nightingale is a politician's boutonniere; in which the formidable Nawab Sahib is four feet tall and most of the courtesans are drag queens—in short, in which tragedy is replaced by farce—we propose that this set of inversions and diminutions adds up to a cinematic construction of one kind of national space as defined against another.

Amar Akbar Anthony's vision of the Bombay suburbs as a space of middle-class optimism is made possible by the shadow of antique Lucknow. Of our three heroes, the baby brother's singular achievement is the triumph of the modern over history. At the film's end, as Akbar drives his brothers and their brides into the sunset, he does so to the tune of the one song in which his part is *not* sung by Mohamed Rafi. "Anhoni Ko Honi Kar De": Let's make the impossible possible.

This Is True, It's No Story

Phir bhi, as one says in Hindi and Urdu, "then again." If that is our argument's conclusion, we are yet left with at least two more ifs that deserve some resolution.

The bifurcation of space in films such as *Mere Mehboob* and *Palki* invites comparison with the way *The Wizard of Oz* (Victor Fleming, 1939) stages its technicolor land of fantasy against the black-and-white realism of dust-bowl Kansas. While not a fantasyland in precisely the same sense as Oz, the Lucknow of the Muslim socials is nevertheless the dreamlike spectacle on which the films are centered—the enchanting face that is paradoxically made visible by the cinema's own special *parda*. But if the movies demarcate Lucknow as the realm of a romantic past by contrasting it with spaces of modernity—trains, a university campus, a big industrial city (Bombay itself in *Palki*)—what sort of space is it that *Amar Akbar Anthony* is constructing against its own little neighborhood Lucknow? In other words, if the Muslim Quarter is but a dream, is what the film shows us of the rest of Bombay the waking reality? And if the achievement of Akbar-as-actor, ultimately, is the conquest of Lucknow, how is that narrative end related to the musical truth told by Akbar-as-voice?

Here is our answer to both of these ifs: Whatever Rishi achieves, Rafi takes further. The Bombay of *Amar Akbar Anthony* is not meant to be real any more than Manmohan Desai meant his film to be realism. The Muslim Quarter the story exposes is merely one false front in a city that turns out to be almost entirely fabricated of appealing but deceptive surfaces. The implication of Akbar's truth-telling power, as manifested within the film by the Sufi poetry voiced by Mohamed Rafi, is that the worldly sphere through which all the characters chart their various courses is a superficial, even meretricious falsehood.

Let's conclude this chapter's argument about song and truth, story and falsehood, by running back through Akbar's solo numbers—the moments in which the voice of the poet intervenes within the narrative—and comparing their effects. In fact, let's rewind one step earlier, with a second look at Akbar Ilahabadi.

The Urdu poet, it will be recalled, won a reputation as a satirist by calling out the artificiality of aspects of the modernity introduced by the Raj and embraced by mentally colonized Indians. For Akbar, it was not illusion in a cosmic sense but the condition of colonial modernity that was phony and therefore comic. And its phoniness resided in its distortion of something that was authentic—a natural order of human relations. Thus, British jurisprudence diverts the course of justice with layers of paper; photography interposes a static imprint between lover and beloved. Mediation by representational veils or masks gets in the way of intimacy, of romantic union. The comedy of *Amar Akbar Anthony* works in a similar way.

The object of humor for *Amar Akbar Anthony* and for Akbar Ilahabadi is not the worldly sphere, even if the most pertinent religious teachings would formulate things this way.[55] To transpose the question from metaphysics to cinema: diegesis itself is not the disguise; rather, it is one site within the worldly sphere—the modern city—that is the domain of serial misrecognition. When at the film's end Amar, Akbar, and Anthony overcome the barriers of social segregation to unite and dispel the reign of illusion, they demonstrate their mastery over it by manipulation of their masks. *This social identity, scripted elsewhere, is just a disguise—underneath it I look like my brothers, and like you.* But if within this layer of phoniness there is scope for comic masquerade, implied behind it are pain and alienation that surely resonate with viewers in India's cities and villages alike. For in a sense, to be a modern individual is precisely to be denied union—to be a frustrated lover.

Opposed to this labyrinth of curtains and mirrors, the film shows us two distinct spaces and two models of social relations. The first alternative space is the Koliwada, the original family home. The second is the frontier of suburban development, where the film situates the promise of a modern Indian society, its citizens undivided by caste or creed. This mapping of national history onto the diegetic city—beleaguered community in the past, urban anomie in the present, utopian suburbs of the future—has been laid out in the introduction. The two social formations are the patriarchal family and the class of the urban poor. On these points too, much that is germane to Akbar's case is also argued elsewhere in this book. But together, these four sites of alternative vision will prove useful as coordinates by which we can steer to this chapter's end.

Now let's compare the moments when each brother penetrates the veil of illusion first identified in song by Akbar. The Hindu brother and the Catholic brother both perceive ruptures in the fabric visually (as does their Hindu patriarch, Kishanlal). When near the end of the movie Amar returns to the Koliwada, his eyesight fogs over at the ancestral site. The optical effect mediates a flashback to the scene in which Amar-as-child buries the pistol that his father has gifted him. Following a logic often cited in origin stories about Hindu temples, Inspector Amar pursues his vision and digs at the spot indicated to unearth a clue of divine presence. In this case, it turns out to be what we who are clued in to Akbar's mystic stratum now recognize to be not a child's toy but a real gun—a sign of its reality as the key to the character's identity and dharma.

Anthony, on the other hand, is first granted a vision of what's true when his own beloved, Jenny, walks into the church and his eyes multiply her image like a kaleidoscope. Again, it is this very distortion that indicates a privileged order of reality. The second time he is visited by this effect is toward the end of the "My Name Is Anthony Gonsalves" number. In his *deewanapan,* his intoxication by love—abetted by alcohol—Anthony ascends to a point of mystical breakthrough (even as he meets with defeat in the world of appearances, at the all-too-phenomenal fists of Zabisko). He succeeds in warping the song's mise-en-scène—the camera deploys a variety of special effects—such that Jenny is invited to see the world through his eyes. The miracle appears all the greater in that his own lyrics set up the feat as a challenge; we have been informed that the poor (Anthony himself) know how to recognize true love, whereas the rich (the beloved, Jenny) can hardly be expected to. Here Anthony takes on some of the attributes of the Sufi as truth-teller. The rhetoric that privileges the poor and lowly over the rich and mighty in matters of the heart is well combined with the performer's demeanor as a love-crazed and tipsy gadfly.

Akbar's own entry in this vein is the raucous "Tayyab Ali Pyar Ka Dushman." Having assembled his scandalous chorus of *hijras,* the poet-hero calls out the Shaikh. Tayyab Ali's surface is revealed to be false on two counts. The outwardly respectable businessman is himself a lover.

And beyond that, he can't recognize the right of those humbler than he to experience love, because the very pride and comfort that come with his social standing have blinded him to their plight.

In style and affect, these two songs differ a good deal, but they come together in the image of the sort of visionary who speaks the truth that ruptures illusion. For alongside the elegant poets of the Muslim socials there are more ragged examples—madmen, drunks, and mendicant *qalandars*—whose integrity is indexed by their disregard for convention. *Palki*'s impoverished hero Naseem comes close to the type, but cinema's best-known illustration is surely the unkempt sculptor played by Kumar in the historical epic *Mughal-e-Azam*. When he emerges from the crowd in his rather monastic-looking robe to defy the assembled might of the Mughal Empire, what bold truth does he affirm with the words "Zindabad Zindabad" (Long Live, Long Live)? That of the power of love, of course. And whose voice delivers the words? That of Mohamed Rafi.[56]

Nevertheless, when it comes to musical ruptures of narrative illusion in *Amar Akbar Anthony,* pride of place belongs to the *qawwali* numbers. They mirror each other, both thematically and in terms of their effects on the narrative. "Parda Hai Parda," as we have observed at some length, is seminal. Akbar takes center stage and lays out the paradigm: there is a veil, and behind the veil there is a beloved. For the film's audience, the veil is outmoded Muslim stereotypes, as projected on the movie screen. Thus Akbar launches the Muslim subplot, whose conflict hinges on his desire to win parental consent to a match that is already a fait accompli.

And here, at last, we have assembled the terms by which to set up the following point. The modernity that awaits on the other side of tradition is not exactly a liberal vision. When the subplot's resolution exposes the film's exemplary node of phoniness—the dead weight of Islamic custom—what stands exposed are not radically autonomous individual subjects. Tayyab Ali is no longer a *nawab,* but he is still a father. And the "secular" young Indian lovers do not awake into some putative heaven of freedom from all hierarchy or ideology. Their own consent is actually a subjection to the patriarchal family, which the film reveals as the authentic model of human relations.

Before the subplot wraps, Akbar presents us with "Shirdi Wale Sai Baba." In this second *qawwali,* our mystic seeker delivers on the Sufi symbolism he deployed in the first—the paradigm that underpins our theory of not only the Muslim subplot but the entire urban narrative as illusion. In contrast with his throwdown in "Parda Hai Parda," Akbar addresses the holy man from the position of a supplicant. The character has made a long journey. From the earlier song's prideful refrain, "And if I don't succeed . . . / Then my name isn't Akbar," he has arrived at: "To attempt an account of your deeds of mercy / How would Akbar even dare?" And having thus enacted his submission before the representative of divine order, his words carry through his heart's desire.

Once again—and conclusively, we propose—the voice penetrates the veil. But what sort of veil is named in this song? And what is the reality thus revealed? It is in bringing about the great pivotal miracle of "Shirdi Wale Sai Baba," we contend, that Akbar's voice reveals that the reign of illusion extends beyond the Muslim Quarter. It blankets the whole wide city, which has hosted the action of *Amar Akbar Anthony*'s improbable plot, and whose streets Bharati has traversed for years, blinded. In this solitary, pathetic figure we have come to recognize legions of fellow travelers, poor people who appear to be cast adrift in the city but whose very poverty, perhaps, keeps them morally grounded. And when the veil is lifted at last from the wanderer's eyes, the truth revealed is that of the patriarchal family, within which she is restored to the one role that allows her to make sense of her identity—that of mother.

And yet all this was foreordained in the film's very first song. When the title and credits roll over the blood-transfusion scene it is to the accompaniment of Mohamed Rafi's voice. The opening lines of "Yeh Sach Hai Koi Kahani Nahin" go like this: "This is true, it's no story. / Blood is blood, it isn't water."

So tell us: What's true, Brother Akbar? This story isn't true—that is to say, *story* isn't true. But once we get beyond narrative, what are we left with? The answer, it seems, is blood: brotherhood, family, union. *Mashallah,* that's what's always been true, at the beginning and in the end.

3

Anthony

AMAR AKBAR IRONY

. . . .

Don't think he's dishonest. It's quite the opposite. He has a very
strict code of ethics and for him it is the state that is corrupt. He
won't let himself be compromised by cheating policemen or tax
officials. This unofficial economy—which is basically the entire
economy—runs on a different moral system.

—Rana Dasgupta, *Capital: A Portrait of
Twenty-First-Century Delhi*

THIS CHAPTER, like Desai's film, brings together a mix of inter-
locking "items." Each of the six items engages an aspect of Anthony's representation, within the film and outside it. And taken as a whole,
the argument we present here coalesces around three themes. The first
theme is the diegetic person of Anthony Gonsalves and the ironic logic
he compels, traced in allegory as a sequence of Catholic rites of passage as
the subject moves from boy to man. The second theme takes up the charismatic capital that surrounds Amitabh Bachchan—likely India's best-known
living citizen—and the Anthony character as the perfect complement to the
star who plays him, a role that refracts the extradiegetic meanings of Bachchan's stardom. The third theme is the way Anthony's portrayal resonates
both inside and outside the film, and the character's resemblance, when
studied as a Christian figure, to what Ashis Nandy has theorized as "the
intimate enemy."[1] Far more than a grab bag of cinematic and cultural
stereotypes of the Christian, the Anthony character—and the force of
the actor behind him—compels us to come to terms with the way the

film engages cultural politics, the Indian state, and a peculiarly Indian predicament of the self.

Amar Akbar Anthony may be a film about national integration, but from Anthony's point of view, the project of national integration has been a failure. He finds a place neither in Nehru's vision of the centralized socialist state nor in Gandhi's vision of the nation as a community united under a benevolent, "secularized" Hinduism. (As such, he has been let down by two father figures—do we already detect a certain pattern developing here?) We argue that our hero embodies this failure, showing us how much is marginalized and erased in India's fantasy of itself, cinematic or otherwise. Anthony disentangles "nation" from "state" in that the character has created an alternative sociopolitical order in his own little neighborhood. The nation, Anthony seems to tell us, survives *despite* the failures of the state.

And before we get started, one more thing. These analyses take for granted what is well known to anyone who has seen this film, or even heard of it: Anthony is the film's protagonist. The previous chapters may have presented ideas to the contrary, but this chapter (like Anthony's name in the movie's title) follows the others not as their subordinate but as their summation. In the end, Anthony is really what this movie is all about, *hai ki nahin?*

Item Number One: "I Am Alone in the World"

The film's best known and most quoted song is "My Name Is Anthony Gonsalves," in which the character laments, "I am alone in the world."[2] With this ironic assertion, Anthony defines his romantic quest: he is an orphan setting forth to win the love of Kishanlal's daughter. Yet this quest is based in falsehoods, as the audience well knows. Far from being an orphan, Anthony is in fact in the midst of his biological kin, although the bonds of family are invisible to him until the end of the film. His love interest, Jenny, is similarly an embodiment of irony, for we know she is not Kishanlal's real daughter; Kishanlal abducted her from Robert when she was an infant. Even as Jenny and Anthony fall in love, we viewers are aware of their connection.

And their connection is complicated, to say the least. Jenny is Kishanlal's adopted daughter,[3] and Anthony is Kishanlal's lost son. Anthony and Jenny are in a sense in the same family, connected by Kishanlal, although they are tied by an immoral and illegal act (abduction) and a twist of fate (itself precipitated by various immoral and illegal acts) that has separated Kishanlal from his children. They are lovers brought together by evil actions. In fact, they are the product of sin in the Christian sense, in which all people, especially a man and a woman in love, re-create the event of original sin. And their sin is a sin of origins—of not knowing their true original contexts. The core romance of the film involves two individuals whom fate has estranged from their own people and joined together in love, as if to test whether the power of their choice can overcome the vexed reality of history. If not in quite the same way as Adam and Eve (the carriers of sin in Christian teaching), Anthony and Jenny essentially share a father. Isn't it ironic that of all the women in the world, Anthony should end up with someone who is (almost) his sister?

But if hero and heroine actually knew the truth of each other's identity, how could their young love bloom? Charade is the very basis of their love—perhaps of all love, the film might insist. What's more, to follow Anthony's lead through the film is to find, at its heart, a bold promise: We can be who we present ourselves to be. We are not beholden to the facts of biology or blood, nor to the strictures of social expectation. We can own the fictions of our self-fashioning—break old molds, recast ourselves as new kinds of subjects. It's an optimistic gospel, charged with both a certain Me Generation spirit and the star power of the Bachchan persona . . . but here we're running ahead of ourselves.

Self-invention notwithstanding, there is indeed a deterministic degree of truth—of prophecy—to be traced in the genealogies of Anthony and Jenny. Jenny's abduction in childhood reverses the usual route that a woman takes to enter her husband's family in patrilocal India. Rather than get married and then move into her husband's home, Jenny moves in first (abducted by Anthony's biological father), and then gets married much later to the son of her guardian (and erstwhile kidnapper).[4] Thus Anthony was never "alone," and certainly not when he sang his song at the Easter party; it seems his marriage was cosmically, or karmically, arranged for him in childhood. When Anthony sings "I am alone in the world," there is a deep and strange irony behind the statement; if not for the slapstick framing that makes it so funny, the discordance here might give us pause.

And there is yet another irony here beneath the surface, for we also know our hero's original name was *not* Anthony Gonsalves. When Anthony was abandoned at the age of three, he presumably would have known and remembered his name, as most three-year-olds do quite well, but a brief mention of "fever" indicates he may have suffered memory loss. Nevertheless, we viewers know that he was born a Hindu—as such, the bearer of a Hindu name—and Anthony surely suspects as much himself. Kept in his pocket as a kind of talisman is the letter that Bharati wrote to Kishanlal when she abandoned the family (see Figure 20 in Chapter 4). The signature on the note would signal to Anthony that his mother was a Hindu ("Bharati" would be an unlikely way for a Christian or Muslim woman to identify herself). In the course of the narrative we learn the original names of Amar and Akbar—Amar and Raju, respectively—but the middle brother is never named. The most the movie gives us is *Chhota*, "the little one," which is how the child Amar refers to him. Even when he is reunited with his parents, his birth name is never mentioned. Little "Anthony" is a kind of blank slate, waiting for a name—and more.

Naming is a recurring motif in this film; it's also basic to sacraments of induction in many religions. In the Catholic Church, naming is the signifier of baptismal entry into the Church and the accompanying removal of the stain of original sin. It is when the child is baptized (offscreen, at some point) that he has become, at once, Anthony and a Christian. But twenty-two years of diegetic time have passed when he testifies to this identity in "My Name Is Anthony Gonsalves."[5] This self-declaration can be understood as something akin to the sacrament of Confirmation, when an adolescent chooses a new, Christian middle name and is confirmed as a Catholic. The song-ritual is Anthony's rechristening, his Confirmation as someone other than who he was at birth. And it's in this musical moment that the love between Anthony and Jenny—the love that is both sin and salvation—is fully kindled. This irony is perhaps not lost on Catholic observers (observant ones, at least).

The character also affirms his identity during the title sequence, when, alongside his brothers in their hospital beds, he announces his

FIGURE 13. The egg

name; and yet again at the end of the film, when each brother names himself during the "Anhoni Ko Honi Kar De" song sequence. But it is no accident that the occasion on which Anthony chooses, ceremoniously, to espouse his name is a holiday that celebrates rebirth and renewal, and it is no mere joke that this rebirth is enacted when Anthony emerges from an egg (Figure 13). Like an Easter chick (or an upper-caste Hindu),[6] he is "twice born," born first of Maa and then again in the Catholic Church. For a Catholic like Anthony, who is mired in a kind of original sin—which is the sin of the father (in this case, a father who chose gold, in his covetousness, over his children)—renewal and rebirth are essential. Yet the sin of one father must still be atoned for by the blood of the other father: the Padre must die so that Kishanlal can achieve redemption.

With so much blood and sin and patrilineal confusion wrapped up in this character's composition, it is no wonder that when film scholars invoke the national allegory, they regularly focus on Anthony. And when the film comes up in popular culture, it is generally Bachchan's role that is summoned.[7] Anthony's dominant position in the film is statistically apparent from his screen time. He appears in 44 percent of the film's scenes, whereas Akbar appears in 35 percent, and Amar in a mere 19.5 percent. Moreover,

Anthony is what links the brothers together. He carries on a relationship with Amar (as his antagonist) and with Akbar (as something like the president of his fan club), but Amar and Akbar do not speak to each other until late in the film, when Akbar goes to the police station for help in tracking down Kishanlal. Even this meeting, however, is perfunctory, and neither character shows any sense of recognizing the other or even introduces himself. On their own, Anthony's two brothers have little connection other than the matrilineal blood transfusion that inaugurates the main portion of the film's narrative. Amar and Akbar are connected to each other through Anthony—Anthony is their one degree of separation. It is again ironic that Anthony—the middle child, the local "fixer," the middleman—is the last to be reunited with the nuclear family, even though he is its center.

When *Amar Akbar Anthony* was released, the media likewise recognized the primacy of Anthony, Bachchan's character. Bombay's famed English-language tabloid *Blitz* (now sadly defunct) remarked, "Amit[abh Bachchan] monopolizes the picture, he is sheer delight as the drunk and dancer." The *Herald* commented, "It is . . . Amitabh Bachchan who gets the major montage of the film, and, to say the least, he steals a march over the rest of the artistes." The *Deccan Herald* stated, "It is Amitabh [Bachchan] who offers a delicious cameo as Anthony." The *Times of India* put it simply: "The main attraction of the film is undoubtedly Amitabh Bachchan." And in one publication, a reporter who "took to the streets" to ask people about the film cites one informant named Sakharam from the Bombay neighborhood of Dadar as opining: "[Anthony] was just like my brother, who is the *dada* of our locality and my brother and I get priority in everything, even movies and all. And we'll get someone like Parveen Babi too!"[8]

As the film's central character, Anthony is the meeting point of all the overdetermined tropes that make up this circular comedy. *Amar Akbar Anthony* ends where it begins; it reverses roles, replicates plots, recycles visual motifs, and connects the brothers in a highly stylized spiral of fate.[9] At the axis of the action there is Anthony. And as is clear from the reviews, which conflate the character of Anthony with the actor Amitabh Bachchan, if we look closely at Anthony, we find Bachchan just waiting to hatch from the character's shell.

Item Number Two: One Is a Lonely Number

"My Name Is Anthony Gonsalves" is a musical scene that is playful, ribald, even sensitive at points, yet it ends with a fight in which Anthony gets his clock cleaned. Compressed here in a single song-item number is the portfolio of a remarkably versatile actor, one who could seemingly do it all. The moody young hero of melodrama could also be the king of comedy. Combining action, romance, slapstick, and pathos, Bachchan's Anthony number was a one-man introduction to the ascendant *masala* genre (as identified in our introduction) as well as the new contours of 1970s stardom. It was also a master class in irony. Onscreen the character announces his loneliness, and in the audience Bachchan fans meet the announcement with rapturous applause. The irony was registered in the first edition of the film publication *Movie,* published in London in 1983. It ran a lead story on Bachchan titled "One Is a Lonely Number."[10] Ah, the loneliness of an actor beloved by a billion people!

Amitabh Bachchan became the "angry young man" of Indian cinema,[11] spokesperson for a generation of the lumpen masses, even while his background was anything but lumpen. Bachchan came from privilege, the Delhi University–educated son of a poet and a socialite. The actor behind Anthony has two master's degrees, and had stardom not worked out, he is said to have considered a career as an engineer. The fetish the public has made of Bachchan's characters, with their youthful disillusionment, shapes a complicated figure: an idol of the working (not to mention unemployed) young men of urban India played by a scion of the intellectual elite.[12]

Whereas the masses could see reflected in *Amar Akbar Anthony* their own yearnings for insurgent release, the middle class—poised for their tasty first bite of the Maharaja Mac in the dawn of economic liberalization fifteen years in the future—could consume the film as a comedy about the incipient demise of the poor and powerless, the dethronement of the "people" as the central concern of the Indian state. Through Anthony, Bachchan emerged as a social polyglot, and has now ascended to the status of something like India's cultural pope. It is as if the Anthony-Bachchan sandwich had been designed as part of a government Five Year Plan in anticipation of the move to a neoliberal model of development: a figure who in life represented the aspirations of bourgeois India to realize the full measure of what market ideology had to offer, and who in film could cathect the experiences of disenfranchised "heroes" on the street hoping to catch a break. At least through the 1980s, Bachchan and his many subsequent characters provide the missing link in public culture between the toiling masses and the prosperous "classes."

As such, Amitabh Bachchan—the biggest movie star in India if not the whole world—embodies a parallel text that accompanies the film.[13] Bachchan is likewise at the center of what film and media scholars have recently termed a "media assemblage."[14] Indeed, given the power of his public persona as a national and international superstar—a robust signifier for the evolving concept of globalized fame—he is anticipated and overshadowed in the transnational projection of Indian cultural forms perhaps only by the Mahatma himself. Gandhi is India's most recognizable face, but right behind him is Amitabh Bachchan.[15]

This chapter is not a thoroughgoing study of Amitabh Bachchan. But in a sense the film is itself a study of him. As Susmita Dasgupta observes in *Amitabh: The Making of a Superstar,* Bachchan's tremendous onscreen and offscreen charisma inspired Desai to craft many of the signature elements of his films.[16] Yet just as Bachchan's enormous star power can "deconstruct the text [i.e., film] in which he is [a] star,"[17] an analysis of the character of Anthony goes far in deconstructing the star himself, the actor in the world outside the movie. Indeed, *Amar Akbar Anthony* harnessed the charisma of Bachchan in such a way that it "dissolved Amitabh's pride in his uniqueness" because Anthony was "the only image [of a film character] that Amitabh could never convey in real life. . . . Anthony bhai remained out[side] Amitabh's reach forever."[18]

Bachchan enters our movie ready-loaded with extradiegetic baggage. The role of Anthony he steps into is not able to contain the star—but nor is it overwhelmed by him. This is Dasgupta's point. What we see here on the screen is not just Bachchan, as is the case with many of his other movies;[19] we see Bachchan and simultaneously we see Anthony. And the secret behind this Amitabh-Anthony amalgam is *masala.* Anthony is a highly complex character, perhaps not so much in the depth of his psychology (the conventional measure of complexity) but in the breadth of his multivocality. He encompasses within his person diverse moods, genre elements, and tropes; he embodies the ironic sensibility of the movie, whose every message is served up with a surplus of meaning. Is he all things to all people? We'd say rather the opposite: far from being a bland, anodyne hero—a product pitched at mass markets and satisfying to none— he is a bold mix of flavors indeed. Anthony steps out to the world, and does so in high definition; he is every bit as real as Bachchan's carefully crafted public persona. It is to the shape and significance of this remarkable character that we now turn.

Item Number Three: Anthony and Jesus, Fifty-Fifty

As a character, Anthony is central to the movie's action. And to the degree that he functions, like his brothers, as the metonym of a religion, we would expect to see Christianity as central to the world of diegesis. Yet the film's depiction of Christianity—of Roman Catholicism, to be precise—is defined by a certain lack of definition; what it shows us is perhaps not as notable, in the end, as what it leaves out.

Let's begin by examining Anthony's personal devotion to Jesus, a theme the film does shape attentively through image and narrative, almost as a character in its own right. The relationship is introduced in the scene that allows the film to jump twenty-two years, from the brothers' childhood in the film's prologue to their adulthood in the diegetic present. The scene begins in a confessional in the church that Anthony has called home. First we see Anthony as a child, confessing that he has sold his schoolbooks to pay for a dead stranger's coffin. In the course of the priest's remonstrations, time leaps forward; the juvenile Anthony is transformed into a full-grown specimen, and the formidable figure of Bachchan fills the confessional's frame. Anthony's priestly guardian scolds him for fighting and trading in bootleg hooch. Anthony retorts that he has a liquor license—a dubious claim[20]—and that he sells a quality product, but the Padre is not placated. He tells his ward to quit this hustle *(dhandha)* of his or be reported to the police. Anthony is indignant: "Then along with me, make sure you file a complaint about him." The camera follows his hand as he points to a statue of the infant Jesus in His mother's arms. The priest asks in English, "What nonsense are you talking?" Anthony explains, returning to his *apun tapun* Bombay Hindi, "Look, Father, whatever I make, fifty percent of it goes in the donation box, am I right?[21] The priest then accuses him of bribing Jesus, which Anthony rejects. As our hero explains, "Whatever He gives to me, I give back fifty percent for the poor. That's an understanding between us." Turning to the image of Jesus, he adds, "Am I right?"

The Padre's charge of bribery evokes several associations connected to church and state. For example, throughout Christianity one finds the "ten percent" rule (that is, giving 10 percent of one's income), but here there is an implication of something closer to a payoff. One can pick up echoes in this exchange of the archaic practice of indulgence—a doctrinal relic that allowed individuals to buy their way out of purgatory, which was understood to be a kind of tollbooth, or *check naka,* on the way to heaven. But the more immediate referent is the deep corruption of the Indian government's so-called License Raj, the years of planned economic policy during which bribery, or *baksheesh* (also known by other, more Bombay-ish words, like *hafta* or *supari*), became a regular feature of transactions both official and commercial.[22]

In his book *Emergency Retold,* Kuldip Nayar argues that corruption in the Indian state apparatus became endemic during the period of the Emergency. It displaced a civic state structure, and what emerged was a more or less formalized system of corruption—a broad-based culture that engulfed officialdom, from petty bureaucrats all the way up to India's most powerful politicians.[23] Anthony can be understood as a kind of response to this deep crisis of the state and the strain it put on civil society. Although not a state actor, Anthony still lives in a world of kickbacks and payoffs. What makes Anthony different isn't that he avoids paying tribute; he just pays it to an unlikely source. He labors under the authority of Jesus, and he shares all his proceeds accordingly. Recall how later in the story, at the Easter party, he walks in the air (as if on water?), and at the film's denouncement he shuts the curtains of Jenny's bedroom simply by waving his blessed hands. These details are light touches—"Easter eggs," if you like—but by the same token they drop a heavy hint. Anthony's business isn't illicit or immoral; it's divine.

Anthony's arrangement with Jesus thus signals a connection with the experience of everyday life during this period. Whether poor or middle class, anyone seeking to obtain some sort of basic service in an office—a ration card, a telephone, a pension check—could expect to pay a bribe. But the scene's primary function is to establish Anthony's moral character—his rationalization, as it were, for a life outside the strictures of the formal state. This is a life led under the laws of a different government (the government of the Christian God), which oversees a civil society oriented around Anthony himself. Thus, from this point onward, to accept the moral force of Anthony—to accept him as "good"—is to recognize that although he is a kind of hero in one corner of society, he is also an outlaw before the Indian state. As seen through Anthony's eyes, the state is outside the boundaries of our film's moral universe. Anthony—part hustler, part Hegel—has developed a new philosophy of right.

This rejection of the state, however, is not an embrace of anarchy, for Anthony accepts another hegemon. Anthony is a man of faith—faith not in politics or government but in Jesus. And his deal is with Him. Anthony is "secular" in a very Indian sense, for in India secularism entails the state's accession to the civic and cultural demands of religion (as opposed to religion acceding to the demands of the state). It could be said that India does not have a freedom *from* religion (along the lines of, for example, the United States and France) but a freedom *of* religion, in which the state encourages religious life and protects the sentiments of religious communities.[24] In other words, the state serves religion, but is mandated to do so impartially.

When *Amar Akbar Anthony* was released, several Christian groups nevertheless protested the film's portrayal of their faith. They took umbrage at various scenes having been shot in a church, particularly the murder of the Padre. They also alleged that Anthony places his foster father's body upon the altar, although in fact Anthony places the Padre's body on a low table along the side of the lectern in a chapel enshrining the Sacred Heart. In any case, these criticisms led to a decision by Bombay's archbishop that producers wishing to film in churches must first file for permission—a protocol still in force today. Another irony: a film about the primacy of religion over the power of the state prompted a religious institution, the Catholic Church, to ask the state to intervene regarding its portrayal.

These extradiegetic issues aside, Anthony takes the Catholic Church seriously, for he emulates its institutional structure in his own dispensation. His higher authority is Jesus, who is also his business partner, and he is himself, in his own way, the bishop of a diocese. Anthony has cleared a space for his own civil society. He is the master of his small locale, his *basti*, which at one point in the film is called "Anthony *Nagar*" (or "Anthonyville") and at another point "Anthony *Wadi*" (Marathi for "Anthony's neighborhood"). This is Anthony's sovereign territory, which he maintains by throwing out people who sell bad liquor and cleaning up the area. Anthony is an outlaw from the point of view of the state; otherwise, he is the benevolent sovereign of his own polity, whose organization, centered as it is around a charismatic personality, seems more feudal than modern. Anthonyville is a hamlet of the past—although it may also harbor the future of urban India.

The community recognizes Anthony's authority, which he exercises in association with the church and in supersession of the state. After Anthony tells the Padre of his fifty-fifty business arrangement with Jesus, a young man runs into the church to report that there has been an accident on the street just outside. The young man does not address the Padre, as one might expect, although he is standing next to Anthony. The priest is the institutional authority, and the accident has occurred on what is essentially his ecclesiastical property. But whom do you summon in emergencies if not the Man in Charge? Anthony, in his capacity as local executive, fixer of problems, righter of wrongs, takes control of the situation and brings the accident's victim (it's Maa!) to the hospital. He even donates his own blood for her survival. Thus Anthonyville encompasses the local church, not the other way around, and Anthony, not the Padre, represents this alternative rule of law.

Importantly, although Anthony has taken over the Church's authority, he is not allowed to exceed his religious affiliation. That is, the narrative—and the peculiar moral-legal dispensation it has set up around him—cannot permit Anthony to be other than Christian, even though his "true" nature, as we know, is Hindu. To understand how the character has been constructed around his Christian identity, we must examine some of Christianity's varied faces in India.

Item Number Four: My Name Is Anthony Gonsalves

Christianity is an Indian religion. It has existed in India for as long as it has existed in Europe; according to tradition, Saint Thomas the Apostle brought Jesus's teachings to South India around 52 CE. According to historians, Christianity was present in India by the second century CE. From the fourth century onward, Catholic merchants and missionaries began arriving in waves from the Mediterranean world. In the sixteenth century, the Portuguese targeted India in their efforts at trade and conversion (two sides of the coin of colonialism), directing their activities from their base in Goa. And by the eighteenth century, Protestant (especially Anglican) teachings and institutions had become established on the subcontinent, along with the machinery of mercantile capitalism.

In the present day, India's Christianity is of diverse varieties, and although a majority of Indian Christians are Catholic, there are large congregations of Syrian Christians, Anglicans, Presbyterians, Congregationalists, Methodists, Baptists, Lutherans, and Pentecostals, as well as small groups of Seventh-Day Adventists, Unitarians, Jehovah's Witnesses, and Mormons. In Bombay, a large portion of the indigenous Koli population is Catholic (and it is in a Koliwada, or "Koli neighborhood," that we find the original diegetic home of our three brothers and their parents). The Indian landscape is filled with churches, memorials, relics, and places of worship sacred to Christians. There is even a popular tale that Jesus himself lived in India and is buried in Kashmir. India, as such, is a Christian land as much as it is Hindu, Muslim, Buddhist, or anything else.

Taken together, these denominations make Christianity the country's third largest religion, with some 24 million followers, roughly 2.3 percent of the population.[25] Yet Christianity has a much higher profile in India than the number of its adherents would suggest. A disproportionate number of India's public charities and service institutions, such as hospitals and orphanages, are Christian organizations. What's more, when it comes to higher education, many of India's best schools are Catholic institutions, such as St. Stephen's College in Delhi, Loyola College in Chennai, Christ University in Bangalore, and St. Xavier's College in Bombay. And at the secondary level, even today, education in a "convent school"—where as a rule English is the language of instruction—signals access to India's elite worlds. In part a legacy of colonialism, the association holds true regardless of the nature of the connection (if any) a given school might have to the colonial era. Christianity thus bears the irony of having its institutions and the primary language with which it is associated perceived as indicators of elitism, while its actual adherents rarely number among India's elite.

Given this set of facts—that India has long been home to a thriving Christian population and that Christianity disproportionately accounts for key public services, especially those related to health care, child welfare, and education—Christianity's profile on the diegetic landscape seems strangely attenuated. *Amar Akbar Anthony* shows us a church, but no school, orphanage, or hospital run by Christians is depicted. Indeed, the name of the medical facility where the brothers give their blood to Maa after her accident is Nanavati Hospital, which in the real Bombay is located in the suburb of Vile Parle. This is a secular hospital with a Gandhian ethics of public service, and its publicity materials proudly note that the first patient was "a man from the Harijan community"—*Harijan* being a Gandhian term for so-called Untouchables—who was "treated free of cost."[26] It might have burdened the already heavily laden symbolism of the prologue to have the brothers attend their mother in a Christian institution, but the very choice and naming of this hospital suggest something of the strategic placement of Christianity within the diegesis.

Given the filmmakers' interest in highlighting the "charity" produced by Anthony's outlaw activities, perhaps no room could be found in the narrative for the actual contributions of the Catholic Church. In other words, it is left to Anthony himself—and the civil society he creates in Anthonyville—to stand in for the social ethics of the Church in India. And the result, plainly put, is farce. The keynote of Brother Anthony's Catholic mission is discord. Anthony runs his operations in consultation with Jesus—but he seems to do as much squabbling with his "partner" as anything else. Far from supporting his ward in his efforts to look after the weak and helpless, the Padre is a vocal critic. Anthony enforces a policy of permitting only high-grade hooch (his own) to circulate in the parish, and although he does represent this as a public-spirited measure, it makes sense as Christian outreach only insofar as Christians tend to be stereotyped in the movies as drinkers. Yet none of this contests the sincerity of Anthony's personal devotion to his deity. It seems doubtful that Desai would have been familiar with the important distinction in Christian teachings between faith and works. But what his film gives us by way of its Christian character's commitments turns out to emphasize a personalized model of faith over a piecemeal handful of works.

Amar Akbar Anthony thus offers a twofold view of Christianity. On the one hand, Christianity is an interiorized site of meaning and as we will see shortly—personal transformation for Anthony. On the other hand, externalized as a presence in the diegetic world, Christian culture is represented through a patchwork of images, most of them comic, and many re-sourced from cinematic antecedents. We will see this even more shortly. And to the extent that Desai is engaging here in bricolage, his project comes curiously close to something he once identified as a quintessentially Christian practice.

In a 1988 interview in the *Times of India*, Desai aired some ideas about how Indian Christians use language. He seemed to believe that all Christians are brought up with English, even though the mother tongue of a Christian is determined in pretty much the same way it is for any Indian—primarily by geography and secondarily by class and education.[27] Thus it is that the characters in *Amar Akbar Anthony* most closely associated with English are Christians—the Padre, Robert, Jenny, and Anthony.[28] But Desai also imagined Christians to be linguistic magpies, theorizing that they somehow crafted a secondhand language to suit their culturally hybrid selves. "I would give a lot of credit to Catholic boys for evolving Bombay talk," he said.[29] This is the argot of Anthony, of course, created through the mixing of the city's vernaculars: Hindi, Marathi, Urdu, Konkani, and a dash or two of English.

However tenuous his grasp on the lived contexts of Indian Christianity, Desai had a definite idea about the origin of his Christian hero. "My Name Is Anthony Gonsalves" is one of the best-known songs in Indian film history, and yet it turns out there is more than one answer to the question, Who is this Anthony Gonsalves? According to the maestro himself, the character was modeled on a gangster and neighborhood dandy in Khetwadi whom Desai knew in his youth. But it also bears mentioning that there is a prominent memorial on a street in Bandra to one Antonio Gonsalves, who died in 1824.[30] And then there is the most famous Anthony of all: St. Anthony of Padua, whose shrines dot India's sacred landscape from Tamil Nadu to Goa to Jharkhand, and who helps supplicants find lost things—now, there would be an appropriate namesake for the hero of this lost-and-found story!

But the most common understanding of the character's antecedents is both more conventional and more odd. Anthony Prabhu Gonsalves, a Catholic from Goa, was the music teacher of Pyarelal Sharma and R. D. Burman, two of Indian cinema's most famous composers, and through them teacher to the last two generations of the Bombay industry's music directors. Anthony Gonsalves was a violinist—like his namesake in the film—and a pioneer in film music orchestration from the mid-1940s to the early 1960s, working on films such as *Kismet* (Gyan Mukherjee, 1943), *Mahal* (Kamal Amrohi, 1949), and *Dholak* (Roop K. Shorey, 1951). He was known for blending Western and Indian musical forms in his orchestral arrangements—a style later copied by Kudalkar and O. P. Nayyar, among many others, and firmly established in the present day in the work of artists like A. R. Rehman. Nevertheless, Gonsalves disappeared into obscurity. At the height of his fame in the 1960s he left the world of *filmi* music to pursue a fellowship at Syracuse University.[31]

While Goan Catholic musicians like Gonsalves played an essential role in creating Hindi film music, their work is now largely forgotten.[32] Instead one mostly hears about the influence of figures from the 1930s and 1940s like Naushad Ali and Anil Biswas, who emerged from classical Hindustani backgrounds. But the ability to fuse Indian and Western musical styles to form the signature sound of Hindi cinema was accomplished in large part by Goan Catholic musicians who could effectively bridge this divide, in part because of their religious and social position as being "in between."[33] We find the trace of these musical pioneers in the regular association of Christian characters with music in Hindi cinema.[34] This influence is likewise reinscribed with Pyarelal Sharma's gift of his music teacher's name to Desai's Catholic character.

The Portuguese-derived name Anthony Gonsalves clearly indicates a genealogy that is Goan Catholic—a constituency that makes up a majority of Bombay's Christians. Portuguese Catholics, in fact, have a long history in the region; they were some of its early settlers, long before the British. The Portuguese claim to the territory of Bombay (then islands) was established in 1534 with the Treaty of Bassein. The area was held as a Portuguese possession until it was transferred to Charles II of England as part of the dowry of Catherine of Braganza, and then it was leased to the Honourable East India Company in 1668. Many of Bombay's neighborhoods were originally Catholic enclaves, such as Mahim (which houses St. Michael's Church, one of the city's oldest), Worli, Sion, Wadala, Parel, Chembur, and most notably Bandra, which provides the landscape for much of *Amar Akbar Anthony*. Even the etymology of *Bombay* may be traced, according to some, to the Portuguese for "good bay." The port's Christian history grew ever more layered as it developed under British control. India's most cosmopolitan city, Bombay is also, historically speaking, its most Christianized.

In spite of their prominence in Bombay's colonial past (or perhaps, in part, because of it), Christians have tended to be depicted in Bombay cinema through a collection of stereotypes—superficial, generally unflattering, and in combination incongruous. Christianity is the go-to religion for criminals and the morally corrupt in films from the 1950s through the 1980s, and also, paradoxically, the religion of unshakable moral resolve, as the Padre's dying plea that his killer be forgiven reflects. Matters of license—drinking, premarital sex—are naturalized vices when Christians indulge in them; the same acts would be grave moral lapses (or antinomian gestures) if committed by Hindu characters. No "Christian social" exists as a genre of Indian film; there is, of course, a "Muslim social," as we discussed in Chapter 2, and almost every other film is in some sense a de facto "Hindu social." Those exceptional films that have highlighted the lives of Christians have not tended to meet with approval within India's Christian community.

Take the film *Julie* (K. S. Sethumadhavan, 1975), for example, in which Julie is an Anglo-Indian Christian woman who falls in love with a Hindu man, becomes pregnant out of wedlock, has the baby in secret, gives the baby up to an orphanage, reunites with her boyfriend, gets the child back, and castigates everyone for giving the couple a hard time. Sex and alcohol abound. Julie's Christian father is a drunkard, although tenderhearted. Julie's premarital proclivities raise questions about her morals, especially for sexually conservative Indian viewers. Although the film's resolution implies a social consent to interreligious unions, the portrayals of promiscuity and alcoholism build on long-standing stereotypes of Christians. Christian men are comical figures, boozers, or petty criminals and

FIGURE 14. Congas

yet at the same time are somehow virtuous, driven by the high moral ideals of their religion. Christian women, like Julie, are sexually available. Christians protested the release of *Julie* in 1975—although this didn't stop Deepak Shivdasani from remaking the film in 2004 with Julie reinvented as a prostitute![35]

Or consider India's top-grossing film of 1973, Raj Kapoor's *Bobby*. This movie, like *Julie,* tells the story of its eponymous heroine, the daughter of a Goan Catholic fisherman who—you guessed it—likes to hit the sauce. Julie falls in love with Raj (Rishi Kapoor, otherwise known as Akbar), who is the son of a rich Hindu businessman (Pran). Here dramatic tension follows the axis of class rather than religion. Believing Bobby to be a gold digger, Raj's father tries to pay off Bobby's father as a way to end the relationship. This scenario hints at the economic deprivation and prejudice that a real-life Anthony might struggle against as a poor Catholic, and there is a clear eroticization of domination, both economic and social.

Given such portrayals, it's no wonder that Indian Christians have often lobbied filmmakers and government censors about their representation in cinema. In fact, now think of *Amar Akbar Anthony*'s own Christian stereotypes as depicted at the Easter party, with their drunkenness, flirtatiousness, and—note the graphic on the wall of the African playing the drum—association with colonial racism. The African drummer even calls to mind another site of Christian missionizing and colonialism—on another continent but coeval, with the same historical project and a similar legacy (Figure 14).

Yet the question of what it really means to be Christian in India, unlike the same question posed in relation to being Hindu, Muslim, poor, Southern, low caste, or female—all the usual social vectors of Indian cinema—remains unexamined in the movies. In fact, there is something about Christianity that seems to transcend social and historical contexts. Through decades of cinema, its adherents retain two reified qualities: novelty and neutrality. Indian film—and public discourse more broadly—has structurally emplaced Christianity as a foil to Hinduism, the implicit norm, and Islam, with its well-defined particularity.[36] And this ironic duplicity—of stereotypical particularity and generality—defines a dynamic at the heart of the erasure of Christianity as an Indian religion.[37]

Item Number Five: The Irony of Anthony as Apotheosis

Let's try a thought experiment. Consider how Desai's national allegory would be altered with a Sikh in Anthony's place—an *Amar Akbar Arvinderjeet*. Instead of a meeting of three religions that are in effect neutralized by the film's feel-good secularism, the characters' sectarian identities would likely signal distinct ideological agendas. In the Indian nationalist imaginary, Sikhism is not politically neutral.[38]

What makes Christianity different? A popular folk interpretation of the symbolism of the national flag is telling in this regard. The light orange, or saffron, band on top is identified with Hinduism. The band along the bottom is the green of Islam. In between there is a white space, a buffer that keeps apart the two antagonists; this white space is Christianity.[39] And consider this: in an interview from 2003, the Bollywood superstar Shah Rukh Khan was asked about the Babri Masjid–Ram Janmabhoomi controversy. Referencing the site where the Babri Masjid (a mosque erected to honor the sixteenth-century Mughal emperor Babur) was destroyed in 1992 by Hindu fundamentalists (who claimed it as the birthplace of Lord Rama), Khan hypothesized, "The Gods must be saying, if it is causing such a problem, give it to Christ."[40]

At the start of this chapter, we analyzed the semiotic operations of the Anthony character in terms of a surplus of meaning. Yet the crucial (so to speak) attribute of Anthony that situates him within the film's nationalist allegory—his Christian religion—is defined more by what it's not than by what it is. It's not Hinduism; it's not Islam; it's that other thing. If the dynamic Anthony is a cyclone of signification, this is what we find when we look into the eye of the storm: an empty signifier.

To respond, then, at the same time to the friends of the flag and to Shah Rukh Khan: to look to Christianity as a "white," neutral term, as a sort of disinterested and thus honest broker that can mediate the volatile and codependent Hindu-Muslim relationship—this is not so much to assign Christianity a color as to make it a blank. Khan's solution to the Babri Masjid question is to put it in limbo—to cast it outside the purview of an authentic Indian dialectic. The curious emptiness of Christianity's representation in *Amar Akbar Anthony* goes well beyond a cinematic device, for the film taps into a consensus in India's communal self-understanding: Christianity, despite two thousand years of residence, is the true Other, and its emptiness renders it a mute bystander to the national story. The impetus behind this "othering" of Christianity is surely the rejection of the colonial regime with which the religion was long associated. We move from original sin to the mark of Cain: in embodiment of colonialism's transgressions, it seems, Indian Christians have been condemned to exile in their own country.

It's true that some postcolonials are more colonial than others. In Indian popular understanding, Christians tend to be divided into two groups: Anglo-Indians, the offspring of Indian and British (or otherwise European) parents or ancestors, and Indian Christians, born without apparent "non-Indian" blood in their veins yet beholden to a "non-Indian" deity and religious system. If the quotient of authenticity here is to be measured by the distance traveled from the center of an authentic Indian ontology, then we would expect to find Anglo-Indians, at once of "mixed blood" and Christian, subjected to the greatest ostracism.[41] And this is indeed the case. Anglo-Indians faced hardships of different kinds in the colonial period and afterwards, for under British rule their status in the racial hierarchy was ambiguous at best, but it was after Independence that most Anglo-Indians left India. They have immigrated mainly to Australia and the UK; those who remained have faced a precarious position.[42]

India's Christian community is the only segment of the population other than Muslims to be governed by a distinct personal code of law. But Christian personal law covers the personal and familial aspects of life for *both* Christians and Anglo-Indians. What is interesting here is that an elision is embedded at the Constitutional level between the category of the "mixed-race" Anglo-Indian (who may or may not be Christian) and the Indian Christian (who may have no genealogical relationship to whiteness). This collapsing of two distinct, if related, categories of identity is likewise evident in *Amar Akbar Anthony*.

Zabisko, for example, seems to be Anglo-Indian—perhaps of a mixed white American and Indian descent. His exotic name comes from a Polish wrestler popular in the United States in the early twentieth century, Stanislaus Zbyszko (1879–1967), who was routed in the world championships in 1910 by India's famed Great Gama (1880–1963).[43] Gama's triumphs still had cultural currency in India in the 1970s, and the two battles in the film between Anthony and Zabisko just might recall this contest.[44] *Zabisko*—a clearly foreign but linguistically dodgy sobriquet—is meant to signal a dangerous hybridity.[45] We are led to understand in the wedding scene that he is Christian; all along we have suspected he is not "purely" Indian.[46] Zabisko is a mysterious muscleman of depraved ethics and uncertain ethnicity. He maintains a dungeon, where he threatens captives with leather straps, and he wears unattractive ponchos—both signs of impaired judgment.[47]

Robert embodies national and religious hybridity even more clearly. He is obviously a Christian, as his name indicates, and his home décor features a painting of Christ, among other religious items.[48] It goes without saying that Robert is not a good Christian in the ethical sense. (And yet as we have indicated, the film's interpretation of Christian ethics is not its strong suit. Recall that Anthony himself—not only a man of faith but an enthusiastic petitioner of divine power as accessed through icons—is a bit shaky when it comes to the doctrine of good works.) Robert exhibits a superficial and hypocritical piety in proximity to Christian symbols, but he is primarily marked as a Christian to the degree that he embodies Christian stereotypes: he is a whisky-drinking underworld figure.

Where Robert's portrayal really comes into sharp definition is as a stereotype of an Anglo-Indian. If Anthony's argot—his mix of Hindi, Marathi,
and English—grounds him as authentically local, a true product of the
Bombay streets, then Robert's verbal peculiarities identify him as being
from another country, or at least affecting the accent of someone from another county. Robert either is foreign or wants to be seen as such; Anthony
is our hometown boy made good. Robert's racket involves adulterating the
Indian economy with gold smuggled in from an overseas source. Less
obvious clues have been planted as well. The cars driven by Robert—and
in one case by Kishanlal in his own capacity as smuggler boss—are American station wagons, outfitted with steering wheels on the left, the wrong
side for Indian roadways. This points toward Robert's foreignness as well
as to the veneer of the foreign that Kishanlal appropriates when he emulates Robert.[49]

But Robert's overseas connections are most clearly established when
we encounter his twin brother, Albert (also played by Jeevan). It is a scene
and plot device of great strangeness. Albert, we learn, lives in London
(Vilayat) and works for the English national bank. Passing through
Bombay on his way to Hong Kong for a meeting, he gets kidnapped by
Zabisko, who holds him captive in a dungeon. When Robert comes to meet
him, Albert tells his twin brother that he hates him, and makes it clear that
he considers himself to be honorable and his brother to be a murderer.
Zabisko has abducted Albert to ensure that he will get to marry Jenny, for it
is on that condition that he will let Robert take Albert's identity and flee to
London, thus escaping the Indian police. As for Albert, Zabisko indicates
his intentions by menacingly snapping a leather strap: "I'll look after him."

This scene functions not only as a rationale for Robert's agreement to
marry off his daughter to a reprobate but also to drive home the villain's
identity as a transnational figure. His brother lives in London and is presumably British. Robert himself is perhaps making up for his own lack of
actual metropolitan polish by adopting a flamboyantly plummy British accent in Hindi. This scene also reminds us that not all Anglo-Indians are
drunken rascals; some are, as Albert appears to be, upstanding and admi-
rable citizens of the world. Furthermore, the antagonistic relationship
between these biological brothers serves as a kind of inversion of the relationship among Amar, Akbar, and Anthony. The former, bound by

blood—the blood of identical twins, no less—are "brothers" only in name; they evince mutual hatred. They are not just opposites but also antagonists. Our three heroes, on the other hand, think of themselves as brothers only in the context of the civil society of their neighborhood because they do not yet know the truth of their biological fraternity. Brotherhood, as the film reminds us, is a choice more than a biological fact, which is all the more important when identity is reduced to charade.

Robert's Anglo-Indian identity is made apparent again when Kishanlal—who has no connection to Britain or any other foreign land—sends Jenny abroad to be educated, as if to honor Robert's genealogy, not only of religion but also of general cultural orientation. Unlike the Padre, who raises Anthony to be a Catholic, Kishanlal does not impose his religion on Jenny, nor does he impose on her a new name. In this regard Kishanlal practices a secularism patterned after that of the Indian state. He raises Jenny with a "personal law" that matches her father's religion and ethnicity, not his own. When Kishanlal sends Jenny to the West, he is supporting her cultural inheritance—and cultural hybridity—as an Anglo-Indian. It seems a principled decision, for changing Jenny's name and raising her as a Hindu would have gone a long way in disguising her identity and preventing Robert from finding her. Yet by allowing Jenny to remain Anglo-Indian, he also extends the charade that he, as her foster father (or "uncle"), is Anglo-Indian as well. All this might make us wonder: Is the film proposing that, at bottom, Anglo-Indian identity can be reduced to a matter of performance? And if that's the case, the question then becomes: How is Anglo-Indian different from any other kind of ethnic or religious identity?

Underlying all this business is the suggestion of conversion—more specifically, the image that haunts Indian political discourse about Christianity, the specter of "forced conversion." The good Padre chooses to raise Anthony as a Christian. The act of taking in an abandoned child apparently comes attendant with the charge to raise the child as a Christian. The coupling of social service with conversion is at the forefront of critiques of Christian charitable enterprises in India. For example, in Christopher Hitchens's scathing book *The Missionary Position,* he accuses Mother Teresa and others of using charity as a coercive tool among India's most susceptible populations.[50] Likewise throughout Asia one hears the derogatory term "rice Christians" to refer to those who are presumed to have converted merely to access the charity—the free rice—given by Christian organizations.

Many have written on this issue, from leftish political commentators like Hitchens to critics on the Hindu right. Indeed, it can seem as if most scholarly studies of Indian Christianity are concerned with conversion, as are most appearances of Christians in political news coverage.[51] And this is not without reason. One need only consider the thinly veiled anti-minority sentiments behind the legislation proposed—or enacted—by several Indian states to criminalize forced conversion. Where legal, the act of conversion is discouraged at the state level through various penalties, such as a divestment of claims for the maintenance of women in the case of divorce.[52] And this politics of paranoia sometimes spills over into violence, especially in states where right-wing organizations—such as the Bharatiya Janata Party (BJP) and the Bajrang Dal—dominate political culture. Human Rights Watch, for example, drew a direct connection between the reestablishment of a BJP government in Gujarat in 1998 and a sharp rise in violence that year against the state's Christians.[53] Violence against Christians has also become common in Orissa, Gujarat, Jammu and Kashmir, Andhra Pradesh, Madhya Pradesh, Kerala, and Karnataka.[54]

Animating this anti-Christian activity is the ideological proposition that Indian Christians (although not necessarily Anglo-Indians) are Hindu in essence—an idea that follows from a line of reasoning laid out in the context of twentieth-century nationalist politics by the radical theorist V. D. Savarkar. In *The Essentials of Hindutva* (later published as *Hindutva: Who Is a Hindu?*), Savarkar presents Indian Christians as having "original Hindu blood," while Christianity is an "alien adulteration." Savarkar constructs a political ontology, which he called *Hindutva* ("Hinduness"), by arguing that all "true Indians" (or "we Hindus," as he often wrote) share a natural love of India as their "fatherland." They also share a biological genealogy—a collective racial "Indian" being.[55] Incumbent upon true Indians, therefore, is a "common homage" to Indian civilization, which he ties to Sanskrit and the Sanskritic word for "culture," which is *sanskriti*.[56] For Savarkar, India is not only a "fatherland" but also a "holy land" *(punyabhumi)*. Following this logic, Christians meet the first requirement of blood and common land, but by their adherence to the doctrines of Christianity they, like Muslims who adhere to Islam, orient their "common homage" outside India. They direct their "real" devotion to religions of non-Indian origin—their "holy lands" are not in India. Clearly Savarkar did not take the many sacred sites of Christianity and Islam located throughout India as serious counterpoints. It must be said that his chief interest was in drawing a line of exclusion against Muslims, but his logic accomplished the same end with Christians.

The question of conversion loomed large for Savarkar, for he believed that the ancestors of modern India's Christians and Muslims had been forced to convert as "unwilling denizens of their new fold."[57] The fact that Savarkar was an atheist and had little interest in promoting the Hindu religion in any soteriological, devotional, or ethical sense makes this political strategy all the more pernicious, for it constructs all Indians as bodies without agency. They are members of a single race divided by a single question: whether they are oriented toward a recognition of their organic bond to the homeland or not.[58] The only agency allowed by Savarkar's political theory is the "choice" to renounce an alien orientation and return to "the Hindu fold."[59] And so to identify Christians (and Muslims) as victims of forced conversion is to imply the imperative of counter-conversion. An Indian Christian is a person with a Hindu body who has been coerced into viewing the world through a Christian lens; to liberate that person from the distorting lens is to restore that body to its natural place and orientation. Reconversion is repatriation.

The theme of conversion is, of course, a structuring element of the plot of *Amar Akbar Anthony*. The film, however, does not have a single hero and villain but rather two teams in opposition to each other—a regular feature of Bollywood's "multi-starrers." The team of protagonists consists primarily of the three brothers; joining them are their foster parents, their love interests, and in the end their birth parents. On this team are Hindus, Muslims, and Christians. Although we know the core players to have been born Hindu, the team is multicultural—the Indian term, of course, is *secular*. If you've followed the arguments of this chapter so far, you'll agree that the leader of this group is Anthony, the film's chief character. And so the protagonists' team, diverse as it is, has for a leader a Christian. The antagonists' team is led by Robert. In addition to Zabisko (who turns out to be a self-serving free agent), Robert calls on a large supply of henchmen. Outfitted as they are in Western fashions, they are not visually coded as belonging to any particular religious community.[60] Among them are a Pedro but also a Raghu, and joining Robert's gang as his lieutenant is the slimy Hindu stepbrother of Lakshmi, Ranjeet. Nevertheless, in the person of its leader and in the atmosphere of its headquarters, with its Christian art and iconography and general air of barely postcolonial decadence, Robert's team is visibly Christian—and, as the preceding argument shows, implicitly Anglo-Indian Christian.

One way to read *Amar Akbar Anthony,* then, is as a film in which one Christian challenges another Christian—a Goan Catholic neighborhood tough goes up against an Anglo-Indian Christian racketeer, a Christian son of the soil takes on a deracinated Anglo-Indian gangster. And it is here that the film enacts a critique of its own representation of Christians, for it divides a community that it also conflates, pitting Christian against Christian. In a sense, the film deconstructs its own caricature of Christianity (inherited primarily from its antecedents in Bombay cinema) by pitting Anthony against Robert. And Robert is not only the source of trouble but also the model for trouble: when Kishanlal wants to give some of that trouble back, he takes on the persona of our Anglo-Indian gangster. Robert is also the force that compels the conversion of Akbar and Anthony in childhood. As Anthony leads the charge against Robert, he is, in a sense, undoing this wrong. Finally he is paying for the sins of the father—his biological father. But he does not "reconvert." Although Anthony and Akbar now know their "true" origin (in Savarkar's sense), they don't return to Hinduism. The film rejects the political narrative that casts Christians (and Muslims) as wayward, misled Hindus, even while it appears to support the idea that all Indians have some essential "secular Hinduism" at the core of their being.

This conflict also moves our film toward a postcolonial critique. Robert is the colonial remnant, the British Indian subject unreconstructed; he is what the ardent British colonialist Thomas Babington Macaulay, in his notorious "Minute on Education," called "Indian in blood and colour, but English in taste, in opinions, in morals, and in intellect."[61] Anthony's battle with Robert mirrors the postcolonial battle in the Indian psyche to rid itself of its colonial detritus.

The idea of a psychic internalization of colonialism has been powerfully theorized by one of India's most prominent intellectuals, Ashis Nandy, in his book *The Intimate Enemy: Loss and Recovery of Self under Colonialism*. In this work Nandy, who happens to be a Christian, analyzes the contemporary predicament of the Indian "self," which reached a state of self-loathing in colonialism and now suffers under the condition of regression. To expose this psychological damage, Nandy chronicles how European, and especially British, colonialism constructed a bifurcation of the Indian and the British-European sense of the social individual by means of a gender/power differential. Under the epistemic regime of colonialism, the British were masculine and hence both mature and powerful, and thus came to dominate their Indian colonial subjects, whom they construed as feminine, childish, or even childlike.[62] In this equation, Indians had little agency or power; they needed protection and guidance to reach Western modernity, which in Nandy's analysis is the projection of a global kind of "maturity" (or to use another nomenclature, the condition of being a "developed" nation in more than infrastructure).

Nandy here makes use of the well-known argument of Edward Said's *Orientalism*,[63] particularly Said's ideas about the discursive gendering of an "Oriental" subject, and applies it to India through the lens of psychology. He argues that Indians internalized this British construction and hence came to see themselves as submissive, infantile, and disempowered in relation to the British, yet also potentially capable of accessing superior qualities by emulating the norms of British masculinity. Nandy thus argues that colonialism was accomplished not simply by mercantile, political, and military might, but by a kind of social-psychological programming, which contemporary Indians must still unravel.

Throughout Nandy's discussion of the social and psychological colonialism of the British in India, we are told about Christianity's role in this history. Nandy observes that the genesis of modern subjectivity in colonial India involved, as Macaulay argued, a certain process of Westernization in which Christianity was vital. Christianity in this regard could be both overt and covert. Overtly, colonialism and missionizing went hand in hand. The details of this relationship are complex and at points highly vexed, but it is clear that colonial authorities and Christian missionaries had an enabling relationship (and the enduring prestige of Christian schools at all levels of learning in India attests to this fact). Covertly, Christianity sent a subliminal message to the Indian psyche in the colonial period, particularly to those who aspired to ascend socially and economically: Westernization, modernization, and Christianity make the modern man.[64] They are the requisites of his success.

Nandy focuses on Christianity because it plays a crucial role, he argues, in the way the self is understood by a pantheon of colonial-era Indian elites—Gandhi, Tagore, Vivekananda, Michael Madhusudan Datta. These historical figures posited Christianity as Hinduism's opposite, if not opponent, and identified Christianity with masculinity. In Christianity, put simply, a supremely powerful male God rules *everything*. Christianity valorizes the masculine, and this cosmic masculinity gives Christians a sense of their own masculine power, granting them the will to feminize and dominate the Other. Therefore, the struggle over the "Indian" psyche is a struggle for the Hindu, male, Indian self.

The Indian thinkers that Nandy engages responded to this colonial construction of selfhood by trying to unsettle its reification of gender identities. One could embrace this feminization as an empowerment, as did Gandhi, or devise a program to "masculinize" the Hindu subject, as did Savarkar and his political scions. Nandy concludes by identifying this neurosis—an insidious fixation on masculinity—as a residual psychic ill of colonialism. The "intimate enemy" for Nandy is not Christianity in the abstract but its instantiation in the subcontinent in the form and practice of Indian Christianity. The question at the heart of this formulation is equality: Indians can convert to Christianity, just as they, like Robert, can wear the coat and shoes of a British dandy, but they are not the equals of their Christian colonial counterparts.

Carefree, exuberant *Amar Akbar Anthony*—but have the smiles been shielding a private neurosis? It is coming to seem all too likely. Robert is the cinematic and comic exemplar of Nandy's "intimate enemy."[65] He is a figure constituted by lack—short on both courage and manliness. Fortune favors the brave, and it doesn't favor Robert. He wants to be something he cannot be. The psychological and psychosocial reverberations of colonialism and Christianity permeate his character. Robert is immature and weak, he is dishonest and disloyal, and he is multiply emascu-

FIGURE 15. Zabisko strikes a pose

lated. He is dominated by the hypermasculine and vaguely foreign Zabisko (Figure 15), who undermines Robert's only redeeming quality—his love for his daughter, Jenny—by compelling Robert to offer Jenny to him in marriage. Zabisko, like Kishanlal before him, comes and takes the person Robert loves the most but cannot protect. This represents not only the loss of Robert's masculinity but also the surrender of his patriarchy. By agreeing to let Zabisko marry his daughter, Robert loses everything that had given him the façade of power.

Configured around Jenny are the winners and losers in this tale. Anthony wins Jenny and Jenny's hand, and Kishanlal remains Jenny's benevolent patriarch—a relationship to be made official with her marriage to Anthony. On the other side are arrayed the losers: Robert loses Jenny for good as she marries into the house of Kishanlal, and poor Zabisko is left alone with his "fantastic muscles."

Anthony, a hybrid Indian subject, appears as the logical hero of Nandy's work—the antidote to the psychic illness of the intimate enemy. He is a Christian who can fight Western Christianity to regain a Hindu-Christian hybrid masculinity. Anthony has unraveled his own identity to expel, finally and fully, the colonial Christian occupation that

Robert exemplifies: the occupation of the self. Robert is the pre-Independence Christianized Indian hegemon through whom the structures of colonialism endure. Anthony is the hero of a new Indian secular modernity, who can hold a "Hindu" identity in union with a Christian faith without contradiction. For if Robert is the intimate enemy, Anthony is the intimate hero—the nation's pugilistic superego—and the greatest foe he vanquishes is the one inside himself.

Item Number Six: The Hemoglobin in the Atmosphere

Religion, nationality, ethnicity, masculinity—it all comes together around an egg. In the very middle of *Amar Akbar Anthony* appears the film's most iconic song-and-dance sequence: Anthony, dressed in a European-style formal suit, bursts out of an egg at an Easter party, gets drunk, and launches into "My Name Is Anthony Gonsalves" with the lament, "I am alone in the world." The scene became a defining moment in Amitabh Bachchan's career. Coupled with the brilliantly comic scene that follows, in which Anthony drunkenly tries to apply a Band-Aid to his bruised face (Figure 16), it proved that Bachchan could do it all. In earlier films he had shown that he could be angry, heroically tragic, and fight well; now the world learned that he could dance, sing (sort of), and be immensely funny.[66] Bachchan's star was ablaze. Anthony Gonsalves and Amitabh Bachchan, fifty-fifty; this was their mutual moment to shine.

Hatching from his egg, reborn, Anthony declaims in English:

> You see the whole country of the system is juxtapositioned by the hemoglobin in the atmosphere because you are a sophisticated rhetorician intoxicated by the exuberance of your own verbosity.

Benjamin Disraeli was prime minister of Great Britain in 1878 when he spoke something close to these words.[67] In addition to providing the source for this esoteric pronouncement as well as the apparent inspiration for Anthony's costume, Disraeli gives us a way to understand the political valences of Anthony's character. He was a principal architect of the 1858 India Act that formalized British rule over most of the subcontinent, and he also devised the statute that designated Queen Victoria

FIGURE 16. Anthony and Amitabh

Empress of India. To the extent that he resonates in Indian popular culture, it is as an agent of high imperialism. Yet Disraeli, like Anthony, was also a convert to Christianity—in his case, from Judaism to the Church of England—and as such was beset by suspicions throughout his life that he had converted for political rather than spiritual reasons. And as someone who was believed to be "not quite" Christian, the imputation followed that he was "not quite" English either.

This association with Disraeli hints at the anti-Christian mode of this film's postcolonial critique. Anthony dresses as the arch-imperialist prime minister and tries to sound like him. He is literally wearing the garb of imperial authority and speaking its language to a group of Christians at an Easter party. Is this meant to be ironic? We viewers understand this to be so, but does Anthony? He seems almost innocently unaware of his semiotics. Yet his costume and words are a parody, perhaps even a parody of a homily, even if not diegetically so. Does the speaker know what his words mean? Does he know their source? Are we to laugh with him, sharing in his sense of play and his jibes at the British Raj, or are we to laugh at him—the fool who has dressed in his Sunday best and holds forth in fancy English? At one level, the scene ridicules Anthony and other Indians who assume the props—linguistic or sartorial—of colonial mimicry.

On the other hand, careful attention to his lyrics and costume provide a clue that Anthony may not only be in on the joke but also its artful master. Flirtatiously, he invites his audience to visit him on the "Lane of Love, house number 420." As he sings out the number, he shows that he has it emblazoned twice on the inside of his morning coat—across the left pocket and behind the tails. The number marks someone as a trickster and cheater, referencing Section 420 of the Indian Penal Code and also Raj Kapoor's picaresque classic, *Shree 420* (1955). Kapoor's star turn in that film was as a con man with a heart of gold, and perhaps that's an apt description here of our silver-tongued hero. At one point in the song Anthony sits pompously on a chair as if it were a throne and wags his finger as he pontificates (the line seems to be derived from the first Disraeli reference): "You see the coefficient of the linear . . . is juxtaposition . . . by the hemoglobin of the atmospheric pressure in the country." At each pause in his delivery, partygoers kneel down in front of him, assuming the postures of a congregation at their pews. Is Anthony hustling the rubes with his hocus-pocus? Or is he ministering to the Christian flock? (Or are these two things somehow the same?)

This moment of masquerade foreshadows the film's climax, when Anthony will disguise himself as a priest. If our hero is indeed in control of what he is saying, we can applaud his clever intervention, which is to outwit his opponent with words that insult and confound. But at the same time all this happens at a dance in observance of Easter, the quintessential Christian festival. And hints of colonialism's melding of political domination and religious conversion are not to be ignored in the Christian gymkhana. In addition to the ghost of Disraeli, there is a floor-to-ceiling decoration showing an African man playing a drum (see Figure 14). It's the only graphic image displayed in the space, and it's literally larger than life. Anthony pretends to join the man in his drumming, mirroring the African's posture; he enters the tune that already has the other in its thrall.[68] What's more, let's not forget that Anthony is sloshed—he's the one who's intoxicated, and not only by his own verbosity.

In between the Easter party and the film's climax, Anthony dons a curiously intermediate disguise, halfway between the secular garb of Disraeli and the priest's vestments he will wear to the final showdown. As Kishanlal and Jenny flee the former's home and try to escape from Robert, Jenny runs into a sugarcane field, with Robert's goons chasing after her. Anthony is waiting there to protect her, disguised as a scarecrow. With his arms outstretched, he invokes the cross and crucifix, which have been symbolic mainstays for him throughout the film. The crucifix has appeared as a pendant on his chest, an icon in the church, and a shrine in the center of Anthonyville, where he beseeches Jesus for help in beating up Amar. Anthony is now a savior too, like his foster fathers—the Padre and God Himself.

And in the end, appropriately, Anthony dons the costume of a priest—the trappings of an official intermediary between man and God. But this is not the first instance of the character being positioned between the human and the divine. The film features three scenes in which Anthony talks to an image of Jesus, and these three moments chart a chronology of the life of Jesus as well as the life of Anthony. The first scene, as mentioned previously, is the one in which Anthony describes his fifty-fifty profit-sharing arrangement with Jesus. There he addresses an infant Jesus in Mary's arms. When he mixes it up with Amar, he again asks for help from his heavenly associate. This time we have Jesus in metonym, symbolized by the cross that bears the abbreviation for "Jesus of Nazareth, King of the Jews." On the cross we see the nails that held Christ to the wood, the crown of thorns that circled His head, the Sacred Heart, and the chalice that symbolizes blood sacrifice.[69] We have moved from birth/childhood to death. And finally, when he discovers the Padre's lifeless body and confronts Jesus for having done nothing to stop the murder, we see Jesus in His risen form—eternal in heaven—the earthly trial complete. He is baring His chest, exposing His heart, and offering it to Anthony. Like Jesus, Anthony has now transcended, or perhaps ascended; and having suffered the death of his father, Anthony renews his conditional relationship with God by demanding to know the identity of the Padre's killer.[70] With the death of his foster father, Anthony has reached his own actualization as a full-grown man. Our hero is now ready to do battle with his nemesis and his past.

When Anthony dons the priest's vestments (Figure 17)—becoming in a sense his own father, now that the latter has passed—he does so fully aware

FIGURE 17. Father Anthony

of his own nature. This isn't a disguise as much as it is the efflorescence of Anthony's religious sentiments. Even when masquerading as a priest he is still himself, retaining his name as "Father Anthony." It is a reminder that Anthony always serves his flock, the citizens of Anthonyville. Anthony chooses who he wants to be and with whom he wants to be; his disguises are authentic expressions of aspects of his being. He finds the "self" that Nandy identifies as lost under the weight of colonialism's psychic effects, and he embraces it.

The final fight in Robert's lair is the double of the Easter party—another moment of combat for the love of a woman. These two scenes are also symmetrical in that in both instances Anthony dresses like one of his foster fathers. At the Easter party, he offers a one-man pantomime of Christian colonialism as encoded, sartorially and verbally, by the historical figure of Disraeli. In the final scene, he dresses like the Padre. And in this case, because he has learned something important about the nature of his "self"—a classic trope of the romantic figure—he wins the fight and the girl and becomes the hero. Anthony must first become the "intimate enemy"—an experience he enters as the hatchling Disraeli—so that he can reject it at the movie's end.

Anthony Gonsalves has undergone more than one conversion in this story: from Hindu to Christian, from boy to man, from single to coupled, from orphan to family man. To go by the ethnographic record, conversion in India is understood more as an accretion than a replacement, experienced more as an accumulation of identities than a switch from one identity to another. In this way, Anthony has resolved the contradictions of the "intimate enemy" by internalizing them, embracing them, and mastering them all.[71] Of these markers of selfhood, religion seems to plague Anthony the most, for he is the only character with a crisis of faith. But he is also the only character in the film who proclaims a belief in multiple religions. The chain of events that leads him back to his biological father—the bestowal on him by Maa of the gift of a flower to present to the "judge" he is sent out to meet—culminates with him offering (along with the flower), this declaration of faith to Kishanlal: "Sahib, do you believe in God? I'm a straight-up believer. . . . I believe in all religions. I go to the temple, I go to the mosque, I go to church, I go to the *gurudwara*. And sometimes, Sahib, I get mixed up and put in time at the police station." The character of Anthony holds all these "faiths" together, and this is precisely what empowers him: he is Christian and Hindu, righteous and lawless, gentle and violent, outside the state and a state unto himself. He contains multitudes; that's why he's the hero of the film.

4

Maa—!

. . . .

Men are what their mothers made them.

—Ralph Waldo Emerson, "Fate"

"My country, right or wrong" is a thing that no patriot would think
of saying except in a desperate case. It is like saying, "My mother,
drunk or sober."

—G. K. Chesterton, "In Defense of Patriotism"

A BOLLYWOOD MOVIE always involves romance, and as is usual for
Bollywood (and most other cinemas of the world) the structuring
principle of romance is heterosexual love within a heteronormative world.
Amar Akbar Anthony presents us with multiple love stories between men
and women, but—as we have discussed in detail in the chapters about
each brother—it also delves into the politics of the family. Absent from
those chapters, however, is a study of the figure at the center of the film's
partitioned, alienated, and ultimately reunited family. It's time to take a
good look at the boys' mother, Bharati.

This chapter is titled *"Maa—!"* in homage to the moments of crisis and
resolution in which grown men cry for their mothers—in this movie and,
it seems, in just about every other melodrama shot in Hindi during this
period. Through Maa, cursed with the metaphorically rich condition of
blindness, we theorize beyond the text toward some of *Amar Akbar Anthony*'s ideological and religious implications. We also investigate the
presence and absence of the other female characters, consigned largely
to the margins but nevertheless vital to the film's logic and allegorical dimensions. Replicating the structure of the book, this chapter is divided
into four sections, with three organized around Bharati's relationship with

each of the brothers and a final section in which Maa stands alone. Maa doesn't dance, she doesn't sing, and she barely acts—in the sense of her character displaying any agency—but she does exhibit a knack for showing up at just the right moment.

Anthony and the Bad Mother

Nirupa Roy (1931–2004), the actress who played the role of Bharati in *Amar Akbar Anthony,* was in real life the mother of two children, but on the screen she raised two decades' worth of sons as well as some daughters. She appeared as the mother of Amitabh Bachchan in at least eight films.[1] Perhaps the most celebrated pairing of Bachchan and Roy as mother and son was in *Deewaar* (Yash Chopra, 1975). In that famous film's most famous dialogue, the Bachchan character, Vijay, boasts of his ill-gotten wealth to his brother, Ravi (Shashi Kapoor), a straight-arrow police officer. "Today I have a mansion, a car, money . . . what do you have?" In reply, Ravi levels a zinger: "I have Maa." And yet we know this to be an ironic statement, for the mother of these star-crossed brothers loves her wayward son the best, as the ending confirms with an iconic image: Vijay's death in her arms.[2]

The stock character role of the Mother came to Roy in the middle of her career. She appeared in almost five hundred films from 1946 to 1999, a highly prolific career by any standard. From the 1950s to the 1970s, before she became the quintessential Bollywood matron, Roy made her name playing Hindu mythological figures, especially goddesses, such as Parvati, Lakshmi, Kali, and Sita. It was in the 1970s that Roy became indelibly associated with the figure of the Mother. Eulogized widely in the Indian press following her death in 2004, it was for her work as Mother—as India's "Cine-Ma," to recall a rather lowbrow epithet—that she was invariably remembered.

Roy's role as Maa in *Amar Akbar Anthony* was anticipated by a great many movies, but her turn in *Deewaar* alongside Bachchan two years before is the one that casts the longest shadow. In *Deewaar* as in *Amar Akbar Anthony* (and in other films before and since), her interpretation of Maa was as a figure of suffering; Indian filmmakers and critics used to refer to Roy as "the queen of misery." But in *Amar Akbar Anthony* she also imported some intertextual charisma from her earlier role as a goddess—as an agent of power to whom one could appeal in a time of suffering, but who would herself mete out suffering as chastisement. The movie affirms the link between mother and goddess through some explicit referents.

Two figures of the divine feminine are made visible in the film. The first is the Virgin Mary, Mother of Jesus, revered by many Christians throughout the world as the divine mother. She has been venerated since at least the fourth century CE, even while Catholic orthodoxy has rejected the idea of Mary as a godlike figure on par with the Father, the Son, and the Holy Ghost. (It might be said that Mary has come up against a kind of theological glass ceiling with the Trinity). The Virgin Mary has a very limited referential ambit in this film, concentrated in the first scene of the diegetic present, when we meet the adult Anthony and hear of his fifty-fifty deal with Jesus.[3] She is holding the infant on her lap, the object of Anthony's address. She too is a "queen of misery," for the Virgin Mary is likewise a mother perennially placed in a state of sadness. She is the Mother of Sorrows, of Perpetual Suffering, of the Pietá—the mother who bears the body of her dead son, the mother who condemned Him to die by giving Him birth.[4]

In addition to this mother of suffering, there is also a mother of "satisfaction," or *santosh*. Santoshi Maa is a modern Hindu goddess who was in large part invented in the cinema world. Although the origins of her worship can likely be traced to rural areas of northern India in the 1960s, her prominence in Indian public culture is the result of the film *Jai Santoshi Maa* (Vijay Sharma, 1975), in which the goddess delivers her faithful servant, Satyavati, from the jealousies and sabotages of men and gods alike. To gain this divine aid, Satyavati must carry out the vows (*vrat*) she has pledged to the goddess, including exacting fasts. The film suggests that a deal is struck between Santoshi Maa and any devotee who keeps her promise to worship her with such vows and fasts. A similar contractual scenario is invoked in *Amar Akbar Anthony*, but with Anthony and Jesus taking the place of the principals and Anthony the bearer of the *vrat*. Santoshi Maa nevertheless appears in the film in a form that corresponds to that identified by scholars of the previous film: a composite goddess of benevolence, assembled in the modern period from characteristics of earlier goddesses, especially Lakshmi, Parvati, and Kali.[5] The villain Robert identifies this divine feminine power when he grabs the pendant of Santoshi Maa from around Kishanlal's neck and declares, "So this is his special power." The word he uses is *shakti,* which is both a feminine noun that means "power" and the name of another composite deity, the goddess of power, Shakti.[6] Like most goddesses, she is customarily addressed as "Mother" by her devotees. Mother and power: this is one of the most common formulations of divinity in Hinduism, and when the combination appears in *Amar Akbar Anthony* it is with a certain Hindu resonance.

We can see the link of divine power move through the film by following the peregrinations of the Santoshi Maa pendant. We first see this item hanging from Bharati's neck when Kishanlal returns from prison only to find that his family is destitute and his wife is deathly ill. Santoshi Maa, it seems, did not do much to help in his absence. The pendant next appears along with the letter Bharati leaves him: it now stands in for the absent wife and mother as well as for a goddess whose efficacious power we might well doubt. But Kishanlal keeps the pendant with him and, having strayed onto a crooked path, nevertheless manages to steer past its perils, as though someone else were looking out for him. He exacts vengeance on Robert and collects wealth through illicit means, although by contrast with his nemesis he remains generous to the poor and needy; championing the humble is also part of the goddess's portfolio of attributes.

The pendant appears again when Anthony is reunited with his father. This meeting also encodes a supplemental, one-degree-of-separation reunion between Bharati and Kishanlal. Anthony had taken a flower from Bharati to offer his "father" (Anthony's colorful term for the judge he has been scheduled to stand before in court), and as things transpire he ends up delivering it to Kishanlal, his actual father. When Anthony lunges violently at the gangster and is thwarted, he excuses himself by claiming to be reaching for the icon's blessing, and then proclaims his faith in all religions, a statement we pondered in Chapter 3. We next see Santoshi Maa in the operating theater scene, when Robert snatches her from the unconscious Kishanlal and declares that he now possesses his enemy's *shakti.*

But at that moment Bharati enters the room and reenters her husband's life. Kishanlal now has Bharati; Santoshi Maa can move on to help others.

The goddess's final appearance follows the Padre's murder. The pendant has fallen from the dead priest's hand. This is a moment of collusion, we may presume, between Santoshi Maa and Jesus, although possibly with help from *His* Maa, the Virgin Mary. Anthony demands that Jesus reveal the killer, and the pendant of Santoshi Maa now stands as evidence of criminal activity. While Anthony reprimands his partner for not intervening in his guardian's hour of need, we are also shown that Santoshi Maa was present at the scene too—and did nothing. Anthony and Jesus had an agreement, but no agreement had been made between Anthony and this Hindu goddess, and so he ascribes no guilt to her. Together, however, Jesus and Santoshi Maa appear to team up in order to enact an ecumenical miracle and point toward the Padre's murderer. Santoshi Maa leads Anthony to Kishanlal, and she allows him to infer that Kishanlal is his father (Figure 18). In a sense, Santoshi Maa is now a partner as well.

For Anthony, Santoshi Maa now stands in for the absent mother. It seems ironic that the film's Christian character should have become so entangled with the miraculous movements of a Hindu goddess. The reason here may be that Anthony, by diegetic logic, is the only one of our three heroes who definitely does not have a foster mother. Although we never see a wife for Inspector Khanna or Haider Ali, we may presume these characters to be married—or to have been married and subsequently widowed. (Perhaps we never hear of the partners of Inspector Khanna or Haider Ali because they "failed" as mothers, for we see no evidence that they produced biological sons.) We could not presume such domesticity for the Padre, however, since all Roman Catholic priests currently take vows of celibacy, as they have for centuries. If phantom surrogate mothers exist for Amar and Akbar, none is implied for Anthony, at least not a mortal one.[7] He is truly a motherless child, and perhaps for this reason the Anthony character, the middle brother, is the least mothered of the three siblings. This is, of course, the complaint of many middle children: the first child gets the love born of novelty, the last gets the love due the family's baby, the middle child gets taken for granted.

FIGURE 18. Anthony, Kishanlal, and Santoshi Maa

Perhaps even more conclusively than in *Deewaar,* the Bachchan character once again does *not* get Maa. But is this such a bad thing for Anthony?

What kind of mother is Bharati, anyway? Consider her actions and decisions in the film. She abandons her sons when she contracts an illness, leaving them with nothing more than a note. She runs willy-nilly into a storm and is blinded, we are signaled, by the hand of God. At the same time she abandons Santoshi Maa, passing off the pendant and thus breaking her vow of personal devotion—and the goddess is known to be jealous in such matters. And even when Bharati is briefly reunited with baby Akbar, when she is rescued by the Muslim tailor in his vintage auto, she cannot make out the cries of her own child who sits in the seat right in front of her. As we reflect on her narrative trajectory, we see that she has done nothing to follow up on her family's fortunes, although she has recovered from her tuberculosis. Blinded, she has made herself helpless and essentially useless. She apparently sells flowers, although we never see her make a sale, only give away her inventory for free. She appears to

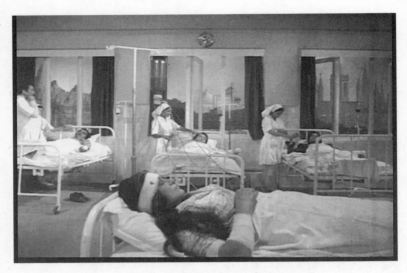

FIGURE 19. Blood transfusion

be resigned to be an object of pity and a drain on the meager resources of charitable agencies. By the end of the film's prologue, when we see Maa with her three boys all linked intravenously (Figure 19), she has become a parasite, a vampiric mother literally drawing out the life force of her children, their youth and vitality, and taking advantage of their generosity. Maa, in short, *is not a good mother.*

And she is especially not good to Anthony. Anthony actually carries on his body an artifact of his mother's withdrawn love. Recall the note, scrawled out by a feverish Bharati as she leaves her children in the midst of a furious storm (Figure 20). Maa's note becomes a talisman of loss and return for Anthony, even while it proves to be a powerful tool—much like a *yantra*—for acquiring and reacquiring fathers. When Kishanlal, on the run from Robert, comes to collect his family, it is this note that informs him that Bharati has fled. When Anthony collapses on the steps of the church, the Padre finds the letter in Anthony's pocket and surmises that Anthony's mother has committed suicide, prompting the man of God to take in the destitute child. And when Kishanlal and Anthony suspect each other's true identity at the film's end, it is Kishanlal's knowledge of the note that Anthony uses as proof of paternity. Yet the note does not circumscribe Anthony's identity or compel him; he is its master. Having

FIGURE 20. Maa and letter

read the note, he knows that his mother is named Bharati, so he also knows that his mother was a Hindu (Bharati would be an unusual name for a Christian or Muslim woman). Yet Anthony wholeheartedly adopts Christianity. Anthony is raised as a Christian, but in a sense he actively *converts* to Christianity, for he knows his religious origins—his "mother faith," his Hindu roots. To the extent that Anthony rejects Hinduism, then, does he also reject his literal and figurative mother?

At once hapless and feckless, Bharati even challenges "one of the most tenacious rules of Hindi cinema," in Rosie Thomas's words: "that it is 'impossible' to make a film in which a protagonist's . . . mother is villainous or even semivillainous."[8] And *Amar Akbar Anthony*'s departure from the norm is especially radical when read against a second way the film constructs Maa. For in this film, as in many that preceded it, the mother figure is embedded in the mythography of the nation.[9] Indeed, all by itself the character's name demands that we see her as an allegory for the nation-state. And this is key to understanding what it is that makes Maa so bad to Anthony, and what makes her absence central to the crafting of Anthony's identity.

"Bharati" is a common name for Hindu women and is derived from the same source as the masculine "Bharat," which is the name of a hero-king of antiquity, the scions of whom are the principal characters within the Hindu epic, the *Mahabharata*. At an early period in the history of the subcontinent, the king's name came to stand in for the territory associated with his dynasty. Bharatavarsha—the land of Bharat—became shortened to "Bharat," which in modern times has become one of the nation-state's two official names; "India" is, of course, the other name. Thus the name of Amar, Akbar, and Anthony's mother directly invokes the name of the country. And on an etymological note we may add that *Bharati* is derived from a Sanskrit root meaning "to bear or carry"—an apt citation for this character so burdened with a metaphor of Himalayan proportions.

Maa, Bharati, is thus also "Mother India" (Bharat Mata), although the figure of Mother India is much older than this movie.[10] The debut of the nationalist concept of motherland as Hindu goddess is conventionally traced to the poem "Vande Mataram" in Bankim Chandra Chattopadhyay's 1882 novel *Anandamath*, which was musicalized by Rabindranath Tagore, among others, and officially adopted as India's "national song." But as a visual icon, Mother India comes into her own as an artifact of colonial-era bazaar culture. At a time when the use of mass-produced devotional images, or "god posters," was becoming normalized among Hindu consumers, presses began marketing similar graphics to those who might wish to direct their adoration at the nation. (The Hindi word for patriot, *deshb-hakta,* neatly combines the religious term *bhakta,* a devotee, with *desh,* or country.) By 1977 the personification of the nation as a goddess, complete with an iconography involving flags, weapons, and the outlined form of the subcontinental landmass, was an image long established in Indian public culture. Like Santoshi Maa, then, Bharat Mata is a distinctly modern goddess, one given iconic form through mass media. In short, the film's engagement with the boys' own Bharati Mata signals an allegory of the modern Indian nation.

As we argued in Chapter 3, Anthony is a figure set explicitly outside the confines of the rule of law that governs and forms the state. He is an "outlaw" who inhabits a slum-land frontier zone, where he encounters occasional police officers as an equal, exchanging cordial *salaams.* He seems to have granted himself an official license as well as the liberty to take civil matters into his own hands. The solution to his extrastate status has been to carve out his own one-man state, with his own territory (Anthonyville), his own social services (he's the guy you go to if there is trouble, like if a woman gets hit by a car outside a church), his own enforcement arm (his arm), and his own system of taxation (50 percent to Jesus). Anthony has been abandoned not just by his biological mother, Bharati, but also by the nation-state.

Left as a little boy in the trusteeship of a statue of Gandhi, Anthony rises to the status of a headman-like figure in something akin to an urban version of the Gandhian village. But then that idyllic conception of civil society, like many of Gandhi's ideas, lies outside the boundaries of the state as well. It is no mere coincidence that when the family is repatriated and reunited—when Anthony finally meets his mother again—the encounter happens in a jail.[11] Imprisonment is a radical figuration of placement in the bosom of the state, and it bookends the film: jail in the beginning, jail in the end. And in between, the state has done precious little to take care of Anthony; it merely stands by passively—like Maa, like Mother India. The film seems to be telling us that the children of Bharati and Bharat cannot rely on their mother *or* their father, their *maa-baap,* a term used colloquially in India for the government in general.[12]

So where's the *shakti,* the Hindu promise of divine feminine power? How might its operations in the movie be connected to Bharati—Hindu goddess and Indian nation in one? And if this force is indeed derived in some way from the national essence, is Anthony deprived of it because of his conversion?

At first glance, the only woman in the film who appears to show any sort of fierce-goddess fury is Jenny's doppelgänger who appears at the airport, a nameless character we dub the Decoy in our synopsis. Yet even considered alongside the various non-Hindu inhabitants of the film, this character must count among the least Hindu—and least Indian. She is portrayed in a cameo, or "special appearance," by Helen, an actress-dancer who made her career in the movies by portraying sexy women who were raced as exotic Others. Helen was herself born in Burma of a Spanish-Burmese mother and French father and came to India as a refugee during World War II.[13] The character she plays is not marked in terms of religious affiliation, but between her arrival on an overseas flight; her chic, Western-style outfit; and her ease with English, not to mention small firearms, she functions in the audience's eyes no less than in Robert's as an effective stand-in for his not-quite-native Christian daughter. As with this film's other "special appearances," Helen is really entering the film as herself, or as her own star text. And as such, she is embedded as a sort of hyperlink to minority identity and its associations—among them Christianity, as we have discussed in Chapter 3.[14] Helen is the Other woman, by turns Continental femme fatale and Oriental dragon lady. If two decades' worth of such roles have typecast her as anything by the time of *Amar Akbar Anthony,* it is as the very opposite of Mother India. She wriggles with sex appeal but bears no progeny. She tempts men, but does she actually win their devotion? To the point of self-sacrifice?

As it turns out, however, Helen does sacrifice herself in the film. The Decoy baits Kishanlal's trap, a maneuver in which she allows herself to be taken to Robert's lair, where she apparently means to put an end to the villain with the pistol she pulls on him. Another performer in a cameo role, Ranjeet, playing a sleazy second-tier villain also named Ranjeet, foils the plan. As Robert instructs his henchman to take away "Kishanlal's gift," the boss hints at the dark acts of retribution, possibly involving sexual violence, that await her.[15] Add to this list of victims Anthony's foster-father Padre, and it is clear that the most extreme violence in the film is meted out to characters who are marked as neither Hindu nor Muslim. True to her cabaret-artist origins, Helen teases us with the promise of righteous fury fulfilled—hers is the only female character who gets to handle a gun—but the gun is seized before she can fire it. Exit Decoy, to an unspeakable end.[16]

Now consider Jenny, who is at once the least national and has the least agency of the three heroines. She has been abducted in infancy, shipped overseas in childhood, placed on return in semi-confinement under the charade of her "uncle's" care, and then re-abducted only to be forced (almost) into marriage with a muscle-bound associate of her biological father. We are not far off here from old-time chattel laws: a woman as property, traded and negotiated into relationships regardless of what she might herself think, want, or say.[17] With the Hindu Lakshmi, the bad girl made an honest woman through marriage, a cultural stereotype of middle-class respectability is reaffirmed; with the Muslim Salma, the female doctor, a cultural stereotype of repression is dismantled; but with Jenny, there's just a dizzy damsel in distress, waiting to be saved by someone else.

Thus when it comes to Jenny, there is no *shakti*—no feminine power—and neither Santoshi Maa nor Mother India comes to her rescue. How could they? In spite of the logic we have begun to trace here, that a woman's *shakti* seems to decline in proportion to her lack of true Indianness, it seems clear that the Mother India of this movie is a complete flop— incapable of helping herself, let alone rescuing others. Maa, the Virgin Mary, Jenny—the three women most prominent in Anthony's life—all appear entirely helpless. As for Anthony himself, he remains an orphan, a Christian convert, all but abandoned by Santoshi Maa, an exile at home from the Indian state, and the least beloved of his own on-screen mother. If Maa—and the swirl of symbolism she generates around questions of gender and power—is to attain redemption in our film, it will have to be found somewhere else.

Akbar and the Wayward Mother

Which of the three brothers steps forward to bring about Maa's deliverance? The question doesn't seem hard to answer. "Akbar, today because of your faith and Baba's miraculous powers my eyesight has come back to me" (Figure 21). With these words, spoken at the end of the "Shirdi Wale Sai Baba" miracle sequence, Bharati reasons through the dissolution of what we define in this section as a divine test—a twenty-two-year trial of abjection and anomie.

Blindness, both diegetic and metaphorical, will prove to be central to Akbar's account of what happens in the film to his mother. And the most important thing about the symbolism of her blindness is that it is not an exceptional condition; on the contrary, Maa's case is but an exaggerated example of a predicament the film poses as endemic to modern India. If the cast contains a character possessed of insight, as Chapter 2 has argued, it is Akbar; and we will move on shortly to discuss why it is that he should be the one to deliver Bharati, in the words of his miracle-song, from the "black night of sorrow." But first, in order to set up our approach to the

FIGURE 21. Vision restored

problem of blindness, it will be helpful to examine a related condition, the other aspect of Bharati's penalty that takes shape through the narrative: her homelessness.

In terms of *Amar Akbar Anthony*'s organization of space, homelessness means she has been cast onto the streets of the city. But our film's principal female character is also homeless in that she has become deprived of the family ties that had defined her as a socially integrated person—the wife of a healthy husband, the mother of three sons—until her flight to the forest. Furthermore, Bharati is the cause of the homelessness of Kishanlal and their sons. As the mother, the heart of the heteronormative traditionalist home, when she abandons that home she removes the possibility of "home" itself. Until her husband and sons reinstate her within the fold of the nuclear family, home is not an option available to any of them. The film combines these constructions of homelessness in a complex weave.

Right at the story's beginning, on the Fifteenth of August, Bharati sets out to kill herself. Stricken with tuberculosis, she has waited for her husband to return from prison so he can take over the family's care, and as soon as he arrives, he leaves again. Then she absconds, leaving the chil-

dren with a suicide note. The night is dark and stormy, and as Bharati
runs through the forest, she meets with disaster—although not the one
she seeks (it is never made clear just how she intended to do herself in). A
lightning bolt from above fells a tree branch, knocking her unconscious.
Providentially, Haider Ali is heading back home through the forest with
the son he has just unwittingly adopted from her. He rescues Bharati in
two ways. First he lifts the branch off her body, and second, when she
wakes to find her eyesight has been taken from her, he offers words of
wisdom (more on this later). Her Muslim deliverer then brings her home,
and once she is back on her own threshold, a neighbor mistakenly informs
her that her husband and children have perished in an accident: "I saw it
with my own eyes." Bharati can no longer see anything with her own eyes,
so she takes his word that she's now bereft of both husband and offspring
and does precisely what the audience would expect her to do. She gives
voice to a despairing *"No-o-o!"* and dashes her wrists at the wall to break
her bangles, symbolic of her married status. Viewers take note: those bangles don't break. Nevertheless, the little cabin in the slum is renounced
along with her wifely status.

At one level, the poor woman is following a time-honored (and con-
tested) religious teaching when she gives up her dwelling place, for according to classical Hindu texts, a widow is to enter homelessness in much
the same way that a man who takes *sannyaas* is to enter the wandering
life, renouncing the worldly sphere for spiritual pursuits. In principle, an
orthodox Hindu widow is a mendicant ascetic—comparable, across traditions, to the ragged *qalandar* of Islam. And while few women observe
the mandate in full, norms of plain dress and living do nevertheless obtain among many people in real life, as they certainly do in the movies.
Following her change of life course, Bharati does not don the white sari
of widowhood (as does Lakshmi's grandmother), but her saris are pale,
featuring modest patterns on a white cotton background so innocuous that
the outfits tend to blend into one another. And her *choli*, or blouse, is always white (except on the fateful night, when her *choli* is dark purple).[18]
Her face displays neither the *bindi* dot nor the vermilion *sindoor* with
which Hindu women across most of India indicate their married status.

A Hindu logic of the widow-as-renunciant goes like this: The dharma
of an adult woman is to serve her husband. When the husband has passed

on, so too has the reason for her role as a social actor. The ethic of self-sacrifice enjoined here has a strong ritual component; thus Hindu wives fast to ensure their husbands' well-being, or take vows as exemplified by *Jai Santoshi Maa*'s Satyavati. And it is possible to read Bharati's original sin as an extreme, if misguided, exercise in precisely this logic. She has learned she has tuberculosis; she fears the illness will take her from serving her family to burdening them; she heads into the forest to sacrifice herself on their behalf.

But Haider Ali sets her right: "Sister, to commit suicide is the greatest sin *(gunaah)* of all. After all, there may be others who also have claims to your life." Bharati accedes to his reasoning: "That's why Bhagvan has given me this punishment, and taken the light from my eyes." When she next speaks the Lord's name—Bhagvan—the stormy sky rumbles as if cued. The thunder echoes the earlier moment when the lightning bolt came down to fell the branch on top of her. It is clear that behind Bharati's injury is a direct agency. This is not the mechanistic system of ethical causality that Indic religious traditions famously theorize as *karma.* God—Bhagvan or Allah, as you please—has taken a personal interest and is calling His subject to task.

But has God handed down a punishment (as Bharati herself states, using the Urdu word *sazaa*)? Or could it be that the judgment is yet to come? Perhaps this ordeal she enters is to be understood in the literal sense of the term—as a period of trial. Either way, in precisely what does her transgression consist?

In terms of dharma, it seems that she has made a sort of category error, for suicide is the opposite of the selfless service she is pledged to as a Hindu wife. It is not for Bharati to take the fate of her husband and sons into her own hands. Her misdeed is an assertion of ego. And indeed, it is in the bonds of service to others—reciprocal service, for the obligation does not run only one way—that Haider Ali locates Bharati's sin. *Your life is not your own to take. Give care to others—and open yourself to their care of you.* Maa is not alone. How wrong of her to act as if she were! It is small exaggeration to say that the sin lies not in a particular kind of individual act but in the commission of any purely individual act at all.

To the extent that her attempted suicide is an extension of her abandonment of her family, so too is her abandonment of her family an extension of the logic of her assertion of autonomy in the first place. *It's my life, and I'll do what I want.* This is the root of the problem: Bharati's bid to make her own move. And note the timing: the Fifteenth of August, Indian Independence Day. Maa has reached an age in symbolic terms that does have a great deal to do with her impulse: her rebellion, we could say, is a symptom of modernity.

Here is another point about the hierarchy of Bharati's sins: While the Lord has averted her suicide attempt, He has permitted the act in which it originates—her abandonment of her loved ones—to reap its consequences. Maa enters modernity as an autonomous subject, deluded into thinking her actions are somehow moral or selfless or family friendly, and alienated from her place within a godly order.[19] As a result of her rebellion, her husband and children have become dispersed. And contrary to her own understanding that she has suffered a punishment in her loss of eyesight, what God seems to have done, at one stroke, is to save her from her own hand and also to lift her debilitating tuberculosis. Maa's blinding, then, is no penalty—much less a curse—but a challenge and a consequence of her freedom. If the wretched woman has chosen the path of wandering, so be it. Let her experience the modern condition in darkness; let her have her Independence Day. This is her trial: How will she find her way back home?

The scenario bears comparison with two famous movies from the United States and Britain, both filmed in 1946. In Frank Capra's *It's a Wonderful Life,* a ruined businessman, played by James Stewart, sets out to commit suicide. Intercepted in a state between life and death, an angel shows him a vision of his hometown as it would exist if he had never been born. In Michael Powell and Emeric Pressburger's *A Matter of Life and Death,* a wounded bomber pilot lingers in a similar state. His fate—is he to remain on earth or be collected to heaven?—is adjudicated at a tribunal beyond the clouds in which the airman, played by David Niven, is made to stand in for Great Britain as a whole. In *Amar Akbar Anthony,* divine intervention permits Bharati to remain on earth, but sets the condition that she live on in the world her sin has created until she is ready to be judged. The time spent in blindness is a trial period, an allegory that turns out to be, likewise, coded unsubtly with nationalism.

In initiating the crisis of the family's separation and dissolution, Bharati's autonomous actions are indeed the original sin that inaugurates our story.[20] The puzzle we confront at this point has to do with the already much-remarked-upon allegory of the nation. If the family (four men, one woman) represent a national collectivity, and narrative developments somehow encode history, how are we to understand what happens to Bharati—Mother India?

First, let's take note of a certain fish-out-of-water quality that surrounds Maa in the big city. Sidharth Bhatia remarks on how "the characters all look urban, but the mother could well be from a more conservative, small-town background. She wears her sari in a very old-fashioned style."[21] We would go further. As an everywoman figure, Bharati strikes us as an overtly rural, even naturalized one. As the film progresses, the character collects visual motifs that cite agricultural and other organic processes— storms, blood, and flowers, to name three of many. To the degree that she symbolizes the national homeland, in fact, Maa figures as a composite of India's human masses with the soil from which they have sprung. And here we make a crucial departure from Anthony's earlier equation of Mother India with the nation-state, for the state is external to this natu- ralized figuration. This distinction puts *Amar Akbar Anthony* in the broad current of nationalist ideology not only in India but also elsewhere in the world, where the relation between nation and state has been defined in terms that are both hierarchical and gendered. (Toward the end of this chapter we take up specific ways the dichotomy has been symbol- ized in India, with an emphasis on Mother India's sons.)

Second: As per our argument in the introduction, the urban geography of *Amar Akbar Anthony* is a representation not just of space—of the city of Bombay as it is constituted outside the film—but also of time—of a mytho- ideological narrative of national crisis and progress. Bharati's own tra- jectory begins in a humble but coherent place of origin: the slum. Un- moored, she flees to the forest, a space of transformation. Her wanderings in blindness traverse a circuit of urban spaces: the streets, the hospital, the police station. The story arc reaches fulfillment with a return to the forest and a second transformation from which Maa emerges restored, ready to advance into the future at the center of a reconstituted family. In our interpretive scheme, the slum is a space of the historical past. The city is the modern present. And the suburbs—more properly the outer suburbs, nascent neighborhoods such as Borivali that were in the process of construction in the 1970s—take shape from the forest as the frontier of future settlement.

Assimilating these two pieces within the allegorical script, then, Bharati's homelessness puts forth the message that India, in the post-Independence years, has fallen adrift. Modernity finds Mother India directionless on the streets, seemingly autonomous yet dependent on the largesse of others, and incapable of recognizing her true sons. Here is the central drama of the allegory: How will her three sons awaken to the truth of their destiny? How will they embrace brotherhood and its corollary—the bond of, and to, their Mother? How will they find, or make, a home?

In the film's present, which can be set more or less at its release date of 1977, Bharati is at large in Bombay. The space she leaves behind on the fateful Independence Day of twenty-two years before is identified as "the" Bandra Koliwada: a Koli village absorbed into the now urban Bandra. Toward the end of the movie, a sentimental Kishanlal will observe that the neighborhood has remained unchanged. Although poor, it was (and is) a close-knit community, where the Bharati of 1955 knew her place and was known in return: a wife and mother recognized to be in good standing even while her husband was away serving a jail sentence.

The Koliwada resembles both a village and a slum, not only in its poverty but also in the character of the patron-client relationships that bind some of its residents. The British sahib–like costume and diction of Kishanlal's master, Robert, suggest that the regime in force in the Koliwada runs along the lines of the colonial system from which its inhabitants are ostensibly celebrating their liberation. And when Kishanlal later returns to the neighborhood as a boss in his own right, we see that while the individual masters may have changed, the neo-feudalistic character of the Koliwada has not. In sum, the old neighborhood is poor and unchanging, cohesive but vulnerable. It is the space of the old order— the domain of social hierarchy in which the poor serve masters who may stand in variously for rural landlords, urban gangsters, or colonial sahibs and their Anglophile understudies.

India has been promised better since her attainment of independence, but according to the film, some years have had to pass for the betrayal of that noble promise to become clear. When the old bonds of servitude are dissolved, Mother India enters modernity. And there, on the streets of the city, is where her troubles really set in.

In Hindu philosophy, the concept of *maya,* cosmic illusion, encompasses all of creation in a formulation that combines ephemerality and lack of essential coherence with a certain attractive, even bewitching quality.[22] One city in particular is recognized as an apt synecdoche for this concept. *Mayapuri,* City of Illusion, is a well-known Hindi nickname that criticizes Bombay's glitz and glamour even as it invokes them.[23] Likewise, as we have seen in Chapter 2, Muslim mystics consider phenomenal reality to be the realm of mere appearances, to be glossed in poetry through esoteric metaphors such as the veil *(parda)* or the picture *(tasveer).* We also argued that Akbar, in his persona of truth-telling poet, takes aim at a specific node of illusion: the dazzle of the modern city, the play of surfaces that enables masquerade.

What does it mean for Bharati to be blind in the City of Illusion? In the Land of the Blind, as the proverb has it, the one-eyed man is king.[24] Conversely, however, in a city of smoke and mirrors, perhaps the blind woman is a step ahead of the game. If there are kings in Bombay, they would be the inhabitants who know that success in the City of Illusion is a matter of disguises: the playfully dressed mob bosses, the trio of costumed brothers at the movie's finale. But again, as the brothers have learned, the whole masquerade is possible because none of the emperors actually has any clothes. Blindness offers Maa no material advantages, but it does signal a sort of rebuff to this pageant: *None of your flimflam will take me in.*

Bharati's life on the streets is ostensibly supported by her work of flower-selling. But while she is described, in Salma's words to Akbar, as a "flower-selling granny" *(phool bechne-wali budhiya),* we never do see her trading her flowers for money. Her so-called selling is closer to begging, with the flowers she offers prompting in their recipients some form of largesse, be it money, food, or acts of care. Such means of livelihood have long been mandated to persons who choose homelessness for religious reasons. This is perhaps the main reason popular attitudes in South Asia toward begging are ambivalent, with a measure of respect for persons whose detachment from society empowers them to bestow blessings or special insight: ascetics, holy fools, certain kinds of folk performers. And as the narrative demonstrates, in her modest way Bharati does offer benedictions along with her flowers, which may themselves be thought of, per ritual convention in all three religions, as blessings in material form.[25]

What is more, however hapless she appears, Bharati's attitude toward others remains grounded in an innocent truth. Not discriminating against people based on their self-presentation, she eschews the hierarchically marked modes of address used by others in the city—Sir, *Seth, Sahib*—in favor of the folksy *beta,* "son." In return, everyone addresses her as *Maa.* To be sure, this is conventional (if familiar) usage among anonymous urbanites as well as villagers. But on another level it is the film's deeper truth: peel away the trappings of diversity and those three funny guys turn out to be brothers, and old Maa really *is* their mother.

In blindness, it would seem, Bharati comes to understand what she had lost sight of earlier. But precisely what lesson has she learned through error and trial? And how long must she wait for the summons to be issued—to give an account of herself before the almighty judge? In symbolic terms the answer is: until she finds the right lawyer to plead her case. In narrative terms the answer is: until the movie's last act, the *qawwali* service at the shrine of Sai Baba. Famously, Gandhi is remembered as having demanded of the British rulers, "Leave India to God or to Anarchy."[26] Bharati's illumination following the "Shirdi Wale Sai Baba" sequence—and the consequent chain reaction of recognitions and reunions—is this movie's way of delivering India back from anarchy to God.

Let's bring this interpretation home with a closer look at the players in the drama of "Shirdi Wale Sai Baba." First there is Akbar, the wielder of the wonderful voice. As Chapter 2 argued, the key to understanding its special power is a concept that is common to Islamic and Hindu teachings: that coming between most of us and a clear perception of the world's essential truths is an obscuring veil of illusion.[27]

Second there is Sai Baba, the Saint of Shirdi, whose antecedents as a Sufi charismatic whose cult has become Hinduized have also been discussed in Chapter 2. As a doctrinal proposition, the famous one-sentence summary of his teachings, *Sab ka malik ek,* "The Lord of all is one," may be understood thus: beyond the world of appearances God is a unity, and whether you address that ultimate quantity as Allah, Bhagvan, or Jesus is your own business. In terms of practice, Sai Baba devotion is centered on adoration of the Master's image. The service at the shrine in *Amar Akbar Anthony,* with its slightly larger-than-life effigy, gives a picture of the ritual setting—albeit an elaborately staged one—and the logic that backs up this practice runs on parallel tracks through Sufi and Hindu metaphysics.

Sai Baba's historical career ran from the last decades of the nineteenth century to 1918. The period coincides with the advent of modern visual media forms and their adoption by Indians for devotional purposes (among other things). In his flesh-and-blood body, Sai Baba provided the followers who recognized him as a *pir* (Sufi saint) or *guru* (Hindu spiritual master) with a fixed access point to divine power. But even before his departure from the phenomenal world, the cult authenticated the use of representations of his visible form as equally direct interfaces— portals to authentic divinity through the shifting veils of appearances.[28] Within its devotional discourse there is, therefore, great concern with illusion in a visual sense. This is generally expressed in the Hindu idiom of *maya* and its companion term *lila,* which denotes divine intervention within *maya* in a mood of wondrous play.[29]

Some pictures, in other words, are *true* illusions, but the image of Sai Baba—a photograph or a poster (or, as in the movie, a statue)—is as efficacious for accessing divine truth as was the Baba's bodily form. The teaching transfers the charisma of the saint's person to his representations. And what this claim to authentic manifestation within the fabric of illusion does to the dictum "The Lord of all is one" is to make of it a bid for recognition. *Do you subscribe to the cult of the saints, within your own tradition?* In India, most Hindus, Muslims, and Christians would say yes. *Then behold the prophet who reveals this truth: the saints of all traditions embody the same divine essence.* If the Lord of all is truly one . . . then what He looks like—whether you call him Allah, Bhagvan, or Jesus—is me. In Akbar's terms, it could be said: Here is the face of the Beloved.[30]

Third, and finally, we have Maa. If the Bharati character has been placed under trial for a transgressive act of ego, how can she gain salvation? If for lack of responsible (and masculine) leadership the Indian nation has gone off course, how will it regain the path of order and progress? The answer to both questions is the same: through submission to, and recognition of, divine will.

FIGURE 22. Maa and Sai Baba

First submission, *then* recognition: the causal relationship proposed here may appear to run backwards, but this is indeed the way the film depicts the operation of grace. Recall the scenario of the inaugural crisis: Bharati asserts her ego, abandoning her family, and is consequently deprived of her eyesight. Following the same causal logic, the error is corrected in the "Shirdi Wale Sai Baba" sequence. This is the second and last point in the film at which Maa performs an autonomous action, and its effect is precisely to reverse the earlier move. The summons has been issued and Bharati heeds the call. Having once turned her back on God in the form of Santoshi Maa, she returns to face Sai Baba (Figure 22). Let's raise the curtain, as it were, on this number and see how it illustrates the principle of the subject's submission.

"In this age, where can a broken picture be mended? / In your court, ruined destinies are repaired." These are the *qawwali*'s opening lines, which greet Bharati in Akbar's voice when, as she hurries through the woods in a replay of the frantic flight of twenty-two years before, the sanctuary of the shrine comes into view. The first line sets up the grand claim of the second line by pairing two unflattering images. "This age" is the present, generally regarded as a time of decadence in South Asian religious discourses; in our own analysis we identify it with the modern and the urban. The "picture" *(tasveer)* can be filed alongside other Sufi symbols like the veil and the curtain, already examined in some detail. Ours, then, is a fallen age—the age of the picture—a time of all flash and no substance.

"In your court / Has arrived a petitioner." This is the *qawwali*'s refrain, and as Akbar sings on, Bharati gains the shrine's threshold. At the narrative level she is clearly the petitioner, but the *qawwal* has assumed the same position in his verbal address. A spiritual charismatic is said to hold "court" *(dar)* on the model of a king, however humble the material trappings, but emphasized in the mise-en-scène here is the complementary image of a courtroom encounter, with the marble Baba seated in the place of the judge. And indeed the juridical scenario is squarely in line with conventions of language and practice current at Islamic pilgrimage sites in South Asia.[31] In effect, Akbar is wording the petition for Bharati; his song is the aural complement to her visible performance of submission. He is a professional pleader, more attorney than messenger. (As we have argued previously, it's when the music starts to play that the Akbar character comes into his own, and his voice projects the power of truth.)

But beyond this task of advocacy he and Bharati have become united, distinctions of ego erased, in common surrender to the Baba: "Prayers on the lips / Eyes full of tears / A heart full of hopes / Yet the pockets are empty." Installed just inside the shrine's entrance, facing the effigy but separated from it by most of the length of the floor, is the stone image of a kneeling bull. Iconographically speaking, this is the sacred mount of the god Shiva, and the bull's placement in a posture of adoration replicates the arrangement in a Shiva temple. But it can also stand in for the buffalo or ox *(bismil)* sacrificed by Muslims on Eid and other occasions and by Hindu votaries of particular deities as well. Bharati stumbles at the step and advances on all fours, her pose mirroring that of the bull. She touches her brow to the ground in prostration, and when she lifts it we see she is bleeding. In fact she holds her raised head with her hand, as if she has suffered a blow, and close attention to the footage will show she has left a puddle of blood on the floor (Figure 23). Her gesture of submission has opened a fresh wound that is linked somehow to the relief of her old wound—her blindness. We could read the red streak here as a *teeka,* the mark that punctuates a Hindu's completion of prayers and attainment of ritual purity. But it also looks like a *ze-bibah,* the sort of "prayer bump" many pious Muslims acquire as the result

FIGURE 23. Blood mark

of five daily applications of the forehead to the floor. Finally, the blood can connote *qurbani:* blood sacrifice in Islam.

"May you reunite the parted / May you relight the dark lamps," Akbar sings on, and we spectators see two little flames kindle in the effigy's eyes and fly across to enter Bharati's. The camera switches to her point of view: a blurry Sai Baba with Akbar kneeling before him is brought into focus, and we know that Maa's sight has been restored. At the lines "These nights of sorrow / These nights so black / Transform them for us / Into Eid and Diwali," flames appear in all the lamps adorning the shrine, and the congregation rises in witness of the Baba's manifestation of power. As Bharati gazes on adoringly, three little figures appear superimposed on the saint's visage: her sons as they appeared twenty-two years before, smiling and beckoning, the baby Akbar particularly fervent with both arms outstretched.

At the song's end she reaches the statue, crawling right past the ecstatically swaying Akbar (it is he who has turned blind to her in the moment). She bows at its feet, placing her head alongside the coconuts and other fruit the Baba's devotees have left as offerings.[32] But the effective gesture of submission, as certified with the spontaneous *teeka/zebibah,* is the earlier spilling of blood. And the reward of submission, as we have proposed, is clear vision—of her long-lost son Akbar and of herself in her proper place in the world, as a respectable mother and wife. *Islam* means "submission" and a Muslim is "one who has submitted." It is small wonder, then, that Akbar's claim to Maa should conclude with her assimilation within a comprehensive order, albeit one imposed under the sign of a heterodox Sufi preacher!

After all that, perhaps it's inevitable that a bit later, when Akbar delivers the dramatic news to Bharati that her husband is still alive, the scene falls somewhat flat. We in the audience have already learned what's important: Maa is back on the right track. And the train of recognitions, to continue the metaphor, swiftly follows her course correction. Beyond the city of appearances the terminus beckons: a rehabilitation of the family unit.

• •

INTERVAL

• •

Amar and the Righteous Mother

Let's restart the analysis by discarding a premise shared by the previous two arguments. To blame Maa for her own troubles, in one way or another, is nothing less than to misrecognize her and misdiagnose her struggles. The real story *Amar Akbar Anthony* has to tell us about Bharati lies embedded within a dense layer of Hindu symbolism. Clearly, this is a job for Inspector Amar: If he can't crack the code, then who?

Serving here as Exhibit A from Amar's file is a sample of informant testimony. In Bombay in 1977, as mentioned in the Introduction, a group of
mass communications students were tasked with interviewing people
from less privileged strata about the *Amar Akbar Anthony* phenomenon.
One student took her inquiries to the Maharashtrian countryside, where
she spoke with a rural fan who worked as a milkman:

> *Gulnar:* The mother of the three heroes suddenly becomes blind and then
>   miraculously gets back her sight in Sai Baba's temple. Do you believe
>   such things are possible in reality?
>
> *Naresh (the milkman):* Yes, certainly. One lady over here had the devil in
>   her and no one could cure her. Then her husband took her to the temple
>   of our big goddess and offered seven coconuts and a dish of fruits at her
>   feet, and the wife soon became all right. So these things are not at all
>   false.[33]

This piece of evidence will come into its own a bit later in the investigation, when we consider specific clues from the movie. Here, let's anticipate that point with two observations. The first has to do with Naresh's
general attitude, which could be described as one of matter-of-fact piety.
Of course divine power intervenes in our world, at discrete places and
times, and in engagement with ritually directed human action. *Of course.*
You just have to be able to see it. But the second has to do with what the
villager has actually seen. When asked a question about a woman's blindness and a saint's miracle, he gives an answer about spirit possession and
goddess worship.

Now, the problem of how to recognize divinity when it manifests
itself in the phenomenal world is a central one for Hindus, as much mythology and folklore attest. Often there is a play on the idea of recognition, and we are called out for our inability to recognize divinity—even
when it is in our midst—and enjoined to be open to such encounters and
respond with devotion. To this end, the gods frequently appear in disguises to test their devotees, to show them the limits of their human
knowledge, and to demonstrate the humor and wonder of divine *lila.*

Stories in which gods pay visits to the world of mortals have inspired
Indian filmmakers to stage some memorable encounters. In *Jai Santoshi
Maa,* not only Santoshi Maa but all the chief deities of Puranic mythology
make appearances as Hindu mendicants on their begging rounds. In

Sant Tukaram (V. G. Damle and Sheikh Fattelal, 1938)—perhaps the greatest Indian "devotional film"—the god Vitthal takes the form of a little boy and, in one comic sequence, a puckish old man. In the satirical *Bawarchi* (Hrishikesh Mukherji, 1972), it is hinted that the humble cook who has managed to straighten out his employer's dysfunctional family is Krishna himself.

What if something similar was the case with Maa? What if the character who seems the most directionless and the least powerful bears signs of divinity? And what if that divine force, in fact, were to be thanked for looking after the children, even steering them onto the paths of their foster fathers? To safeguard the members of Bharati's family and enable them to flourish independently until conditions are right for its reconstitution— that would be a mission worthy of a goddess come to earth.

Here is one line of interpretation, not far removed from our previous discussion of Maa as widow. As we know by the icon on the locket around her neck, Bharati is a devotee of Santoshi Maa. Following the logic of the cult, as per the film *Jai Santoshi Maa* and the countless "vow stories" (*vrat kathas*) that circulate among Hindu women, Bharati takes suffering onto herself as a vow to the goddess.[34] She practices austerities so that the deity takes note and returns blessings, as per convention, not to her devotee but to those the devotee has pledged to serve, generally her husband and children. The deity offers the devotee's family protection, which supplements—indeed replaces—any efforts on the part of the rotary herself. It is a zero-sum game,[35] and so the sons grow straight and strong, and even Kishanlal prospers on the crooked path he has chosen, precisely because Maa denies herself on their behalf. Maa's misery, in other words, is indexed to her men's flourishing.

This reading will not seem peculiar to Hindu viewers, for whom vows and related practices of female piety are a matter of daily life. But there is another interpretation, which sets aside Santoshi Maa just as Bharati herself does when she passes on the locket along with her suicide note. We still discern the handiwork of a goddess; it just isn't Santoshi Maa in her filmic form.

To identify the goddess at work in the film (and in Bharati), let us keep in mind three points about goddesses as a class of Hindu deities: (1) they follow a logic that is divine, not mundane, and as such the blessings and afflictions they bestow may be incomprehensible to their human subjects; (2) they have porous identities, such that a goddess may turn into or even merge with another goddess, and their devotees have similar identities, for the bounds separating divinity and humanity are fluid; and (3) they often implement their divine plans and guide their devotees through the mechanism of possession. As Frederick M. Smith argues in his magisterial *The Self Possessed: Deity and Spirit Possession in South Asian Literature and Civilization,* "Possession is the most common and, at the grass roots, most valued form of spiritual expression in India."[36]

Inspector Amar's investigation will follow this hypothesis: Bharati is possessed by a goddess, and the goddess's divine plan guides Bharati, her family, and the film. This interpretation relies on a complex model of composite personhood. Readers may be reminded of a *matryoshka,* or "little mother"—a Russian nesting doll. On the surface we find India's national Cine-Ma, Nirupa Roy; beneath that we find the character of a Hindu woman, Bharati; and inside that mortal's skin we find another female personality: a goddess. And it is this goddess that is the agent of many of the narrative movements of this composite person.

One strange thing about this identification is that Bharati herself might doubt it, for it is common for the subjects of possession not to recognize the workings of the deity or to experience amnesia with regard to them.[37] Anthony and Akbar would likely doubt it as well. Anthony thinks of Maa as a subject who has failed to take responsibility for herself, not understanding the composite and divine aspects of that self. And Akbar judges her as a lost soul who needs to be reclaimed as a servant of God's will, not understanding that she is already, in a sense, divine will incarnate. Even Manmohan Desai would likely dismiss the notion. But consider a fan of Desai's movies like Naresh, the village milkman quoted above. He understands the mechanisms of possession and the curative power of the goddess. He would surely be more receptive. Perhaps one reason the "masses" championed *Amar Akbar Anthony* even as the "classes" and critics disparaged it was because among them were many like Naresh, who could see that Maa—and indeed the film itself—was divinely guided.[38]

As for Inspector Amar, the process of deduction has led him to an unsettling conclusion. The evidence indicates that the deity that has taken up residence inside Maa is a mother goddess of the sort worshipped by adherents of what is generally known as Village Hinduism. The term is inadequate in that deities within this rubric also claim urban devotees, but the tradition's purview is decidedly rustic, even parochial.[39]

A village goddess such as this one is recognized as the personification of a local settlement in its spatial and natural dimensions.[40] Her main purview is the sort of processes that affect the human organism and the agricultural cycle. It is in this connection that we can most clearly see how the film constructs Bharati as a cosmic force. The motifs and thematic associations that cohere around the character are earthly ones, taken from the portfolio of a typical rural mother goddess. Details that seem arbitrary when encountered serially attest to a pattern once collected in a list: red flowers, thunderstorms, blood marks, snakes, snake holes, anthills. These have come up in our retellings of the story, and will do so again. But first we want to explore several other clues that are key to our identification: homelessness, disease, fever, blindness, trance, and blood sacrifice. Once we have assembled all the evidence, we will find that we have a compelling portrait of a country goddess on a mission in the city.

The Bharati character has entered homelessness in a double sense, as we noted in the previous section. First, she has been deprived of her consort and her dependents;[41] second, she has been denied spatial emplacement. In the context of Hindu goddess lore, both conditions situate her as highly unstable, if not downright dangerous.

To expand on the first point: a consort-less goddess is fierce and also volatile. This is a connection by no means confined to peasant cults; it is well developed in the mythology and iconography of mainstream Hinduism. The classic, and classical, examples are the warrior maidens Durga and Kali, wild-haired and well-armed aspects of the same goddess, Devi. When, by contrast, she is depicted as Shiva's consort under the names Parvati or Gauri, Devi appears demure and domestic—light complected, well groomed, and serene. Glenn Yocum makes clear the connection between this dynamic and the association of goddesses (and the female gender more generally) with natural processes:

> When properly married, i.e., domesticated, encultured, brought under male control, they are benevolent, compassionate, and accessible. The more firmly tied to a deity the goddess is . . . the more decorous her behavior.

In the Sanskritic tradition the association of the goddess with philosophical notions such as *śakti* . . . seems to convey a parallel insight. The goddess's fundamental being is natural. She is homologous with nature, and nature can be uncanny and destructive. Subjected to human control, however, nature is often a source of abundance.[42]

To expand on the second point: a wandering deity is frustrated and thus volatile. As a category distinct from ghosts, the wandering deity can be understood as a spiritual presence that has been divined in a general locality but not seated at a spot where it can receive the ritually guided attentions of humans. One hazard such a spirit presents is that it may make a home for itself by possessing a local human as its material vessel—an experience that can have inconvenient consequences. Manuel Moreno describes an episode in which a form of Kali possessed the daughter of a Tamil villager, Kantacami, and demanded the construction of a temple in which she could take up permanent residence. This Kali

> lacked a dwelling place, just as humans often do. She was in a state of "need" . . . ; she sought relief from a state of wandering. A place where she could be worshiped was rightfully hers. She therefore called upon Kantacāmi to rectify this undesirable situation. This state of deprivation and constant flux altered the bodily constitution of the goddess, making her extremely "hot."[43]

Bharati's situation and behavior look quite different if we diagnose her own homelessness as an effect generated on a human host by a restless deity. In fact, it is tempting to read this deity's tale as an allegory for the struggle of the labor migrants who move to Bombay in such large numbers: she has become exiled from her home in the village-like Koliwada, cast onto the profane terrain of the city, and now tries to take root. But the goddess also has divine work to do. And remember: the goddess's actions may seem mysterious, for they don't stem from human concerns, but the concerns of a village-based mother goddess are indeed *earthly.* And it this formulation that helps us make sense of Maa's tuberculosis.

Disease is central to the phenomenon of possession in goddess worship—specifically, contagious diseases that can spread from village to village. Indeed, this connection is so important that in many places the identities of goddesses are keyed to distinct maladies. Symptoms like rashes and blisters that swell and mark the skin (including boils, which are glossed as red "flowers," or *phool*) are read as indices of the "mother" who has taken up residence within. To be sure, this form of possession is an ambiguous blessing, for a surge of *shakti* may well prove fatal to the mortal so chosen.

In many villages across India, mother goddesses actually come in teams, with great variation in the names and job descriptions of the individual deities.[44] But two of the best-known figures often operate solo. These are Shitala Mata (or Shitala Maa), long worshipped across Hindi- and Bengali-speaking areas as the force manifest in smallpox blisters, and Mariamma (or Mariamman), her primary counterpart in South India. When in the aftermath of the virus's eradication—as announced by the WHO in 1977—Margaret Trawick Egnor set out to ask "What the Smallpox Goddess Did When There Was No More Smallpox," Mariamman, she found, had been assigned a second brief: tuberculosis.[45]

How do infection, motherhood, and the village community come together in the cultic imagination? When a disease invades the boundaries of a settlement, these foreign pathogens trigger the *shakti* warrior that is a latent aspect of every normally serene goddess. The poised, Parvati-like figure enters fierce Durga mode. Among the red flags that signal "goddess on the warpath" are pox and other symptoms that mark the skin, but these are not the malady itself. The true cause is invasion or infiltration by invisible outsiders—demonic and male-gendered agents of chaos. What reads as "disease" is the battle waged to expel them, which is a sign that the goddess has roused herself to address a problem that cannot be handled by normal means. When the local deity rallies, it is both an enactment of territorial sovereignty and the move of a matriarch to put her house in order. As for the village's human inhabitants—at once subjects of a goddess and children of a collective mother—their own bodies constitute the site of the mother goddess's operations. And a protectress who fails to stamp out an epidemic with dispatch may be rejected, her image dethroned from the village's temple.[46]

Now we can identify the next two clues. Fever, with its flame-like surges and spells of dreaminess, is the deity's emanation of energy—in other words, *shakti*. And blindness—or inward-directed vision—is both a symptom and a signifier of possession, in this film and across South Asia.[47] Lastly, the final two clues: trance and blood, specifically the ritual offering of blood to the deity. Because these both figure prominently in events at the start of the movie, let's review the opening sequence to see how this evidence fits together and what it portends.

Bharati is a humble Hindu woman based in a village-like environment. While her husband is in jail, having abandoned his family to oblige his evil boss, she contracts tuberculosis. This may be a sign that the goddess has arrived to protect her charges, for her sons seem remarkably healthy when we meet them, in spite of not having eaten for two days.[48] For Bharati, however, the blessing is not easy to bear: she is bent over and coughing when Kishanlal comes back to her from jail. She touches his feet, signaling her devotion, but her hotheaded husband is home for only a few minutes before he leaves the family again—not to appease his boss this time but to seek vengeance.

Bharati had kept up her strength thinking that with Kishanlal's return, order would be restored to the fold. But her hopes are dashed. The threat from outside has not been defeated. Far from severing his connection with Robert, as she had wished, her husband's continued engagement with him aligns him with the forces of chaos. She succumbs to the strain, and the goddess rages; Bharati burns under the burden.[49] She pens Kishanlal a farewell note. Taking from her own neck the icon of Santoshi Maa, she attempts to transfer to him the goddess's protective power, which she has built up as a ritually observant wife, leaving him the locket.

Then she flees, abandoning the pale of human settlement for the jungle of Borivali Park, which may be considered a liminal wilderness in relation to the city. There she mistakenly thinks she has thrown off the yoke of the goddess, as though taking off the locket were enough. But the fever—the hot goddess energy—moves to take a different form. A lightning bolt from heaven pins her under a branch (Figure 24). When she later arises, her altered condition can be understood as a kind of trance. Maa is destined to wander the same space as others while inhabiting a distinct world of perception, blind to the world and its hierarchies.

Independently of her and of each other, her three young sons happen into rescue's way. But note that none of them is in command of his senses. Amar panics, rushing into traffic in a frenzy reminiscent of his mother's, and is knocked onto the sidewalk, where Inspector Khanna finds him unconscious. (Another hint that Amar's impetus carries with it

FIGURE 24. Maa blinded

something of the goddess's blessing: the accident leaves him with a red streak on his forehead.) The future Akbar is seized by a crying fit that draws Haider Ali from his prayers. And the Anthony-to-be is unable to respond when the Padre cradles him on the steps of the church; he has gone senseless, notes the priest, with fever. As adults, their memories of these events and what preceded them are wiped away—yet another sign that the goddess was the prime mover behind their actions.

All this is established in the lengthy opening sequence. When the credits finally roll, they do so, famously, over the bodies of the three grown brothers in their hospital beds, connected to their mother by the tubes delivering her their blood (see Figure 19). How does this scene's meaning change once we recognize the presence of an additional party to the transaction? For one thing, we can identify the agency behind a development that would otherwise have to be attributed to "fate" *(daiva)*, or some similarly fuzzy formulation.[50] There is a goddess here, exerting her *shakti* to bring about a reunion. For another thing, we discover a ritual dimension to this exchange that endows it with a powerful symbolic charge. For in cultic practice in peasant communities, mother goddesses of the sort that combat disease are propitiated through blood sacrifice: *balidaan*.

We propose that the goddess arranged for Bharati's accident to satisfy her own needs. The deity's consumption of blood is what sustains her through the righteous conflict, which in the case of this film—at the culmination of twenty-two years' time—is about to enter its final chapter. In the straightforward reading of this scene, the transfusion enables our three heroes to restore health to their mother's body, giving her enough vitality to resume her wandering. But if at the same time they are presenting an offering to the goddess within to carry the battle on through to the end, one peculiar implication is that they are actually prolonging the host body's trance—their own mother's blindness. At this level, we might say, the transfusion works as trance-fusion.

What follows the title sequence, of course, is the main portion of the narrative—the story of how the three brothers court their brides, recognize their kinship, and defeat their common enemies. But it is little exaggeration to say that once we have reached the credits—nearly twenty-five minutes in—and the film finally introduces its cast of players, we have already learned most of what we need to know about how their roles will come together in the national allegory.

Recall that the definitive event that leads a mother goddess to take possession of a human host is the invasion of a village by an epidemic. The goddess mobilizes in defense of the community she personifies, and the battles of this war are fought in the infected bodies of its members. In principle, the combat fought through possession of an individual subject is being waged for the integrity of the whole. To recapitulate this in the movie's terms: the goddess descends to roost in the entranced Bharati, and her person is made the site of an internalized struggle whose stakes are the cohesion of a consanguineous network—not an entire village, in this case, but the nuclear family.

And then again, as a synecdoche Bharati's dispersed household can be made to stand not only for a village but also for an entire nation. But beneath the surface of this well-worn trope, we now detect the stirrings of a distinctively Hindu *shakti*. Here there is a clear departure from Akbar's argument that Mother India symbolizes the national populace, the teeming masses of India. In the Amar-centric view, Mother India is a village goddess on a national scale—ancient tradition rooted in the very ground—recast and reinvigorated to embody something new. Hers is the

maternal face on an ideological conflation of cultural heritage with geographical terrain: a veritable "heartland."[51]

And so we have the Indian motherland, Bharati, and the sons of the
soil, her children. They have come under assault by foreign pathogens:
Robert and, at one remove, other degenerate moderns who have denied
their own *deshi* birthright. Postcolonial leadership, Kishanlal in this
case, has fallen down on the job. Corrupted—indeed, infected—by greed,
he has become a parody of the Westernized Robert, even more foppish
than the original. In her travails Bharati is subjected to the stern guard-
ianship of the goddess, representing traditional Hindu lifeways. The
goddess shields her subject from the dazzle of Western-style modernity, and by concentrating the struggle within one woman's body, she
frees her children so that they can grow up uncorrupted and uncompro-
mised. This deity fights the good fight for twenty-two years and is made
newly flush, via a timely blood offering, to carry through to the final effort.

As telegraphed in the title sequence, Mother India will in due course
be revived through the service of three modern yet pure-hearted sons;
these are the representatives of a diverse yet fraternal civil society.[52] But
before Amar, Akbar, and Anthony can come together in realization of their
brotherhood, each must first resolve his own narrative conflicts, and here
the goddess is bound to expend her *shakti* to ensure that they succeed
with integrity.[53] To posit a goddess contained within Bharati is thus to
recast the logic of the Hindu mother's vow, or *vrat,* in an agonistic mode.

What's more, to read the scene in this way as a foreshadowing gesture
is to frame the transfer of blood as a kind of debt to be repaid—the obli-
gated party here being the goddess. A comparison with a pledge drive
might be helpful here. The goddess has raised a set of pledges from do-
nors, and now she has to make good on their donations—now she has to
run the marathon. In support of this interpretation, we can even cite
(somewhat against the overall tenor of the lyrics) a line from the song "Yeh
Sach Hai Koi Kahani Nahin," which plays over the scene: "Shouldn't the
price of this be redeemed? / Blood is blood / It isn't water." And as with
the ritual precedent of *balidaan,* the brothers' gift of their blood is in fact
a transaction—a down payment on further trance-action.

There is, however, another side to this allegory: Mother India needs
to shed her temporary residence and find a permanent home, just as

Lakshmi did when she moved from her stepmother's house to Amar's
bungalow. The goddess has made use of Bharati as the human command center for her divine mission, but when her work is finished, she
will need to find another residence. This isn't easy, however, in the film's
representation of Bombay, which is a landscape notably lacking in Hindu
holy places. The challenge the goddess now confronts (and into which she
propels Bharati, willy-nilly) is this: How will she navigate this bewildering terrain to become seated in a stable place? And, to further the allegory: How will she overcome modernity's trials to meet the promise
of the future?

The when and where of the matter are easy enough to identify. We have
discussed the Sai Baba miracle in Chapter 2 (Akbar's chapter) and again
in the Akbar section of the present chapter. But in its symbolic richness,
the scene has even more to yield.

In retelling Maa's encounter with Sai Baba, we begin with an earlier
scene, for the goddess's eventual departure and Bharati's restoration—her
personal and social reintegration—is prefigured in a sort of wake-up call.
And it comes from an unlikely source: the villainous Robert. In the hospital, Bharati surprises him in the act of abducting someone whom she will
discover to be her long-lost husband. "That's Kishanlal's wife," exclaims
Robert in his English accent, calling her out in her correct relation to the
world, her position within the traditional value system.[54] Foolishly, he believes this is his moment of triumph. Both the Santoshi Maa locket he has
seized from his enemy's breast and his enemy's flesh-and-blood wife are
in his clutches. What he's failed to realize—and it's an indictment of how
far he has severed himself from Indian tradition—is that trying to hold
live *shakti* in your grasp is, literally, playing with fire.

Discarding their surgical scrubs, Robert and his lieutenant Ranjeet
take Bharati for a ride. The poor woman seems nearly senseless with
fear—or is it some other force? Now we watch as the *shakti* rises out of
the motherland's very soil to see the goddess's servant to safety. Ranjeet
loses control of the car and rams it into a mass of earth resembling an ant-
hill or termite mound, which is a telltale mark of ground blessed by a
goddess's presence. Bharati escapes from the wreck and flees through a
landscape whose topography and vegetation shield her from her pursuers,
even though she can't see which way she is going. The woods recall the

wilderness of her fateful flight of twenty-two years before, but this time the terrain offers her safe passage. When she gains the threshold of the shrine, inside of which her youngest son is singing a song of deliverance, a cobra appears at the gate and wards off the wicked trespassers.[55]

"One who has been rejected by everyone / Is given nurture by you," sings Akbar. These lines, offered in praise of Sai Baba, describe the condition of the desperate Bharati crawling to the saint's feet. We can also understand them to apply to three foundling brothers, abandoned by their parents and adopted by the Lord of all, most obviously represented here in the iconic form of Sai Baba. But the lyric can also be read as praise for another divine Provider,[56] whose identity explains the shock of recognition that occurred when Bharati's head touched the shrine's floor.

Who is this divine agent? What has become of the goddess that possessed Bharati? And what is the connection between these two questions?

In our previous discussions of Sai Baba, we had made clear his origins as a Sufi charismatic and stressed the Unitarian principles of his doctrine. But for many of his devotees, including the most influential ones, the Baba has long been absorbed within the mainstream of Hinduism. Pilgrims to Shirdi, the Maharashtrian village where the saint lived among his original, eclectic group of disciples, worship inside a thoroughly Hindu temple structure; inside, a marble image in his likeness is attended by brahman priests who follow an orthodox ritual protocol. We observed earlier that the Baba's ontological relation to the Lord, whose power he dispenses, is open to complex interpretation. But for his more conservative Hindu followers the question is straightforward. Sai Baba is God incarnate—an avatar of Shiva.[57]

Iconographic detail in the movie confirms this sectarian claim. We have already remarked that Shiva's mount, the stone Nandi bull, is stationed at the entrance to the temple. We also noted the threshold was guarded by a snake—a cobra, like the one Shiva wears around his neck. In addition, to the left of the Baba statue (a replica of the original at Shirdi) is installed a black stone *linga,* the classical, aniconic form in which Shiva is seated in a Hindu temple. And on the wall behind the *linga* can just be seen a framed devotional print depicting Shiva and his consort Parvati (see Figure 22). In Chapter 2 the shrine was decoded as a site of national "secularism," and earlier in this chapter it was connected with the Sufi trope of the *dargah* in the wilderness. But the iconography here tells us otherwise. The structure is a Shiva temple, and it is the only Hindu house of worship that is featured in the movie.[58]

What are the implications of this shadow narrative? Here theology delivers the big reveal. By the same logic of encompassment that absorbs a local charismatic like Sai Baba into the orthodox cult of Lord Shiva, canonical Hindu literature teaches that all mother goddesses native to India's villages are encompassed within the pan-Indian Great Goddess, Devi.[59] And Devi belongs in Shiva's house. In her respectable, civilized persona as Parvati, she is married to Him. If the goddess inside Bharati is a local, rustic form of Devi, and if Sai Baba is a form of Shiva identified with modernity and with the Bombay area, then the story of how the goddess travels in her human vessel—across the span of many years, around the dazzling streets of the great city, until she finally arrives at this temple—becomes the story of a homecoming.

Let's return to the bloodstain on Bharati's forehead, read this time as the mark of a married woman. A proper Hindu wife bows in veneration before her husband, and Bharati/Devi is certainly such a wife. When Kishanlal returns from prison, Bharati touches his feet; even though he abandoned her to take the rap for Robert, she has stayed true to him. Now Devi makes a similar gesture. Long separated from Shiva, the first thing she does on encountering Him is to prostrate herself, acknowledging that she is His wife and that she serves Him. And this requires not merely a foot touching, as when Bharati was reunited with Kishanlal, but a "five-limb prostration" *(pañcāṅga praṇāma)*—knees, hands, and forehead—demonstrating full subservience. This is nothing less than her moment of rehabilitation. Shiva is her lord, and she has returned to settle back down after her wild, hot, untamed period of *shakti*-struggle. Bharati raises her head, and we see a scarlet streak—once again she is wearing the *sindoor* of a married woman (see Figure 23).

Even as Devi departs her vessel to rejoin Shiva in His home, Shiva (via Sai Baba) restores to Bharati her eyesight. When the blindness finally lifts, a vision of her three sons as they were when the goddess entered her body

FIGURE 25. Sai Baba and the three brothers

welcomes her return from the trance state into the present (Figure 25). Bharati is once again in command of her senses. And Devi is reunited with her beloved, just as Akbar sings of Diwali and lights miraculously blaze throughout the sanctuary. The Hindu festival of lights marks the union of god and goddess; it also commemorates the return from exile of heroes who have fulfilled epic quests—Rama and Sita in the *Ramayana*, the Pandavas in the *Mahabharata*.

This, then, is the story of an exile that culminates in the establishment of a new home. Recall the discussion at the start of this section in which we delineated the characteristics of our goddess. She was a consort-less deity (restless and volatile because single) and she was also a wandering deity (restless and volatile because homeless). Recall too the example we gave in illustration of the rootless goddess category: the rustic Tamil form of Kali, who, stymied by her lack of station in the coconut grove, possessed a peasant girl in order to make her demand known for a proper temple. We excavate a similar script from *Amar Akbar Anthony* to present a drama in which our own invisible goddess is the star.

It is 1955. A small nuclear family, symbolizing the nascent nation-state, resides with difficulty in the Koliwada, the site of exploitative systems of social organization—colonialism and feudalism—that are understood to have prevailed into the post-Independence period. The native deity of this "backward" milieu fits the profile of a parochial mother goddess, although her symbolic domain embraces the whole of India's territory. With the straying of Kishanlal (the state part of the nation-state partnership), Bharati (the nation) becomes dislodged into the bewildering conditions of modernity. The animating agent here is the goddess, and while her quest ends up taking a circuitous path, it is actually anything but aimless.

In this reading, the blind Bharati who stumbles on the Sai Baba shrine is the possessed Bharati who has been driven all the way there by the goddess. Here on the city's outskirts, the deity alights at a consecrated spot where she can finally settle. In the process, she discharges the faithful mortal who has long served as her vehicle, or "mount," releasing her into a future in which they can both inhabit their correct stations. Bharati's story is thus a journey through history mapped in space—from the village/slum through the anonymous city to the suburbs of the developed future. And implied in the journey is a telos of modernization and self-improvement—the proverbial "uplift"—not only for Indian society but for Hindu deities as well.

The film's penultimate scene shows us Bharati as the resplendent Hindu matriarch of three sons and three brides. She is adorned not only with a *bindi* on her brow and vermilion in her hair but also with a third matronly accessory, a *mangalsutra* necklace (Figure 26). And she has traded in her rustic cotton sari for a handsome, upscale number in gold. Domestic fulfillment thus comes packaged together with social success. There were a number of stumbles along the way, but Maa has finally moved on up from the slum to the suburbs.

So here's to you, Mrs. Kishanlal: your guardian spirit has done right by you, perhaps more than you could know. Yet Bharati in her turn has surely served the deity well. In the film's parallel text, where religion meets nationalism, the mother goddess of folk Hinduism's myriad local cults has successfully moved through her human vessel to become assimilated with Devi, the Great Goddess of the classical tradition. And in accomplishing this—*Om namah Shivay*—she has found domestic contentment, at last, through union with Lord Shiva.

FIGURE 26. Reunited at the jail

Maa and the Cosmic Mother

Ek minute, Amar beta, we can imagine Maa saying. *Take a good look at who's standing with whom in the scene of our reunion. I'm backed up by my sons— nice boys that you are—each paired up with a bride. But that so-called father of yours, still tricked out in his English threads—he's on the other side of the jailhouse bars, with the likes of Robert and Zabisko.*

Fulfillment through submission to my husband? It might be time to check your theology. I began this movie as a devotee of a mother goddess, and that's the way I'll end it. Don't you get that when I call on Bhagvan to bless you, I'm not talking about the Lord—I'm talking about the Lady.

Amar and Bharati represent diverging tendencies within Hinduism, each with its own constructions of gender, history, and territorial sovereignty, and each with its own prescribed methods for combating cosmic disorder. Amar is the rational masculine element, while Bharati is the naturalized feminine. He is the state that has been mandated to advance its interests, while she is the organic, eternal nation. He is the public face of the Hindu religion as an abstract set of principles, while she is the repository of ritual and tradition. In fact, Amar, Bharati, and Anthony can each be seen to have their own dispensations, with their own laws, and their own mechanisms for rewarding those who follow their laws and punishing those who don't. Anthony is a renegade, the architect and enforcer of a set of laws that are in opposition to the state, while Amar is the religion of the state, or perhaps the state as religion. Bharati is the traditional antecedent to the modern state along the lines of customary law or *panchayat* (village council) rule. She can collaborate with the state, even complement it—and if she so chooses, she can supplant it.

In "Diglossic Hinduism: Liberation and Lentils," Vasudha Narayanan stages a gently polemical encounter between the two tongues of Hindu tradition represented by Amar and Bharati. In the one corner, Liberation: a set of discourses centered on soteriology, based on Sanskrit learning and a long tradition of philological and philosophical exposition. This is, broadly speaking, the Hinduism of asceticism and associated yogas, with great concern for karma and *moksha*. In the other corner, Lentils: a complex of practices and associated narratives, symbols, and dispositions. This is Hinduism as experienced by what you consume, and when and how you taste it, as opposed to the teachings you espouse. Alongside cooking, eating, and other oral matters, Narayanan lists aspects of religious life in which participation is mediated through different parts of the sensorium: music, dance, and practices salient in goddess worship, including possession.

Having identified two camps, Narayanan argues that the prestige historically enjoyed by the Liberation side has only become magnified in modern times by academic study—to the corresponding marginalization of Lentils. It is in this context that she asks her fellow scholars the big question:

> Who then speaks for Hinduism, and whom should we listen to more attentively? I would say, listen to the goddess—not the demure, circumspect ones but the dynamic ones who possess and who are progressive.[60]

Well, of course. Amar beta, are you listening?

Not all schools of Hinduism teach that Devi is subordinate in the end, a mere consort to Lord Shiva. The theological case is made most systematically by the Shaktas, goddess devotees with a prodigious intellectual and literary tradition (and corresponding standing in the Liberation camp). According to these servants of *shakti,* the Goddess Herself is the ultimate entity. All others—gods, mortals, and everything else—are by definition subordinate to Devi inasmuch as She encompasses illusion and reality within Herself.

Amar's patriarchal Hinduism wants to modernize the goddess by domesticating her. He believes that a woman's place is married and in the home, be she mortal or divine—Lakshmi his human wife or Lakshmi the goddess. But not all women need or want male minders, and the Shaktas are far from alone as a voice within Hinduism that valorizes an independent Devi. Mother Santoshi is one example of a thoroughly modern goddess whose mythology holds no place for a divine husband. Another example is the figure with which Amar was ostensibly concerned, but to which he gave the merest lip service: Bharat Mata, Mother India.

Well, you got one thing right. Amar Akbar Anthony is a story about a composite person, Mother India. And in this story, just as in real life, it seems Mother's work is never done. Nine months each was enough for the three of you. I carried that goddess inside of me for twenty-two years. Twenty-two years—and this is all the thanks I get? I'm sitting here in the dark at the end of the book. May as well still be blind, boys. What was all that struggle about?

Step one in restoring the Devi to primacy is to complicate the nature-culture dichotomy. It is by no means uncontested among Hindus—historically or in the present day—that the two domains are divided neatly between goddesses and gods. Readers of the pox-goddess scenario as introduced in the previous section may have noticed a certain slippage between the figuration of the deity as a force of nature and her mission as the guardian of the village. The village, in fact, is a site of divine order—that is to say, of civilization as defined against the natural wilderness. And in this Hindu sacred geography, with every village a frontier outpost, it is precisely the civilizational center that is gendered as female and the "natural" periphery that is roamed by demons and other aggressive male agents of chaos.[61] This is what the struggle is about. If Bharati's "village" is India, then Robert and the other gangsters—yes, even Kishanlal—are the demons.

It follows that the notion of "soothing" or even "civilizing" a raging goddess who is inflamed with *shakti* by introducing a stabilizing masculine element may be unwise. Field research conducted in contemporary Orissa found a broad consensus among ordinary Hindus that "a woman derives her power from her natural substance but such power gathers its full significance only because it is subject to cultural . . . control that originates from within herself."[62] And across India, the same model of internally generated and administered *shakti* can apply to female deities as well. This can be observed at the cultic level. Generally speaking, the male ritual specialists who attend a village goddess at a moment of crisis don't attempt to tame her *shakti* by inviting the intercession of a god. The purpose of their ritual attentions is to supplicate and propitiate her from a position of submission. To that end, they offer sacrifice.

Step two in giving the Goddess her due is to examine properly what goes on in the hospital scene at the ritual level. It is a sacrifice. Here, in looking to the mythology and iconography of established mother goddesses for context, we find that Santoshi Maa is not a helpful example except by way of contrast. Her wants are vegetarian and famously modest—her prescribed offering is *gur-chana,* brown sugar and chickpeas. Mother India, on the other hand, sets the bar high.

Historically speaking, Mother India came into her own as a distinct goddess persona in the late colonial period with the circulation of mass-produced graphic media. In her book *The Goddess and the Nation: Mapping Mother India,* Sumathi Ramaswamy devotes a chapter to the male patriots who appear in many of these graphics, generally in supporting roles or, if foregrounded, then basking in her blessing or even framed in her maternal embrace.[63] This class of devotees is dominated by nationalist leaders such as Gandhi, Nehru, and Subhas Chandra Bose, "big men" whom Ramaswamy situates in relation to the national goddess (and the iconized national map) in a "love-service-sacrifice" nexus.[64] It is the firebrand Bose, along with a cast of lesser big men such as the young militant Shaheed ("Martyr") Bhagat Singh, whose enactments of sacrifice are of particular interest here. In citation of their warlike acts of service, their pictures feature red streams of blood. Blood flows from their wounds—and often from the stumps of their beheaded necks—as an offering to Mother India. Ramaswamy reproduces a number of pictures that show Bose and other votaries serving up their own heads on platters, and in one lurid image from 1931, a whole row of nationalist leaders, with Gandhi himself in the lead, queues up before an axe-wielding Bharat Mata—very Kali-like amid the severed heads.[65]

It feels odd to be describing *Amar Akbar Anthony*'s take on anything as subtle, but given antecedents like these, the scene over which the credits roll comes across as a model of understatement. It consists of a largely static tableau: the three brothers lined up in their hospital beds, Maa laid out in a fourth bed in the foreground.[66] Tubes connect our fraternal trio to a bottle that collects their blood and feeds it into Bharati (see Figure 19). It is largely by means of camera movements that trace the blood's course from each donor that Desai succeeds in injecting some dynamism into the scene. And yet however restrained, the citation of the visual code of the "big men's" self-sacrifice is apparent.

The narrative purpose of the scene hinges on a problem of recognition. We spectators recognize a mother attended by her three sons. We might even recognize a goddess attended by three votaries. And on both levels, we see the authenticity of the relationship proven by the test of blood: the transfusion *works,* organically and ritually.[67] But on the mundane level, the boys don't recognize the old woman as their mother (let alone one another as brothers), and the mother doesn't recognize her sons.[68] And this has got to be more than a little frustrating on the supramundane level, where the deity who has brought about the whole ménage knows she is not recognized. To the extent that the whole, long movie this scene kicks off comes down to a drama of recognition—How will our three heroes discover their kinship? Unmask their parents? See through illusions?— then we can likewise trace the goddess's own trajectory as a quest to be recognized.

"Maa is not just a mother. / She's also something more than that." These are the lines that launch the opening song, "Yeh Sach Hai Koi Kahani Nahin."[69] The three brothers' offering should be as much about recognizing that there is in fact "something more"—a divine presence within—as it is about recognizing that she is their biological mother. As we have just observed, it is crucial for the narrative that no conscious recognition pass among the four as family members. But then again, this particular plot point is not just a plot point; it's also something more than that. It is a musical number, an alternate diegetic temporality in which emotional truths are laid bare.[70] Above and beyond mere narrative exposition, the symbolism of the scene's Mother India iconography stakes out a triple claim: the relation of loyal sons to their mother parallels the relation of loyal subjects to their country, which parallels the relation of Hindu devotees to their deity. It's time to set aside Amar's rather mechanical and instrumentalist model of ritual. There is nothing transactional about this sacrifice; this is a paradigm of servitude.

And now let's run the film back through the allegory machine for a last hurrah. Not long after Independence, India finds the condition of modernity (represented visually and spatially by the city of Bombay) to be a challenge to its organic unity. The central problem of modernity, as this rather conservative critique has it, is the distortion of community. And this can be understood in optical terms: a certain blurring of Indians' capacity for mutual recognition has scrambled the hierarchical and gendered principles that used to define their roles in relation to one another. The result is a chaotic disordering, which echoes the fears that Arjuna voiced to Krishna in the beginning of the *Bhagavad Gita* (and which the latter goes on to reject): "The sins of men who violate the family create a social upheaval and erode the eternal laws of caste and family duty."[71]

We have already diagnosed Bharati's blindness as a sign of the struggle she hosts so that her children may thrive. An implication is that the malady concentrated inside her has a potentially epidemic reach. So too, then, does the pathogen that triggered the response. If not for Maa's self-sacrifice—or, more precisely, the goddess's valiant struggle within her—all of India might succumb to blindness. Indeed, there is an implication that it already has.

Consider this: Bharati's sons seem to have grown to adulthood with their faculties intact. Nevertheless, they remain impaired when it comes to essential truths: who their brothers are, who their parents are, and where the *shakti* that protects them comes from. How will Christians, Muslims, and modern Hindus come together if they can't recognize the matriarch from whom all three have sprung? As laid out in the previous section, this is a debate basic to Indian nationalist discourse: Is civil society even possible without the acknowledgment of common origins?

But let's wrap up this final section on Maa by recentering the challenge around the deity's own perspective and motivations. Now the question becomes, What can she do to make herself visible? How can she gain the recognition that is her due in the modern order? It seems that the rules of the game have changed a bit since village days. For twenty-two years she has possessed a faithful mortal, and yet for her pains—for the pains of both of them!—she has received precious little attention in the city. How, in short, will this overlooked and disrespected peasant goddess come into her own as Mother India?

What does a goddess want? In narrative terms, what she wants is a room of her own.

The dénouement of our revised goddess drama occurs at the same point as in our previous telling. There, we identified the sacred site on the city's frontier as a Hindu temple dedicated to Shiva in His most ecumenically welcoming aspect, namely Sai Baba. Shirdi's saint as avatar, Shiva's "secular" mask—that is already fairly complex. But in fact more typical of the history of Hindu holy places in Maharashtra would be for a rustic site like this to have originally been consecrated to a mother goddess. Over the past two hundred years, many such cultic centers have been adopted by upper-caste Hindu patrons. In the typical pattern, temple structures are built on top of sites that might have started out as sacred rocks, anthills, or snake holes.[72]

Is the goddess, then, simply reclaiming what was hers by right? In vacating her host at the "Sai Baba temple," our wandering goddess accomplishes a feat of assimilation into the presiding deity. And here let us follow the Shaktas in identifying that sublime presence as the Great Goddess. After all, why should the miracle be attributed to Shiva, any more than to an ecumenically minded Muslim fakir? The text provides ample support for yet another interpretation. In the end, it's not so hard to see that our goddess does all the work by herself.

Shakti, as we have noted before, manifests itself as heat. As such, first our goddess was fever, then she was lightning, and perhaps in this climactic scene she is fire.[73] Bharati enters the temple crawling; she lowers her head to the floor, and when she raises it we see, of course, the much-discussed bloodstain. And we noted how, in anointing the woman's brow with her own blood, as it were, the deity reinscribes the wound from the fateful night of twenty-two years before—the last time Bharati went running through the woods, the last time a Muslim served as witness in an hour of need—and breaks open the old aperture.

So this is what the blood really marks: an exit wound. Demonstrating the overwhelming heat the goddess can generate—the very fever-heat liberated from her human host—flames light up in Sai Baba's eyes. The deity has left her mount to enter the idol. Now the effigy has become "charged" and can dispense *shakti* to the assembled faithful. A portion of fiery energy flies back to clear the gaze of Devi's chosen servant, and then flames erupt in all the lamps hanging among the congregants. The Goddess's temple is open for business!

The movement traced here is argued theologically and prefigured narratively in the central scripture of the Shakta tradition, the sixth-century *Devi Mahatmya*. The Great Goddess can assimilate or disseminate discrete goddesses depending on Her divine needs. But in the end, She is the divine totality. When confronting the demon Shumbha—a particularly troublesome male adversary—the Goddess Herself schools him on this point, and does so in spectacular fashion:

"I alone exist in this world. Who else is there besides Me?
Look, Evil One, at these manifestations of mine as they merge
  back into Me!"
Then all the goddesses, led by Brahmani, merged into the body
of the Goddess. And all that remained was the Great Mother.[74]

As the trump card played at the culmination of this chapter's game of hermeneutical one-upmanship, the statement has a certain finality to it.

*Nice try, boys . . . although you really should say one-up*woman*ship. But after one more song and dance involving goddesses and demons, Mahatmas and civil society, your old Maa asks you to recognize one last thing.*

Yes, if there's to be a last word with which to close this chapter, it belongs by rights to Maa. Not to any superhuman or supernatural personality—a mother goddess, or even the all-encompassing Goddess—but to the poor, mortal woman Bharati. We have given thoroughgoing attention to the movie's withholding from Bharati of her eyesight but not to the way it deprives her of her voice. If she were invited to reflect on her own role in this story—on her long, strange journey from tradition into a golden future—what would she say?

We imagine it going something like this:

I'm a simple woman, beta. I'm not educated—it's not for me to make films or write books. But when lettered people talk about "giving women a voice," often what they're saying is, they've forgotten to listen. If what the film shows you is a mother who seems irrational and passive—dependent on some outside force to give her shakti—*that's because the folks in charge haven't left any room in their fancy movie for ordinary, everyday conversations.*

When we talk amongst ourselves, Hindu women know different. We know all about shakti *in our everyday lives. We know as a matter of fact that the thing that sets us apart is that inside each of us there's natural energy of all kinds—and the men know it too. It didn't take a goddess to give us what we've already got:* adya shakti *(primordial power),* matru shakti *(mother's power),* stri shakti *(women's power).*

That's what gets a woman up in the morning. And that's how—listen up, boys!—a woman goes about her daily business. Every day, in little ways, whether you're paying attention or not: making asadhya *(the undoable) into* sadhya *(the doable),* asambhav *(the impossible) into* sambhav *(the possible) . . . all in a day's work for Maa.*[75]

"The impossible into the possible" . . . yes, the phrase has got a ring to it.

Conclusion

EXCUSE ME, PLEASE

. . . .

T O MAKE the impossible possible . . . ," sing the three brothers in the famous first line of the finale number. And then, "Together in one place, we three united / Amar Akbar Anthony!" Our translation here of those first words—*anhoni ko honi kar de*—is idiomatic, conveying something of the original but masking an interesting ambiguity. Complicating this single line will be the last task we undertake in this lengthy study of Manmohan Desai's epic.

Amar Akbar Anthony's finale sequence is the justly celebrated culmination of a narrative extravaganza. When the brothers finally join forces to infiltrate the robbers' den, the rabbits come leaping out of Desai's hat; it is the feat of a showman at the height of his powers. The "Anhoni Ko Honi Kar De" song to which the action unfolds is well known and well loved—a musical metonym for the film and the secularist ideals for which it is remembered. And yet, up to this point in the book, we have shown the finale relatively little attention.

The theme of this musical number is cooperation, or as the Indian national motto would have it, Unity in Diversity. Once the brothers are united, with their diverse talents and powers combined, they become invincible. In the end—as far as the narrative struggle against the racketeer Robert goes—the heroes realize their heroism by putting their interdependency to work. Indeed, at a superficial level, the whole movie might be thought to conclude with the lesson that the three brothers, although different, are equal.

Yet each of the chapters representing a brother has already laid claim to the finale. We have championed Amar's encompassment as the one-man band that incorporates India's multitudes, Akbar's disguise as a means of mastery over illusion, and Anthony's manipulation of the priest's vestments as a kind of self-mastery. In each case, the emphasis has been on the truth hidden beneath the masquerade. Each brother's disguise says something about that character, and we have followed what the implications of this play with identity might be for reading the text as a whole.

Our interest in the first line of their song together concerns a related question of illusion and reality. But here we pursue the inquiry on a level that goes beyond personal or social identity and enters more "meta" territory. What are the conditions of possibility that Amar, Akbar, and Anthony are singing about?

In terms of narrative, the dialogue that cues the brothers to burst into song is initiated by Zabisko, who is stymied by Jenny's refusal to marry him. How can he persuade her to consent? "What does she like?" asks "Father Anthony" in English, stepping in to offer counsel. "She likes . . . *nachna* (dancing), *gana* (singing)," says the heavy, and when Akbar advises him to dance and sing, he sadly confesses he isn't capable of either. "No problem, my son, absolutely no problem," Anthony assures him, and switches back to Hindi. "To get her consent for your marriage, *I'll* sing." "I'll dance," says Akbar. "And I," says Amar, flourishing his accordion, "will play." "Thank you," Zabisko answers humbly. "But Father—how's this all going to happen? It all seems impossible *(anhoni)*." "To make the impossible possible . . . ," Anthony begins, ". . . that's our business," completes Akbar. Amar vamps into a waltz, and the brothers kick off the film's last dance.

But what is the referent of "impossible"? What is this "it" of which Zabisko speaks, the "it" we understand to be qualified by *anhoni*—"nonexistence" or "nonpotential"?[1] What do our heroes propose to convert into a condition of *honi*—"existence," "that which will come to pass"? To stay at the level of narrative, it would appear that this something that's not in the cards is a causal disjuncture: the proposition that three motley strangers singing and dancing will make Jenny decide to marry Zabisko.

And to be sure, that doesn't seem to make a whole lot of sense—for who would consent to marry the brute Zabisko, even with his fantastic muscles and groovy poncho? "It" is indeed an implausible proposition . . . in the real world, or even in a fictive world conditioned by realism.

In the world of *Amar Akbar Anthony,* however, characters do break into song and dance. And the shift into music does have the power of rupturing narrative logic (the seemingly prescripted, foreordained, *honi*) and creating something unpredictable. In fact, by the movie's own terms, it's hard to think of anything other than the introduction of music that could make a change of heart in Jenny feasible! Of course, it's only certain characters in the story that command music in this way: the three heroes and to a lesser extent their ladyloves. So one way to read the statement is as Zabisko's protest against the fantastic world in which he finds himself trapped. Nearly three hours in, does he *still* expect the film's course of events to follow the norms of realism? What a hopeless square.[2]

Another construction of *anhoni* situates it on the ideological plane. In the film's allegory of the nation, what is "unfeasible" to an antinational villain like Zabisko or Robert is the secularist vision of Hindu-Muslim-Christian unity. India's diverse communities overcoming their divisions in recognition of something more authentic—their shared national essence? Bah! *Anhoni hai*—not gonna happen. The possibility of national unity is the enemy's blind spot, precisely what the villain in a film like this never bargains for. His schemes are built on the assumption that true patriots will never get it together.[3] Note that this interpretation lends a certain stirring resonance to the bit of dialogue that launches the song. Anthony begins, "To make the *anhoni, honi* . . ." His brother, the model Muslim, delivers the call to arms: "that's *our* business." Hindu, Muslim, Christian, all in business together.

So far, so good. But the Hindi of Anthony's spoken line runs thus: *Anhoni ko honi karna.* And the first line when the brothers burst into song runs thus: *Anhoni ko honi kar de.* The distinction is one of verb forms. *Karna* is the infinitive: "to do" or "to make." *Kar de,* on the other hand, is an imperative: "make [it so]." What's more, a rather complex grammar permits Hindi speakers to pack a good deal of affective and context-sensitive fine-tuning into concise formulations. To choose *kar de* over an alternative imperative form, like *karo,* is to shape the message, address it, and deliver it in specific ways. *Kar de* is familiar, but not necessarily rude. And embedded in the form is a request, an implicit "do me a favor." The song's first line, then, is less an order than an exhortation, or an intimately phrased plea: "C'mon, let's make the impossible possible." There is also the suggestion of an invocation: "C'mon, let's bring the impossible into being."

The question now becomes, Who is being addressed? To whom is agency being assigned in this quixotic project of making that-which-will-not-come-about actually come about? Are the brothers even voicing this from their own perspective? Whose words are these, and how are our three heroes positioned as speakers?

One possibility is that they are paraphrasing Zabisko's own request to themselves. Translating this variant involves placing quotes within quotes. "'Let's make the impossible possible, the possible impossible.' Once we have all three in one place: Amar, Akbar, Anthony." In this reading, what the brothers are doing is voicing an incantation or magic spell on behalf of somebody else: the tongue-tied Zabisko, and perhaps by extension everybody else, diegetic and extradiegetic, who wants to watch the wonder-workers bend the rules of realism.

Our masqueraders are thus also ventriloquists. A complementary way to open some distance between the brothers and the words they speak—to question their "authorship" or "ownership" of the statement—would be to interpret these lines as a poetic declamation. The string of names at the end then corresponds to the "signature line" *(maqta)* in which an Urdu poet delivers his or her nom-de-plume *(takhallus)*. Compounding the distancing effect is the way the film sets up this self-naming moment as an extension of the masquerade. For to go by the narrative logic, at this point the brothers are still trading in aliases: "Amar" is the leader of the "Amar Lal and Brothers Band"; "Akbar" is his own fictive "uncle," the tailor; and "Anthony" is of course "Father Anthony." The narrative reveal happens after the song. "Who are these people?" demands Robert, and our heroes step up and discard their disguises: "Inspector Amar." "This unworthy is known as Akbar Ilahabadi." "Anthony. Anthony Gonsalves."[4]

There is another possibility, a more radical interpretation that can be put on *Anhoni ko honi kar de.* The phrasing *kar de* configures the recip-ient of its request as both singular and intimately familiar. For Hindi-speaking Hindus, Muslims, and Christians alike, it is a form appropriate to prayer. Could it be, then, that our heroes are calling on God—the divine agent the three address by different names, but have now come to recognize as the unity ruling them all?

"Bring the impossible to pass, cause what is written to be unwritten. Here present before You, we three [servants]: Amar, Akbar, Anthony." This would explain the visual performance of the three supplicants. As they sing and dance their way through the number, each time the chorus returns and the brothers name themselves, they face the camera while assuming a posture of prayer: namaste, salaam, the sign of the cross.

The Almighty! In the last analysis, it is surely He (or, to return to the end of the previous chapter, She) who is the ultimate arbiter in these matters of possibility: the working of miracles within the film as well as the unifying of Indians who persist in calling on the Lord by different names. But in fact, at the risk of courting the charge of blasphemy, we three authors propose an additional, yet more final analysis. We draw attention to the most naked example in the film of a character breaking the fourth wall in an appeal to the audience. It occurs in the middle of the "Anhoni Ko Honi Kar De" number, when the heroes first fall to their knees in prayer. Amar sings out his name and turns his head to the right, winking at Akbar. Akbar follows suit and turns his head to wink at Anthony. And then Anthony turns his own head to face directly into the camera. Who is he winking at? He's winking at *you*.

This book has documented many instances when the film's characters communicate with deities. When the divine presence is mediated through a visual artifact—the images of Jesus and Mary, the Sai Baba effigy—*Amar Akbar Anthony* follows Hindi film convention in alternating close-ups of the icon with the supplicant's face, giving the camera, and thus the spectator, a god-like view of human devotion.[5] And in two scenes in which there is prayer but no icon—when Akbar rescues Salma from the flames and she gives him news of his family, and when Kishanlal revisits his old home in the slum and offers a prayer to Bhagvan—the characters face the camera to exhibit their reverence. Anthony's wink likewise cites this convention of frontal address. But at the same time it pushes the proverbial envelope. It might be thought of as an interpellating gesture, a "hailing" of the viewing subject, an invitation to enter the ideological world of the film.[6] *Oh, hi there—are you laughing? Then you're already in on the joke.*

FIGURE 27. Jalopy

And with that, we are back to our first, cajoling translation: "C'mon, let's make the impossible possible." For the spectator truly is endowed with godlike power when it comes to the credibility of the film. The success of the whole *Amar Akbar Anthony* enterprise rests on the viewer's suspension of disbelief—her or his willingness to let go of the norms and hobbled horizons of realism, both aesthetic and political. Pertinent in this regard is the Urdu word *musafir,* "fellow traveler," often used in address to the audience of poetry or song. Friend, will you laugh with us? Will you travel with us beyond what's practical or reasonable? Come! Follow us through cinematic illusion as we expose the realist project itself as illusion. It's then that a new world—a new Bombay, a new India—will become possible: a society of the future, in which Hindu, Muslim, and Christian recognize each other as true brothers. And as our heroes, and their ladies, ride off in an old jalopy into India's future (Figure 27), we hope their wish comes true: let the impossible become possible.

APPENDIX

•

NOTES

•

BIBLIOGRAPHY

•

ACKNOWLEDGMENTS

•

INDEX

•

Appendix

FILM SYNOPSIS

This synopsis of the film's narrative is offered as a comprehensive guide to help orient readers as they navigate the book's arguments. *Amar Akbar Anthony* is a long film that tells a complicated story. The story is unrealistic—we could even say antirealistic—but it is not illogical or incoherent. However, both its narrative logic and its comic effects rely on the dense accumulation of many details. Appreciating the film in its full coherence requires unpacking these details in relation to one another and in their citation of signifiers external to the text. In short, although this synopsis is a summary, it is a long and textured one. To readers interested in a more streamlined account we recommend the second chapter of Sidharth Bhatia's *Amar Akbar Anthony,* which delivers a lively plot synopsis, and the sixth chapter of Vijay Mishra's *Bollywood Cinema,* which provides a structural breakdown of the text, scene by scene.[1]

Along with narrative, this synopsis takes note of several other aspects of *Amar Akbar Anthony.* We have emphasized the film's organization of space, with matches and disjunctures noted between the Bombay of diegesis and its geographical coordinates in the world beyond the text. We have been attentive to visual symbolism, especially motifs that encode social difference as defined by religion and class. And we have been correspondingly interested in language use. In the Bombay of *Amar Akbar Anthony,* as in real life, the way people speak is another important index of social difference.[2]

Prologue Sequence: The Historical Nation as Slum

Following the official notice of certification by the Central Board of Film Censors (release date: May 10, 1977), the screen is filled by another official-looking notice: "Central Jail." A newly free KISHANLAL (Pran) emerges from the prison gate. Dressed in a white servant's uniform, he holds some meager funds in his hand. He returns to his neighborhood, a humble-looking settlement to be identified as a Koliwada—an ethnic enclave marked by features of both villages and slums[3]—in the Bombay suburb of Bandra. The lanes are decked festively with miniature Indian flags, for the date is August 15, Indian Independence Day. If the bulk of the film is understood to take place in the present—that is, 1977, the year of the film's release—calculations voiced by the characters would place this anterior sequence in 1955. Kishanlal is welcomed back by a neighbor who offers a Muslim salaam, but a Hindu neighbor, Gangu Bai, warns him of the parlous state in which he will find his family.

Kishanlal arrives home to find his three little sons starving—and squabbling—and his wife, BHARATI (Nirupa Roy), afflicted with tuberculosis. He offers sweets to placate the children, as well as gifts: a toy cart to the MIDDLE SON (Master Ravi), a toy cricket bat to the YOUNGEST SON (Master Tito), and what appears to be a toy pistol to the ELDEST SON (Master Bittu).[4] The boys go right back to their quarrel, with the second son now demanding the gun. The pitifully coughing Bharati informs her husband that his boss had neglected to provide for her, as promised, during the period of Kishanlal's confinement. But she would have refused the money anyway, since she didn't want to raise her children on what she considers the wages of sin.[5] On the pendant around her neck we can see the image of a Hindu goddess. On his way to confront his treacherous boss, Kishanlal encounters his eldest son burying the rather realistic-looking pistol in a bed of earth across from their crude little cottage. "If my little brother sees it, he'll want it for himself," the boy explains.

"Happy Birthday" reads the icing on a fancy cake, part of a celebration for a BABY GIRL (Baby Sabina)—evidently her first—that also involves a private movie show with a home projector. The lifestyle trappings of Kishanlal's dandyish boss ROBERT (Jeevan) are at once luxurious and Westernized. His daughter's birthday would appear to be coincident with that of the nation, although the Indian colors are nowhere to be seen in his home. As the film (whatever it is) winds down and the lights flash on, he hands the baby to a nanny in a short-skirted dress. He sees a newcomer has entered the scene.

But the drama of Kishanlal's return is deflated by Robert's declaration to his guests—who seem to consist entirely of his henchmen, clad mostly in suits and ties[6]—that he doesn't recognize his former driver. His tone is cold, peremptory, and English accented. Frank and emotional by contrast, Kishanlal reminds him of his service, introducing a brief flashback that reverses the roles: an agitated Robert, dressed in a foppish chalk-striped suit, comes rushing to Kishanlal's humble door. He pleads with Bharati to see her husband. "You are a faithful servant," he informs his chauffeur, "and it's the duty of a faithful servant to help his master." In a development that all-too-realistically cites a recurring scandal of life in Bombay, the rich man has killed a poor man with his car and wants his driver to take the blame and the jail sentence.[7] Robert vows to look after the family, maintaining them at a rate double Kishanlal's pay—a promise that Kishanlal increases to triple post-flashback.

"Triple—forget it," Kishanlal laments, back in the master's mansion, "you didn't give them so much as one anna."[8] Turning his back, the boss refreshes his drink at the private bar. "I was wondering why this whisky didn't taste quite right. Silly me—I forgot the ice." Robert has no time for useless talk. He disavows any personal obligation, but stands by the principle that honest work is always due fair compensation. Staining his own shoe with whisky, he thrusts it at the desperate Kishanlal to polish with his sleeve. By way of payment, he offers a single anna. "To you the misfortunes of the poor are no more than a joke. . . . Robert *Seth,* you're drunk—not with liquor but with your own wealth. I swear on my children someday I'll get even with you!"[9] Fighting off the goons tasked with ejecting him, Kishanlal seizes a pistol from one of them and fires several rounds into Robert. The villain cackles, revealing the chain-mail vest shielding his chest. Kishanlal makes a break for it, crashing through a window, fleeing to the garage, and taking off in a car that a dismayed Robert realizes is carrying a stash of gold in the trunk. He sends a second car after it.[10]

The chase begins at night, running through a suburban landscape marked by middle-class housing developments and adjacent lots that have the look of future construction sites. The pursuit car runs aground in one of these empty lots; the fugitive Kishanlal catches his breath back in the lanes of his slum neighborhood. Awaiting him at home is a note from his wife, passed on by his eldest son. In it Bharati announces her decision to kill herself so he won't feel bound to spend money on her care; whatever he earns should instead be dedicated to the support of their sons. To replace her own wifely care, she leaves him her amulet of the goddess Santoshi Maa.[11] Distraught, Kishanlal gathers his children and continues the flight in Robert's car. He is seen by Gangu Bai and another local resident who works as a police constable.

Robert's heavies are back on his tail. Kishanlal races through the slum—still strung with its patriotic bunting—and arrives at a gated garden with a statue of Mahatma Gandhi in the middle and a Catholic church fronting one side. By this point, it is perhaps very early in the morning. This location is identified as the entrance to Borivali National Park, although the site is a cinematic composite bearing no resemblance to its nominal referent in the real city. A desperate Kishanlal pulls up behind a vintage auto with green detailing, hurries his children into the park, and unloads them at the statue's feet, instructing the eldest to wait until he returns. But the boy resists the abandonment; he runs into the street after his father's car and is promptly hit and thrown to the side by Robert's men, who don't even slow down. He collapses on the pavement, a red streak marking his forehead. The camera shifts to Bharati, who is shown running wildly through a dark forest. (This location is also to be identified as Borivali Park, which it does indeed resemble, although the actual park is too far from Bandra to reach on foot however wildly one may be running.) A bolt from the heavens fells a branch on the unhappy woman, who collapses beneath it, a streak of blood on her forehead.

"*Ahiṃsā paramo dharmaḥ,*" reads the Sanskrit inscription on the pedestal of the Gandhi statue, a favorite phrase of the Mahatma: Nonviolence is the supreme law.[12] Announcing to the youngest that he will return with food, the second son now strays from the meeting place. Meanwhile the chase has continued into a hilly, forested area. Kishanlal loses control of his car, which tumbles down the hillside, crashes, and catches fire. Robert's men start after it on foot—the crate of gold visible in the wreckage—but a truck full of policemen arrives on the scene, and the hoods, who disavow any connection with the crash, are warned away by the officer in charge. One of the constables is Kishanlal's and Bharati's neighbor. Recognizing the car, he sadly concludes that his friend has perished in it, along with his three children.

Cut back to the garden with the Gandhi statue, where a bearded and capped Muslim man, HAIDER ALI (Shivraj), kneels in a bamboo grove quietly praying. Interrupted in his devotions by the squalling of a baby, he discovers the youngest of the three boys. Framed with the child in his arms and Gandhi in the background, he addresses Allah: "What strange people there are in Your creation! They give birth to children, and when they can't provide for them, they abandon them." He tucks the baby into his car—a jalopy trimmed in green—and drives off just in time to miss the middle child, who has rushed back to the park with some bread for his brother.[13] On his way home through the woods, Haider Ali comes across a woman lying on the road beneath a fallen branch. He helps her up; her forehead is still red with blood. And when she discovers she can no longer see and despairingly repeats her wish to die, he offers a gentle admonishment: "Sister, to commit suicide is the greatest sin of all. After all, there may be others who also have claims to your life." In the background the baby wails from the car. "Perhaps you're right," answers Bharati. "That's why Bhagvan has given me this punishment, and taken the light from my eyes." Haider Ali guides her into the car and offers to take her back home. An exhausted Bharati rests her head on the seat in front of her, unaware that the crying child who sits in it is her biological son.

There follows a sequence of short cuts. We see Kishanlal, recovering from under the bushes where he has been thrown by the wreck, discover the crate full of gold ingots. We see Haider Ali, Bharati, and the third son together in the vintage car. The Muslim man describes how Allah has written the little boy's care into his own destiny, and the Hindu woman calls on Bhagvan to preserve them both in happiness; as if in response, the skies thunder anew. We see the middle son seek refuge in the doorway of a church. Haider Ali drops Bharati off in the old neighborhood—toy flags still fluttering, one day later—and when her neighbors greet her, the policeman reveals the sad news: he has seen "with [his] own eyes" how her husband and children perished in an accident. *"No-o-o!"* shrieks the blind woman in agony. The denial, as we all-seeing spectators know, is of course quite correct—and corroborated diegetically by a telling detail. In a typical Bollywood gesture, Bharati beats her wrists at the wall to shatter her bangles, an adornment that marks a woman's married status. Watchful viewers will notice the bangles don't break.

Back at the church, white-robed priests exclaim in English at the sight of a child, ill with fever, collapsed on their front steps. The senior PADRE (Nazir Hussain) finds a letter in the little boy's pocket: Bharati's suicide note. Concluding that the mother killed herself and the father abandoned the child out of poverty, the priest gathers him in his arms. "Come on, son," he says, "God will protect you." An ecclesiastical organ swells in the background, and the camera pans up to the statue in the foyer: Mary cradling the infant Jesus.

Finally we are taken back to the spot on the curb where the first of the three boys lies unconscious, red streak of blood on his face, after having been hit by his father's pursuers. A police jeep enters the scene, INSPECTOR KHANNA (Kamal Kapoor) at the wheel. Although taciturn by contrast with the other two foster fathers, he duly rescues the child, instructing the attending constable to lay him safely in the jeep. When a bedraggled Kishanlal returns on foot, his crate of treasure in his arms, he sees the jeep approaching and turns to face a roadside wall, pretending to urinate.[14] The gold has exerted an unhappy effect. Blinded in his own way—or perhaps intoxicated, like his nemesis, by wealth— Kishanlal misses the chance to reunite with his son. He blunders back to the Gandhi statue, where a freeze-frame captures his anguish as he calls out the missing boy's name: *"Amar—!"*[15]

Time Lapse into the Present

The next scene is established with an exterior shot of the most famous Catholic site in the greater Bombay area, Bandra's Mount Mary church. (It is implied that this church is distinct from the one portrayed before, which adjoins in some way the park with the Gandhi statue, fictitiously located in the outer suburb of Borivali. The Bandra church's name is given toward the movie's end as St. Thomas, a reference to the Apostle Thomas, whom many Indian Christians believe to have brought the Gospel to the Subcontinent.) The middle brother is shown in the confessional, tidy in his school uniform. He confesses to the Padre that he has sold his schoolbooks, following up with an explanation: he used the money to buy a coffin for a pauper who had died on the street. The priest is moved by his generosity, but gently instructs his ward that the correct course would have been to inform the police. "What?" booms a deep voice, "No, Father, I don't go to the police station," and in revealing the confessional's occupant to have grown into the strapping and stylish ANTHONY GONSALVES (Amitabh Bachchan), the camera accomplishes a time lapse of some twenty-two years.

Anthony gives the law a wide berth. Given his appearance and manner—he projects a certain streetwise swagger—he can't expect a fair reception from the police. No sooner would he show his face than he'd be tossed in the lockup. The priest retorts that it would do him good to spend time there. It seems his ward routinely embroils himself in neighborhood brawls. Anthony protests that his last antagonist, a dealer of bootleg hooch, had it coming to him. Sure, he follows a similar line of work, but he has a license and his product is quality—perhaps the Padre would like to try some? His guardian is not amused, warning Anthony that if he doesn't give up the hustle, he will file a complaint with the police himself. "Then along with me," Anthony retorts, "make sure you file a complaint about Him," and gestures at the baby Jesus in Mary's arms that adorns the altar. Anthony tithes 50 percent of his earnings to the church for the upkeep of the poor; he considers Jesus his business partner.

It becomes clear that Anthony is a sort of informal community leader—a *dada,* or big brother figure—when a young man enters the church to seek his help in an emergency. Just outside the gates, a hit-and-run driver has knocked down a woman.[16] A crowd of onlookers has gathered around the prostrate figure. Anthony summons a taxi to take her to the hospital and looks with compassion on the gray-haired woman, simply dressed in a drab sari, on whose face the place of the red *bindi* dot and vermilion streak that would mark her as a married Hindu woman has been taken by a streak of blood. We spectators recognize the victim as his own mother, Bharati, although Anthony does not.

News of the accident also reaches a slick-looking young police officer, who receives the details on his office telephone. He proceeds to "Nanavati Hospital" (located close by his office in the diegetic Bandra, although the real Nanavati is up the road in Vile Parle). The scene shifts to an office inside the hospital, where a pretty female doctor is going through the motions of giving a checkup to a flashily dressed young man. Calling on Allah's mercy, he names his afflictions in poetical Urdu: "Pain in my heart, pain in my waist, pain in my liver. . . ." These are the thoroughly modern and professional SALMA (Neetu Singh) and her flirtatious admirer, AKBAR ILAHABADI (Rishi Kapoor).[17] There is nothing the matter with Akbar except his inconvenient desire to spend time with Salma, who's either busy at the hospital—hence his habit of calling on her as a patient—or confined at home under the thumb of her traditionalist father. But as he explains, today's errand is a special one. He is a singer of *qawwali*, a music genre whose lyrics follow a poetic tradition originating in the symbolism and teachings of Sufism, and he has brought her an invitation to his concert. The playful Akbar is thus revealed as an individual with an exceptional gift. Tonight is impossible, Salma begins to protest: either her father will forbid her from attending or he will insist on bringing the whole family. Then a nurse interrupts to say that an injured woman whose treatment Salma is monitoring needs blood for a transfusion. Salma recalls that Akbar's is the right blood type. "My blood—that's nothing!" Akbar exclaims, rolling up his sleeve. "If it's for your sake, your slave is prepared to give up his life."

Title Sequence and First Song

A white-coated colleague addresses Salma as the transfusion gets underway. "What are these people's names?" "Amar," says the police officer AMAR KHANNA (Vinod Khanna), lying in the leftmost of a row of three beds. "Akbar," says the man in the middle. "Anthony," says the donor on the right. The credits roll, starting with the three stars' names, and with the title's appearance the singer Mohamed Rafi's voice bursts forth on the soundtrack, inaugurating the first of its seven songs, "Yeh Sach Hai Koi Kahani Nahin" (This Is True, It's No Story), which celebrates the bonds of family. "Blood is blood / It isn't water," the singer repeats, as the camera follows the tubes that mingle the blood of the three and flow in one stream to the mother, Bharati. "Flowers are recognized by their color and scent / People are recognized by their blood . . . . / All who have produced this blood have drunk the milk of their mother. / Shouldn't the price of this be redeemed?" The nurses attending the patients wear Western-style uniforms with skirts that end below the knee. The look, as well as profession, is typical of Christian women. But the most conspicuous marker of religious affiliation in this scene is the view from the windows that back each of our three heroes in their beds. Amar's window opens on a grand and antique-looking Hindu temple, Akbar's on a domed mosque, and Anthony's on a church with Gothic towers.

Neighborhood Antics and Second Song

We see Anthony in action as the enforcer of his own law in the corner of Bandra people have begun to call Anthonyville.[18] Sprung from jail, the locality's previous boss, RAGHU (Hercules), has been making a nuisance of himself in the saloon he used to run. This is a dark, raw space that serves not only liquor but also meat, shown sizzling in kebab form on a griddle; at the same time the walls bear Catholic devotional art alongside pinup girls, and there is a small personal shrine. Anthony is looking tough in a green leather jacket (although it does sport a stars-and-stripes patterned patch in the shape of a peace sign). He makes short work of his rival with acrobatic moves that include throwing him through a brick wall (English words are scrawled to one side: "Jesus Loves Me") and pummeling him from a large, chandelier-like light fixture in the shape of a wagon wheel.[19] The endgame takes place outside, where we watch along with other spectators, mainly neighborhood children, as the rival is disposed of in a rubbish-hauling truck. A sign on the building shows how the business has changed hands: "Anthony's Country Bar, License Number 108."[20]

"Allah be praised, Brother Anthony!" The folksy and unmistakably Muslim figure who approaches, marked by his skullcap and *lungi* wrap, is the boyish Akbar. In a pleasantry that draws on the civic rhetoric of the Indira era, he compliments the kingpin on the success of his neighborhood cleanup drive. It seems a while has passed since their last meeting— possibly the blood transfusion—and Akbar has spent that time preparing for another concert, to take place that very night. He offers an invitation card to Anthony, who volunteers his services in the matter of moving any unsold tickets. "By the kindness of Allah," responds the artiste, "we've got a completely full house."

The scene outside the recital hall, South Bombay's Birla Krida Kendra, is lively indeed. Akbar drives up with his musicians in his adoptive father's old car, which now sports red rose-and-crescent motifs to complement the green trim. It has also been inscribed with the potent 786 of Islamic numerology and with a comic couplet he reads to his fans through a mouth stuffed with paan: "Take Allah's name first / Then open the door." Placards and signs proclaim Akbar Ilahabadi to be "King of Qawal."[21] All the members of the crowd, including young women and girls, are dressed in Western-style attire. The sole exception is a blind flower vendor in a modest sari: Bharati, who approaches the young star and addresses him, per convention, as "Son." She has come to repay his kindness to her in the only way she feels capable—by offering him her blessing. Akbar responds by calling her "Mother" and asks her to tie a string of flowers around his wrist.[22] He heads into the theater, and Bharati busies herself seeking a ticket. "No, Mother," comes the reply, "there are no tickets left." But a tall fellow in the crowd recognizes her and makes himself known: it's another benefactor, Anthony Gonsalves.[23] Learning that she hasn't been able to obtain a seat, he offers her his own. He'll escort her inside as the holder of a "special pass" and sit down on the floor.

The curtain rises. The musicians and chorus are seated before a backdrop centered on a big green heart inscribed with Urdu letters: *Akbar.* Swathed in Islamic green, the star makes his entrance with verve, leaping out of the wings. We watch with him from the stage as Salma's father TAYYAB ALI (Mukri) enters the theater, a diminutive Muslim gentleman turned out in an old-fashioned wool cap and frock coat. He leads six orthodox-looking women veiled in black, of whom the first can be seen, through the gauze, to be Salma. As they take their seats, Anthony and Bharati also arrive. Akbar launches into his number, "Parda Hai Parda" (There Is a Veil).

The lyrics of the *qawwali,* and the features of its production, are replete with Sufi symbolism. But on the narrative level, his flirtatious reiteration of the theme that "Behind the veil / There is a beloved / And if I don't succeed in unveiling that object of desire / Then my name isn't Akbar" has the effect of evoking reciprocal gestures of desire from Salma. First she unveils herself in answer to his declaration of love (and his flamboyant launch of the rose into her seat), then veils herself again in offended modesty, and finally approaches the stage to silence her suitor with a finger at his lips—to the ineffectual outrage of her walking stick–shaking father and the general delight of the other spectators. Also of note: as Akbar is singing of the veil motif, with successive layers of fabric floating before him, he is met by the answering gazes of the women who love him. His bride-to-be Salma watches him through the film of her own veil, and his mother Bharati strives to view the source of the wondrous voice through the obscuring veil of her blindness. To these two adoring fans may be added a third: Akbar's veiled affine Anthony, first among responders in the characteristic call-and-response pattern of the *qawwali* performance.

Enter Lakshmi: Romance and the Redemption of Middle-Class Hindu Respectability

Amar is summoned to the office of his foster father. Inspector Khanna gives him an assignment: A girl has been flagging down motorists on the highway and waylaying them to rob with her confederates. Her last victim was a photographer, who managed to take a snapshot of the offender. Amar dons a fawn-colored Perma-Prest suit and sets out in a civilian car. On the road he finds LAKSHMI (Shabana Azmi), correspondingly modish in a floral blouse and bell-bottom slacks. She addresses him forthrightly in English-studded urban Hindi, concluding a request to be dropped at the next crossing with a faux-demure "Please." Amar offers her a lift to her home. "I have many homes," she says, rattling off a list of Bombay neighborhoods. "If you give me the word, I'm even ready to come to your home." He plays along, replying that his own (implicitly respectable) house is not an appropriate place. He says he's keen to move on with her, but he's also anxious about the police. "I'll take you to the kind of place the police don't come," says Lakshmi, and directs him to a suburban construction site.

Once alone in this seemingly isolated spot, she makes a move for his wallet. When Amar resists, she threatens him with an accusation of rape and calls loudly for help. Her thuggish stepbrother RANJEET (Ranjeet, in a "special appearance") appears, along with several other hoodlums, and makes a blustering attempt to extort the money. Amar responds by flashing his police ID. This precipitates a melee, in which the young officer handily disposes of the chain- and knife-wielding baddies, although Ranjeet escapes. When police reinforcements arrive in a jeep, Amar is suavely wiping the dust off his aviator lenses. He is intrigued to find that Lakshmi has chosen to remain at the scene, her head bowed becomingly. "Please arrest me, Inspector Sahib," she implores.[24] Custody would at least offer respite from the shame of the life into which she has been forced by her wicked foster family. "Come with me," says the chivalrous Amar.

Lakshmi returns to her suburban seafront home and falsely informs her shrewish STEPMOTHER (Nadira, "special appearance") that Ranjeet has been arrested. Her stepmother slaps her in the face and berates her for failing to live up to the promise of the name Lakshmi—Goddess of Wealth. Scheming after the means to raise bail for her biological son, the Stepmother resolves to sell off the gold earrings that are the only adornment—and property—left to Lakshmi's widowed GRANDMOTHER (Protima Devi).[25] Over the Grandmother's protests that they are the one item she's saved for Lakshmi's dowry, she tries forcibly to remove the earrings. As the struggle ensues Amar steps in, backed up by a couple of constables.

"You seem to have a fondness for wearing jewelry," he says, producing a pair of handcuffs, "and what better jewelry than this?" Exit Stepmother, to indignant protests. When the Grandmother expresses her concern that Ranjeet—still at large—will return to exact his revenge, Amar offers his assurance that the police will place the house under twenty-four-hour surveillance. But the lease is in the wicked step-relatives' names, Lakshmi explains. What's more, with the rent in arrears, the landlord has served notice to evict all of them. "Fine, then. Why don't you both come with me?" says Amar, repeating his line from the previous scene. And to the Grandmother's query "Where?" he spells it out: "To my home." "*Ji?*" presses an emotional Lakshmi, her use of the honorific syllable heavily laden—it's tempting to say "pregnant"—with longing. "*Ji,*" confirms the sexy yet respectful sub-inspector.

Reversal of Fortune: Kishanlal and Robert

On a deserted shore a line of smugglers are hard at work offloading contraband. One struggling coolie, clad in a white servant's uniform, is tripped up by a smartly booted foot. Surprise! In the menial position is Robert, and the new chief racketeer, resplendent in the ensemble of dark suit, red waistcoat, and red Teddy Boy tie last seen on Robert, is none other than the beneficiary of his ill-gotten gains, Kishanlal himself. Whereas Robert has lost his proud, colonial-style mustache, Kishanlal has acquired a goatee, signaling the subcontinent-wide association of facial hair with masculine prowess. Turnabout is fair play: Robert's stumble has spilled the drink Kishanlal has been carrying onto his shoe, and in a freshly acquired English accent the parvenu sahib commands his lackey to polish it with his sleeve. "Where is my daughter?" begs the agonized Robert, his own accent completely gone. A brief flashback reveals that at some point on the fateful night of the origin tale a bedraggled Kishanlal had stolen into Robert's bedroom and abducted his daughter, the birthday girl, leaving only a note in his pajama top. "Have you remembered?" he begs. "Yes, now I remember." Kishanlal repeats a familiar line. "I was wondering why this whisky didn't taste quite right. Silly me—I had forgotten the ice." And now the icing on the cake: Kishanlal reaches into his vest and produces a one-anna tip, spelling out to Robert that it's the identical coin with which the latter had delivered the original insult many years before.

"Forgive me," pleads Robert. "Only tell me where my daughter is." Never, retorts Kishanlal: Robert has separated him from his family, abandoning them to penury, and he has committed himself to revenge by ensuring his nemesis suffers similarly. Nevertheless, Kishanlal claims he is not on Robert's level. He has sent the girl to be educated overseas and is looking after her as if she were his own child. Indeed, she is due back in Bombay imminently. Concluding this revelation by tossing his dregs in Robert's face, Kishanlal advances to the head of the column. In yet another recapitulation from the pre-credit sequence, Robert seizes a pistol from one of the boss's henchmen and pumps the contents into Kishanlal's back. Gloating, Kishanlal removes his shredded coat. Revealed is the bulletproof vest he has donned against just such a move—worn to protect not his chest but his back. At this point the cops, led by Inspector Khanna, arrive in a jeep. In the ensuing chaos Kishanlal and Robert flee in different directions. Having gotten his hands on another pistol, Robert is able to shoot down the inspector when the latter accosts him and to escape with a familiar prize: a crateful of contraband gold.

In his flight through a murky slum-like area, however, Robert gets tripped up for a second time. His obstacle this time is the long-legged Anthony. "Life gets a man running like that for two reasons," observes Anthony in full tough-guy mode, rhyming: "an Olympic *race,* or else a police *case.*" He notes the contents of the crate, some of which have spilled on the ground, describing them facetiously as imported biscuits. Robert appeals to him for a hiding place. Anthony calculates that if he turns in the malefactor he'll be awarded 20 percent of the recovered amount, on top of which he'll get his picture in the papers, "a first-class hero." A government jeep zooms past, and when the two emerge from the bushes, Anthony demands the fugitive's assurance that he hasn't raised his hand in violence against the police. "No, no, I swear." A businesslike Anthony lays out the terms of his protection: one third of the gold for Robert, one third for himself, and one third for his "partner" in heaven. After some waffling, Robert assents. Pressing his brow to the chunky crucifix at his new ally's chest, he swears "by Jesus" that there won't be any monkey business.

The uniformed Amar strides into a hospital room occupied by several female nurses, garbed Western style, and a bespectacled male doctor. In the bed, hooked up to a drip, is Inspector Khanna. His critical condition is corroborated in English by the doctor, who offers Amar the not-so-reassuring Indian line of reassurance: "We are trying our level best." Amar informs the doctor—and reminds us—that he was separated from his parents in childhood and that Inspector Khanna raised him as his own. "I don't want to become an orphan again," he says, a hard look on his face. The scene switches to a police dungeon, where the young officer, backed up by a pair of glaring electric lamps, confronts a lineup of low-lifes, small fry from Kishanlal's gang. Punctuating his words liberally with slaps, he declares that if anything happens to his "sahib" he won't let any of them escape with their lives. He demands to know who shot Inspector Khanna, concluding with a punch that topples the whole row like dominoes. The strong-arm tactics yield fruit, and after being snatched off the ground and faced with Amar's menacing fist, a prisoner names Robert as the culprit. A witness in the precinct office states that he has seen Robert in Anthonyville.

Amar and Anthony: Fictive Brotherhood
between Real Brothers

Amar comes roaring in his jeep into Anthonyville. He dispatches his constables into the neighborhood and turns his attention to a tall loafer decked out in high Seventies street fashion next to the sign *Anthony's Country Bar.* Rattled, Anthony turns his back to the police, but there's no evading the officer's gaze. After some back-and-forth involving Amar's no-nonsense questions and Anthony's attempts to put things on a friendlier basis, the policeman recognizes his evasive interlocutor as the fellow who had joined him not so long ago in donating blood to an old woman. A fellow, it comes back to him, named Anthony. "Where's Robert?" Amar presses, and when the cricket-based joke offered in response—"Robert? The fast bowler Andy Robert?[26] Oh, when the match ended he went right back to the West Indies"—fails to fly, Anthony finds himself literally collared in the officer's grasp. The wise guy loses his cool. He's lived in the area twenty-two years, he declares. Over that whole span of time he's been at pains to be cordial—on terms of *salaam*—with many men of the law. None has ever disrespected him as Amar has: "You're the first and last man [to do so]." Amar responds by shoving him to the ground. A crowd begins to collect. The setting is the same as that of Anthony's previous pugilistic triumph. Picking himself up, the local hero warns Amar that the only thing standing between him and a righteous beatdown is his own respect for the uniform.

Against the backdrop of a semiurban neighborhood—old-fashioned tiled-roof dwellings, modern apartments, and rude storage huts—Amar throws it down.[27] If the uniform is all that's holding Anthony back, he'll just take it off. Stripped down to their undershirts, each with a medallion around his neck, the two heroes square off. A local crowd gathers to watch: young men in Western dress, a sprinkling of older people, women, Muslims. In a rollicking sequence in which Anthony's comic banter and the theatrical moves of both are accented by musical quotes from cowboy movies and Hong Kong kung fu films, Amar submits Anthony to a thorough public drubbing. The outcome is put briefly in doubt, however, when Anthony is cast onto a large public cross and calls on his celestial partner for help. "Can we go fifty-fifty in this rumble too? . . . It's a question of honor." He gets in a few licks. But the lawman (and older brother) carries the day, and before the eyes of his neighborhood constituency, Anthony finds himself lifted on the shoulders of his shorter but beefier opponent, flung into a palm-leaf shack—flushing a variety of livestock—and retrieved, only to be thrown unceremoniously into the back of the jeep, just as he had tossed his rival Raghu into the refuse truck in a previous sequence.

Revived with a splash of water in the holding cell, a bruised Anthony acts largely unrepentant, bantering through the bars at the desk-bound Amar until the cop barks at him to shut up. A calming note is introduced when a drably clad woman enters the office: Bharati, bearing a walking stick and a basket of flowers. "Amar, son, I made sure to bring your favorite flowers today." Amar thanks her affectionately, remarking on the trouble she goes to in order to visit him daily. Recognizing her, Anthony calls "Mother!" from the cell, and the blind woman identifies his voice. Learning from Amar that Anthony has been locked up, she protests, "But son, he's a very good boy. He also gave his blood for me. He's as much of a son to me as you are." Behind the bars Anthony laughs. "What are you saying, Mother? He's your son, I'm also your son—thinking like that will turn us into brothers."

Bharati pleads for his release, but Anthony scoffs. "Even if we were real brothers, that one's not going to let me go. He's a real hard case." The chimes of a clock signal that it's time for his hearing. As he is taken from the cell he makes a request of Bharati that relies on a complicated logic of mediated kinship. "Look, Mother. Here we are, my first time ever at the police station, and you've made me the inspector's brother. Now it's going to be my first time at court. Will you let me have one of your flowers? For good luck? I'm thinking when I get there, if the man I face there turns out to be as hard as that one, I'll pass him your flower, and that'll make him my dad." Bharati gives him the flower, and he crosses himself with it, then touches her feet. She invokes the Lord's name in blessing: "May Bhagvan keep you in happiness."

Anthony is in the paddy wagon, heading to court through palm-shaded neighborhood streets. Suited toughs emerge from the bushes and set off smoke bombs. Anthony and his escort are caught in a cloud that both chokes and obscures. When the police halt the van they discover their prisoner has been whisked away. But where? "Untie the band," commands a familiar voice, and as his blindfold is removed we see with Anthony that the goons have brought him to a private bungalow, where at the far end of the table in a posh dining room a gray-haired man sits eating with a knife and fork. "Who are you, *maai-baap?*" asks Anthony, addressing his elder as "Mother-Father," an old-fashioned way of honoring an authority figure.[28] "Forget the 'Mom.' It's your Daddy," says Kishanlal, a line which, however literally true, is delivered by the character in the colloquial sense to emphasize who's boss. (He has lost the affected accent he used earlier when addressing Robert.) Anthony advances toward the head of the table to take an adjacent seat. Struck by a thought, he presents Kishanlal with his flower: "I was just telling Mother that if some Daddy came my way, I'd give him this rose-flower. Take it, Sahib." Kishanlal invites him to eat, and Anthony assents: "Why not? If Dad's offering food, of course his son's going to have a bite."

But Kishanlal's interest in Anthony turns out to be distressingly similar to Amar's: "Where's Robert?" Anthony makes a desperate lunge but is intercepted by henchmen and finds himself facing a gun in Kishanlal's hand. Unconvincingly he tries to cover himself: "I was just trying to get Mother's blessing." He indicates the Santoshi Maa locket Kishanlal wears at his chest—a token, of course, of his lost wife, Bharati. "Sahib, do you believe in God? I'm a straight-up believer. . . . I believe in all religions. I go to the temple, I go to the mosque, I go to church, I go to the *gurudwara*. And sometimes, Sahib, I get mixed up and put in time at the police station." A liveried waiter arrives with Anthony's meal. It's that Indian emblem of sophisticated upscale dining, a sizzler. Kishanlal presses on with his demand for Robert's whereabouts. He makes threats, but the young man's banter seems to charm him. Called away to some other business, he has an electric fan put on and, instructing his stooges to wait on the answer and to make sure their charge is well fed in the meantime, leaves Anthony with a pat on the head. Our hero wastes no time. He uses the fan to spray chilli pepper from the condiment tray into his minders' eyes and takes a flying leap across the table. Some acrobatic moves and well-placed punches see him into the garden, out of the clutches of numerous thugs, and away . . .

. . . all the way back to the lockup in the police station, where he resumes his old place on the bunk. When Amar asks him why he didn't flee when he had the chance, Anthony responds that he didn't want to place his keeper's position in jeopardy. "Thing is, Mother told me that you and me are both like her sons. What that means is we're brothers, am I right? And you don't cut out on your own brother." Amar is exasperated. On the one hand, Anthony insists on calling him his brother. On the other, he refuses to help him track down the criminal who shot his Sahib. "What kind of a brother are you?" The revelation that Robert attacked a police officer comes as a real shock to Anthony. So the villain lied to him! His change of heart is immediate. "Let's go, brother. I'll tell you where Robert is. Let's go."

But when he leads the officer to the cellar beneath his bar, he finds the helper he had left in charge of Robert nursing a sore head. The wanted man has flown the coop. An irate Amar instructs Anthony that if he fails to turn up Robert within one month he'll find himself back behind bars. And no sooner have the police left the scene than Anthony's priestly guardian enters in full I-told-you-so mode. "Yes, Father," says the young man, thoroughly abashed. "Will you do as I say?" "Yes, Father." "Then get yourself married right away." "Yes, Father—no, Father! Marriage? That I can't do." And when pressed on what his problem is, Anthony waxes romantic, explaining that the woman to share his life must be someone very special indeed. "I mean, Father. It's like, I'd see her and violins would automatically start playing inside me. Bells are going to go off in my mind—ting-tong, ting-tong. It's got to feel like this—Father— like a fairy from paradise, flying in a plane, is touching down for a landing at the airport of my heart."

Enter Jenny: Christian Hybridity and Third Song

Cut to a Swissair jumbo jet, just touched down at Santa Cruz Airport. Among the stylish crowd disembarking on the tarmac we see blond-haired foreigners as well as a proper Indian lady in a sari. The camera zooms in on an attractive young woman in Western dress, who is soon joined in line by a second. The first woman wears a red and white outfit with a wide sun hat, and the second woman wears blue and yellow. Inside the terminal the sinister Robert makes his reappearance in the uniform of a baggage handler, now with a pair of red muttonchop whiskers that accentuate the general colonial sahib effect. The plummy accent is back. He is attended by two similarly uniformed lackeys, who ask how he will recognize the long-lost daughter who's due to return to India that day. It's simple, he replies. She will be whichever girl engages the man waiting over there in the long black coat.

He indicates Kishanlal, who has met the occasion by amping up his neo-Edwardian look with a Teddy Boy frock coat, creatively accessorized with sunglasses, walking stick, cigarette holder, and lamb's-wool trilby hat.[29] The chic woman in blue approaches. This is the DECOY, a "special appearance" by the dancer and actress Helen.[30] Kishanlal presents her with a bouquet, and following an affectionate exchange, the two proceed to his limousine, where they are accosted at gunpoint by Robert and his confederates. Haplessly crying "Uncle! Uncle!" the Decoy is manhandled into a getaway car, which zooms off. An unruffled Kishanlal reaches through the car window, withdraws a fresh bouquet, and calls in the direction of the terminal. "Jenny! Come, my daughter. Come now."

To the strains of a romantic brass solo, the lady in red, JENNY (Parveen Babi), makes her entrance through the glass doors. Addressing Kishanlal as Uncle, she smilingly takes the flowers but expresses puzzlement at what she has just witnessed. "That was all a show," explains her sponsor, "put on to keep you safe." Then he spins another fabrication: that the man she saw fleeing the scene is her father's murderer (although we spectators know, of course, that Robert is her actual father), whose intent had been to kidnap her. As they drive through suburban Santa Cruz in his shiny black car, Kishanlal fills Jenny in on a lightly edited version of his tale. "Twenty-two years ago, on the Fifteenth of August, I was on the run for my life from that very same man. I had my three sons with me. I hid them in Borivali Park and ran on. His people were hot on my tail. When by one trick or another I managed to shake them off and I made it back to the park, there was nobody there. I lost all three of my sons." He is sobbing. "I am sorry, Uncle," says Jenny, "but if Bhagvan wills it, you will surely be brought back together with your sons. And that man will be paid back in his own coin."

In his new headquarters—a high-ceilinged mansion no less lavish than his roost of twenty-two years before—Robert has indeed found himself on the brink of comeuppance. The Decoy is holding a pistol to his head. Robert has lost the red sideburns, part of his disguise, but he's dressed again in the dandyish style he favors. It looks bad for him as Kishanlal's agent marches him down the stairway that opens onto the great hall. His own goons stand frozen, their hands raised over their heads. But a side door opens, and the sleek but odious hoodlum Ranjeet—last seen pimping his own stepsister—enters to intercept the Decoy at the point of his own gun. Robert congratulates his recruit—and himself, on having had the good sense to take him into his gang. Instructing his new lieutenant to take away "Kishanlal's gift," he vents relief at his narrow escape: "My God."

A light-complected, Western-looking bodybuilder in a leather jerkin is introduced with a shot of him bending an iron bar around his shoulders and a line from Kishanlal: "And this is ZABISKO" (Yusuf). The forth-right Jenny can't restrain herself from running a hand over his arms. "Hi," says Zabisko. "Fantastic muscles," responds Jenny. Kishanlal has hired the muscleman as her personal bodyguard; wherever she goes, he'll go too. And first among the stops on her circuit is Easter Mass, where Anthony, neat in a white leisure suit, turns around from the candles he's been tending to encounter the dumbfounding vision of his dream girl walking up the aisle. Bells chime in to complement the choral music on the soundtrack; Jenny, clad in a canary yellow outfit with a mantilla-like lace headdress, advances through the congregation and genuflects. Anthony shifts to the organ as the service begins. Strangely, when he looks at her the object of his desire multiplies in his eyes and spins, as though seen through a kaleidoscope (or with the impaired gaze of a drunkard, or possibly the inspired gaze of a madman).

An antic violin takes over the soundtrack as the Mass concludes. Anthony follows Jenny through the church interior and out to the iconic front of Mount Mary (whose actual interior looks quite different).[31] "Excuse me, please!" calls Anthony, producing a canary yellow handbag from somewhere in the crowd and presenting it to her. In the flirtation that follows, much humor is generated by the contrast between Jenny's self-assurance and Anthony's boyish awkwardness—along with the additional contrast we spectators draw between that awkwardness and the swagger we've come to associate with Anthony in other situations.

Jenny rejects the purse, which isn't hers, and her nervous beau falters; he presses the purse on a different woman in order to take a red flower from her hair, but when Jenny rebuffs that in turn—the flower doesn't belong to her either—he rallies. Forging yet another link in the narrative's chain of symbolically laden flower-giving, he offers, "No, this is mine. Keep it. It will suit you very well." He manages to ask her to an Easter dance, but Jenny declines, explaining that she will be attending with somebody else. Then, nonplussed for only a moment, he asks her to wait for him and goes racing back inside the church. But even as Anthony hustles the Padre to the door, babbling of how the bells in his mind have finally rung, the burly Zabisko appears at Jenny's side. The bodyguard points to his watch: it's time to go. When the smitten Anthony reaches the gate of the church, he's greeted by the sight of a canary yellow Volkswagen Beetle driving off down the road.

The next scene is set in a banquet hall of the sort in which well-to-do Christians of real-life Bandra might very well hold a community Easter party (in the previous dialogue, Jenny names it as the "gymkhana"). But the hall's flashy décor and the guests' flashy dress contribute to a high Seventies disco effect. Turbaned waiters roll an enormous egg on a platform through service doors. The egg is decorated with red ribbons and tape that spells the words *Happy Easter*. Before the fascinated eyes of the revelers—who include Zabisko, in a white blazer with a red boutonniere, and Jenny, who has changed into a red dress that matches the red flower from Anthony she wears in her hair—the waiters slide open a panel in the egg. "Wow-w-w!" The crowd approaches with enthusiasm: inside is Anthony, turned out in a European-style formal suit even more elaborate (and parodic) than the neo-Edwardian rig favored by Robert and Kishanlal. Along with a black cutaway and striped trousers he wears a top hat, white gloves, and even a monocle, and in place of a walking stick he carries an English-style umbrella.[32] "Wait! Wait! *Wait—!*" he admonishes the crowd, and follows up a stream of learned-sounding English verbiage by stepping smartly out of his capsule and lighting into his anthem, "My Name Is Anthony Gonsalves."

In narrative terms, what happens during this musical number can be summed up as follows. Singing of his uniqueness and consequent aloneness, the egg-hatched foundling boy woos his lady on the dance floor. He takes the red flower from Zabisko's lapel to present to Jenny. Not amused, the bodyguard circles the couple and pulls Anthony's top hat over his eyes. Our hero rights himself and coyly evades Jenny's play for the flower he still carries, passing it to another woman only to have it recovered by Zabisko, who clouts him on the head. When Anthony opens his eyes the strange kaleidoscope effect has again scrambled his vision. He refocuses, delivering another set of lyrics: in that very place, he's found the one companion who can redeem his loneliness, but it seems she's holding back for fear of someone else. And as he develops the theme, flirting with others who don't try to steer clear of him, he reverses the optical illusion: he wields his umbrella like a magician's prop, struts around in a state of levitation, and somehow conjures up a condition in which he and Jenny end up racing toward each other in dreamy slow motion while Zabisko stands by frozen and all the others dance on at a normal speed.[33]

Alas, the enchantment doesn't last, and the strongman interposes himself and shoves Anthony away. In the last set of lyrics, Anthony makes a distinction between the poor, who are endowed with the gift of true love, and the rich like Jenny, whose understanding is obscured. He executes an aerial backflip into his shell, where, isolated again, he has all but concluded his tune . . . when Jenny, mustering her resolve, approaches him to deliver his own English catchphrase: "Excuse me, please." "Oh yes!" exclaims Anthony, and jumps down to make a triumphant exit with his lady. But he walks straight into Zabisko's fist, and as he sprawls on the floor trying to recover, chugging hastily from a flask, the bodyguard mocks him and challenges him to stand up and fight. Unfortunately the kaleidoscope effect shows him multiple Zabiskos, and he badly whiffs his punch. In the roughhousing that follows, a disoriented Anthony is clownishly incapable of maneuvering as he would like, and an ineffectual Jenny can offer little help. Anthony ends his big night packed back up in his egg, and his thuggish rival slides the shell closed.

Three Models of Romance and Fourth Song

Back at his home, which no longer contains the accoutrements of a bar or cellar, Anthony considers his disheveled and bruised self in a full-length mirror. Drunkenness has played tricks not only with his vision but with his sense of recognition; we as spectators don't see things through his eyes in this scene, but we are treated to the comic spectacle of Anthony haranguing his own reflection as though it were a separate person. First he berates his alter ego for drinking, which has made him weak. "Hey, Brother Anthony, you know you can take ten men all on your own. . . . But take a look how you've been whipped. You look like a straight-up idiot." Next he gets some medicine to disinfect his wounds, applying the tincture to the surface of the glass, huffing in vicarious pain, and following up with two carefully placed Band-Aids. Finally, once again addressing his reflection as Brother, he bids it good night and walks into the corner.

The scene that follows has a certain formal similarity. We are shown a close-up of Jenny through a pattern that turns out to be the screen of a confessional. Jenny begins her confession: she feels sorry to have been the cause of the beating visited on Anthony. She admits she is very fond of him. In fact, she begins, "I—I think I—" "Do you love me?" asks the face on the other side of the screen—Anthony, stylish in another white leisure suit, who has been cleaning the confessional box. Jenny, flustered, protests that it's a sin to listen to somebody else's confession, but his response is a charming shrug: "I'll have to ask my partner for forgiveness." Anthony tries to deliver an avowal of his own, but Jenny would rather hear him out somewhere outside the church. Out front, though, Zabisko can be seen impatiently waiting (for some reason he has donned a South American poncho over pink coordinates). "What can I do?" Jenny sighs. "He's my bodyguard." Anthony steps up: "Hey. From today, consider me your bodyguard." They slip out together through a side exit.

With the shot of a phallic motorboat plowing through frothy waters we—along with all three brothers and their destined brides—are plunged into the musical number "Hamko Tumse Ho Gaya Hai Pyar Kya Karein" (Can't Help Falling in Love with You). Anthony, at the wheel, and Jenny, helping him steer, appear carefree and ardently romantic. The city on the shoreline furnishes a glamorous backdrop to this attractive and modern young couple enjoying leisure time together. It's an aspirational image of middle-class recreation. In this musical sequence the city takes shape as a cosmopolitan oasis, a space that promises room and prosperity enough for lovers of all religious communities to court, settle down, and build the Indian families of the future. The ensemble number showcases each couple expressing love in a distinct style representative of its community. Thus we are first shown the Christian couple in their Western fashions (white for him, pink ruffles for her) sporting on the water, then shifting to a pony cart they race down the beach. They dance as a couple; his arms caress her body. Associations here are youth, transnational sophistication, sex appeal, and leisure.[34]

The next segment underscores that the Hindus are the grown-ups in this ménage. It opens with a framed black-and-white photograph of Amar in his uniform, which is picked up and lovingly contemplated by a figure at once familiar and transformed: Lakshmi. By contrast with the bell-bottomed floozy of the movie's first half, the new, bindi'ed Lakshmi is the image of a demure Hindu housewife, her hair secured in a bun and her figure secured in a black-and-silver sari, the sartorial equivalent of the tastefully understated middle-class dwelling she now inhabits. When the camera follows her to the garden, the master of the house, in a spotless white *kurta pajama,* is seen relaxing with a book in the hammock. The message could hardly be clearer. The fallen Lakshmi has been redeemed through domestication by this paragon of clean-cut masculinity, and even as she sings she moves on to attend to the laundry she has hung out to dry in the yard. The musical arrangement has taken on a softer, *raga-*inflected tone.

In a return to the frenetic, Akbar, a camera draped around his neck, climbs acrobatically from a station platform into the open side of a miniature tourist train. In the car, occupied primarily by other women, is Salma, distinguished from her Western-attired fellow passengers by her peach-colored *salwar kameez.* The rhythm picks up, evoking the sort of hypnotic regularity characteristic of *qawwali;* her bench-mates clap the beat as Salma and her suitor dance around each other. One car back, Salma's pint-sized father, very much the middle-class tourist in an outfit that combines sunglasses, a newsboy's cap, and a pair of binoculars, looks on and seethes. He attempts to halt the train by waving a red flag, but Akbar counters with green (a more properly Islamic color) and thwarts Tayyab Ali by decoupling the rear part of the train. The lovers continue their frolic. Salma manipulates the *dupatta* scarf that goes with her outfit to burlesque the way a hijabi woman flirts with her veil. The train passes through a dark tunnel, and when it emerges, we see the couple dancing merrily on the train's roof—as does Tayyab Ali, furiously aiming his binoculars from a bridge over the track. The number's concluding shots return us to Anthony and Jenny, driving their cart up the beach during a glowing sunset; then to Amar and Lakshmi, seated dreamily on the verandah with their backs to each other as rain drenches their garden; then to Akbar and Salma, embracing atop the toy train; and finally back to Anthony and Jenny.[35] The sun sets.

Interval

Muslim Social Subplot and Fifth Song

In a dark, rudely constructed interior, whose bare timbers recall the family home in the slum (as well as Anthony's Country Bar), Akbar appears at a gap in the wall, camera dangling at his neck. It seems to be evening, but he imitates a rooster crowing; Salma appears on the balcony of the house across the alley. Akbar's camera is a new purchase, and he wants to inaugurate it by taking a photo of his beloved. But she shushes him. Her father is in the house—we hear his voice calling her name—and she can't get away. She'll try and make it tomorrow. Disgruntled, Akbar moves on among the beams of what we now see is actually a timber warehouse, part of Salma's father's business. A servant approaches Tayyab Ali and murmurs something that perturbs him. He gets up from his accounts and hustles outside to the warehouse, wearing a sheepskin hat and embroidered white *kurta,* looking like a North Indian Muslim aristocrat. He has been summoned to a rendezvous with the courtesan he patronizes, BIJLI (Madhumati, "special appearance").

Akbar catches sight of the furtive meeting and eavesdrops. In sarcastically polite Urdu, Bijli explains that she has come to check up on her lover, whose "moonlike countenance hasn't appeared in [her] boudoir to shine for many days." Tayyab Ali tries to shoo her off, but the flashy, paan-chewing Bijli is implacable. She demands six months' upkeep, "otherwise I'll show you how the angel standing before you turns into a devil." Akbar seizes the moment to try out his camera, and the flash from behind startles Tayyab Ali. "It seems lightning must have struck somewhere," he says nervously. Punning off her own name, which means "lightning," the mistress makes her parting threat: "I think not, dear sir. On the day that Bijli strikes, she'll burn your honorable establishment down to ashes for you."

Now it's daytime, most likely the very next day. Akbar paces, frustrated, at the crossroads in front of Tayyab Ali's house and business. The set, representing a commercial area in Bandra, suggests the integration of communities, with signage in Urdu, Hindi, English, and Gujarati. Replicating the conceit of the hospital windows during the title sequence, the view down one street leads to a church, down another to a temple, and the background of the block facing Tayyab Ali's is dominated by a mosque.[36] Akbar is approached by a band of *hijras,* transgender performers often referred to as "eunuchs," and he gains their support in his project of publicly shaming Salma's recalcitrant father. They act as backup dancers and chorus for the song "Tayyab Ali Pyar Ka Dushman" (Tayyab Ali Is the Enemy of Love).[37]

Riffing off a well-known proverb, Akbar repeats the refrain: "Boy and girl are both agreed / It's only the judge [*qazi*] that won't sign off," and mocks his oppressor by dangling his fingers under his chin like a beard.[38] The *hijras* advance to Tayyab Ali's door and taunt him, flushing him into the street. Akbar sings out his threat to expose Salma's pious father as a clandestine sponsor of—"Want me to name names?" "No, no, no, *ji!*" "Want me to show pictures?" "No, no, no, *ji!*" But even as Akbar announces that he's not the sort to drag people's good names through the dirt, the old man loses his temper. He pays a trio of neighborhood toughs—burly Muslim guys in *lungis*—to dispose of his tormentor. Much to the distress of Salma, who rushes down from her balcony, they give Akbar a thrashing and throw his unconscious body into a nearby dovecote. But retribution, in the long-legged form of Anthony, is swift to arrive. He thrusts a pole through the plate glass of Tayyab Ali's office and, seizing the merchant, totes him out to the street, where a taxi awaits. He tosses the little man onto the luggage rack and gets in the back seat. As Tayyab Ali wails for the police, they drive off through a crowd of skullcapped onlookers. A poster on the street corner advertises a film with a graphic of two men standing together and the title *Dosti,* or "Friendship."

Enter Anthony, again carrying Tayyab Ali and berating him all the while, into a hospital ward. In one of the beds lies Akbar, with his face bandaged. Salma stands by in her capacity as doting girlfriend, not doctor. (She is still dressed in the outfit seen in the musical number, although she is to reappear later in a white coat). Anthony has also dragged in a reluctant third: a proper *qazi,* or Islamic judge, with a long beard and fur hat. "Now we'll get you and Salma married," Anthony announces. "This minute!" Comic bickering ensues with Tayyab Ali. Salma smiles, but Akbar is not amused. He declares that under the circumstances he refuses. Anthony protests that he has brought the *qazi* all the way from a different wedding. But Akbar is insistent. "I could have raised a hand too, if I had wanted to. But hitting people's not my way, Brother Anthony. If I'm going to win someone over, it's through the power of love." "I've been hearing that in church my whole life," counters an exasperated Anthony. But his friend refuses to get married unless Tayyab Ali offers his daughter's hand of his own free will. And, in spite of Anthony's threats, he refuses to consent to the match. Anthony blows his stack. "Shorty here's going to marry off his daughter to somebody else. And when that happens don't you come running to me, all, 'Brother Anthony, I've been robbed in love, I'm done for!' Because what I'm going to do is kick your ass. And from here on out, we're not talking. Go to hell!'" He storms out, muttering to himself, "In this country, I can't get any respect."

Zabisko Makes His Move

Back at Kishanlal's bungalow, Jenny is decked out in a black and yellow Western-style outfit, the long skirt slit to the top of her thigh. Humming happily, she's all set to go out, but the loutish Zabisko blocks her way and demands to know where she is going. "It's none of your bloody business," Jenny retorts, and when he presses on with his suspicion that she's off to meet that good-for-nothing Anthony, she reminds him angrily that he's only her bodyguard. "Oh, I'll be guarding your body your whole life," he says unpleasantly, "so that no one besides me is ever going to touch it. . . . I'm the one you're going to marry." "You bastard!" screams Jenny, but the heavy blocks her from slapping him and throws her into the adjacent room. She sprawls on the floor, distressed, in a pose that has been suggestively arranged to show her bare legs and underwear.

An ornately decorated, antique-looking phone rings on a side table by Robert's sofa. A well-dressed henchman answers it and passes it to the boss, who remains, true to form, sharp-looking in cream-colored suit pants and waistcoat. "Mister Robert," says Zabisko, "I have your daughter with me." Robert, shocked, demands to know whom he's talking to. "Zabisko," is the laconic answer. Flexing a bicep for his own admiration, the rogue bodyguard goes on to ask what price the other might pay to be reunited with his daughter. Would he, for example, be prepared to offer his daughter's hand in marriage? In contrast with Tayyab Ali, Robert pauses hardly a beat and gives his consent. "Then come immediately to 325 Silver Beach," says Zabisko, and hangs up as his boss's big black limousine pulls up in the driveway.[39]

The Silver Beach bungalow's drawing room conveys a picture of the good life: it has windows that open onto the sea, a well-stocked bar in one corner, and a stool made out of an elephant's foot. Kishanlal enters, looking as foppish as ever in a new Teddy Boy suit (slate blue) and accessories: cigarette, sunglasses, swagger stick, and black wool trilby. He carries a beribboned gift box. "Good Morning, sir," says Zabisko. Kishanlal asks after his charge. Jenny is out; she's gone to meet her boyfriend, the bodyguard lies. "Boyfriend?" asks Kishanlal. Zabisko explains that there appears to be a man Jenny likes to meet on the sly. Then he softens the news by stating that Gracie has accompanied her. Unseen by the two of them, Jenny, bound and gagged in the upstairs room, is struggling to make some statement of her own. "Are you Jenny's bodyguard or is Gracie?" demands an angry Kishanlal. (We are never shown Gracie, or told anything more about her, although it can be inferred that she is a Christian member of the household.)[40] "I want no more mistakes of this kind."

Leaving the gift on the coffee table, he heads back out to his car. But upstairs Jenny has managed to snag the window shade on one of her high-heeled feet, and by rapidly opening and shutting the venetian blinds she succeeds in flashing Kishanlal a signal that something is up in her room. He returns and gives Zabisko a number to dial. With the goon's back turned, he applies some chloroform to his handkerchief, pulls a gun from his waistband, and efficiently knocks out his disloyal servant, leaving him sprawled on the floor with the hanky draped over his face. Then he rushes upstairs to discover someone else on the floor—Jenny. Even as he unties her, Robert's hireling is opening the gate to the compound. A long, sea-green, American-looking station wagon and a jeep—a convoy of thugs—roll up the driveway behind the parked limousine. (Adorning the front lawn is a pair of bronze statues of female nudes.) Kishanlal and Jenny hurry to the back of the house. Robert enters with his minions through the front to encounter the supine form of Zabisko. "Oh my God," he re-marks, sniffing the handkerchief. Meanwhile, his daughter and his enemy have reached the getaway car in the garage—another American station wagon, this one in red—and Kishanlal guns the engine, barreling through the garage doors.[41]

What follows is a car chase through a largely barren landscape, where the trees seem to have been replaced with streetlights and electric towers; it's the picture of a suburban highway zone in the early stages of develop-ment.[42] Kishanlal's red vehicle goes careering up the road, annoying the occupants of the car in front of it—a familiar-looking jalopy with green accents. Akbar, at the wheel, wears a loud shirt in a floral print and has a blue bandana on his right wrist. Anthony is dressier, in a flat cap and a black bolero worn open to show the cross at his chest. Akbar signals for the honking wagon to pass, and his friend quotes his own rhyme from a previous scene: "Life gets a man driving like that for two reasons—an Olympic race, or else a police ca—*Jenny?*" Now there are four cars in the chase: the red and green station wagons—the latter carrying Robert—the jeep full of hoodlums following them, and finally the Akbarmobile. Kishanlal senses crisis. He instructs Jenny: as soon as he finds a place to stop, she's to get out and hide. He'll lead the pursuers away.

He exits the highway onto a tree-lined country road, where a big banyan stands next to the turn. Jenny hops out and finds refuge in a hollow in the trunk. Relieved to see Robert's car and the jeep racing past, she glances down and discovers . . . a cobra! Screaming, she kicks at the snake and it slithers away, but Jenny has backed away from the tree and the jeep's driver sees her in the side mirror. Robert follows the jeep in reversing direction; ahead, Kishanlal sees the maneuver and turns too. Jenny flees down a dirt road that leads through woods and into a sugar-cane field, with all three cars in pursuit. (And what's become of Akbar and Anthony?) She runs past a railway crossing and the barrier comes down after the jeep, cutting off the station-wagon rivals. But the goons in the jeep are relentless; they hound her along the trail and off it, and when Jenny risks a leap down a slope that knocks their ride out of service, two of the thugs get out and continue on foot. She's just about at her last breath when she enters a clearing in the cane and swoons at the feet of a scarecrow.

Its face, hands, and long legs are covered in straw, and it's costumed in the patched remains of a formal morning suit. As soon as the two hoods arrive and bend over the prostrate Jenny, the scarecrow whacks them senseless—one outstretched arm each—and shrugs, revealing Anthony's face. Another goon catches up, and Anthony, his cruciform pose resumed, toys with him, tapping him first on one shoulder and then the other before smacking him down. Meanwhile, Kishanlal has pulled up in his red station wagon alongside Robert in the green one. Robert's driver side-swipes the red car and sends it off the road, where it slides on a pile of rocks and flips over. Kishanlal staggers out and collapses, clutching his body and groaning in pain.

His plight is seen by two people: Robert, who orders his driver to run him over, and Akbar, sitting in his own car, presumably waiting for Anthony. Akbar drives down a trail through the cane field and interposes his car between Kishanlal and the green station wagon bearing down on him. Robert's driver swerves and loses control. The station wagon goes somersaulting into a pit and lands upside down with a splash, in the water at the bottom. Anthony appears from the canes with an unconscious Jenny in his arms. "Hey, Akbar! You look after that guy. I'm taking Jenny away. Okay?" "Fine, Brother," responds Akbar, carrying the likewise comatose Kishanlal to the car. "Let's go, Pops." The final shot in this sequence shows a soggy Robert emerging with his driver from the water.

We see an English sign on the façade of an old-fashioned colonnaded building: Sawant General Hospital.[43] In spite of the name change—and the lack of resemblance between the exterior we are shown and that of the actual Nanavati Hospital—we are given to understand that this hospital is the same as the one shown in the blood-transfusion sequence. At the admissions desk Akbar, with a supine Kishanlal propped on his shoulder, argues with a nurse in a white uniform sari, who claims that all beds are full. What about Number 102, asks Akbar. "That one belongs to Akbar Ilahabadi," says the nurse. "I'm Akbar Ilahabadi," he explains. "I vacated that bed two hours ago." The nurse asks the name of the injured man she's admitting. Akbar hardly pauses a moment. He sees a word tattooed on the older man's left arm, just below the spot where he has tied his own bandana as a makeshift bandage: "For his name, please write 'Kishanlal.'"[44]

Robert has made it back to his mansion looking none the worse for his dunking. The great room in which he addresses his minions has the appearance of a miniature castle. It features a high ceiling with bare timbers, stonework walls, and a winding stairway that leads to a mezzanine.[45] He stands in the foreground, irate that Kishanlal has escaped. Now when will he be reunited with his daughter? In the background are a dozen thugs, most of them in jackets and ties. The middle ground is occupied by Ranjeet and Zabisko. The muscleman approaches the boss. "Don't worry, Robert," he says, "if not today, we'll have Jenny back tomorrow. But all of that comes with the promise of my marriage. Remember . . . ?" "What rot!" exclaims Robert, in fine Anglophile form, claiming not to remember any such thing. Zabisko is unfazed. How quickly Robert seems to forget his promises, he says. But that very day he'll introduce Robert to a person who'll give him ready cause to remember.

In a cellar somewhere—a spooky space with a black, coal-like texture on the walls—Zabisko flips the lights on a wincing prisoner. It's Robert's twin ALBERT (Jeevan), whose chief marks of difference are a beard and mustache, and a less affected accent in Hindi. (His dress sense, however, is if anything more daring than Robert's; he's paired a shirt and tie with a lapel-less jacket of contrasting panels.) Albert composes himself and addresses his brother coolly, accusing him of planning his kidnapping. Robert denies it: "I swear, my brother." "Don't call me your brother," retorts Albert, "I hate you!" They may share the same parents, he concedes, but he knows Robert to be a murderer and a smuggler, whereas he is an honorable man. "But how has my brother—who's been the manager of the English national bank for ten years—ended up here?" Robert wonders aloud. Zabisko leads Robert to one corner of the cellar, whose chief adornment is beer crates stenciled "Hamburg Pils." It seems Albert had traveled to Bombay to attend a World Bank conference. "We had a chance encounter, and ever since then he's been my guest." Zabisko lays out his plan. The police are on Robert's trail, and if they catch him he'll surely hang. The only way for Robert to escape this fate is to marry Jenny off to him. Then Zabisko will let Robert take Albert's identity and flee to London to take his place. "As for Albert," says the heavy, menacingly flexing a strap in his hands, "I'll look after him." And observing that Kishanlal must surely have been admitted to some hospital, he advises Robert to find him and learn Jenny's whereabouts.

The Scales Fall from the Eyes:
Bharati's Redemption and Sixth Song

In the very hospital ward that offers the multifaith views from its windows, male orderlies transfer Kishanlal from his bed to a gurney. Just as they wheel him out of the ward, Bharati enters, a bundle of red flowers in her hand, and finds her way to the bed—"Akbar, my son"—only to discover it is empty. A sari-clad female nurse explains to her that the bed's occupant has been removed for his operation. "But I've brought him flowers from the *dargah*," protests Bharati, and asks the direction of the operating theater.[46]

Flash! Another powerful lamp reprises an effect used in the Albert sequence and in the early scene in which Amar bullies his detainees. The prisoner this time, however, shows no response to the glare: Kishanlal is lying unconscious in the operating theater. He is oblivious to his harassment by Robert, disguised in a surgeon's scrubs, who threatens to throttle him if he won't reveal where his daughter is. "No, sir, you won't get him conscious that way," says the similarly garbed Ranjeet. He goes to retrieve a prisoner from the room next door. This is a real white-coated doctor—Salma, gagged hospital-style with surgical tape. (She has evidently remained at the hospital to begin her shift after seeing Akbar out earlier.) Ranjeet marches her past two other gowned gangsters to the patient: "You're the doctor. Make him come to—quick!"

Under duress, Salma goes to work with a respirator apparatus. With rhythmic inhaling aggravating the tension on the soundtrack, the camera zooms in on the mask over Kishanlal's face . . . and over to what covers his chest: the medallion of Santoshi Maa, the amulet Bharati had left him with decades before. Robert snatches it, snapping the chain: "So here's the secret of his power—what's been saving his hide all this time."[47] Yet in spite of this apparent coup—and the doctor's best efforts—Kishanlal remains unresponsive. And someone keeps knocking on the door from outside; some woman has arrived with blessed flowers for the patient, and she means to deliver them. Robert loses his patience. He mutters at Ranjeet to let the intruder in. And even as Bharati exhibits her blindness in her uncomprehending stance, Robert recognizes her from their long-ago encounter. "That's Kishanlal's wife," he exclaims within earshot of Salma. "Now I'll find the way to my daughter." Impulsively he ditches the still-unconscious husband for the wife.

Robert and Ranjeet take the terrorized Bharati for a ride. They've discarded the scrubs—Robert for a dark, sailor suit–like ensemble—and Ranjeet drives yet another station wagon, this one in blue. The scene is chaotic. Robert threatens Bharati with a drawn revolver. Ranjeet races along the highway. A Volkswagen bus pops up in an inopportune spot, and swerving to avoid it, the station wagon flies off the road and piles into a mound of raised earth. The goon sitting next to Ranjeet is thrown from the vehicle. Driver and boss are both stunned, and Bharati manages to exit the car but, in her blindness, trips over the stooge's prone body and goes rolling down a slope. Ranjeet stirs and in turn rouses Robert. The two set off in pursuit of Bharati, whose seemingly hapless tumble has delivered her from the barren roadside down into a verdant, garden-like space. The soulful tones of a *qawwali* singer flood the soundtrack. She sets off in the direction of the music.

When we are shown the source of the singing—which of course Bharati herself cannot see—we recognize a destination forecast in the allusion to the *dargah* she had just left. A building rises before her in the wilderness, and as the camera zooms ahead past the crude mud enclosure that screens it we see a little sanctuary styled with Islamic arches but crowned with the saffron flags seen on Hindu temples. We return to the wicked pursuers, shown in the same frame as Bharati, who remains continuously masked from them by foliage—it's as though the earth itself is acting to protect her in her moment of need. Then the lens advances through the shrine's entrance to present us with the object of veneration: the slightly larger than life-sized statue of a thin, bearded man, garlanded and draped in saffron-colored cloth. This decidedly Hindu-looking image is of Sai Baba of Shirdi, a Sufi holy man whose claim to embody divine power is recognized by members of both communities.[48] Immaculate in a white frock coat, Akbar leads the mixed congregation of Hindus and Muslims, men and women, in a rousing *qawwali* in the saint's praise, "Shirdi Wale Sai Baba." As he sings on, a desperate Bharati gains the sanctuary. Robert and Ranjeet are not far behind, but as they approach a cobra drops from atop the gate in the wall and flexes its neck in the threat posture. Robert concedes defeat; he gestures Ranjeet away.

This is but a foretaste of the Baba's favor, and of Bharati's redemption.[49] Bharati follows the music up to the threshold of the shrine. She stumbles at the step and advances on all fours. She touches her brow to the ground in prostration, and when she raises it we see she is marked on the forehead with blood. "May you reunite the parted / May you relight the dark lamps," sings Akbar, and we spectators see two little flames kindle in the effigy's eyes and fly across to enter Bharati's. The camera switches to her point of view: a blurry Sai Baba with Akbar kneeling before him is brought into focus, and we know that Bharati's sight has been restored. At the lines "These nights of sorrow / These nights so black / Transform them for us / Into Eid and Diwali," flames appear in all the lamps adorning the shrine, and the congregation rises in recognition of the Baba's power. As Bharati gazes on adoringly, three figures appear superimposed on the saint's visage: her little sons, smiling and beckoning her with their hands. At the song's end she reaches the statue and bows her head to its feet. She greets Akbar before the image. "Akbar, today because of your

faith and Baba's miraculous powers my eyesight has come back to me."
She explains that she has escaped from grave danger. Akbar invites her
to come away with him.

Haider Ali rolls up his prayer rug amid his living-room sofa and chairs.
Akbar enters with Bharati, whom he introduces to his father as "the mother
with the flowers." Haider Ali rises and returns Bharati's namaste gesture.
As Akbar describes the miracle that has given Mother back her sight,
Haider Ali studies her face, dons his glasses, and confirms his identification: She's the very person he encountered in a parlous state twenty-two
years before. "You remember, don't you, sister?" "How can I forget that
black night—the night I lost my husband and my three children? Why, that
same night you yourself had found somebody's lost child. He must be
pretty well grown by now." "Thanks to Dad's love and your blessings, he
is pretty well grown up, Mother," says Akbar, walking over to a black-and-
white photo of Haider Ali cuddling a little boy on the wall. "Dad lovingly
calls him 'Abbu.' You call him Son. And the world knows him by the name
Akbar Ilahabadi." Bharati in her turn makes her own identification: "But
this picture can only be my littlest child Raju—" "Your son?" asks Haider
Ali. "O! Thou Provider!" he exclaims piously. "Sister, this is what's meant
by Allah's glory. When He took away your eyes, He took your child away
too. Today He has restored your eyes, and restored your child too."
There is a tearful embrace.

Akbar and Salma United, Kishanlal and Amar Reunited

Akbar's day—recall it began at the crossroads in front of Tayyab Ali's
house—is still not over.

A blaze lights up the night sky in the Muslim Quarter: Bijli has indeed
struck. "Let's go, Mother dear," she says to an older woman, perhaps the
madam, "our work here is done." Inside, surrounded by flames, Salma
cries out for her father. Akbar runs through the mob that has collected
around the fire but is pulled back by police constables; a Muslim neighbor
informs him that father and daughter are both trapped inside.[50] Our hero
makes an end run around the crowd and appears on top of a wall behind
the conflagration. This is the neighborhood where religious buildings
mark the skyline, and here Akbar is framed against the mosque. He throws a

rope with a grappling hook across to the burning house and swings to the balcony Tarzan style, calling fervently on Ali to see him through the trial.

Inside, he finds the house blazing furiously. "Akbar—!" cries Salma from under a fiery bed. Akbar maneuvers acrobatically across the room, extracts her, and attends to another call for help: "Yah Allah!" Akbar completes the rescue by ushering his beloved and her father past fast-collapsing beams to the balcony, where his rope is still hanging. Before the agitated crowd, he swings with them both clinging to him (it is unclear where the rope is suspended from at this point), crossing back to the wall in front of the mosque. Addressing him as "Son," Tayyab Ali thanks his deliverer. "Nothing to thank me for, Tayyab Ali *Seth,*" says Akbar, "that was simply my duty." But I should have done my own duty to you before it came to this, is Tayyab Ali's graceful response, and he joins the lovers' hands, wishing Allah's blessing on the couple. "What a strange day today is," says Salma, beaming at the night sky with her hands raised in the posture of prayer. "First, Father's given his consent. And the other thing—you know that flower-selling granny, the one you like to think of as your mother? Today her husband was admitted to the hospital." In fact, she reveals, he turns out to be the very man Akbar himself had brought in that morning. Akbar stares in his turn at the sky—in the direction, perhaps, of God (and certainly that of the audience). "A mother . . . a father . . . both. . . ."

It's the next day. Akbar hurries into a rough but nevertheless tidy interior. Bare poles line the ceiling; it's a space much like the family's original home in the slum, and although the location of this room is unclear, it's where Bharati keeps house. Akbar greets his mother in a state of high excitement. "Mother, look—I've packed a lifetime's worth of happiness into this little box for you." Bharati's puzzlement turns to something like offense when he shows her the pillbox's contents: *sindoor,* or vermilion powder, conventionally worn by Hindu women in northern India to signify their married status. Akbar spells it out: her marriage is still preserved. He explains that when she brought the flowers to the hospital the previous day it had been not him but his father who had been taken in for an operation. Again he urges the *sindoor* on his mother, who, deeply moved, dips her fingers and applies the red to the part in her hair. She begs him to take her to her husband. Unfortunately the sari-clad nurse at the hospital's Enquiries desk declares that Kishanlal has been discharged that morning and no further information is available. Apprehension passes over Bharati's face. Akbar reassures her: he'll go to the police station and have a report filed.

Seated at his desk in the station office, Amar is all business. "What's the name?" he asks Akbar, filling out the official form. "Kishanlal." "Where did he live?" "In the Bandra Koliwada." Now the policeman sits back, looking pensive. "Somehow the name seems familiar." He gives Akbar his assurance that he'll look into the case. The scene shifts to Kishanlal, on a visit back to the old neighborhood.[51] He has returned in his capacity of racketeer boss, however, and we catch him in the act of smacking down a minion who has failed to distribute funds Kishanlal had set aside for his local dependents. Backed by two heavies, the godfather declares he can forgive a murder, but not the abandonment to hunger of anybody's wife and children. "I'm no Robert!" he roars at the flunky he holds by the collar. "Take him away." Gently he apologizes to the mother who stands at her doorway with two shirtless children. He hands her some cash and makes the promise to return every month to deliver the money in person.

As he turns in the lane, we spectators take in his view of the Koliwada. It looks the same as it did twenty-two years ago—an impression confirmed by his voiceover. "Not a thing back here has changed. But how much I've been changed in the world. Yesterday's Kishanlal—how happy he was in this neighborhood, together with his family!" Even as Amar drives into the lane in his police jeep and makes inquiries about where a man named Kishanlal may have lived, the boss enters his old home. His reverie ends in a prayer: "Bhagvan, everything You've sent my way since—take it all away. But once—just once—bring me back together with my lost children." He is rattled by the sight of a police officer approaching the door. But an uncanny foggy effect seems to have softened the little house's contours in Amar's vision and he turns to consider the spot opposite, where the fog clears to show him a flashback: a young boy with a realistic pistol in his hand, digging a hole in the dirt. Before Kishanlal's amazed eyes, the officer scrabbles at the rocks and earth, clearing them away to recover the gun.

"Amar, my son," gasps Kishanlal, and approaches the policeman to ask how he knew it was there. "Twenty-two years ago, on the Fifteenth of

August, my father gave me this pistol, and to hide it from my brother I buried it here. . . . But why are you asking me this?" "You remember the pistol your father gave you, yet you don't remember the father who gives you his heart?" There is a tearful embrace. Again Kishanlal invokes God. "All the earnings that Bhagvan took twenty years ago He has returned to me today with interest. My son has become a police officer!" He asks Amar about his two brothers. Amar realizes that he had met the younger one just that morning. The only mystery left is the middle brother. . . .

Anthony Loses One Father and Regains the Other

At Haider Ali's tailor shop, the master tailor is measuring Jenny for a wedding dress. To comic effect, Anthony fusses over details of the design while the paan-chewing Akbar harangues Anthony for haranguing his dad. Akbar sees them out to the street and to a waiting taxi. Bantering all the way, the brothers have failed to note a menacing figure watching from a nearby phone booth: Zabisko. The taxi delivers the couple to Mount Mary, the diegetic "St. Thomas's Church." Anthony drops Jenny off with the crowd heading into Mass; he's going on to check up on the wedding band.

Inside, the Padre finishes up his sermon with a personal announcement. Tomorrow, he says, will be the most important day of his life. He invites the congregation to join him in celebration. "Twenty-two years ago, on the Fifteenth of August, Independence Day, when everyone was observing the happy occasion, I found a three-year-old innocent foundling child, unconscious with fever and holding a note in his hands, on the steps of Borivali Church, where someone had abandoned him. Under the protection of our Lord and under this roof, that innocent child flourished and grew. You know him by the name of Anthony. Tomorrow he weds this lovely girl, Miss Jenny, who is sitting here among you." Amid the happy stir, Jenny rises from her seat and heads through a side exit to the pay phone installed on the outer wall. Kishanlal answers, a cigarette in his lips. "Congratulations, Uncle," says Jenny in English. She reminds him how he had told her the story of his separation from his three children.[52] Well, one of them has been found and what's more, she's about to get married to him. And his name is—

"Jenny! Hello! Hello!" bellows Kishanlal, but someone on the other end has cut off the connection. Jenny's startled gaze turns to the unassuming-looking man who's pressing down on the receiver hook. He's her dad, he says, come to take her back. "I don't believe you," says Jenny, and Robert replies, "You must believe me, darling. I'm your father!" When she resists, Zabisko appears with another goon. Just as they pick her up to carry her off, the Padre happens on the scene. Robert sends off his muscle with Jenny and confronts the priest, who defies him: "This is a house of God.[53] Your knife won't get you anywhere here." But Robert raises the blade in his hand and the camera cuts to a brightly colored effigy of Christ on the cross. Offscreen the Padre cries in pain and speaks his last words: "Oh Lord, forgive him." A bright red streak trickles down Christ's body.

A prim young Hindu housewife comes walking up the road by the church: it's Lakshmi. She encounters a teal Volkswagen bus parked awkwardly in the road. Waiting outside it, smoking a cigarette and clearly up to no good, is her stepbrother Ranjeet. Lakshmi darts behind the van and watches: Zabisko and his thuggish partner arrive carrying Jenny, followed by Robert. The gangsters bundle their victim into the getaway vehicle and drive off—but not before Lakshmi has stowed away in the back. The van drives up to Robert's mansion, grandly ornamented in colonial style. Lakshmi waits for the others to exit the van and then attempts to sneak off, but Ranjeet turns out to be a step ahead of her. "Why, Sis—where might you be going, ditching your own brother like that?"

Anthony struts into the church, now unoccupied but for the Padre who can be seen from the back, bowed at a little side chapel. "Look at me, Father," says Anthony, showing off a gleaming-white three-piece suit. "They tell me, 'Brother Anthony, you're looking very handsome today. Someone's definitely going to throw you the evil eye.'" From this day forward he'll be turning over a new leaf. No more strong-arm tactics, hooch peddling, mischief of any sort. Taking his guardian as his example, he pledges, he's going straight. Annoyed by the lack of response, he jogs the priest's shoulder. The body falls back, showing a chest wound at the spot indicated on the crucifix image. Anthony cradles the dead Padre, distraught. "Don't leave and make me an orphan a second time . . . Father, please." He raises reddened eyes to the image enshrined in the chapel: the Sacred Heart of Jesus.

Laying out the corpse in front of the image, he addresses his "partner." "Here, right in front of You, they came into Your house, they came to Father and—" he gestures at the body. "And You—I guess You just stood there and watched it all happen. If You had wanted to call someone up from out of this world, You could have called me. Hey, You could have had me sent up! There's no need for the likes of me in this world. No need. But him—there was a need for *him*." Brandishing the tattered paper he keeps in his pocket—Bharati's farewell note to Kishanlal—he echoes the priest's words, reminding the icon how he had been abandoned on the church's steps. If not for the Padre, who would have taken him in? And now who will take in the innocent children that continue to be abandoned every day? He's making one last deal. Where is the man who has murdered his guardian? If the Lord won't show him the answer, he vows, he will become such a bad man that no power on Earth will be able to reform him. Something slips out of the body's hands and clatters on the floor. Anthony sees its significance: it's the pendant of Santoshi Maa.

"Do you recognize this locket?" demands Anthony, who has exchanged his festive white suit for a formal black one, complete with a black tie for mourning. Threatened with a knife in his own living room, Kishanlal affirms that it's his. But his greatest enemy, Robert, had taken it from his neck when he was torturing him in the hospital in an effort to find his lost daughter, Jenny. "See what games fate plays with us. Her father is thirsty for my blood. And the one she loves—the man she wants to marry—he's none other than my long-lost son." Explaining how Jenny had telephoned him that very day with the news, he observes: "What a difference between father and daughter! It's the father's doing that I was separated from my offspring. And the daughter is bringing me back together with that very offspring." The wheels are turning in Anthony's mind. Again he withdraws the tattered note from his pocket. "If he's your son for real, then do you recognize this letter?" Not long in coming: a tearful embrace. "What a fortunate man I am today. I've been reunited with all three of my sons."

Masquerade

Akbar minds the tailor shop. Haider Ali's employees ply their craft in the background. Zabisko approaches, looking like a Western tourist in a T-shirt with a whale on the chest. He demands Jenny's wedding gown and, when queried, refuses to identify himself. Akbar smells a rat; in the Indian idiom of his voiceover, "There's something black in the lentils here, Mister Akbar." He explains that the dress will require a final fitting and that his uncle, the master tailor, will need to travel with it back to the bride. Zabisko returns to Robert's mansion leading, none too gently, a gray-bearded Muslim gentleman by the arm. Beneath the fez, Nehru coat, glasses, and whiskers it is of course Akbar. Making the most of his old man persona, garrulous and fussy, Akbar castigates Robert in rapid-fire Urdu: "By your appearance you seem a person of quality, but for all that I must say that your manners appall me." On the great room's exposed stairway Zabisko and Akbar intersect with Lakshmi, whom Ranjeet is manhandling down the stairs. "My name is Lakshmi. I'm being held here by force," she appeals to the tailor, who merely continues to natter as he is brought up to the bedroom on the mezzanine level where Jenny is being confined.

Jenny reacts with fury at Zabisko's appearance and at his insistence that she try on the wedding dress. Akbar tries to get close enough to reveal himself by posing as Zabisko's advocate but Jenny is having none of it. What is this "Akbar, Akbar" he's whispering, she wants to know; the tailor covers by repeating piously, "Allahu akbar." Seeing he's getting nowhere, Akbar announces he has seen enough to finish the dress and makes a bid to leave, but Robert prevents him: "No, no, no. You're not going anywhere until this wedding is over." "Why? Do you think that, old as I am, you're going to get me to dance a *mujra*?"[54] "Oh, shut up," says the exasperated Robert. Akbar follows Robert to the phone, where he is taking a call from his associate PEDRO (Mulchand). Robert arranges to have a priest and a wedding band sent to a spot where they can be picked up. Akbar takes note of the rendezvous—five o'clock at Hotel Naaz in the plush South Bombay neighborhood of Malabar Hill—and heckles Robert until he agrees to let him send a message back to his shop, ostensibly for the materials needed to finish the dress.

"I am writing this note in Urdu because nobody here knows Urdu. Jenny and Lakshmi are in danger. Immediately deliver this message to Amar and Brother Anthony," reads Akbar's voice as Haider Ali scans the note handed him by Ranjeet. The tailor takes it behind the shop to his living quarters and shows Salma, who takes charge. He is to bring the news to Amar and

Anthony. She'll join Akbar with the sewing machine and the trim. "O Provider," invokes Haider Ali. When Ranjeet asks to know who she is and why she insists on personally delivering the tailor's equipment, she says with pride, "I'm his lady."[55] She joins Akbar in the thieves' den. In the meantime, a tall priest in a white cassock and a shorter man equipped as a one-man band are waiting in a park-like location.[56] No sooner do we see the similarly sized pair of Anthony and Amar approach with an elaborately casual air than we sense the final masquerade in store; when a long, low Chevy pulls up, one of Robert's toughs at the wheel, the padre and bandsman who get in are only shown from the rear. The time appointed for the wedding is indeed fast approaching.[57] Ranjeet drags Lakshmi to Jenny's room. He warns Lakshmi to see that the bride is dressed within ten minutes. The groom, Zabisko, has also entered the room, looking clownish in a tuxedo with a ruffled shirt and big red bow. He informs Jenny that Lakshmi will be her bridesmaid. Sleazy as ever, Ranjeet concludes his threat with a moist-sounding air kiss; the men leave. Miserably, Lakshmi holds out the wedding gown to Jenny: "Please put this on. Otherwise my brother won't leave me alive. Please."

The father of the bride has changed into a formal gray morning suit. He paces impatiently. Where are the band and the padre? No sooner has Robert voiced his frustration than, with a crash of cymbals, the one-man band appears at the entrance. "The Amar Lal and Brothers Band reporting, sir!" But where are the brothers? Robert wants to know. "Oh, sir! I'm three-in-one. Everybody here is my brother. Hindu, Muslim, Sikh, Christian—all of us are brothers." He embraces Akbar, and in response to Robert's continued doubts states: "By the Lord's blessing, I'm the equal of twenty men. Just give me the opportunity. I'll play a whole band's worth all by myself." But where is that son-of-a-Father, Robert frets. "Not 'son-of-a-Father.'" Anthony enters in the priest's cassock. "Son, *Father* is what you call your dad, and it's your Daddy who's standing here in front of you." Pretending to mistake Robert for the groom, the false-whiskered Anthony kisses him effusively. Then, when Zabisko is pointed out as the real groom, he comically withdraws the kisses from Robert's cheeks with his hands and plants them on Zabisko's. "What a personality! What a personality!" Anthony dispatches Robert to fetch the bride. Akbar and Salma greet the padre, and Zabisko expresses interest in their prior relationship.

Anthony makes everyone smile with a Muslim joke about having offici-
ated at no fewer than four of his friend's weddings.

Seventh Song and Finale

Upstairs, the white-gowned Jenny loudly rebuffs Robert's entreaties.
"Father Anthony" takes note and announces that the bride must consent
before he can conduct any wedding. Zabisko is stymied: How can he con-
vince her? "What does she like?" the padre queries. "She likes . . . dancing,
singing. . . ." But, the lummox confesses, he's not much good at either.
"No problem . . . absolutely no problem," Anthony assures him, "I'll sing."
Akbar: "I'll dance." Amar, with a flourish of his accordion: "And I will
play." "Thank you," says Zabisko. "But Father—how's this all going to
happen? It all seems impossible." "To make the impossible possible . . . ,"
Anthony begins, ". . . that's our business," completes Akbar. At the
padre's cue, Amar strikes up a waltz melody, and the two other brothers
seize their partners—Robert and Zabisko—and initiate the last dance.

"Anhoni Ko Honi Kar De," they sing, "To make the impossible possible / The possible impossible. / Together in one place, we three
united: / Amar Akbar Anthony!" As each brother names himself, he
assumes a posture emblematic of his religious community: namaste, salaam, the sign of the cross. The brothers dazzle the assembled hoods with
comedic and musical hijinks. The scene switches briefly to Pedro, whose
work at the garage that he operates is interrupted by an agitated priest and
an unpantsed musician. Back at the mansion, the brothers bring on a
reprise, pantomiming prayer this time as they name themselves, each
winking at the next, with Anthony's wink reserved for the audience. The
final verse involves a move up to the mezzanine. Salma advances ahead of
the trio to join the other two brides. Once Anthony succeeds in flashing
Jenny his face beneath the false whiskers, all six have been united in the
ruse. They dance together back down the stairway, to the obtuse satisfaction of Zabisko and Robert.

Now "Father Anthony" stands Jenny and Zabisko next to each other
and leads the couple through their wedding vows. The groom affirms his
intent, but when it's her turn, the bride swoons and faints. Ranjeet, Lakshmi, Anthony, Robert, and Zabisko all kneel around the prostrate Jenny.

With real concern in his voice, Robert calls for a doctor. "No need to call a doctor. I'm a doctor," says Salma. She checks Jenny's pulse and makes her announcement, accompanied by a riff on Amar's accordion: "Congratulations! Your daughter is going to be a mother."

Venting the culminating groan of a whole film's worth of exasperated moments, Robert launches into recriminations. No wonder you gave her hand so readily, Zabisko retorts. Anthony acts the mediator as his brothers amp up the tension with frenetic fiddling and accordion music. Placating the enraged racketeers by promising he'll get the girl to confess, Anthony ascends to the bedroom where Salma and Lakshmi have taken Jenny. Dismissing the guard posted at the glass doors, he enters the room and, humming a liturgical tune, enacts a minor miracle: the curtains on the doors shut themselves without aid of human hands. Then he embraces Jenny, produces a coil of rope, and tells the women to escape through the window and send police as quickly as they can.

Pedro arrives at the mansion accompanied by the real priest and one-man band. The game is up. An astounded Robert demands, "Who are these people?" In a moment that echoes the title sequence during the blood transfusion, we are introduced to each brother anew. Amar snaps to attention, doffing his hat and peeling back his beard: "Inspector Amar." Akbar discards fez, wig, and beard, and declaims: "This unworthy is known as Akbar Ilahabadi." Anthony steps onto the mezzanine and tosses his padre's hat to the stooge at the bedroom door. "Anthony," he says, "Anthony Gonsalves," and knocks the goon out with one blow. This inaugurates a general melee, in which Anthony vaults down from the balcony to aid Amar in taking on all comers, and the gentle Akbar recuses himself to accompany their fisticuffs on Amar's accordion and bongo drums. Amar defeats Ranjeet, and Anthony subdues Zabisko. The boss, however, has exited the building, stepping over the prone form of Pedro in his urge to escape. He opens the gate to confront a police convoy, sirens blaring, with three righteous brides in the lead jeep's passenger seat. Making an about-face, he encounters Amar's and Anthony's fists, finally—and literally—clasped together. And when, after a good dose of slapstick punishment, Robert manages to flee back into the house, the third brother trips him up. "O Lord, until today when I've raised my hands it's always been to pray. But today, for the first time, I ask Your forgiveness"—and the peaceable Akbar delivers a roundhouse punch—*"Yah Ali—!"*

The camera gives us Robert tumbling straight into a jail cell, to land—in the classic South Asian posture of submission—at the feet of the man who already occupies it: Kishanlal. "I've begun this whole story with you, and today I'll complete it with you." They are joined by the remnants of Robert's gang: Ranjeet, Zabisko, and the thug played by Hercules. Kishanlal approaches the bars, on the other side of which his whole family stands reassembled. "Bharati. Why are you crying? Today you should be happy. You had lost three sons, hadn't you? But today, along with your three sons, Bhagvan has given you three daughters-in-law. Inspector Sahib, just once, I would like to grasp my three sons to my breast." A fully recovered Inspector Khanna assents. There is a fond embrace.

The final sequence shows us a quaint-looking jalopy, the front seats occupied by three hearty brothers, the back seats packed with three beaming brides. Merrily reprising the final song, they drive through a wooded landscape into the sunset—and India's future.

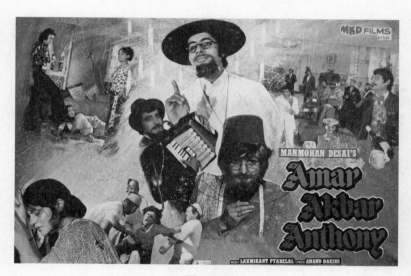

The End

Notes

Introduction

1. For more on the experience of moviegoing, see Lakshmi Srinivas, "The Active Audience: Spectatorship, Social Relations and the Experience of Cinema in India," *Media, Culture and Society* 24 (2002): 155–173. See also Pankaj Rishi Kumar's documentary *Kumar Talkies* (2000), which explores the connections between life in impoverished small-town North India and the world of rebellion and romance in the films at the town's lone movie theater.

2. The film has made its way into successful novels, like Vikram Chandra's *Sacred Games* (New York: Harper Perennial, 2007), and influential memoirs, like Suketu Mehta's *Maximum City: Bombay Lost and Found* (New York: Vintage, 2005), as a kind of stand-in for a Bambaiya ethos of the past. The film is likewise embedded in histories of modern India, as in Ramachandra Guha's massive *India After Gandhi: The History of the World's Largest Democracy* (New York: Harper Perennial, 2008), where a publicity still of Anthony in his illicit liquor den is the only image from a film selected as an illustration for the book (fig. 48). And to the extent that imitation is a form of flattery, consider that it took Pakistan only one year to produce a cinematic response with *Akbar Amar Anthony* (Haider Chaudhary, 1978). In India itself there has been *Ram Robert Rahim* (Vijaya Nirmala, 1980) in Telugu and *John Jaffer Janardhanan* (I. V. Sasi, 1982) in Malayalam, and there are always rumors of additional remakes. England has also joined the filmic procession with its own *Amar Akbar & Tony* (Atul Malhotra, 2014), an homage to the original but shot in London.

3. *Amar Akbar Anthony* is featured in various blogs and fan websites, and it is mentioned in many books on Indian cinema, as will be clear from what follows. Sidharth Bhatia, *Amar Akbar Anthony: Masala, Madness and Manmohan Desai* (Noida, India: Harper-Collins, 2013) provides an excellent introduction to the film; we have made grateful use of his research and insights.

4. Rachel Dwyer praises *Amar Akbar Anthony* as "one of the great *masala* films" and one of her own "favourite films of all time." Rachel Dwyer, *100 Bollywood Films* (London: British Film Institute, 2008), 14–15. M. K. Raghavendra calls the film "one of the boldest exercises in storytelling in Indian popular cinema." M. K. Raghavendra, *50 Indian Film Classics* (Noida, India: HarperCollins, 2009), 197. And Tejaswini Ganti lists *Amar Akbar Anthony* among the "key films" of post-independence India, and notes that it is "now considered a classic." Tejaswini Ganti, *Bollywood: A Guidebook to Popular Indian Cinema* (New York: Routledge, 2004), 163. Even an outlier to the world of Indian cinema like *The Rough Guide to Comedy Movies* lists *Amar Akbar Anthony* as a "near perfect *masala* film" that displays "Bombay cinema at its playful best." Bob McCabe, *The Rough Guide to Comedy Movies* (London: Rough Guides, 2005), 255.

5. Vijay Mishra, *Bollywood Cinema: Temples of Desire* (New York: Routledge, 2001), 176. Mishra argues that *Amar Akbar Anthony* confirms the resilience of the secular nation-state in three ways: (1) through "the grammar of the eternal dharma, the ultimate Law of the Father" embodied in Amar; (2) through "the figure of the mother, who confirms the primacy of blood," which Mishra relates to Partition and the ability of the prologue's transfusion scene to assuage "for the Indian spectator" the fear that the rupture of the family here (and by extension Partition) will not be uncorrected in the film; and (3) through "the iconography of Gandhi" as the metonymic referent for both "Indian independence and Indian secularism," where "the secular can be celebrated provided that (Hindu) dharma remains intact." Ibid., 176–177.

6. Jyotika Virdi, *The Cinematic ImagiNation: Indian Popular Films as Social History* (New Brunswick, NJ: Rutgers University Press, 2003), 36–37, 75.

7. Rachel Dwyer, *Filming the Gods: Religion and Indian Cinema* (New York: Routledge, 2006), 143, 144.

8. Philip Lutgendorf, "Amar Akbar Anthony," *Philip's Fil-ums: Notes on Indian Popular Cinema,* accessed April 8, 2015, www.uiowa.edu/indiancinema/amar-akbar-anthony.

9. Another thing we like about the allegory is that in its many tellings, it is itself understood to be many different allegories. Jains, for example, have used it to illustrate their "doctrine of manypointedness" *(anekāntavāda),* while Buddhists have used it to explain the multiplicity of non-Buddhist views and the "right" view of the Buddha. For Sufis, the parable illustrates the ultimate inadequacy of poetic language—however inspired—to express mystical experience. The elephant has a long and rich history in South Asia as a repository of symbolic values: the ears, wisdom; the feet, royal power; the tusks, writing; and the trunk, you guessed it, a phallus. The story was made popular among English speakers in the nineteenth century by John Godfrey Saxe's poem "The Blind Men and the Elephant."

10. "Amar Akbar Anthony: Blow to Prestige," *Film World,* August 1977 [NFAI Archive no. 43625-A].

11. "Cinema: Of Saints and Sinners," *Times of India,* n.d. [NFAI Archive no. 96042-A].

12. "Indian Films in City: Amar Akbar Anthony, a Hilarious Comedy," *Deccan Herald,* June 25, 1977 [No NFAI Archive no.].

13. Shalini Pradhan, "Amar Akbar Anthony: Birds of the Same Blood Group," *Filmfare,* June 10–23, 1977 [NFAI Archive no. 96011-A].

14. "Amar Akbar Anthony," *Dream Star,* July 1977 [No NFAI Archive no.].

15. A parallel can be seen in the way that reality television was first evaluated within the existing genre of the "documentary;" it was disparaged, and only later came to be recognized as a genre unto itself. See Susan Murray, "I Think We Need a New Name for It: The Meeting of Documentary and Reality TV," in *Reality TV: Remaking Television Culture,* eds. Susan Murray and Laurie Ouellette (New York and London: New York University Press, 2008), 65–81.

16. The other four nominations were for Best Film, Best Director, Best Lyricist, and Best Male Playback Singer (for Mohamed Rafi's "Parda Hai Parda").

17. "9-Cinema Jubilee" [NFAI Archive no. 41985-XI]. If a film is shown continuously in cinemas in one city for twenty-five weeks, it earns a silver jubilee; fifty weeks earns a golden jubilee, and seventy-five weeks or more earns a platinum jubilee.

18. "Amar, Akbar Anthony on UK TV," *Indian Express,* October 10, 1980 [No NFAI Archive no.]. See also Rosie Thomas, "Indian Cinema: Pleasures and Popularity," *Screen* 26, no. 3–4 (1985): 117.

19. This economic decline and subsequent recovery correlates, to some extent, with the beginning of Emergency Rule and the years after its end. See Atul Kohli, "Politics of Economic Growth in India, 1980–2005: Part I: The 1980s," *Economic and Political Weekly,* April 1, 2006: 1251–1259.

20. "Amar Akbar Anthony: Man's Master-Blend," *Blitz,* June 4, 1977 [NFAI Archive no. 45280-A].

21. "'Amar Akbar Anthony'—Delectable Escapist Fare," *Goa Herald,* June 21, 1977 [NFAI Archive no. 72489-A].

22. "Amar Akbar Anthony: Blow to Prestige," *Film World,* August 1977 [NFAI Archive no. 43625-A].

23. Pradhan, "Amar Akbar Anthony."

24. "'Amar Akbar Anthony'—Delectable Escapist Fare."

25. NFAI Archive no. 31236-A, no title, author, publication date, or publication source. Much like the film critics quoted before, the professor's comments about his or her rationale for the project gesture to English-speaking India's alienation from the masses: "We make so many glib statements about what the masses like, and I wanted them to have some first hand experience of what they were talking about. But I also want the students, most of whom come from the middle class, to have the experience of talking to people about issues they don't know. I particularly like them to talk to working people. It is a surprise for them that even peons have views: In fact, one peon said that he was far too busy to have time for such interviews, and the student was 'amazed by his air of superiority.' Nevertheless, he finally agreed, and over a cup of tea, he told her precisely what he thought of the direction, the acting, the location, the stars, the message."

26. Bikram Singh, "Amar-Akbar-Anthony: Absurd, but Funny," *Times of India,* May 30, 1977 [NFAI Archive no. 69998-A].

27. A few years earlier, *The Poseidon Adventure* (Ronald Neame, 1972)—a star-studded Hollywood affair that likewise appealed to the masses and not the critics—was similarly dismissed as "strictly formula hokum but reasonably diverting" (*Washington Post,* January 5, 1973, B7/4). Here too "hokum" connotes a melodramatic and overdetermined performance; it was a criticism that would increasingly be leveled throughout the 1970s at Hollywood and Bollywood both.

28. Singh, "Amar-Akbar-Anthony."

29. For more on the genres of Hindi film, see Rajinder Dudrah, *Bollywood: Sociology Goes to the Movies* (New Delhi: Sage Publications, 2006), 175–180. For more on 1970s cinema, see Priya Joshi and Rajinder Dudrah, eds., *Special Issue: The 1970s and Its Legacies in India's Cinemas, South Asian Popular Culture* 10, no. 1 (2012).

30. Harish Kumar Mehra, "Future of Multi-Starrers: Amar-Akbar-Anthony—a Test Case!" *Current,* April 23, 1977 [NFAI Archive no. 47005-A].

31. "Amar Akbar Anthony," *Dream Star.*

32. Pradhan, "Amar Akbar Anthony." Desai's *Parvarish* also came out in 1977. Many films produced under the Emergency were only released after it was lifted.

33. NFAI Archive no. 96055-A, no title, author, publication date, or publication source. One can, however, see a "/77," presumably added in by the press-cutting service to signify the date.

34. NFAI Archive no. 96055-A.

35. "Cinema: Of Saints and Sinners."

36. "'The Three Musketeers' with a Planned Destiny," *Indian Express,* June 7, 1977 [NFAI Archive no. 96048-A].

37. Sunki Laxminarayan, letter to the editor, "Hindi Films," *Sunday Standard* (ND/BY), February 12, 1978 [NFAI Archive no. 49634-A].

38. Ibid.

39. Tailpiece, "Secularism—'Filmi' Style," *Indian Express* [NFAI Archive no. 43834-A].

40. Ibid. The reference here to the paan shop—the local tobacco stall—is a close cognate in India to the European cafés that Jürgen Habermas describes in *The Structural Transformation of the Public Sphere* (Cambridge: Polity Press, 1989).

41. Thomas, "Indian Cinema," 124.

42. "'Amar Akbar Anthony'—Delectable Escapist Fare."

43. "Amar Akbar Anthony: Man's Master-Blend."

44. "Amar Akbar Anthony: Blow to Prestige."

45. See, for example, Colleen Taylor Sen, *Curry: A Global History* (London: Reaktion Books, 2009). See also Sharmila Sen, "Looking for Doubles in the Caribbean," *Massachusetts Review* 45, no. 3 (2004): 241–257.

46. Raghavendra, *50 Indian Film Classics,* 197.

47. Ibid., 194.

48. See, respectively, M. Madhava Prasad, "This Thing Called Bollywood," *Seminar* 525: 2003, accessed January 21, 2014, www.india-seminar.com/2003/525/525%20madhava%20prasad.htm; Ravi Vasudevan, "The Meanings of 'Bollywood,'" in *Beyond the Boundaries of Bollywood: The Many Forms of Hindi Cinema,* eds. Rachel Dwyer and Jerry Pinto (New Delhi: Oxford University Press, 2011), 3–29; Ashish Rajadhyaksha, "The 'Bollywoodization' of the Indian Cinema: Cultural Nationalism in a Global Arena," *Inter-Asia Cultural Studies* 4, no. 1: 25–39; and Tejaswini Ganti, *Producing Bollywood: Inside the Contemporary Hindi Film Industry* (Durham, NC: Duke University Press, 2012), 12–15.

49. As Dudrah and Desai note, "*Masala* films are often the ones mistaken to represent all Bollywood films as formulaic or 'the same' in uninformed commentaries on Indian and popular Hindi cinema." Rajinder Dudrah and Jigna Desai, eds., *The Bollywood Reader* (Berkshire, UK: Open University Press, 2008), 11.

50. Prasad, "This Thing Called Bollywood."

51. H. R. F. Keating, *Filmi, Filmi, Inspector Ghote* (Garden City, NY: Doubleday, 1977), 40.

52. "Contact," on H. R. F. Keating's official webpage, in reply to a query on November 29, 2009, accessed December 15, 2014, http://hrfkeating.com/contact/#comment-26. For more on Bevinda Collaco's claim that she invented the term, see Anand, "Wordspeak: On the Bollywood Beat," *Hindu,* March 7, 2004, www.thehindu.com/lr/2004/03/07 /stories/2004030700390600.htm. See also "Community News," *Goan Voice Newsletter,* March 4, 2004, www.goanvoice.org.uk/newsletter/2004/Mar/issue1. The filmmaker Amit Khanna has also taken credit for originating the term, but he didn't use it in print, so this too is as much hearsay as evidence. *Telegraph,* April 1, 2005.

53. Ganti, *Producing Bollywood,* 369, note 20.

54. These love stories have parallels with the medieval heroic romance, which have a long history in India, Europe, and the Middle East. They generally involve a quest of self-discovery or spiritual transformation, usually of a male hero, often directed toward reuniting with or otherwise winning the love of a heroine. Such stories are often circular, with the hero finding himself back where he began but renewed, changed, and wiser. As such, these stories are also metaphorical, simultaneously romantic journeys and religious ones, connected to Christianity, Islam, Hinduism, and so on. See, for example, Aditya Behl's introduction to the *The Madhumalati,* a sixteenth-century Sufi romance from India. Aditya Behl and Simon Weightman, trans., *The Madhumalati* (New York: Oxford University Press, 2001), xi–xlvi.

55. Jyotika Virdi puts it succinctly: "The concept of the nation subtends the imagination in Hindi films and centers its moral universe." Virdi, *Cinematic ImagiNation,* 9. See too Sumita S. Chakravarty, *National Identity in Indian Popular Cinema, 1947–1987* (Austin: University of Texas Press, 1993); K. Moti Gokulsing and Wimal Dissanayake, *Indian Popular Cinema: A Narrative of Cultural Change* (Stoke on Trent, UK: Trentham Books, 1998); Ashis Nandy, ed., *The Secret Politics of Our Desires: Innocence, Culpability and Indian Popular Cinema* (Delhi: Zed Books, 1999); Ravi Vasudevan, ed., *Making Meaning in Indian Cinema* (New Delhi: Oxford University Press, 2000); Rachel Dwyer and Christopher Pinney, eds., *Pleasure and the Nation: The History, Politics, and Consumption of Public Culture in India* (New Delhi: Oxford University Press, 2001); Gayatri Chatterjee, *Mother India* (London: British Film Institute, 2002); Rachel Dwyer and Divia Patel, *Cinema India: The Visual Culture of Hindi Film* (New Brunswick, NJ: Rutgers University Press, 2002); Rajadhyaksha, "'Bollywoodization'"; and many others. For challenges to the nation-state centrality of Indian cinema, see Priya Jaikumar, *Cinema at the End of Empire: A Politics of Transition in Britain and India* (Durham, NC: Duke University Press, 2006); and, to some degree, Mishra, *Bollywood Cinema.*

56. Lalitha Gopalan, *Cinema of Interruptions: Action Genres in Contemporary Indian Cinema* (London: British Film Institute, 2002).

57. For more on the aesthetic and political reasons for Indian melodrama, see Ravi Vasudevan, "The Melodramatic Mode and the Commercial Hindi Cinema: Notes on Film History, Narrative and Performance in the 1950s," *Screen* 30, no. 3 (1989): 29–50, and *The Melodramatic Public: Film Form and Spectatorship in Indian Cinema* (New York: Palgrave Macmillan, 2011); Ashish Rajadhyaksha, "The Epic Melodrama: Themes of Nationality in Indian Cinema," *Journal of Arts and Ideas* 25–26 (1993): 55–70; and

M. Madhava Prasad, *Ideology of the Hindi Film: A Historical Reconstruction* (New Delhi: Oxford University Press, 1998): 135.

58. Prasad, "This Thing Called Bollywood."

59. Rajadhyaksha, "'Bollywoodization.'"

60. Nandy, *Secret Politics.*

61. Virdi, *Cinematic ImagiNation.*

62. Sumita S. Chakravarty, "The National-Heroic Image: Masculinity and Masquerade," in *The Bollywood Reader,* eds. Rajinder Dudrah and Jigna Desai (New York: Open University Press, 2008), 86–87.

63. Amit Rai, *Untimely Bollywood: Globalization and India's New Media Assemblage* (Durham, NC: Duke University Press, 2009).

64. Mishra, *Bollywood Cinema.*

65. Ranjani Mazumdar, *Bombay Cinema: An Archive of the City* (Minneapolis: University of Minnesota Press, 2007).

66. Anandam P. Kavoori and Aswin Punathambekar, eds., *Global Bollywood* (New York: New York University Press, 2008).

67. Benedict Anderson, *Imagined Communities: Reflections on the Origin and Spread of Nationalism* (London: Verso, 1983).

68. Linda Hutcheon, *Irony's Edge: The Theory and Politics of Irony* (London: Routledge, 1994). Irony has also been identified as a dominant feature of modern historical writing. See Hayden White, *Tropics of Discourse: Essays in Cultural Criticism* (Baltimore and London: Johns Hopkins University Press, 1986).

69. Roland Barthes, *The Pleasure of the Text,* trans. Richard Miller (New York: Hill and Wang, 1975).

70. Raghavendra, *50 Indian Film Classics,* 196.

71. Connie Haham, *Enchantment of the Mind: Manmohan Desai's Films* (New Delhi: Roli Books, 2006): 23.

72. "For Desai," Bhatia notes, "Satyajit Ray was a metaphor for seriousness and authenticity which had no place in Desai's world view." Bhatia, *Amar Akbar Anthony,* 49.

73. Haham, *Enchantment of the Mind,* 107.

74. Ibid., 56–57.

75. A comparison with the festival of Holi here is apt. It too creates a temporary transgressive and cleansing disorder, a subversively curative release from the constraining rules of propriety. And what fuels this reprieve, as McKim Marriott notes in his famous essay, is love: "Boundless, unilateral love of every kind flooded over the usual compartmentalization and indifference among separated castes and families. Insubordinate libido inundated all established hierarchies of age, sex, caste, wealth, and power. . . . [But] the Holi of Krishna is no mere doctrine of love: rather it is the script for a drama that must be acted out by each devotee passionately, joyfully." McKim Marriott, "The Feast of Love," in *Krishna: Myths, Rites and Attitudes,* ed. Milton Singer (Honolulu: East-West Center Press, 1966), 212. Not surprisingly, scenes of Holi celebrations are often featured in Bollywood films, including many Amitabh Bachchan classics, like *Sholay* (Ramesh Sippy, 1975) and *Silsila* (Yash Chopra, 1981).

76. Haham, *Enchantment of the Mind,* 144.

77. Bhatia, *Amar Akbar Anthony,* 76.

78. See too Haham, *Enchantment of the Mind,* 146–148.

79. One might think of these as "kinship emotional fantasies," for Desai uses family ties to heighten affective response. As the screenwriter K. K. Shukla explains, "Kinship emotion in India is very strong—so this element always works—that's what 'lost and found' is about. It doesn't work so well with educated audiences who go several days without seeing their families, but it works with B and C grade audiences who get worried if they don't see a family member by 6:30 P.M., whose family members are an important part of themselves and their experience of the world." Thomas, "Indian Cinema," 126.

80. Bhatia, *Amar Akbar Anthony,* 48.

81. Haham, *Enchantment of the Mind,* 144.

82. Ibid., 115.

83. See the work of Louis Althusser on ideology, especially his seminal essay "Ideology and Ideological State Apparatuses," in *Lenin and Philosophy and Other Essays,* trans. Ben Brewster (London: Monthly Review Press, 1971), 121–176.

84. Desai also claimed that children were his target audience: "Children form a majority of my audience. I aim my films at them especially, and then for all ages. It is my attempt to provide clean stuff." Ibid., 96. Desai's films are certainly childlike in their sense of wonder and play, although their appeal is more to the working stiff than to the child.

85. Thomas, "Indian Cinema," 120.

86. Bhatia, *Amar Akbar Anthony,* 130.

87. Thomas, "Indian Cinema," 119, citing Iqbal Masud in *Cine Blitz,* July 1981.

88. Ibid., 123.

89. Ibid.

90. Speaking of one such mix of moods, Desai explains, "*Coolie* is first half comedy; first three reels are emotional, comedy, comedy, comedy, then trrrrraaa . . . : emotion, drama, action, everything going in like this in correct portions." Haham, *Enchantment of the Mind,* 62.

91. Haham, *Enchantment of the Mind,* 68–70.

92. But the recycling continues. Recently released was a Bhojpuri film with the same name (Harry Fernandes, 2012), and following Desai's *masala* formula it was a multi-starrer, with fights, car chases, item songs, and a Holi scene. It was a huge production with grand aspirations, but like its predecessor, it underperformed in theaters (Kathryn Hardy, personal communication).

93. Rosie Thomas, "Melodrama and the Negotiation of Morality in Mainstream Hindi Film," in *Consuming Modernity: Public Culture in a South Asian World,* ed. Carol A. Breckenridge (Minneapolis: University of Minnesota Press, 1995), 163, 164.

94. Ibid., 163. Thomas offers this elaboration: "One is more likely to hear accusations of 'unbelievability' if the codes of, for example, ideal kinship behavior are ineptly transgressed (i.e. a son kills his mother, or a father knowingly and callously causes his son to suffer) than if a hero is a superman who single-handedly knocks out a dozen burly henchmen and then bursts into song." Thomas, "Indian Cinema," 128.

95. Reginald Dyer, who was an Indian Army brigadier when he ordered his troops to fire on a civilian crowd in the enclosed space of Jallianwala Bagh, became one of the folk villains of Indian nationalism. A well-remembered aspect of his career is the enthusiastic reception that greeted him in England in the massacre's wake. A Hindi film called

Jallian Wala Bagh (Balraj Tah, 1977), released in the same year as *Amar Akbar Anthony*, shared two of its stars: Vinod Khanna and Shabana Azmi.

96. Philip Lutgendorf, "Mard," *Philip's Fil-ums: Notes on Indian Popular Cinema,* accessed April 8, 2015, www.uiowa.edu/indiancinema/mard. Desai offers a similar criticism of political leaders in *Dharam Veer* (1977), where there is likewise a mapping of the present on the past, as Raani Maa, a Mrs. Gandhi–like figure with the requisite streak of gray hair, mediates a palace full of corrupt and scheming officials. Protesting the "eye for an eye" law that exists in the kingdom, and the capricious way it is applied, the poor yet noble Dharam (Dharmendra) offers this rebuke: "If you continue to play with the lives of the poor, this reign will not continue. The fires of revolution will flare up in the hearts of the poor, and this palace will be consumed." Cf. Haham, *Enchantment of the Mind,* 132–133.

97. Bhatia, *Amar Akbar Anthony,* 113.

98. The official names of these two landmarks have been, for some time, Chhatrapati Shivaji Terminus and Hutatma Chowk, respectively. These are products of the campaign of Marathi-ized nomenclature that rebranded the city as *Mumbai* in 1995.

99. And perhaps in Delhi as well. Writing about India's capital and its own encounter with development and modernity, Rana Dasgupta likewise observes, "We tend to think of migration as movement in space; but in some ways this kind of migration is a sideways step within the far grander, onward exodus that everyone who lives amid the churn of capitalism is part of: the migration across the plains of time." Rana Dasgupta, *Capital: A Portrait of Twenty-First-Century Delhi* (Noida, India: HarperCollins, 2014), 48.

100. One possible candidate is Akbar's auditorium, the Birla Krida Kendra, a real South Bombay location that happens to announce its name on a sign across its façade. But the name is never spoken or otherwise indicated in the film.

101. For readers more familiar with the geography of New York than of Bombay, the concept of *outer boroughs* may be helpful.

102. The suburbs are bookended by Bandra on the inner end and Borivali on the outer. A glance at the map will complicate this equation, but these are the names impressed daily on the minds of commuters on the Western Line of the Bombay rail system.

103. Amar mentions the hospital just before the film's title sequence, but its exterior is shown only after the great car chase in the second half: it turns out to be a colonnaded building with an Edwardian, South Bombay look, and it bears a sign with a different name: "Sawant General Hospital."

104. It is unclear whether yet another hospital-bed scene, when Amar visits his wounded foster father, was filmed on the same set or not. Other interiors belonging to the hospital include Salma's office and the operating theater.

105. At first glance, the Muslim Quarter gives the impression of being part of a densely built up downtown area, but the impression is misplaced. The Muslim Quarter is the film's own parodic version of the old-fashioned pleasure quarter of a North Indian city like Lucknow, and this association—which is one of the keys to *Amar Akbar Anthony*'s allegory of the nation—is developed in Chapter 2. But its location in the suburbs, as opposed to Bombay proper, is made clear by a circular pan that follows Akbar as he sings on top of a ladder in the "Tayyab Ali Pyar Ka Dushman" number. The Quar-

ter's whole skyline can be seen, with no big downtown buildings to rival the spires of the three religious structures.

106. Perhaps owing to its proximity to the church, Anthonyville has an obvious Christian presence, such as the public cross on which Anthony lands in the middle of his fight with Amar.

107. Bombay's coastal neighborhoods are dotted with such settlements. The real Bandra, historically and in the present day, contains more than one.

108. Café Naaz, which closed in 1999, drew customers from across the city, perhaps more for its spectacular view than for its Irani menu. Bollywood film crews were known to go there for setting up elevated shots of the city.

109. A few miscellaneous sites remain: the bungalow—modest but with a view of the sea—that Lakshmi's wicked stepmother rents could also be in Bandra, but just as well in Juhu or another coastal suburb. Robert's magnificently kitsch second mansion could really be anywhere, although the glimpse we get of the ornamented colonial-era exterior suggests a location in an old downtown neighborhood. The dungeon where Zabisko has imprisoned Robert's twin, Albert, is yet more elusive—underground in more ways than one.

110. Visual details indicate that the Muslim Quarter also contains Hindu and Christian communities in residence; they do not, however, appear within the film's plot.

111. To be sure, some residents of the city do enjoy lavish comforts, but the great homes we are shown as examples of the high life all belong to crooks. Diegetically, wealth is connected to immorality, and making money and having it are indexed to hardheartedness or inhumanity. See, for example, Chapters 1 and 2 for what money brings to two of the film's father figures—Kishanlal and Tayyab Ali.

112. Haham, *Enchantment of the Mind,* 38.

113. Tailpiece, "Secularism—'Filmi' Style."

1. Amar

1. Khanna, in addition to being the surname of Amar's adoptive father, is the actor's real-life surname as well as a stereotypical surname for a Hindu police officer. Amitabh Bachchan, for example, plays Inspector Vijay Khanna in *Zanjeer* (Prakash Mehra, 1973) and Inspector Karan Kumar Khanna in *Geraftaar* (Prayag Raj, 1985).

2. In childhood, however, Amar does bear the mark of some kind of divine protection. In the scene when he buries the gun (see Figure 4), he is shown wearing a protective amulet around his neck. It is a cylindrically shaped hollow tube, silver in color, tied and knotted with black thread. Such objects are known as *taveez* (and *kavach*), and are used by a variety of religious communities in India. They are empowered according to the objects placed inside of them—either sanctified materials or bits of sacred text, such as from the Qur'an or from Hindu scripture. As such, Amar is protected by a divine power, but the identity of that divine power is concealed. This also references a millennia-old practice associated with Tantra in South Asia in which amulets, often containing some text, impart supernatural protection.

3. As Connie Haham notes, "Desai himself had no second thoughts and no regrets about his portrayal of the prisoner-beating police officer. To his mind, such practices were

both commonplace and justifiable. He was apparently immune to any concern that police brutality, with its contempt for human beings, might corrupt society as a whole." Connie Haham, *Enchantment of the Mind: Manmohan Desai's Films* (New Delhi: Roli Books, 2006), 117.

4. Max Weber, *Weber: Political Writings,* ed. Peter Lassman and Ronald Speirs (Cambridge: Cambridge University Press, 1994), 300–311.

5. Kishanlal just might have given Amar a real gun, which could help explain the latter's "loaded" relationship with guns in the movie. Kishanlal arrives home from prison with a box of sweets, a wrapped package, a large plastic truck, a toy cricket bat, a toy cart, and a gun. Distressed and disoriented at the pitiful condition of his family, he sits with his literally starving children. He absentmindedly sets aside the plastic truck, giving it to no one, and then hands out the bat, the cart, and finally ("You," he tells Amar, "take . . . this") the gun. Still frazzled, he then sets down the wrapped package (a gift for his wife?) and distributes the sweets. One possibility is that the truck was intended for Amar, which would have been an appropriate gift, and for some deliberate or unconscious reason he instead gave him the gun, which he had brought home for his own protection.

6. See, for example, Alok Bhalla, ed., *Stories about the Partition of India* (New Delhi: HarperCollins, 1994); Intizar Husain, *A Chronicle of the Peacocks: Stories of Partition, Exile and Lost Memories,* trans. Alok Bhalla and Vishwamiter Adil (New Delhi: Oxford University Press, 2002); Bhaskar Sarkar, *Mourning the Nation: Indian Cinema in the Wake of Partition* (Durham, NC: Duke University Press, 2009).

7. Salman Rushdie, *Midnight's Children* (New York: Knopf, 1981), 243. As Saleem explains elsewhere, "My inheritance includes this gift, the gift of inventing new parents for myself whenever necessary. The power of giving birth to fathers and mothers." Ibid.,108. According to one scholar, "If one adds the multiple surrogate or symbolic parents and parent figures [of Saleem], one arrives at approximately seven maternal characters and thirteen father figures." Matt Kimmich, *Offspring Fictions: Salman Rushdie's Family Novels* (Amsterdam: Rodopi, 2008), 56.

8. Rushdie, *Midnight's Children,* 552. This formulation is reminiscent of Claudius's words from *Hamlet* (act 3, scene 2): "Your father lost a father / And that father lost, lost his, and the survivor bound / In filial obligation for some term / To do obsequious sorrow."

9. Rushdie, *Midnight's Children,* 118.

10. On paternity and "elective filiation" in Rushdie's work, see Kimmich, *Offspring Fictions,* 23. Such moments of elective filiation are, to be sure, not limited to fiction and film or to the Indian subcontinent. Consider this refashioning of paternity in the autobiography of the rap star and entrepreneur Jay-Z: "We were kids without fathers, so we found our fathers on wax and on the streets and in history, and in a way, that was a gift. We got to pick and choose the ancestors who would inspire the world we were going to make for ourselves. That was part of the ethos of that time and place, and it got built into the culture we created. Rap took the remnants of a dying society and created something new." Jay-Z, *Decoded* (New York: Spiegel and Grau, 2010), 255.

11. Kishanalal is a kind of Robert-lite. Just out of jail, Kishanlal chastises Robert for not making the payments promised to his poor family: "To you the misfortunes of the poor are no more than a joke . . . . Robert *Seth,* you're drunk—not with liquor but with your

own wealth." Twenty-two years later, looking just like Robert, he is livid when one of his underlings fails to pass on money to a poor family. The man begs for forgiveness, and Kishanlal berates him: "Kishanlal can forgive a murder, but he can't forgive a person who lets someone's wife and children starve!" Then he bellows, "I'm no Robert!" Kishanlal is a crook, but he isn't drunk with wealth, and he does care for the poor. Also unlike Robert, he doesn't shoot people in the back . . . or shoot police officers or stab religious leaders.

12. In this way, Jenny also joins the ranks of midnight's children, for she too is reborn on Independence Day, with Kishanlal as her new father. Unlike the other chosen fathers in the film, however, Kishanlal raises his new offspring not in his own religion but in that of his new charge. Jenny remains a Christian, unlike Kishanlal, who is a Hindu by birth.

13. When Kishanlal steals Jenny from Robert's bed, he places a note in the pocket of Robert's pajamas, no doubt telling him that it was he who stole Jenny, and that Robert brought this grief on himself. The note is never discussed, but it functions as an inversion of the suicide note that Bharati had left Kishanlal earlier that same day.

14. At Jenny's birthday party, no other family besides Robert is present, and when Kishanlal steals Jenny later that night, she is sleeping alone with Robert in his bed. There is no evidence that the bed was ever shared with a wife.

15. Robert's twin, Albert, is a respectable bank manager living abroad, who is later kidnapped by one of Robert's allies so that Robert can take his place and escape to England while Albert is forced to take Robert's place in jail for his murder of the Padre. There is little love between the brothers. This plan exhibits the film's tendency to replicate and reverse plot points: Robert will switch identities with Albert, just as Kishanlal had previously done with him, and Albert will serve time in prison for a murder Robert committed, also following Kishanlal's example.

16. Akbar and Salma are oddly reticent with each other, due perhaps to the extraordinary circumstances: Akbar had just saved Salma and her father from dying in a house fire, and her father had just approved their marriage.

17. The absence of any family members in Robert's life other than Jenny prompts us to wonder: Was his daughter perhaps adopted? Or, in line with Robert's character, stolen?

18. Anthony's adoptive father then tries to stop the kidnapping, but Robert stabs him, killing him on the day before he would celebrate his adopted son's wedding and Jenny's transformation into his daughter-in-law. The film juxtaposes the dead priest with an image of the bleeding Jesus, for the Padre was likewise blameless and died for the sins of others. Contrary to Kishanlal's claim, Robert wasn't Jenny's father's murderer—but he is the murderer of Anthony's.

19. The brothers joke and jest with one another in an intimate way, but this "fraternity" is more social than familial. Akbar and Anthony call each other "brother" and call their mother "Maa," terms of endearment that suggest deep friendship and intimacy. This naming can also be read as a kind of aspiration on their part, a desire for more family, and it also serves as an ironic harbinger of the later denouement. Amar, however, doesn't use such familial terms. He is more restrained than his brothers, conflicted perhaps about embracing others who are younger, weaker, and on the margins of the workings of the state.

20. Whereas classical texts speak of this in terms of *varna,* or what we might think of as "caste," here the difference is one of class. Salma is a doctor working at a hospital and surely has a better salary than Akbar, a sometime singer of *qawwali.* Jenny is foreign educated and awash in wealth, not a petty criminal like Anthony.

21. NFAI Archive no. 31236-A, no title, author, publication date, or publication source.

22. *Chhalia* was a success for Desai, and it did reasonably well at the box office, although it suffered because it was released the same week as K. Asif's monumental *Mughal-e-Azam.*

23. For more on representations of the historical events of Partition in Indian cinema—and especially on the theme of familial partitions—see Kavita Daiya, *Violent Belongings: Partition, Gender, and National Culture in Postcolonial India* (Philadelphia: Temple University Press, 2008); Sarkar, *Mourning the Nation.*

24. Ironically, the actor who played Kewal—Rehman—was himself born in Lahore to a Pathan family of royal lineage that then immigrated to India, and the actor who played Abdul Rehman Khan—Pran Kewal Sikand, *Amar Akbar Anthony*'s own Pran—was born in Delhi.

25. Following the censors' intervention, the lyrics to "Chhalia Mera Naam" were changed to "Fraud is my name / Fraud is my name." The censors forced many changes on the song, as is evident from a comparison between the original audio release and the edited version contained within the film. The censors were clearly uncomfortable with Chhalia's "game"—the fact that he's a thief—and most of the changes seem to have been designed to make him seem less like a con man and more like a do-gooder.

26. Philip Lutgendorf, "Ramayana Remix: Two Hindi Film-Songs as Epic Commentary," in *Ramayana in Focus: Visual and Performing Arts of Asia,* ed. Gauri Parimoo Krishnan (Singapore: Asian Civilizations Museum, 2010), 147.

27. There is a long tradition in the subcontinent of using the *Ramayana* in this way to make arguments that are both political and religious. As Sheldon Pollock notes, "In fact, it may be doubted whether any other text in South Asia has ever supplied an idiom or vocabulary for political imagination remotely comparable in longevity, frequency of deployment, and effectivity." Sheldon Pollock, "Rāmāyaṇa and Political Imagination in India," *Journal of Asian Studies* 52, no. 2 (1993): 262.

28. The song's original audio release, before it was bowdlerized by the censors, makes this explicit. In the original release, for example, Chhalia sings, "I am prince of the streets. / What I want, I take. / Princes play with swords. / I play with scissors." In the film, however, he says, "I am prince of the poor. / What you ask for, I give. / Princes play with swords. / I play with tears." Nevertheless, the line "I play with tears" plays over an image of Chhalia picking up a pair of scissors and thrusting them forward in a cutting motion. The censors no doubt recognized something incorrect in Chhalia—as a self-proclaimed "saint," he certainly went "against the grain" of normative Hinduism. Their goal was to turn him into an Indian Robin Hood.

29. In the movie, Abdul Rehman Khan's chivalry—more specifically, the Pathan code of Pashtunwali—is much more effective than the state in combating familial disintegration, but it has its limitations. Abdul Rehman offers asylum to Shanti but later becomes incensed that his sister has never returned from India, and therefore goes to Delhi for justice. He battles Chhalia, with whom he has a prior score to settle, and tries to avenge

his sister by abducting the love of Chhalia's life. Since he has never seen Shanti's face, he doesn't recognize that the woman in Chhalia's home is the same woman he housed so honorably for five years. When Shanti calls out for him to stop, he realizes his terrible mistake. He has failed doubly: he hasn't avenged his sister's honor, and now he has lost his own. On Abdul Rehman's train ride back to Pakistan, however, an older Sikh gentleman approaches him and asks if he is going to Pakistan. The Sikh explains that he has looked after someone else's charge, treating her "as his own daughter," but now he is old and wants to reunite her with her brother in Pakistan so that he can face God with a clear conscience. He then calls over his de facto daughter, who is in full purdah, and she turns out to be Sakina. Brother and sister are reunited. In all, the state (which is all but absent from the film) is a less effective moral agent than Pashtunwali, which is less effective than the Sikh moral code, which is less effective than Chhalia's saintly fraud.

30. Lutgendorf, "Ramayana Remix," 147, 151; emphasis added.

31. Ibid., 145.

32. For one example of police corruption during the Central Recovery Operation, see Kirapāla Siṅgha, *The Partition of the Punjab* (Patiala: Punjabi University, 1972), 171.

33. As one reluctant woman explained, "I have lost my husband and have now gone in for another. You want me to go to India where I have got nobody and, of course, you do not expect me to change husbands each day." Urvashi Butalia, "Muslims and Hindus, Men and Women: Communal Stereotypes and the Partition of India," in *Women and Right-Wing Movements: Indian Experiences,* ed. Tanka Sarkar and Urvashi Butalia (London: Zed Books, 1995), 65. For more on such experiences, see Ritu Menon and Kamla Bhasin, *Borders and Boundaries: Women in India's Partition* (New Brunswick, NJ: Rutgers University Press, 1998).

34. U. Bhaskar Rao, *The Story of Rehabilitation* (Delhi: Department of Rehabilitation, Government of India, 1967), 15.

35. Butalia, "Muslims and Hindus," 71–74. As one member of parliament explained, making this *Ramayana* logic explicit: "If there is any sore point or distressful fact to which we cannot be reconciled under any circumstances, it is the question of the abduction and non-restoration of Hindu women. We all know our history of what happened in the time of Shri Ram when Sita was abducted. Here, when thousands of girls are concerned, we cannot forget this. We can forget all the properties, we can forget every other thing, but this cannot be forgotten. . . . As descendants of Ram we have to bring back every Sita that is alive." Ibid., 72, citing *India: Legislative Assembly Debates 1949,* 752).

36. In Valmiki's *Ramayana* 6.103.15–16, Rama makes this clear: "Bless you, but let it be known that it was not for your sake that I undertook this war effort, which has now been brought to completion by the heroism of my allies. Instead, I did all this to protect my reputation and to completely erase this insult and dishonor to my illustrious lineage." And then, in what follows (6.103.21), he makes his argument bluntly: "The reason you were won back was so that I could reclaim my fame. I don't love you anymore. Go wherever you like, but away from here." References follow *Ramayana,* critically edited by G. H. Bhatt et al., 7 vols. (Baroda: Oriental Institute, University of Baroda: 1960–1975).

37. Even Anthony knows that the institution of the police is a religion unto itself. As he explains to Kishanlal: "I'm a straight-up believer. . . . I believe in all religions. I go to the temple, I go to the mosque, I go to church, I go to the *gurudwara*. And sometimes, Sahib, I get mixed up and put in time at the police station."

38. *Ramayana* 3.35.13.

39. For more on Sanjay Gandhi's involvement in blocking the release of *Kissa Kursi Ka*, see J. S. Bright, *Allahabad High Court to Shah Commission* (New Delhi: Deep and Deep, 1979), 43–44.

40. Desai was familiar with the film and impressed by it as well: "I saw only one film, *Garam Hawa* (by M. S. Sathyu). I was thrilled by it. It was brilliant. It moved me. I was not bored to death." Haham, *Enchantment of the Mind*, 26. Sathyu, however, was scathing in his criticism of Desai: "Desai's films are devoid of any kind of sensibility. As he himself admits, there's no logic in his films. He just plays with the weaknesses of people." *Filmfare*, 1–15 May 1984; cited in ibid., 24. For more on *Garam Hawa* and its account of post-Partition trauma, see Sarkar, *Mourning the Nation*, 190–199.

41. Butalia, "Muslims and Hindus," 64.

42. See, for example, Sumita S. Chakravarty, *National Identity in Indian Popular Cinema, 1947–1987* (Austin: University of Texas Press, 1993); Rachel Dwyer, *All You Want Is Money, All You Need Is Love: Sex and Romance in Modern India* (London: Cassell, 2000); Ashish Rajadhyaksha, "The 'Bollywoodization' of the Indian Cinema: Cultural Nationalism in a Global Arena," *Inter-Asia Cultural Studies* 4, no. 1 (2003): 25–39.

43. There was significant pushback against this campaign, as witnessed by the opposition's inversion of another of Mrs. Gandhi's political slogans. As Arthur Klieman notes, "Among villagers as election day [in 1977] neared the slogan became, instead of '*garibi hatao*' (abolish poverty)—which had been Mrs. Gandhi's 1971 election theme—'*Indira hatao, indiri bachao*' (abolish Indira and save your penis)." Arthur S. Klieman, "Indira's India: Democracy and Crisis Government," *Political Science Quarterly* 96, no. 2 (1981): 255.

44. Emma Tarlo, *Unsettling Memories: Narratives of the Emergency in Delhi* (Berkeley: University of California Press, 2003), 88.

45. Ibid., 165. And what the young man goes on to say is likewise instructive: "They were looking for one or other excuse. Those who didn't have [sterilization] slips were pressurised on that account; those who had not paid their rent were threatened on that account; those who had purchased plots were threatened on that account; those who had already had the [sterilization] operation had to have it again." Ibid.

46. Mohandas K. Gandhi, *The Collected Works of Mahatma Gandhi*, vol. 15 (Delhi: Publications Division, Ministry of Information and Broadcasting, Government of India, 1958–80), 43; cited in Joseph S. Alter, *Gandhi's Body: Sex, Diet, and the Politics of Nationalism* (Philadelphia: University of Pennsylvania Press, 2000), 3.

47. Alter, *Gandhi's Body*.

48. See, for example, Wendy Doniger, *Asceticism and Eroticism in the Mythology of Śiva* (New York: Oxford University Press, 1973); Sudhir Kakar, *Intimate Relations: Exploring Indian Sexuality* (Chicago: University of Chicago Press, 1990); Joseph S. Alter, "Seminal Truth: A Modern Science of Male Celibacy in North India," *Medical Anthropology Quarterly* 11, no. 3 (1997): 275–298; Joseph S. Alter, *Moral Materialism:*

Sex and Masculinity in Modern India (New Delhi: Penguin Books, 2011). The research of George Morrison Carstairs—"Hinjra and Jiryan: Two Derivatives of Hindu Attitude to Sexuality," *British Journal of Medical Psychiatry* 29 (1956): 128–138, and *The Twice-Born* (London: Hogarth Press, 1958)—which was conducted among high-caste Hindus in northern India in 1951, is particularly instructive. Carstairs notes that it was "assumed that every doctor must know that *jiryan,* a loss of semen, is the commonest cause of bodily weakness," and as such, "celibacy was the first requirement of true fitness, because every sexual orgasm meant the loss of a quantity of semen." Carstairs, "Hinjra and Jiryan," 133. Yet as one informant explained, semen loss has two causes: " '*bad-parhez* and *badpheli*—that is, eating what is wrong and doing what is wrong.' Under the latter head he included not only sexual promiscuity, but every sort of violation of Hindu *dharm* such as mixing and eating with people of inferior caste; acting disrespectfully towards one's elders; drinking to excess; giving way to anger or to lustful thoughts, to fear or to excess worrying. In all these cases, what happens is that a man's semen curdles and goes bad and can no longer be retained." Ibid., 134. In short, celibacy is crucial for cultivating healthy reserves of semen, but "true fitness" comes only from following Hindu dharma, which determines one's biology as well as one's future karma, and which encompasses a complex biomoral protocol.

49. Joseph S. Alter, "Celibacy, Sexuality, and the Transformation of Gender into Nationalism in North India," *Journal of Asian Studies* 53, no. 1 (1994): 45.

50. Joseph S. Alter, "Somatic Nationalism: Indian Wrestling and Militant Hinduism," *Modern Asian Studies* 28, no. 3 (1994): 557–588.

51. Anthony reflects that Amar must know karate and kung fu, but Amar simply wrestles and pummels him using his superior strength, not "exotic" martial arts.

52. *Brahmacarya* is also the first of the four stages of the traditional Hindu life cycle. With his marriage to Lakshmi, Amar could be said to transition into the second stage of the traditional Hindu life cycle—the householder's life *(grihastha)*—which likewise enjoins a "nearly" celibate life, with sex only for procreation (which is mandatory), and the dangers of semen loss ever present. See, for example, A. Sumathipala et al., "Culture-Bound Syndromes: The Story of *dhat* Syndrome," *British Journal of Psychiatry* 184 (2004): 200–209. For more on the stages of the Hindu life cycle, see Patrick Olivelle, *The Āśrama System: The History and Hermeneutics of a Religious Institution* (New York: Oxford University Press, 1993).

53. Alter, "Somatic Nationalism," 573.

54. Alter, "Celibacy," 46.

55. Alter, "Somatic Nationalism," 573.

56. Ibid., 574.

57. Alter, "Celibacy," 49.

58. Cited in ibid. The case of night emissions exemplifies the way that the first half of the term "biomoral" can be determinative of the second, with an impure biology creating an impure morality, even if the impurity is unintentional. Alter makes this clear: "I was first surprised and perplexed by the inordinate attention given in the literature on *brahma-carya* to the problem of night emission. My reasoning was that the involuntary emission of semen could not be considered a moral problem since it was purely accidental and related to forces over which the individual could not be expected to exercise control.

However, my logic was backward. I was operating under the false assumption that celibacy was the product of self-discipline, and morality a measure of the strength of one's resolve. Instead, the strength of one's resolve is directly related to the power inherent in semen, which means that it makes virtually no difference how you lose it; the moral effect is the same." Ibid., 53, n. 6.

59. Joseph S. Alter, "Indian Clubs and Colonialism: Hindu Masculinity and Muscular Christianity," *Comparative Studies in Society and History* 46, no. 3 (2004): 502.

60. For more on the various forms of muscular Christianity, see Donald E. Hall, ed., *Muscular Christianity: Embodying the Victorian Age* (Cambridge: Cambridge University Press, 1994); Tony Ladd and James A. Mathisen, *Muscular Christianity: Evangelical Protestants and the Development of American Sports* (Grand Rapids, MI: Baker Books, 1999); Clifford Putney, *Muscular Christianity: Manhood and Sports in Protestant America, 1880–1920* (Cambridge: Harvard University Press, 2001).

61. To the extent that England and India, as the colonizer and the colonized, were mutually constitutive, consider the resemblance between British sportsmanship and Gandhian pacifism: "With the exception of the anomalous members of the lower working class (who never came to the colonies in large numbers), the English are preoccupied with the control of their own aggression, the avoidance of aggression from others, and the prevention of the emergence of aggressive behavior in their children. . . . In the English middle and upper classes this control of aggression would appear to have been a major component in their character for several centuries. In the context of games this control of aggression is called 'sportsmanship', a concept which the English introduced into much of the rest of the world. One aspect of 'sportsmanship' is the acceptance of the outcome unaggressively, neither taunting the vanquished nor showing resentment against the victor. This concept of 'sportsmanship' has long been metaphorically extended from games to almost all situations of rivalry or competition; the reputation of being a 'good sport' is one that is very highly valued by the majority of the English." Geoffrey Gorer, "The British National Character in the Twentieth Century," *Annals of the American Academy of Political and Social Sciences* 370 (1967): 74–81, cited in Ashis Nandy, *The Intimate Enemy: Loss and Recovery of Self Under Colonialism* (New Delhi: Oxford University Press, 1983), 50. For an inversion of this formula in India, the "feminization" of the Parsi, see Tanya Luhrmann, *The Good Parsi: The Postcolonial Anxieties of an Indian Colonial Elite* (Cambridge, MA: Harvard University Press, 1996). For a study of the Indian experience in comparison with Ireland's, see Sikata Banerjee, *Muscular Nationalism: Gender, Violence, and Nationalism in India and Ireland, 1914–2004* (New York: New York University Press, 2012).

62. David Rosen, "The Volcano and the Cathedral: Muscular Christianity and the Origins of Primal Manliness," in *Muscular Christianity: Embodying the Victorian Age*, ed. Donald E. Hall (Cambridge: Cambridge University Press, 1994), 20.

63. J. G. Cotton Minchin, *Our Public Schools: Their Influence on English History; Charter House, Eton, Harrow, Merchant Taylors', Rugby, St. Paul's Westminster, Winchester* (London: Swan Sonnenschein & Co., 1901), 113.

64. As the dreams of one Indian renunciant suggests, "As long as the penis remains, one cannot be a true ascetic. Under the influence of religious practice the penis will have not only to be controlled but to be made to disappear within the body. Until this takes

place nothing will happen." Sarasi Lal Sarkar, "A Study of the Psychology of Sexual Abstinence from the Dreams of an Ascetic," *International Journal of Psychoanalysis* 24 (1943): 173.

65. References to the *Mahabharata* follow *Mahabharata,* critically edited by V. S. Sukthankar et al., 19 vols. (Poona: Bhandarkar Oriental Research Institute, 1927–1959). For more on this story, see Doniger, *Asceticism,* 130–136; and Wendy Doniger, *Hindu Myths: A Sourcebook Translated from the Sanskrit* (London: Penguin Books, 1975), 137–154.

66. David Shulman, "Terror of Symbols and Symbols of Terror: Notes on the Myth of Śiva as Sthāṇu," *History of Religions* 26, no. 2 (1986): 109.

67. *Mahabharata* 12.15, 2–4a. See too *Manusmriti* 7.17–19, for an identical verse and a nearly identical sentiment.

68. Madeleine Biardeau, "Ancient Brahminism, or Impossible Non-Violence," in *Violence/ Non-Violence: Some Hindu Perspectives,* ed. Denis Vidal, Gilles Tarabout, and Éric Meyer (Delhi: Manohar Publications, 2003), 93. Biardeau, ibid., also cites this wonderful passage from the *Mahabharata* (XII.15, 36–43), showing how the Rod applies not only to human society but also to the environment: "If they did not fear *daṇḍa,* birds and beast of prey would eat up livestock and men and offerings meant for sacrifice. The Vedic scholar would cease his studies, milch cows would not be milked and young women would not marry. Negligence would be widespread, barriers would be broken down and it would be impossible to identify one's own if *daṇḍa* did not exist. None would remain in a year-long sacrificial ceremony for the mere fee ordained by law if *daṇḍa* did not exist. None would practice the dharma which conforms to his own stage of life in accordance with Vedic injunctions, nor even would anyone be interested in knowing them if *daṇḍa* did not exist. Only *daṇḍa* ensures that camels and bullocks, donkeys and mules consent to be hitched to a vehicle. But for *daṇḍa,* neither domestic servants nor little children would obey, nor would maidens observe their dharma. All creatures exist owing to *daṇḍa* and fear it: the wise know it. In the eyes of man, the heavens like the very earth are founded solidly on *daṇḍa.*"

69. See, for example, Wendy Doniger O'Flaherty's appropriately named *Tales of Sex and Violence: Folklore, Sacrifice, and Danger in the Jaiminīya Brāhmaṇa* (Chicago: University of Chicago Press, 1985), or just about any of Bollywood's many gangster films, such as *Deewaar* (Yash Chopra, 1975), *Parinda* (Vidhu Vinod Chopra, 1989), or *Satya* (Ram Gopal Varma, 1998). Saadat Hasan Manto, *Bitter Fruit: The Very Best of Saadat Hasan Manto,* ed. and trans. Khalid Hasan (New Delhi: Penguin Books, 2008), depicts this play of sex and power particularly well in his short stories about Partition. They chronicle the physical and psychological torment of Partition's survivors as they struggle to make sense of sexual aggression—or is it aggressive sexuality?—and the contradictions of identity politics.

70. For more on Shiva as ascetic and householder, alternately chaste and sexual, see Doniger, *Asceticism.*

71. Shulman, "Terror of Symbols," 110.

72. Philip Lutgendorf, personal communication. Integral to this construction of brotherhood is hierarchy. Amar's *youngest* brother is a Muslim, and indeed, the trope of Hindu-Muslim brotherhood as a relation between senior and junior partners is

characteristic of the present-day rhetoric of the Hindu right. As one VHP official in the context of the 2002 Gujarat massacres explained, "We do not want the Muslims to shift to Pakistan. They can live here, as part of our family, like our brothers, but like *younger* brothers." Quoted in Rakesh Sharma, "Gujarat 2002: A turning point in modern Indian history?," *Rakesh Sharma* (blog), November 15, 2005, http://rakeshindia.blogspot.com/2005_11_01_archive.html.

73. *Ramayana* 2.16.48.

74. The name itself doesn't bring back his memory. Although Amar writes down Kishan-lal's name and address when Akbar comes to the police station to report his absence, he half forgets the name by the time he arrives in the old neighborhood. We hear a local explain that "it's not Kishan, but Kishanlal that used to live here."

75. One is reminded of the final lines to Philip Larkin's poem "This Be the Verse": "Man hands on misery to man. / It deepens like a coastal shelf. / Get out as early as you can, / And don't have any kids yourself." Philip Larkin, *High Windows* (New York: Farrar, Straus and Giroux, 1974), 30.

76. Now that justice can be served, Amar can take up the Rod of the patriline. When his father originally presented him with the Rod (that is, the gifted gun), Amar rejected it, not wanting its power to fall into Anthony's rebellious hands and not wanting it for himself either. After all, the Rod came from a father who didn't have the proper authority to wield it—something made evident in the next scene, with Kishanlal's failed attempt at homicide, which sets in motion the family's dissolution. Moreover, the Rod appears merely to have been a simulacrum—a fake. And if it was real and gifted to Amar by mistake, that further disqualifies Kishanlal's authority to bestow it in the first place. All in all, Kishanlal shouldn't be bestowing the Rod; he should be subjected to it, and Amar is now in a position to do just that.

77. Kishanlal, as he reminisces, calls it a *basti,* here denoting a neighborhood of the urban poor.

78. When Kishanlal returned home from jail, for example, he found his oldest two sons in the kitchen fighting over the remnants of a plate of food, and the youngest simply crying. When questioned, Amar replied that they hadn't eaten in two days.

79. Bharati tells Kishanlal that even though Robert never paid her while Kishanlal was in prison, she wouldn't have accepted his money anyway because it is "ill gotten" *(haram).* Kishanlal, needless to say, did not share her convictions.

80. This nostalgia is probably best understood as a yearning for a time when there was hope and optimism for the future, not a yearning to re-experience the material conditions of the past. For was there ever a time when Kishanlal, along with his family, was happy *in* the old neighborhood and *with* it as well? As Lauren Berlant explains, "The desire for a less-bad life involves finding resting places; the reproduction of normativity occurs when rest is imagined nostalgically—that is, in the places where rest is supposed to have happened, a fantasy masquerading as screen memory or paramnesia. One might read these repetitions as nostalgia for nostalgia, a kind of desperate regression toward the desire to soon experience an imaginary security one *knows* without having ever had." Lauren Berlant, *Cruel Optimism* (Durham, NC: Duke University Press, 2011), 180.

81. Haham, *Enchantment of the Mind,* 4.

82. Ibid.

83. Ibid., 18.
84. Ibid.
85. Sidharth Bhatia, *Amar Akbar Anthony: Masala, Madness and Manmohan Desai* (Noida, India: HarperCollins, 2013), 135–136.
86. Thomas Wolfe, *You Can't Go Home Again* (New York: Harper and Row, 1940), 602.
87. Haham, *Enchantment of the Mind*, 8.
88. Ibid.

2. Akbar

1. Rishi has debunked the popular notion that Raj Kapoor came up with *Bobby* as a means to launch his son, stating that the film was conceived as a way to pay back debts incurred by *Mera Naam Joker,* which was an epic flop. *Bobby,* whose Romeo-and-Juliet romance involves a rich Hindu boy and a poor Christian girl, will receive some more attention in Chapter 3.
2. Ashis Nandy, "Invitation to an Antique Death: The Journey of Pramathesh Barua as the Origin of the Terribly Effeminate, Maudlin, Self-Destructive Heroes of Indian Cinema," in *Pleasure and the Nation: The History, Politics, and Consumption of Public Culture in India,* ed. Rachel Dwyer and Christopher Pinney (Delhi: Oxford University Press, 2000), 139–160.
3. See another amusingly titled essay in a volume edited by Nandy, Ziauddin Sardar's "Dilip Kumar Made Me Do It," in *The Secret Politics of Our Desires: Innocence, Culpability, and Indian Popular Cinema,* ed. Ashis Nandy (Delhi: Zed Books, 1998), 19–98. Devdas first made his appearance in print as the hero of the eponymous Bengali novel of 1917 by Saratchandra Chattopadhyay, *Devdas: A Novel,* trans. Sreejata Guha (Delhi: Penguin, 2002). He was portrayed by different actors in different versions of 1935's talkie production: P. C. Barua in Bengali and K. S. Saigal in Hindi. The character was revived, his bathos intact, by the contemporary Bollywood superstar Shah Rukh Khan in a lavish (not to say bloated) 2002 production. Finally, in Guru Dutt's autobiographical opus *Kaagaz Ke Phool* (1959), a measure of self-awareness is indicated by Dutt's choice of the movie-within-the-movie that his director-protagonist struggles to create: it is of course *Devdas.* For more on the character's cinematic incarnations, see Corey Creekmur, "Remembering, Repeating and Working through *Devdas,*" in *Indian Literature and Popular Cinema: Recasting Classics,* ed. Heidi M. Pauwels (London: Routledge, 2007), 173–190.
4. Although Amar functions at one level as the embodiment of the state, it should be noted that his speech does *not* favor the stilted and pedantic idiom known as *sarkari,* or government, Hindi. The artificiality of this style is the result of efforts by nationalist officials and academics to purify Hindi by purging it of its Urdu lexicon and emphasizing vocabulary derived from Sanskrit. In real life it is associated with broadcasters on the Indian government networks (and perhaps with foreign students of Hindi). In the movies it is likely to be heard from the mouths of characters who are marked as officious or pretentious, and/or as traditionalist Brahmins.
5. The line is *"Jiski zubaan Urdu ki tarah."* Our translation is adapted from one by Meredith McGuire. Harish Trivedi offers a slightly different gloss of the first two lines: "*'Ho*

yaar mera khushboo ki tarah/Ho jiski zubaan Urdu ki tarah' (May my lover be like a fragrance/And his/her language rather like Urdu): that is to say, not quite Urdu but suggestive of Urdu and redolent of it." Harish Trivedi, "All Kinds of Hindi: The Evolving Language of Hindi Cinema," in *Fingerprinting Popular Culture: The Mythic and the Iconic in Indian Cinema*, ed. Vinay Lal and Ashis Nandy (Delhi: Oxford University Press, 2006), 64–65.

6. Mukul Kesavan offers a more scholarly illustration, providing a history of the ways Bombay filmmakers have used Urdu to evoke heightened moods. He locates the origins of Hindi cinema in Urdu theater, which calls attention to the historically contingent character of the distinction between dialogue and song. "In fact it could be plausibly argued that Urdu didn't simply give utterance to the narratives characteristic of the Hindi cinema, it actually helped create them. Certainly the conventions of early Urdu theatre bear a remarkable resemblance to those of the Hindi film. For example, the Urdu plays performed by the Parsi theatre . . . were entirely sung, a reminder that the song and dance format of the talkies has theatrical roots. More than that, like latter-day films where the hero and heroine blithely change costumes and locations half a dozen times in the space of a single song, early Urdu theatre was marked by a fine disregard for the classical unities of time and place." Mukul Kesavan, "Urdu, Awadh, and the Tawaif: The Islamicate Roots of Hindi Cinema," in *Forging Identities: Gender, Communities, and the State in India*, ed. Zoya Hasan (Delhi: Kali for Women, 1994), 249. (Incidentally, Mani Ratnam's *Dil Se*, released four years after this essay was published, is a perfect example of this pattern.) It should be added that Trivedi's "All Kinds of Hindi" delivers a nuanced critique of Kesavan's thesis that the main language of "Hindi cinema" should be recognized, more often than not, to be Urdu.

7. Jayson Beaster-Jones, *Bollywood Sounds: The Cosmopolitan Mediations of Hindi Film Song* (Oxford: Oxford University Press, 2014) is a recent, production-oriented study of Hindi film music across the decades. For an ethnomusicological inquiry centered on devotional songs, see Gregory Booth, "Religion, Gossip, Narrative Conventions and the Construction of Meaning in Hindi Film Songs," *Popular Music* 19 (2000): 125–145.

8. For a brief introduction to *qawwali* music's place in Hindi cinema, see Rashmi Attri, "Qawwali: A Mode of Representation of Muslim Culture in Bollywood," in *Muslim Culture in Indian Cinema*, ed. Jasbir Jain (Jaipur, India: Rawat Publications, 2011), 51–62. Rishi Kapoor's career was associated with *qawwali* numbers in the 1970s; examples include *Laila Majnu* (Harnam Singh Rawail, 1976) and *Hum Kisise Kum Naheen* (Nasir Husain, 1977).

9. See, for example, Faisal Devji, "Gender and the Politics of Space: The Movement for Women's Reform, 1857–1900," in *Forging Identities: Gender, Communities, and the State in India*, ed. Zoya Hasan (Delhi: Kali for Women, 1994), 28–30.

10. An analogy that may work for the nerdier members of our readership would be to recast the brothers as character archetypes from a Dungeons & Dragons adventure (or similar example of fantasy fiction). Amar is the warrior, steadfast in his suit of armor. Anthony is the thief, nimble of tongue as well as fingers. But Akbar is the wizard—and the genre's whole raison d'être is magic.

11. Tejaswini Ganti, *Bollywood: A Guidebook to Popular Indian Cinema* (New York: Routledge, 2004), 84. Songs are also the reason Bollywood movies have such long running

times; take them away, and they shrink to the length of their Hollywood counterparts. One shudders to consider the butchery visited on *Amar Akbar Anthony* by the BBC when they chose it, in 1980, as the first Hindi movie ever to be broadcast on British television—and "adapted" it for UK tastes by discarding all the musical numbers as superfluous to the plot. Rosie Thomas, "Indian Cinema: Pleasures and Popularity," *Screen* 26, no. 3–4 (1985): 117.

12. The film does not support an identification of Ilahabadi as Akbar's family name. The tailor-shop sign bears the name of Haider Ali. In the dialogue with Bharati toward the movie's end, when mother and son are reunited, Akbar declares, "The world knows [me] by the name Akbar Ilahabadi," indicating a name used for public circulation.

13. None other than Emperor Akbar is said to have rededicated the city, which had been known by the Sanskritic name Prayag, to Allah—and Allah not in the strictly Islamic construction but as the mystically conceived Godhead of the esoteric fusion religion developed within his inner circle, the Din-e-Illahi.

14. Shamsur Rahman Faruqi, "The Power Politics of Culture: Akbar Ilahabadi and the Changing Order of Things," *Fourteenth Zakir Husain Memorial Lecture* (Delhi: Zakir Husain College, 2002), 10–21.

15. Ibid., 22–24. Our interpretation of Akbar Ilahabadi's poetry is indebted to Faruqi's essay. We have also relied on Iqbal Husain, "Akbar Allahabadi and National Politics," *Social Scientist* 16, no. 5 (1988): 29–45. For translations of representative verses, along with commentary, see Mehr Farooqi, "'Akbar' Ilahabadi: Satirical Verses and Excerpts from 'Dialogue between Old and New Ways,'" in *Nationalism in the Vernacular: Hindi, Urdu, and the Literature of Indian Freedom,* ed. Shobna Nijhawan (Delhi: Permanent Black, 2010), 269–271; Ralph Russell, *Hidden in the Lute: An Anthology of Urdu Literature* (Manchester: Carcanet, 1999); and Ralph Russell and Khurshidul Islam, "The Satirical Verse of Akbar Ilahabadi," in *The Pursuit of Urdu Literature: A Select History,* ed. Ralph Russell (London: Zed Books, 1992), 129–175.

16. Zulfaqār, Ghulām Husain, and Akbar Allāhābādī, *Mohandās Karamcand Gāndhī: Lisānul'asar kī nazar men* (Lahore: Sang-i Mīl Pablīkeshanz, 1994). We are indebted to Francesca Chubb-Confer for her reading of this text on behalf of our project. A comparison of Akbar's work with Gandhi's own assault on "modern civilization" as delivered in *Hind Swaraj* would turn up many correspondences. Both legal men offered fierce critiques of British jurisprudence, for example (and both had problems with plumbing). See Mohandas K. Gandhi, *Hind Swaraj and Other Writings,* ed. Anthony Parel, Centenary Edition (Cambridge: Cambridge University Press, 2009).

17. The representation of Muslims in Bollywood films of the present day is an equally rich and much-contested issue. For a pair of polemical essays that can be read together as a sort of point-counterpoint, see Pankaj Jain, "From *Padosi* to *My Name Is Khan:* The Portrayal of Hindu-Muslim Relations in South Asian Films," *Visual Anthropology* 24 (2011): 345–363; and Sanjeev Kumar, "Constructing the Nation's Enemy: Hindutva, Popular Culture and the Muslim 'Other' in Bollywood Cinema," *Third World Quarterly* 34 (2013): 458–469.

18. Akbar's disguise in the "Anhoni Ko Honi Kar De" performance is different from Anthony's (a padre) or Amar's (the one-man band). Akbar, we have suggested, is in a sense impersonating himself, or else an obsolete version of himself: an old-fashioned Muslim

type, a received image imprinted in public in no small part through the movies themselves. Akbar's masquerade thus finds its proper correlate in Anthony's earlier mimicry of a Christian type in the "My Name Is Anthony Gonsalves" number. It should be noted that in displaying their manipulation of these stereotypes, the hip young moderns Akbar and Anthony not only destabilize them as defining images of Muslim or Christian identity but also up-end authority figures associated with the not-so-distant historical past: feudal landowners (the would-be *nawab*) and colonial *babus* (the Anglophone dandy).

19. In diegetic fact, of course, behind the disguise, Akbar and his foster father Haider Ali are precisely that: modest bazaar tailors. The very notion of a *khaandaani,* or hereditary, tailor has something comic about it: "People may treat me like a tailor, but I'm actually an aristocrat" neatly sums up a certain kind of Indian Muslim snobbery.

20. *Shatranj Ke Khilari* was one of two films Ray made in Hindi (the other, 1981's *Sadgati,* was also based on a Premchand work) and is in fact the product of a move he was making toward a more mass-market format. We are still a long way from Bollywood *masala,* however. Just how far becomes evident when specific points of comparison are drawn with its fellow 1977 release, *Amar Akbar Anthony,* which employed two of its stars— Shabana Azmi and Amitabh Bachchan (voiceover)—in radically different guises.

21. For a multifaceted exploration of Lucknow's cultural life, see Veena Talwar Oldenburg, ed., *Shaam-e-Awadh: Writings on Lucknow* (Delhi: Penguin, 2007).

22. The latter three films are discussed (along with others) in a very useful essay by Fareed Kazmi, "Muslim Socials and the Female Protagonist: Seeing a Dominant Discourse at Work," in *Forging Identities: Gender, Communities, and the State in India,* ed. Zoya Hasan (Delhi: Kali for Women, 1994), 226–243.

23. See Corey Creekmur's insightful guest post on *Chaudhvin Ka Chand* at *Philip's Filums: Notes on Indian Popular Cinema,* accessed April 10, 2015, www.uiowa.edu/indiancinema/chaudhvin-ka-chand. Another source is Ameena Kazi Ansari, "Hybridity and the Filmic Text: Re-visiting *Chaudhvin ka Chand,*" in *Muslim Culture in Indian Cinema,* ed. Jasbir Jain (Jaipur, India: Rawat Publications, 2011), 161–170.

24. Something of a swan song for the genre, *Pakeezah* was completed in 1972 but may safely be classified as 1960s cinema in that its production (already a long time in the planning) began in 1964, only to flounder with the breakup of the marriage between the director, Kamal Amrohi, and the star, Meena Kumari. Kumari finally returned to the project after a not-so-secret struggle with drink; her death a short while after *Pakeezah* was finally released contributed to its elevation to cult-film status. For more about the film, see Kazmi, "Muslim Socials," and Bandana Chakrabarty, "Celebrating the Courtesan in Hindi Films: *Umrao Jaan* and *Pakeezah,*" in *Muslim Culture in Indian Cinema,* ed. Jasbir Jain (Jaipur, India: Rawat Publications, 2011), 132–139.

25. Meena Kumari's tragic life story resonates with the melancholy timbre of the Muslim social, although the role that most closely parallels her downward spiral is not that of Pakeezah but of Chhoti Bahu, the iconic Little Bride of *Sahib Bibi Aur Ghulam* (Guru Dutt, 1962). This story of the decline of a noble house of colonial Calcutta would be exemplary if not for one inconvenient detail: all the characters are Hindu. Nevertheless, the film deserves mention alongside our representative quartet as a sort of missing link, in that it rounds out a rotating ensemble cast that can give the whole genre the

look of a family business. *Sahib Bibi Aur Ghulam* brings *Pakeezah*'s Kumari together with Rehman, Waheeda Rehman, and Guru Dutt, the triangle from *Chaudhvin Ka Chand*. If the film is a Muslim social in Hindu guise, the reverse could be said of its star, whose birth name was Mahjabeen Bano and who wrote Urdu under the *takhallus* Naaz. In the present day, Meena Kumari has become embraced as a diva figure by many gay men in India.

26. If *Amar Akbar Anthony* throws a wake for the Muslim social, the recent film *Dedh Ishqiya* (Ahbishek Chaubey, 2014) is a full-blown *urs*, or Sufi death commemoration. At once an homage to the genre at the level of style and a skillful subversion of its ideological norms, *Dedh Ishqiya* is at its most deft when exploring the homoerotic dimension of *parda*-regulated desire.

27. Beaster-Jones, *Bollywood Sounds*, pp. 115–118, offers a discussion of "Parda Hai Parda," translated as "The Veil between Us."

28. "By the kindness of Allah, we've got a completely full house," as Akbar tells Anthony the afternoon of the concert. It is of course Anthony who sits in the aisle, having given up his seat to the blind woman who turns out to be their mother. For their own unveiling, Bharati's eyes will have to wait for Akbar's second *qawwali* number, "Shirdi Wale Sai Baba."

29. These five other women could be Tayyab Ali's wives, playing as it does to stereotype, even though Islamic law sets the maximum number at four. The alternative idea that they are all his daughters suggests a different way to make fun of the old Muslim man, since it would mark him simultaneously as virile and yet not quite virile enough to be the father of male progeny. It should be added that none of these hijabi women are ever seen again; when Akbar rescues Salma and her father from their burning house, there is no indication that any other family members occupy it.

30. *Chaudhvin Ka Chand* features a closer counterpart to *Palki*'s "Chehre Se Apne Aaj To Parda Uthaiye" in an earlier number, where it's Rehman who espies Waheeda's face when he peeks through a screen. But in this number, "Sharma Ke Agar Yun Pardanashi," it's the coquettish girlfriends of the character who do all the singing—their theme is how beauty can be both masked and revealed—and the male lead is stymied by the need to keep silent in his hiding place. Rehman never seems to get to sing in any of his films.

31. The only song on the *Amar Akbar Anthony* soundtrack to feature female vocals is the omnibus number "Hamko Tumse Ho Gaya Hai Pyar Kya Karein." Lata Mangeshkar sings for Jenny, Laxmi, and Salma alike.

32. "Remembering Rafi, on His Birth Anniversary." *Hindustan Times,* December 23, 2009, www.hindustantimes.com/entertainment/remembering-rafi-on-his-birth-anniversary/article1-489814.aspx.

33. Connie Haham, *Enchantment of the Mind: Manmohan Desai's Films* (New Delhi: Roli Books, 2006), 80.

34. Ibid., 80–81.

35. Kishore Kumar was in fact also making a comeback in this period. The singer had faced harsh reprisals during the Emergency for not agreeing to promote the government's economic program. All his songs were banned from state-sponsored radio and television, the films in which he was to appear were held up, and all sales of his gramophone

records were frozen. His voice was silenced, and this silencing was meant to send a message to other artistes who might likewise dissent. See Shah Commission of Inquiry, *Interim Report II* (New Delhi: Government of India Press, April 26, 1978), 8–9.

36. The second coming of Rafi, unfortunately, was of no long duration; he died in 1980.

37. Footage of this sequence's shooting in Borivali Park is featured in a short film, *Destination: Bombay* (1976), produced by the Indian government's Films Division for the purpose of promoting tourism from overseas. The film's presentation of Bombay as a well-scrubbed playground for all manner of high Seventies leisure activities makes it an illuminating companion text to the "Hamko Tumse Ho Gaya Hai Pyar Kya Karein" number.

38. The *mahurat,* or inaugural shot, of a feature film is a full-blown ritual occasion in Bollywood. The camera is garlanded, producers hobnob with their investors, and stars make a token appearance on footage that is, as a rule, thrown out.

39. Clearly shown behind Akbar is a poster advertising a production of *Dhola Maru,* Rajasthani folk culture's counterpart of Romeo and Juliet (probably the 1956 Hindi film).

40. Parsi businesses and other properties, prominent in many downtown neighborhoods, are absent as a design element from the Muslim Quarter. The lack of any Parsi presence on the film's landscape is yet another indication that the Bombay of *Amar Akbar Anthony* is not really the old "island city" but the suburbs to its north. (If there is a Parsi-coded character to be encountered in the film at all, the closest candidate is the ostensibly Christian villain, Robert.)

41. Bombay's Lamington Road–Muhammad Ali Road area, not far from Khetwadi, is a case in point. The film's dialogue writer, Kader Khan, grew up in the vicinity.

42. In African American ballroom culture and other Black queer spaces, gay men and transgender women assume a structurally analogous license to "read." Verbal statements may be emphasized with the snapping of fingers or—as in India—the clapping of hands. The world of drag performance and the practice of reading featured in a well-known documentary, Jennie Livingstone's *Paris Is Burning* (1991), which was also celebrated for its slyly self-aware take on ethnographic filmmaking.

43. As we will explore in Chapter 3, Christian characters in film have historically been made to stand in for minority communities in general, and minority-group criminals confront the likes of Inspector Amar with a mirror image: they simultaneously transgress the law (they oppose the state) and violate majoritarian cultural norms (they oppose the nation).

44. Telling in this regard are the reflections of Saeed Mirza, as relayed in *"Albert Pinto Ko Gussa Kyoon Aata Hai," Encyclopaedia of Indian Cinema,* ed. Ashish Rajadhyaksha and Paul Willimen, New Revised Edition (London: Routledge, 1999), 444. A filmmaker in the social reformist "parallel cinema" tradition, Mirza wrote and directed *Albert Pinto Ko Gussa Kyoon Aata Hai "What Makes Albert Pinto Angry?,"* a 1980 film about the constrained circumstances of working-class Christians in Bombay. He later stated that the film used Christian characters in a surrogate capacity because he did not have the courage to make a critical work about the condition of Bombay's Muslims. In 1989 he did, with *Salim Langde Pe Mat Ro "Don't Cry for Salim the Lame."*

45. Mohandas K. Gandhi, *Harijan,* November 24, 1933, 6.

46. Indeed, Akbar's Gandhian-sounding statement about winning over his enemies with love resonates just as much with the rhetoric of Sufism. Compare the words of the exemplary Sufi poet-hero, the love-crazed protagonist of the twelfth-century romance *Layla and Majnun:* " 'If they were enemies,' Majnun replied, 'I could fight them. But as these enemies are my friends, what shall I do? This is no battlefield for me. The heart of my beloved beats for the enemy, and where her heart beats, there is my home. I want to die for my beloved, not kill other men. How then could I be on your side, when I have given up my self?' " Nizami, *The Story of Layla and Majnun*, trans. and ed. Rudolph Gelpke (New Lebanon, NY: Omega, 2011), 59. The year before *Amar Akbar Anthony*, Rishi Kapoor starred in a hit Hindi film based on Nizami's classic; his bruised face and disheveled appearance in the hospital scene cite the way he looked as Majnun.

47. Robert's snap decision to take Bharati hostage is a miscalculation on more than one level. He does not realize that in separation, Bharati and Kishanlal each believe the other dead. Robert's immediate goal is information about his daughter Jenny, but having forsaken Kishanlal, Bharati has no knowledge of Jenny. And as we suggest in Chapter 4, by placing himself in possession of two vessels of the *shakti* that protects Kishanlal—Santoshi Maa's locket and Bharati's person—the oblivious Christian Robert has exposed himself to some fearsome Hindu goddess power.

48. See William Elison, "Sai Baba of Bombay: A Saint, His Icon, and the Urban Geography of *Darshan*," *History of Religions* 54, no. 2 (2014): 151–187. The theological distance between a Muslim saint who contains *barkat* and a Hindu "god-man" who embodies divine essence is—according to Sai Baba's own teachings and personal example—zero. The well-known summation of his doctrine is *Sab ka malik ek,* "The Lord of all is one." The position is at once heretical by the standards of dogmatic Islam and unexceptional in the context of antinomian Sufism.

49. Haham, *Enchantment of the Mind,* 39.

50. As evidence of Congress Party patronage of the Sai cult, Maharashtrians cite an intervention in the holy man's iconography: he is generally depicted in poses derived from his photographs, of which the most popular is a seated posture with crossed legs. In contemporary iterations of this image, it is usual to see his right palm raised in blessing, but the gesture is not recorded in the cross-legged photo or any other. It is, however, the graphic symbol of the Congress, as encountered on campaign posters and ballots (such graphics are especially important as a means of addressing illiterate voters). Congress in fact adopted the hand beginning with Indira Gandhi's comeback election in 1980, too late for *Amar Akbar Anthony,* and the movie's statue sits with its hands draped per the photo, signaling no discernible political endorsement.

51. Another, brief indication of the Congress Party's presence within diegesis is a graffito that can be clearly seen on a wall behind Akbar at the start of the "Tayyab Ali Pyar Ka Dushman" number: the English word *Congress.* Whatever this detail may say about the Muslim Quarter as a neighborhood, it should not be forgotten that the film was made under the Emergency, when Indira's Congress was the only game in town.

52. The drum is a large, pie-pan-shaped *dafli,* a trademark prop of Rishi Kapoor, as famously shown two years later in a song from *Sargam* (K. Vishwanath, 1979), "Dafliwale Dafli Baja."

53. Sidharth Bhatia, *Amar Akbar Anthony: Masala, Madness and Manmohan Desai* (Noida, India: HarperCollins, 2013), 59–60, chronicles how a scheduling conflict with another production prevented Rishi Kapoor from participating in the climactic fight's shooting. A body double appears in some shots. Akbar's accompaniment of the fight on Amar's bongo drums was filmed separately afterwards.

54. The veil is also the central organizing metaphor of W. E. B. Du Bois's *The Souls of Black Folk* (Chicago: A. C. McClurg, 1903). It is for Du Bois a powerful image for thinking through the "double consciousness" of a minority community whose sense of self is mediated through representation by the majority: "the Negro is a sort of seventh son, born with a veil, and gifted with second-sight in this American world,—a world which gives him no true self-consciousness, but only lets him see himself through the revelation of the other world. It is a peculiar sensation, this double-consciousness, this sense of always looking at oneself through the eyes of others." Ibid., 3. The position is at once a predicament and a vantage that offers critical clarity.

55. Just how wide the bounds of the worldly sphere are to be drawn has of course been a matter for debate over the ages. In her analysis of the early modern Hindu saint Mira, Kumkum Sangari tidily historicizes the doctrine of illusion: "The belief that death and *maya* challenge all is a staple of the metaphysic of the high Hindu tradition. Like many other saints, Mira's *bhakti* reinterprets *maya*. From being a cosmic illusion emanating from creation or from god, it becomes more a set of conventional beliefs and attitudes, familial and patriarchal encumbrances, which prevent the meeting between the self and god. . . . *Maya* becomes a condensed sign for invoking a moral order based on moral worth rather than on social institutions and inherited privilege." Kumkum Sangari, "Mirabai and the Spiritual Economy of *Bhakti*," *Economic and Political Weekly*, July 7, 1990: 1469.

56. A close runner-up is the beggar-poet played by Mahipal in *Navrang* (V. Shantaram, 1959), who discomfits some colonial sepoys with the song "Na Raja Rahega Na Rani Rahegi," his prophecy that kings and queens alike (even white ones) will crumble to dust—as indeed, everything does in the end. The voice here is not Rafi's, however, but Mahendra Kapoor's. (Another example has already been mentioned: Majnun, the mad lover of *Laila Majnu*, played by Rishi Kapoor, sung by Mohamed Rafi.)

3. Anthony

1. Ashis Nandy, *The Intimate Enemy: Loss and Recovery of Self Under Colonialism* (New Delhi: Oxford University Press, 1983).

2. The song continues to resonate as a sign of Amitabh Bachchan's success. It signals his triumphant arrival within Indian public culture, and as such, it is something of a symbol to which the arriviste aspires. See, for example, *My Name Is Anthony Gonsalves* (Eeshwar Nivas, 2008).

3. When Kishanlal and Jenny meet after the latter returns from some foreign land on a Swissair flight, Kishanlal greets her by calling her "daughter," and Jenny greets him by calling him "Uncle." It seems that Kishanlal became her guardian but not her foster "father."

4. One wonders, as the jalopy heads off into the sunset at the end of the film, how Anthony and Jenny will resolve these thorny family politics. How, for example, will Robert

and Kishanlal get along as fathers-in-law? By abducting Jenny and marrying him to his own son, Kishanlal has fully "defeated" Robert, for Kishanlal—patriarch of a strange family—gets the girl in the end as much as Anthony does.

5. The other brothers likewise announce their full names as a testimony to their new identities. Akbar proclaims himself Akbar Ilahabadi, destroyer of veils, when he sings the *qawwali* "Parda Hai Parda." Amar proclaims himself to be Amar Khanna when he thrusts his police ID at Ranjeet and then beats up his gang.

6. In classical Hinduism, the "highest" three *varnas*, or "castes" (brahman, kshatriya, and vaishya), are thought to be "twice born" *(dvija)*. Members of these castes, especially brahmans, may undergo a ritual of rebirth as one of many life-cycle rites. Sometimes birds are likewise referred to as "twice-born" because of their two-phase birth process.

7. See Vijay Mishra, *Bollywood Cinema: Temples of Desire* (New York: Routledge, 2001); Ashish Rajadhyaksha, *Indian Cinema in the Time of Celluloid: From Bollywood to the Emergency* (Bloomington: Indiana University Press, 2009), 282.

8. "Man's Master-Blend!" *Blitz,* June 4, 1977 [NFAI Archive no. 45280-A]; "Amar, Akbar, Anthony—Delectable Escapist Fare," *Goa Herald,* June 21, 1977 [NFAI Archive no. 72489-A]; "Indian Films in City: Amar Akbar Anthony, a Hilarious Comedy," *Deccan Herald,* June 25, 1977 [No NFAI Archive no.]; "Cinema: Of Saints and Sinners," *Times of India,* no date given, [NFAI Archive no. 96042-A]; No title given, NFAI Archive no. 31236-A.

9. Mishra, *Bollywood Cinema,* makes a similar point; his treatment of *Amar Akbar Anthony* in chapter 6 has been formative to our analysis.

10. Ibid., 136–137.

11. See M. Madhava Prasad, *Ideology of the Hindi Film: A Historical Reconstruction* (New Delhi: Oxford University Press, 1998).

12. As a character defined by youthful disillusionment, Bachchan's "angry young man" is often compared to the figure of Karna from the *Mahabharata*. Kunti, Karna's mother, had him "out of wedlock" with Surya, the Sun God, so Karna is half brother to the epic's heroes, the Pandavas. The secret of Karna's true identity is one of the poignant tragedies of the epic, for he must fight his own brothers, unaware of the nature of their blood relationship. Karna is thus the classical archetype of the angry young man—heroic, honest, upright, yet in a very important sense on the wrong side of history.

13. Vijay Mishra, Peter Jeffrey, and Brian Shoesmith, "The Actor as Parallel Text in Bombay Cinema," *Quarterly Review of Film and Video* 11, no. 3 (1989): 49–67; Mishra, *Bollywood Cinema,* 125–156.

14. Amit Rai, *Untimely Bollywood: Globalization and India's New Media Assemblage* (Durham, NC: Duke University Press, 2009).

15. See Fareeduddin Kazmi, "How Angry Is the Angry Young Man? 'Rebellion' in Conventional Hindi Films," in *The Secret Politics of Our Desires: Innocence, Culpability, and Indian Popular Cinema,* ed. Ashis Nandy (Delhi: Zed Books, 1998); Prasad, *Ideology,* 14; Ranjani Mazumdar, "From Subjectification to Schizophrenia: The 'Angry Man' and the 'Psychotic' Hero of Bombay Cinema," in *Making Meaning in Indian Cinema,* ed. Ravi Vasudevan (New Delhi: Oxford University Press, 2000); Mishra, *Bollywood Cinema,* 128–129.

16. Susmita Dasgupta, *Amitabh: The Making of a Superstar* (New Delhi: Penguin Global, 2007), 39.

17. Mishra, *Bollywood Cinema*, 152.

18. Dasgupta, *Amitabh*, 41. The way the author stages the superstar against his defining role brings to mind that comic highlight of the film, the mirror scene.

19. One angry young man after another—who remembers their names? The eclipsing force of Bachchan's personal star affects the viewing of films made before *Amar Akbar Anthony* as well as those made after it, in that the effect is something brought to the film by the viewer.

20. Anthony's liquor license, which we see on the bar's signboard just before Anthony and Amar duke it out, is License No. 108—a number with great religious resonance in South Asia, especially among Hindus and Buddhists. Here the number's meaning is something like "good luck," and thus Anthony's "lucky license" indicates more than his authority to sell liquor. He is a purveyor of social good in general. This is likely a license issued not by the official state but by the government of Anthonyville—by its mayor to himself.

21. We'll see this deal negotiated again, later in the film, when Anthony briefly helps Robert escape from the police. For his help, Anthony demands a third of the gold for himself and a third for his "partner."

22. In response to decades of such practices, recent political movements have formed in India to create a civic-governmental ombudsman, or *lokpal*.

23. Kuldip Nayar, *Emergency Retold* (New Delhi: Konark Publishers, 2013). Nayar—a journalist, politician, and leftist activist—is far from unproblematic as a source on the politics of India, but the idea that the Emergency inaugurated newer and deeper levels of state corruption does not seem farfetched. The Emergency greatly altered Indian political and social life.

24. Most state and bank holidays, for example, are religious ones, allotted to India's religions according to a demographic calculus: Hinduism and Islam as India's two largest religions get roughly four each, and every other major religion—Sikhism, Christianity, Jainism, Buddhism, and so on—gets at least one holiday of its own.

25. According to the latest available census figures, Christians constitute 2.3% of the population, Sikhs 2%, and Jains 0.4%. Interestingly, Christians make up almost 35% of the charity, volunteer, and educational sector, whereas more than 20% of military personnel are Sikhs. Bombay's demographics show a larger proportion of Christians: they add up to more than 4% of the population, whereas Hindus make up 68% and Muslims 18%.

26. "About Nanavati Hospital," accessed May 9, 2015, www.indiamart.com/nanavati-hospital/aboutus.html.

27. The possible exception to this formulation is the use of Urdu among India's Muslims, but here too region and class tend to trump religion.

28. In "My Name Is Anthony Gonsalves," Anthony stops singing three times and—leaving Hindi behind—speaks in English, uttering apparently nonsensical statements. In response, the audience of Christians says, "What?!" They ask this question not because they do not understand English—after all, they are saying *what* in English—but because of the semantic incoherence of the sentences. This is much different, for example, from the moment in *Guide* (Vijay Anand, 1965) when Raju (Dev Anand) speaks in English to confound the Sanskrit-speaking brahman priests.

29. "Bombay Bhaasha as She Is Spoke," *Times of India,* November 3, 1988, A22.

30. Our thanks to Priya Joshi for this reference.

31. In the 2000s, a spate of new Anthony films sent journalists through Bombay's back lanes and across coastal Goa in search of Anthony Prabhu Gonsalves, who was found living in relative obscurity in Majorda. Gonsalves tells a story of being sidelined in Bombay's film music scene and moving to the United States to pursue a career as a jazz musician.

32. The reason for the diminished presence of Goan musicians in the film industry is unclear. There is an air of historical inevitability about the decline of the cultural capital of Christian communities in the decades following Independence. But another factor would likely be the spread of Western-style music pedagogy beyond churches and Catholic schools.

33. The most important musicians from Goa in this period learned their instruments while playing in church bands. For a study of Goan Christians and Indian popular music, see Warren R. Pinckney Jr., "Jazz in India: Perspectives on Historical Development and Musical Acculturation," *Asian Music* 21, no. 1 (1989–1990): 35–77.

34. We are thankful to the participants on the South Asia Cinema listserv for this insight, particularly Bhaskar Sarkar, Priya Joshi, Sangita Gopal, and Amit Ray. Philip Lutgendorf raises this point as well in his essay "Amar Akbar Anthony," *Philip's Fil-ums: Notes on Indian Popular Cinema,* accessed April 8, 2015, www.uiowa.edu/indiancinema/amar-akbar-anthony.

35. Consider also the genre of Bombay film noirs in which the villains have Christian names like John and Tony, and the gangster's moll is named Mona, Monica, or Lily, as in the iconic *Zanjeer* (Prakash Mehra, 1973). In *Guide* (Vijay Anand, 1965), the most unsympathetic character is Marco, who is a Robert-type deracinated figure played straight—not a smuggler but a liberal intellectual of questionable moral character. And in another Vijay Anand film, *Johny Mera Naam* (1970), a Hindu character goes undercover as a petty thief and in jail assumes a Christian name (Johny) in order to complete his charade. The use of a Christian name as a complement to the disguise of a criminal likewise occurs in more recent films, such as *Johnny Gaddaar* (Sriram Raghavan, 2007). For more, see Lalitha Gopalan, "Bombay Noir," in *A Companion to Film Noir,* ed. Andrew Spicer and Helen Hanson (West Sussex: Blackwell Press, 2013), 496–511.

36. We do not want to implicate Desai and Bachchan in the cultural-political undertow that, since Independence in 1947, has dragged Christianity out into perilous waters. (Bachchan, in particular, had solid, middle-of-the-road political credentials in the 1970s, and in the 1980s he served a short term in the Lok Sabha from Allahabad on the Congress ticket.) For a clearer understanding of the politics of Desai and Bachchan, one might look to *Naseeb* (Manmohan Desai, 1981), a film that seems to amplify the purported "national integration" message of *Amar Akbar Anthony.* Bachchan's character in the film is named John Jani Janardan, and he reports his genealogy this way: "A Christian mother gave me birth, a Hindu fed me milk, and a Muslim brought me up." Mishra, *Bollywood Cinema,* 152. Now that is communal harmony! The name also resonates with Marathi religious history: Jani or Janabai is the name of a shudra woman who was a devotee of Namdev in the fourteenth century, and Janardan is the name of the Muslim guru of the sixteenth-century saint Eknath (in addition to being a common name of Vishnu).

37. Chad Bauman, "Hindu-Christian Conflict in India," *Journal of Asian Studies* 72, no. 3 (2013): 638.

38. A case in point is the film *Rang De Basanti* (Rakeysh Omprakash Mehra, 2006), in which an interfaith mix of contemporary young Delhiites emulates a similar mix of colonial-era freedom fighters. The chief character—Daljeet, or DJ (Aamir Khan)—is a Sikh who leads his group of Hindu, Muslim, and Sikh friends to fight and die in an attempt to right the corruption of the Indian state. The film was a great hit and highly influential, and as a text it invites comparison with *Amar Akbar Anthony* on several other points: it too mixes religious and nationalist symbolism, and its narrative goal is also national renewal—the redemption of the promise of Independence. But the way *Rang De Basanti* gets there is not through the construction of a brotherly civil society. Its theme is martyrdom for the nation, and the idiom of martyrdom that unites the young idealists is taken largely from the Sikh tradition. Where Hinduism and Islam enter the story, what is made visible are explicitly political dimensions of the two religions: Hinduism as the inspiration for a reactionary, majoritarian, and ultimately corrupt politics; Islam as the face of an insular and beleaguered minority. No Christian character is included, perhaps because the nationalist narrative of the freedom struggle involves few Indian Christian heroes and generally associates Christianity with the other side. For more on the Sikh martial tradition, see Purnima Dhavan, *When Sparrows Became Hawks: The Making of Khalsa Martial Tradition* (New York: Oxford University Press, 2011).

39. This is not the official meaning of the Indian national colors; it is, however, a common interpretation that is related to the flag's origins in 1921 as a symbol of the Indian National Congress.

40. Quoted by Madhu Jain in *Outlook,* September 8, 2003.

41. The term "Anglo-Indian" can have several connotations. Formally, Article 366(2) of the Indian Constitution defines an Anglo-Indian as someone whose father was British or European, and who was born in India; this includes, therefore, people without any subcontinental genetic inheritance, like Rudyard Kipling. In popular usage, however, Anglo-Indian means a person of mixed parentage.

42. To help ameliorate this situation, the Indian Constitution contains Articles 331 and 333, which reserve seats for Anglo-Indians in both the Lok Sabha (People's Assembly) and the State Assemblies, and Articles 336 and 337, which provide special provisions for Anglo-Indian communities, particularly with regard to educational grants.

43. Zbyszko's loss in the world championships was also something of a loss of face. In their first match, Zbyszko hugged the mat defensively for more than two and a half hours, wrestling Gama to a draw. He then failed to show up for their second encounter, forfeiting the match.

44. Unlike Anthony, however, Gama was born a Muslim—his given name was Ghulam Muhammad—and he never converted. He also chose Pakistan over India as his home after Partition.

45. "Zbyszko" itself was also a pseudonym; the wrestler was born Stanislaw Jan Cyganiewicz. Zbyszko was the name of a heroic knight in the Polish historical novel *The Knights of the Cross (Krzyżacy)*, written by the Nobel laureate Henryk Sienkiewicz. Henryk Sienkiewicz, *The Knights of the Cross,* trans. Jeremiah Curtin (Boston: Little, Brown, 1900).

46. In spelling this alien-seeming name, some commentators have even looked to Portuguese, which would secure his Goan bona fides. Vijay Mishra, for example, opts for "D'Bisco." Mishra, *Bollywood Cinema,* 196–197, 200.

47. For more on the poncho fad of the 1970s, see Diane Mullane, "Trends in Consumer Packaging," White paper for Shikantini and Lacroix, November 2009, www.slideshare.net/Jeap18au55/packaging-trends-23163652.

48. Unlike Robert's first home, depicted in the movie's prologue, his second home, acquired after he regains his riches, is decorated with items of Christian devotional art. Has Robert rediscovered his Christian roots? More likely, in a kind of Pascal's Wager, he is trying to shore up his odds against Kishanlal, whom he suspects of having a particular *shakti,* or "power," on his side. Hypothesizing that the *shakti* is contained inside the Santoshi Maa pendant around Kishanlal's neck, he steals it, presumably to add to his collection.

49. Kishanlal's relationship with Robert is peculiar, for while Robert performs an almost vaudevillian impersonation of a British dandy, Kishanlal is but a parody of Robert—his entire world is reduced to emulating his enemy, which means, in part (and with important moral exceptions), becoming like the Anglo-Indian villain he despises. Those moral exceptions include not shooting people in the back, not ignoring poor people with a claim on his charity, and not forcing Jenny to convert to Hinduism.

50. Christopher Hitchens, *The Missionary Position: Mother Teresa in Theory and Practice* (London: Verso, 1995).

51. The scholarly literature on Indian Christianity, past and present, is extensive. Academic studies of its historical, political, and social dimensions almost always engage the question of conversion. See, for example, Gauri Viswanathan, *Outside the Fold: Conversion, Modernity, and Belief* (Princeton, NJ: Princeton University Press, 1998); Corinne Dempsey, *Kerala Christian Sainthood: Collision of Culture and Worldview in South India* (New York: Oxford University Press, 2001); Robert Eric Frykenberg, *Christians, Cultural Interactions, and India's Religious Traditions* (New York: Routledge, 2002); Selva Raj and Corinne Dempsey, eds., *Popular Christianity in India: Riting between the Lines* (Albany: State University of New York Press, 2002); Rowena Robinson, *Conversion, Continuity, and Change* (New Delhi: Sage Publications, 1998); Rowena Robinson and Sathianathan Clarke, eds., *Religious Conversion in India: Modes, Motivations, and Meanings* (New Delhi: Oxford University Press, 2003); Chad Bauman, *Christian Identity and Dalit Religion in Hindu India, 1868–1947* (Grand Rapids, MI: William B. Eerdmans, 2008); Rupa Viswanath, *The Pariah Problem: Caste, Religion, and the Social in Modern India* (New York: Columbia University Press, 2014).

52. See Rowena Robinson, *Christians of India* (New Delhi: Sage Publications, 2003), especially 17–20. See also Bauman, "Hindu-Christian Conflict," 633–653; Viswanath, *Pariah Problem.*

53. Smita Narula, " 'We Have No Orders to Save You': State Participation and Complicity in Communal Violence in Gujarat," *Human Rights Watch* 14, no. 3 (April 30, 2002): 1–68.

54. The heaviest concentration of Christians is in the states of India's Northeast (Arunachal Pradesh, Assam, Manipur, Meghalaya, Mizoram, Nagaland, and Tripura). Elsewhere in India, hate crimes are frequently reported against students from the Northeast, and politics in the region itself is often characterized by ethnic strife over the question of indigenousness.

55. V. D. Savarkar, *Hindutva: Who Is a Hindu?* (Bombay: Veer Savarkar Prakashan, 1969 [1923]).

56. Ibid., 77.

57. Ibid., 82.

58. For a survey of the Hindutva politics that surround Christianity, see Robert Eric Frykenberg, *Christianity in India: From Beginnings to the Present* (New York: Oxford University Press, 2008), 473–478.

59. Savarkar, *Hindutva*, 94. The Hindi term for counter-conversion is *ghar wapsi*, "return home."

60. It might be added, however, that Western clothes are not simply the default choice but rather the only possibility for a Christian character, who has no sartorial alternatives. On the pedagogical charts designed for Indian schoolrooms that show the nation's diverse ethnic types, the Christian is shown wearing Western clothes—"native dress" for the boy who has no native heritage.

61. Thomas Babington Macaulay, "Minute by the Hon'ble T. B. Macaulay, Dated the 2nd February 1835," accessed May 9, 2015, www.columbia.edu/itc/mealac/pritchett/00generallinks/macaulay/txt_minute_education_1835.html.

62. Nandy, *Intimate Enemy*, 16.

63. Edward Said, *Orientalism* (New York: Pantheon Books, 1978).

64. Nandy, *Intimate Enemy*, 14. Although the "Western" and the "modern" are synonymous with Christianity in Nandy's analysis, in the colonial metropole Christianity was viewed as a detriment to modernity, particularly as the call of the "secular" rose throughout the Western democratic states of Europe and North America. See Charles Taylor, *A Secular Age* (Cambridge, MA: Harvard University Press, 2007); Mark Lilla, *The Stillborn God* (New York: Vintage Press, 2008).

65. Nandy has also commented on Indian cinema. See, for example, Ashis Nandy, ed., *The Secret Politics of Our Desires: Innocence, Culpability and Indian Popular Cinema* (Delhi: Zed Books, 1999), in particular his introductory essay, "Introduction: Indian Popular Cinema as a Slum's Eye View of Politics."

66. Amitabh Bachchan provided vocal support to Kishore Kumar in this song, delivering the spoken lines, which have their own lyrical quality.

67. It was in a speech—directed toward his political rival, William Gladstone, and delivered on July 27, 1878—that Disraeli said: "A sophistical rhetorician, inebriated with the exuberance of his own verbosity, and gifted with an egotistical imagination that can at all times command an interminable and inconsistent series of arguments to malign an opponent and to glorify himself." Quoted in the *Times* (London), July 29, 1878.

68. David Chidester, *Savage Systems: Colonialism and Comparative Religion in Southern Africa* (Charlottesville: University of Virginia Press, 1996).

69. On one side of the cross we have the Latin abbreviation, *INRI*, and on the other side, we have its translation into English, *JNKJ*. This again signals the connection between English and Christianity.

70. The slaying of the Padre is the film's sole murder. Dark things are hinted at when Robert orders Ranjeet to take away Jenny's Decoy, and Zabisko's leather-strap snap augurs some serious sadism when we last see Albert, but the only murder in the film—the only

death, in fact—is that of the Padre. Amar's foster father is shot but not killed, Akbar's father is never in jeopardy, but Anthony is—as he fears—"orphaned twice." Amar expresses the same fear when he visits his father in the hospital, but Inspector Khanna will survive; the Padre will not. The Christian Father will die, linking him to his martyred heavenly master, Jesus. This point is made explicit in the film, especially when the Padre is stabbed and the scene cuts to an image of Christ on the cross, with blood clearly marked on the statue's body.

71. As numerous studies have argued, religious conversion in India is not an either/or proposition. It generally does not, for example, change conventions around caste and gender. Viswanath, *Pariah Problem,* has detailed how so-called "Untouchables" who convert to Christianity, despite their new religion, are often still considered to be "Untouchables" by Christians and non-Christians alike. See too Dempsey, *Kerala Christian Sainthood;* Jeffrey Cox, *Imperial Fault Lines: Christianity and Colonial Power in India, 1818–1940* (Stanford: Stanford University Press, 2002); Lamin Sanneh, *Translating the Message: The Missionary Impact on Culture* (Maryknoll, NY: Orbis Books, 2008). For a comparison with the case of Muslim eastern Bengal, see Richard Eaton, *The Rise of Islam and the Bengal Frontier* (Berkeley: University of California Press, 1993), especially chapter 10, "The Rooting of Islam in Bengal."

4. Maa—!

1. *Deewaar* (Yash Chopra, 1975), *Khoon Pasina* (Rakesh Kumar, 1977), *Amar Akbar Anthony* (Manmohan Desai, 1977), *Muqaddar Ka Sikandar* (Prakash Mehra, 1978), *Suhaag* (Manmohan Desai, 1979), *Mard* (Manmohan Desai, 1985), *Gangaa Jamunaa Saraswathi* (Manmohan Desai, 1988), and *Lal Baadshah* (K. C. Bokadia, 1999).

2. It is of course Ravi who has shot Vijay, in the line of duty. There is an earlier scene in which Maa straightforwardly tells her second son, "You always asked who was my favorite. Today I'll tell you. I have always loved Vijay more." For more on *Deewaar,* see Vinay Lal, *Deewar* (New Delhi: HarperCollins, 2011).

3. Mary's first appearance is actually in the form of a similar but larger image that is enshrined at the entrance of a different church, shown in the scene where the Padre takes in the abandoned child not yet known as Anthony. We may also note that it is unclear in this scene whether Anthony makes his pact with Jesus, Mary, or both, although later, when Anthony helps Robert escape from the police, it becomes apparent that Anthony's deal is with Jesus.

4. This theme resonates in *Deewaar* and in many other Hindi films, perhaps most famously Mehboob Khan's epic *Mother India* (1957). For more on the multiple significations of the Virgin Mary, see the classic study by Julia Kristeva, "Stabat Mater," in *The Kristeva Reader,* ed. Toril Moi (New York: Columbia University Press, 1986), 160–186.

5. For more on the goddess and the film, see Philip Lutgendorf's "A Superhit Goddess: *Jai Santoshi Maa* and Caste Hierarchy in Indian Films, Part One," *Manushi* 131 (2002): 10–16, and "A 'Made to Satisfaction Goddess': *Jai Santoshi Maa* Revisited, Part Two," *Manushi* 131 (2002): 24–37. See also Veena Das, "The Mythological Film and Its Framework of Meaning: An Analysis of *Jai Santoshi Ma,*" *India International Centre Quarterly* 8, no. 1 (1980): 43–56; Lawrence Cohen, "The Wives of Gaṇeśa," in *Ganesh:*

Studies of an Asian God, ed. Robert L. Brown (Albany: State University of New York Press, 1991); Kathleen M. Erndl, *Victory to the Mother: The Hindu Goddess of Northwest India in Myth, Ritual, and Symbol* (New York: Oxford University Press, 1993); and John S. Hawley, "Prologue: The Goddess in India," in *Devī: Goddesses of India,* ed. John S. Hawley and Donna M. Wulff (Berkeley: University of California Press, 1996), 3–6.

6. The goddess Shakti in the film *Shiv Shakti* (Jayant Desai, 1952) seems to have been played by none other than Nirupa Roy.

7. One candidate for the position of Anthony's foster mother could be the Catholic Church. The Church is known as the Bride of Christ, and the figuration of the Church as a mother is also well established in Catholic teachings. Baptism into the Church—and thus inclusion within the community of saints—is precisely what takes an unformed subject (somebody who might even be, by the logic of consanguinity, a Hindu) and welcomes that person into an environment where, through education and ritual consecration, he or she is molded into someone bound for salvation. This nurturance is situated against the masculine judgment of God the Father. When the Padre announces Anthony's impending wedding to his congregation, he describes how "under the protection of our Lord and under this roof, that innocent child flourished and grew."

8. Rosie Thomas, "Melodrama and the Negotiation of Morality in Mainstream Hindi Film," in *Consuming Modernity: Public Culture in a South Asian World,* ed. Carol A. Breckenridge (Minneapolis: University of Minnesota Press, 1995), 164.

9. The quintessential example in film is Mehboob Khan's *Mother India* (1957). For a brilliant analysis of the film, see Gayatri Chatterjee, *Mother India* (London: British Film Institute, 2002).

10. The history of the Mother India image as a product of modern visual culture is the theme of Sumathi Ramaswamy's *The Goddess and the Nation: Mapping Mother India* (Durham, NC: Duke University Press, 2010). Some aspects of Ramaswamy's exposition will come in for detailed consideration in this chapter's fourth section. See too the essay by Lise McKean, "Bharat Mata and Her Militant Matriots," in *Devī: Goddesses of India,* ed. John S. Hawley and Donna M. Wulff (Berkeley: University of California Press, 1996). *Mother India* was also the title of a sensationalistic account of Indian men's abuse of Indian women, their own persons, and much else besides by the U.S. journalist Katherine Mayo. The book was not sparing in its indictment of what it portrayed as endemic barbarism and was received with fury among Indian nationalists. Katherine Mayo, *Mother India* (New York: Harcourt, Brace, 1927).

11. Anthony discovers the identity of his father when he goes to Kishanlal's house with the pendant to accuse him of the Padre's murder, but it is a different keepsake that comes into play: Bharati's suicide note. We spectators can infer that his father will go on to tell him that his mother is alive, since Akbar would have brought that news to Amar, and Amar to Kishanlal. The next scene in which Anthony and Maa appear together is in the jail. Amar's reunion with his mother, after learning of her true identity, would appear to be the jail scene as well.

12. Sometimes seen as *man-bap* in colonial-era orthography, as in Paul Scott's *Raj Quartet* (London: Heinemann, 1966–1975), where it signifies specifically the institution of the Indian Army as embodied in the person of a British officer—the Indian soldier's mother

and father in one. *Maa* is nowadays the standard Romanized form of this Hindi equivalent of "Mom," but the vowel is indeed nasalized, per the older spelling. It is a Marathi-ized variant, *Maai-baap,* that is spoken twice in the film, both times by Anthony and with an ironic edge. Encountering his biological father for the first time in adult life, Anthony addresses Kishanlal as *Maai-baap.* Earlier, in the middle of his brawl with Amar, he uses the term to refer to the police.

13. Helen Richardson's stepfather was apparently a British officer who gave her his name but did not accompany the family to India. See the biography by Jerry Pinto, *Helen: The Life and Times of an H-Bomb* (London: Penguin 2006). In 1973, James Ivory and Ismail Merchant filmed a documentary about the actress, *Helen: Queen of the Nautch Girls.*

14. One of the other "special appearances" in the film is that of Nadira, another actress who vamped through a previous generation of films as a Westernized bad-girl figure, in the role of Lakshmi's wicked stepmother. Nadira was of Baghdadi Jewish ancestry.

15. There is a hint of sadism here, as there is when Zabisko threatens Robert's twin, Albert, with a leather strap in his own private dungeon. The outfit Zabisko wears in the sequence is worthy of some attention: tight black pants, black platform heels, and a sleeveless black muscle shirt accented with metal studs.

16. Another contender for the title of most *shakti*-empowered character is Bijli, the implicitly Muslim—and thoroughly wicked—courtesan at whose order Tayyab Ali's house is burned down. (Madhumati's "special appearance" here cites her well-established career as a dancer in Hindi films, a rival to Helen; the film thus imbues its nautch-girl character with dancer's credentials even though she doesn't appear in any dance number.) Following our analysis of the Muslim subplot in Chapter 2, however, we read Bijli's symbolism in terms of the subplot's parody of clichés taken from older films about Muslims. To the extent that the destruction of Tayyab Ali's house is the product of female agency (and not merely prescripted by genre conventions), it is yet another subversion of outmoded expectations.

17. See Eve Sedgwick on homosociality: "Patriarchal homosociality can best be discussed in terms of one or another form of the traffic in women: it is the use of women as exchangeable, perhaps symbolic, property for the primary purpose of cementing the bonds of men with men." Eve Sedgwick, *Between Men: English Literature and Male Homosocial Desire* (New York: Columbia University Press, 1985), 29.

18. All Bharati's saris, with the exception of her outfit in her last scene, appear to be printed cotton. She has four, with modest blue, purple, black, and yellow patterns on a white background. The argument following this one, in Amar's section, presents a different reason why Bharati might want to stick with cotton: women prone to spirit possession choose cotton saris over silk ones because the fabric feels cooler on hot and sensitive skin. See Margaret Trawick Egnor, "The Changed Mother or What the Smallpox Goddess Did When There Was No More Smallpox," *Contributions to Asian Studies* 18 (1984): 24–45, at 35, 38.

19. Maa's assertion of independence can be thought of as an attempt at what Durkheim called "anomic suicide"—simultaneously an assertion of modern autonomy and an index of social disintegration exacerbated by the decline of religious institutions. See Émile Durkheim, *Suicide: A Study in Sociology,* ed. George Simpson, trans. John A. Spaulding and George Simpson (Glencoe, IL: Free Press, 1951).

20. In Hindu scriptures and myths dating back to the Vedic period, the creation of the world—and of human society within it—begins with the sacrifice and dismemberment of a cosmic body that is imagined as anthropomorphic. This separation of a whole into discrete, differently valued, and organically related component parts is the paradigm of creation in Hindu mythology. See Wendy Doniger, trans., *The Laws of Manu* (London: Penguin, 1990), 3–16; Brian K. Smith, *Reflections on Resemblance, Ritual, and Religion* (Delhi: Motilal Banarasidass, 1998).

21. Sidharth Bhatia, *Amar Akbar Anthony: Masala, Madness and Manmohan Desai* (Noida, India: HarperCollins, 2013), 123.

22. "*Māyā* is typically associated with various Vedāntic schools. . . . In purānic texts, however, it is more often described in terms of egocentricity *(ahaṃkāra)*, the magical quality of creation, the very fabric of existence itself." David Kinsley, "Kālī: Blood and Death Out of Place," in *Devī: Goddesses of India,* ed. John S. Hawley and Donna M. Wulff (Berkeley: University of California Press, 1996), 82.

23. Movies themselves are implicit in this formulation of Mayapuri; compare Los Angeles's nickname *Tinseltown.*

24. In Hindi, *andhon mein kana raja,* although the proverb is shared by many cultures.

25. A point in support of the association of the Bharati character with beggars and with the dispensers of powerful blessings (often, as previously noted, the same people): she frequents religious sites, namely the Catholic church outside of which she gets hit by a car, and the Muslim *dargah* (not shown) from which she attempts to deliver blessed flowers to Akbar. (Her apparent lack of interest in Hindu temples will be addressed in this chapter's next section.) The inclusion of Amar's police station on her circuit brings to mind Anthony's statement about his fondness for places of worship: "I go to the temple, I go to the mosque, I go to church. . . . And sometimes, Sahib, I get mixed up and put in time at the police station."

26. Gandhi's full quote, "Leave India to God. If this is too much then leave her to Anarchy," dates back to May 1942, when Congress leaders were drafting the strategy of what would become the Quit India movement. Gandhi was retorting to the British position that the firm hand the Indian masses needed was not to be found among the nationalist leadership. See Sankar Ghose, *Mahatma Gandhi* (Bombay: Allied Publishers, 1991), 290; see also Faisal Devji, *The Impossible Indian: Gandhi and the Temptation of Violence* (London: Hurst, 2012), 151–184.

27. *Saṃsāra,* another way to conceptualize the phenomenal world as essentially illusory, is foundational to classical Hindu and Buddhist thought and resonates with Sufi figurations of the world of appearances. The Sanskrit term crops up in modern Hindi parlance as *sansar,* the idiomatic way of saying "world." Mercator maps can be seen in Indian classrooms bearing the legend *saṃsāra.*

28. In its historical context, this teaching was a radical formulation. Note the emergence of the Mother India icon in roughly the same period, enabled by the proliferation of the same industrial media technologies.

29. See Elison, "Sai Baba of Bombay: A Saint, His Icon, and the Urban Geography of *Darshan,*" *History of Religions* 54, no. 2 (2014): 151–187. The official print organ of the Shri Sai Baba Sansthan, the organization that administers the pilgrimage site at Shirdi, is called *Shri Sai Leela.*

30. The main compendium of the Baba's teachings, the *Shri Sai Satcharita,* outlines two versions of the process by which a visual encounter with the Baba image yields an experience of the divine presence. The first method is to practice contemplation of the image as a focusing diagram *(yantra)* for meditation; see Govind R. Dabholkar (Hedmadpant), *Shri Sai Satcharita: The Life and Teachings of Shirdi Sai Baba,* trans. Indira Kher (New Delhi: Sterling Publishers, 1999), 22:9–25. The second method—whose efficacy is attested throughout the text—is through the ritual of *darshan,* a personalized engagement with the deity through a visual interface in which a mutual recognition is attained: *I perceive divinity given form in Sai Baba, and He recognizes me as a subject.*

31. Carla Bellamy, *The Powerful Ephemeral: Everyday Healing in an Ambiguously Islamic Place* (Berkeley: University of California Press, 2011) is a study, rich in ethnographic detail, of one such site, the "court" of Shiite martyrs at Husain Tekri in Madhya Pradesh.

32. In recent times, the cults of many Hindu deities formerly honored with animal sacrifice have substituted vegetarian offerings, such as coconuts. Etymology attests to the customary homologizing of coconuts with human heads in South Asia: compare the Anglo-Indian term *copra* with *khopri,* the Hindi word for "skull."

33. Interview from a village in Maharashtra, NFAI Archive no. 31236-A.

34. On the theme of the *vrat* in *Jai Santoshi Maa,* see Lutgendorf, "A Superhit Goddess." For more on *vrat katha* literature, see Robert Menzies, "Lucky You; Lucky Me: Revival Based on Women's Ritual Power in vrat kathas," in *Chakra: tidskrift för indiska religioner (tema: medicin och terapi)* (Lund: Fööreningen Chakra, 2004), 58–69. On *vrat* practices, see Anne Mackenzie Pearson, *Because It Gives Me Peace of Mind: Ritual Fasts in the Religious Lives of Hindu Women* (Albany: State University of New York Press, 1996).

35. Zero-sum logic, and its place on the conceptual horizon of Indian village life, is discussed in D. C. Pocock, "The Evil Eye—Envy and Greed among the Patidar of Central Gujerat," in *The Evil Eye: A Casebook,* ed. Alan Dundes (Madison: University of Wisconsin Press, 1992).

36. Frederick M. Smith, *The Self Possessed: Deity and Spirit Possession in South Asian Literature and Civilization* (New York: Columbia University Press, 2006), xxv.

37. Amnesia is a typical feature of spirit possession experiences, much discussed in the literature on South Asia and elsewhere. See Frank R. Ervin et al., "The Pyschobiology of Trance II: Physiological and Endocrine Correlates," *Transcultural Psychiatric Research Review* 25, no. 4 (1988): 277. See also Ronald C. Simons, Frank R. Ervin, and Raymond H. Prince, "The Psychobiology of Trance I: Training for Thaipusam," *Transcultural Psychiatric Research Review* 25, no. 4 (1988): 239–266; Bellamy, *Powerful Ephemeral,* especially 129–171; Sudhir Kakar, *Shamans, Mystics, and Doctors: A Psychological Inquiry into India and Its Healing Traditions* (Chicago: University of Chicago Press, 1982), 53–88.

38. *Jai Santoshi Maa* is merely the most successful example of a whole subgenre of religious films that celebrate the power of Hindu mother goddesses. The phenomenon is especially prominent in South India, where possession by the "mother" (Tamil *amman*) often figures as a structuring element of the plot. See Kalpana Ram, "Bringing the

Amman into Presence in Tamil Cinema: Cinema Spectatorship as Sensuous Appreciation," in *Tamil Cinema: The Cultural Politics of India's Other Film Industry,* ed. Selvaraj Velayutham (London: Routledge, 2008), 44–58. Another essay that focuses specifically on goddess possession as manifested visually through pox is Perundevi Srinivasan, "The Creative Modern and the Myths of the Goddess Mariyamman," in *Religion in Literature and Film in South Asia,* ed. Diana Dimitrova (New York: Palgrave Macmillan, 2010), 83–91.

39. For a short overview, see the "Village Goddesses" section in David Kinsley's *Hindu Goddesses: Visions of the Divine Feminine in the Hindu Religious Tradition* (Berkeley: University of California Press, 1987). A recent, detailed book-length treatment is Sree Padma, *Vicissitudes of the Goddess: Reconstructions of the Gramadevata in India's Religious Traditions* (New York: Oxford University Press, 2013).

40. Diane P. Mines offers this assessment: "In the language of literary tropes, the goddess does not merely symbolize the village metaphorically, as a rose might symbolize love. Rather, as synecdoche . . . the goddess is a part which suffuses the whole of the village: her power (*cakti* [=Hindi *shakti*])—rooted in the earth of the temple grounds—is commonly understood to suffuse the rice-planted soil of the whole village and constitutes its fecundity as well as the reproductive potency of all its residents." Diane P. Mines, *Fierce Gods: Inequality, Ritual, and the Politics of Dignity in a South Indian Village* (Bloomington: Indiana University Press, 2005), 32.

41. According to brahmanical Hinduism, one could even say that "home" itself is destroyed with Bharati's homelessness, not just for her but for her family as well. For example, in the *Caitanyacaritāmṛta,* a biography of the Vaishnavite saint Chaitanya Mahaprabhu, it is said that "a house by itself is not a home, for it is a wife who gives a home its meaning." *Caitanyacaritāmṛta of Kṛṣṇadāsa Kavirāja Gosvāmi,* ed. Radhagovinda Natha, 6 vols., 4th ed. (Calcutta: Sadhana Prakasani, 1958), Ādi 15.27. Maa, in a sense, is the essence of homeness. Other Sanskrit sayings express a similar sentiment.

42. Glenn E. Yocum, "Comments: The Divine Consort in South India," in *The Divine Consort: Rādhā and the Goddesses of India,* ed. John S. Hawley and Donna M. Wulff (Berkeley, CA: Graduate Theological Union, 1985), 280. Yocum is not alone in reading the gendering of Hindu deities in terms of "female is to nature as male is to culture." For another influential discussion, see Lawrence A. Babb, *The Divine Hierarchy: Popular Hinduism in Central India* (New York: Columbia University Press, 1975), 217–229. We will make use of this formulation in the Amar section, but it has met with various counterarguments, especially from scholars who are critically aware of the role the nature-culture dichotomy has played in Western gender ideologies. The dichotomy laid out in this section will therefore, in turn, be challenged by the argument contained in the final section of this chapter.

43. Manuel Moreno, "God's Forceful Call: Possession as a Divine Strategy," in *Gods of Flesh, Gods of Stone: The Embodiment of the Divine in South Asia,* ed. Norman Cutler and Joanne Punzo Waghorne, in association with Vasudha Narayanan (New York: Columbia University Press, 1996), 112. Moreno offers several interpretations of what he calls the goddess's "forceful call" for a temple of her own, including one that has to do with the negotiation of space and status within the village community: "Some socio-

logists would be inclined to read these events as statements on the expansion of caste boundaries to an unsettled territory, accompanied by a forceful claim on Kantacāmi's part to an elevated social status." Ibid., 111.

44. For example, in the Delhi-area village in which they conducted fieldwork in 1977–78, Stanley A. and Ruth S. Freed identified the following: Shitala Mata, smallpox; Khamera Mata, measles; Khasra Mata, scabies; Marsal Mata, mumps; Kanti Mata, typhoid; and Phool ki Mata, or "Mother Flowers"—boils. The Freeds name two others not assigned diseases, for a total of eight, although seven is the typical number. Stanley A. Freed and Ruth S. Freed, *Hindu Festivals in a North Indian Village* (New York: American Museum of Natural History, 1998), 124–125. For a South Indian comparison, see, for example, Henry Whitehead, *The Village Gods of South India* (New York: Oxford University Press, 1921), 29. The author, who was the Anglican bishop of Madras, recorded the following deities (among others) in residence at a single shrine in Bangalore: Maramma, the cholera goddess; Udalamma, the swollen-neck goddess; Kokkalamma, the cough goddess; and Sukhajamma, the local mistress of smallpox and measles.

45. Egnor, "The Changed Mother," 24–45. If now extinct, smallpox *(variola major)* was once endemic in South Asia, as attested by the pockmarks that scar many older people. The attribution to mother goddesses of new diseases—or the advent of new goddesses—is a phenomenon that has been recorded throughout the twentieth century. In colonial days, Whitehead remarked on the rise of Plague-Amma ("Mother Plague") in areas where that disease was prevalent (and identified, presumably, by health officials working in English). Whitehead, *Village Gods,* 21. And in the 1990s, Vasudha Narayanan studied the propagation, under similarly dire circumstances, of the cult of another goddess: AIDS Amma. Vasudha Narayanan, "Diglossic Hinduism: Liberation and Lentils," *Journal of the American Academy of Religion* 68 (2000): 772–774.

46. Many of these cultic features are examined in Satyajit Ray's classic film *Devi* (1960). For a recent and compelling ethnographic account of the pox goddess's activities in rural West Bengal, see Fabrizio Ferrari, "Old Rituals for New Threats: The Post-Smallpox Career of Sitala, the Cold Mother of Bengal," in *Ritual Matters: Dynamic Dimensions in Practice,* ed. Christiane Brosius and Ute Hüsken (New York: Routledge, 2010).

47. The ethnographic record offers many illustrations of this association, like the one indicated to us by Bulbul Tiwari from among the highly ritualized South Indian dance forms she has studied. In the Teyyam of northern Kerala, as in other traditions, the performer initiates the performance in a state of trance that is understood to be goddess possession. The experience of trance is induced and managed in the virtuoso of Teyyam by controlled shielding of his gaze. Both eye-covers and mirrors are brought into use at different points in the performance. The online resource connected with Tiwari's multimedia Mahabharata project has information about Teyyam and related forms, including video footage. See Bulbul Tiwari, "Teyyam, Bhuta Kola, and Mudiyettu," *Maha Multipedia,* www.mahamultipedia.com/forms/6.

48. Alternatively, we could observe that the three boys actually seem a bit feverish, fighting heatedly over scraps in Bharati's kitchen. The youngest wails, relenting only when Kishanlal picks him up. Bharati makes no effort to care for him directly, perhaps

allowing the goddess to work in her stead. Later, when Kishanlal returns to find Bharati's suicide note, the two older boys are fanning and patting the youngest, who is bedridden, likely with fever.

49. The heat of this encounter might explain Bharati's recovery from tuberculosis; her illness was burned off by the intense blessing of the goddess. Her blindness, in other words, marks the end of her tuberculosis, as one blessing supplants another. A more Freudian inference would be that in the absence of a masculine hand to keep her feminine nature in bounds, Bharati has become hysterical. (And if her womb has gone wandering—to follow the logic of early twentieth-century Western gynecology—so will she.)

50. See Julian F. Woods, *Destiny and Human Initiative in the Mahabharata* (Albany: State University of New York Press, 2001).

51. It would be hard to imagine a more vivid illustration of the nationalist formula (Masses + Natural Bounty = Nation) than what Mehboob Khan came up with in his classic film *Mother India:* "In a pivotal scene, after the villagers have succeeded in combating a ravaging flood and in reaping a good harvest out of this difficult land, they break out into song as they thresh their crop. As they do so their produce and bodies form into an outline map of undivided India." Ramaswamy, *Goddess and the Nation,* 243–244.

52. Defining social diversity in terms of religion offers one benefit from the rupture with old village ways: any consciousness the boys might have grown up with of that rival category, caste, has been erased.

53. What sorts of corrupting weakness do the boys resist? Anthony never allows his various extralegal projects to compromise his personal code of honor. Akbar, in the face of provocation, hews to his vow of nonviolence. And Amar, in spite of the opportunities for illicit self-advancement a posting in Bombay might present, remains a credit to the Maharashtra Police (by Bollywood standards, anyway). When Inspector Amar squares off against Anthony, it is the meeting of adversaries from different walks of life—each nevertheless true to his own rules of order.

54. Recall that it was Robert who precipitated the family's ruin in the first place when he viciously withheld recognition from Kishanlal, who had approached him to plead for his rightful back pay. A circuit has thus been closed.

55. This is likely the same guardian spirit that Jenny discovered she was sharing a hiding place with in an earlier scene. The Christian, somewhat deracinated Jenny knew no better than to panic and kick at it; instead of striking at her, the snake discreetly excuses itself. Snakes are local allies of mother goddesses, and snake holes, like anthills, mark goddess territory. Cobras in particular are also closely identified with Shiva, so it is fitting to find one at the shrine of Sai Baba, who as we shall see has Shaivite bona fides.

56. Preservation, maintenance, or nurture is an aspect of divinity much celebrated in both Hindu and Islamic discourse in South Asia. *Amar Akbar Anthony*'s dialogue features the repeated use of *parvarish,* a Persian-derived word meaning "provision" or "maintenance," which is related to *parvardigaar,* Provider, the pious Haider Ali's favorite way of invoking Allah. *Parvarish* is also the title of another Manmohan Desai movie released in 1977, likewise starring Vinod Khanna, Amitabh Bachchan, Neetu Singh, and Shabana Azmi.

57. In his stronghold of Maharashtra, Sai Baba is in fact a secondary avatar of Shiva. Hindus claim him as an earthly incarnation of the god Dattatreya, who is himself a manifestation of Shiva.

58. In the background of both the hospital and the Muslim Quarter, we glimpse the façade of a temple—a composite of two flat background images—but we never see inside it or hear anything about it.

59. In his discussion of the goddess Minatci, William Harman states the general principle: "The perception of divine power in any locale often comes to be associated with a more well-known and pan-Indian deity. This makes the specific appearance more recognizable, more comprehensible, and more available. Local deities are thus understood as forms or aspects of major ones, and major deities are rendered more accessible when portrayed as having specific, local forms." William Harman, "How the Fearsome Fish-Eyed Queen Mīṇāṭci Became a Perfectly Ordinary Goddess," in *Goddesses Who Rule,* ed. Elisabeth Benard and Beverly Moon (New York: Oxford University Press, 2000), 36. And for a detailed examination of the interplay between site-specific goddesses and the Great Goddess, see Cynthia Ann Humes, "Vindhyavāsinī: Local Goddess yet Great Goddess," in *Devī: Goddesses of India,* ed. John Stratton Hawley and Donna Marie Wulff (Berkeley: University of California Press, 1996), 49–76.

60. Narayanan, "Diglossic Hinduism," 768.

61. As David Kinsley notes, "The myths and cults of village goddesses, however, often cast males in disruptive roles and equate the village goddess with the civilized, orderly, and refined realm of the village. Outside the village is the jungle: wild, raw, and chaotic. The village goddess represents the order of the cultivated field and the security of hearth and home. She is preeminently the being who protects the village from attacks by wild, unstable, demonic spirits from the uncivilized outer world. Those demons, furthermore, are often said to be male, and Śiva himself, the deity of the Sanskrit pantheon most commonly associated with village goddesses as a consort, is well known to live on the periphery of civilization, to associate with demons, and in general to have disruptive, antisocial habits." Kinsley, *Hindu Goddesses,* 203.

62. Usha Menon and Richard A. Shweder, "Power in Its Place: Is the Great Goddess of Hinduism a Feminist?" in *Is the Goddess a Feminist? The Politics of South Asian Goddesses,* ed. Alf Hiltebeitel and Kathleen M. Erndl (Sheffield: Sheffield Academic Press, 2000), 164.

63. Ramaswamy, *Goddess and the Nation,* 177–236.

64. Ibid., 181.

65. Ibid., 227.

66. It may be thought that Bharati's humble, even abject portrayal as a woman of the streets makes identification of her as Bharat Mata a stretch. But in fact,*Amar Akbar Anthony*'s depiction of a beleaguered Mother India is squarely in line with iconographic tradition. Historically, the national goddess has often been pictured as weakened or under threat of assault or even mutilation—and thus all the more in need of filial devotion. Many images circulated in the period of British rule show her wearing shackles, and in one celebrated film appearance, in the great pre-Independence hit *Kismet* (Gyan Mukherjee, 1943), the figure is depicted on crutches.

67. Lawrence Cohen, "The Second Kidney: Biopolitics beyond Recognition," *Body and Society* 7, no. 2–3 (2001): 9–29, examines the ideological encoding of blood as a medium of national unification across barriers of religion and caste. Cohen's sampling of Hindi films is a rich one. In addition to *Amar Akbar Anthony,* he discusses *Sujata* (Bimal Roy, 1960), in which an "Untouchable" girl adopted into an upper-caste family turns out to be the only compatible donor for her foster mother, and *Zanjeer* (Prakash Mehra, 1973), in which a Hindu police officer (Amitabh Bachchan) is saved by an infusion of blood from a Muslim racketeer (the ubiquitous Pran). Also worthy of note is *Munimji* (Subodh Mukherji, 1955), which presents a contrasting scenario that nevertheless depends on the same logic of consanguinity. Nirupa Roy, in one of her earlier turns as a mother figure, gives blood to save the life of an arrogant young landowner played by Pran, her husband in *Amar Akbar Anthony.* The Pran character is scandalized to find that his body has admitted the blood of someone he regards as a lower-caste servant. Toward the movie's end, it is revealed that the two are actually biological mother and son.

68. A woman's loss of the faculty of recognition is a full-blown cliché in Hindi popular films. (This would suggest that Maa, as the conventionally afflicted, bears a heavier burden of recognition than her sons—for some viewers, at least.) The record of a single star interpreter of amnesia and coma, Waheeda Rehman, attests to the trope's endurance across the decades: *C.I.D.* (Raj Kosla, 1956); *Palki* (Mahesh Kaul and S. U. Sunny, 1967); *Coolie* (Manmohan Desai, 1983); and *Rang De Basanti* (Rakeysh Omprakash Mehra, 2006). Corresponding most closely to Bharati's case is *Palki,* examined in detail in Chapter 2. Mehro, the Waheeda Rehman character, receives a psychic shock that results in partial memory loss; her sister-in-law attempts to heal her by taking her on a pilgrimage to the shrine of a Sufi saint. Much is always at stake in Waheeda's revival, namely truths about the correct arrangement of relations among the other characters. Truths deferred—to everyone's suspense—in an embodied but unstated condition until she either wakes up or dies.

69. The lines are *Maa sirf mata nahin | Yeh kucch aur bhi hai.* A more aggressive translation would be "Maa is never just a mother. / And this one's something else." The lyrics that follow make plain the theme of recognition, or *pehchaan:* "Flowers are recognized by color and scent. / People are recognized by their blood."

70. For more on this idea of song sequences as a privileged temporal mode, see Chapter 2.

71. *Bhagavad Gita,* ed. Shripad Krishna Belvalkar (Pune: Bhandarkar Oriental Research Institute, 1943), 1.43.

72. Often the icon installed in these modern temples is that of the god Dattatreya. See Charles Pain, with Eleanor Zelliott, "The God Dattatreya and the Datta Temples of Pune," in *The Experience of Hinduism: Essays on Religion in Maharashtra,* ed. Eleanor Zelliot and Maxine Berntsen (Albany: State University of New York Press, 1988), 95–108. Dattatreya, it will be recalled, is the intermediary form recognized between Shiva and Sai Baba, and this yields a yet more complex formulation: Sai Baba as the makeover of Dattatreya as the makeover of a site that was already dedicated to the goddess to begin with.

73. A close examination of the Sai Baba temple will show, hanging over the *linga*—the embodiment of Lord Shiva—a *dharapatra*, a conical pot from which water can continuously drip to keep the Lord cool. Note that in this case the *dharapatra* is empty and the *linga* is dry. Shiva, we can surmise, is burning from the heat of the goddess.

74. *Devi Mahatmya,* ed. and trans. Swami Sivananda, 2nd edition (Tehri-Garhwal: Divine Life Society, 1994), 10:5–6. The translation is our own.

75. Maa's monologue here is a free adaptation of Odissi women's statements as recorded through fieldwork and summarized in a remarkable passage in Menon and Shweder, "Power in Its Place," 159.

Conclusion

1. In more colloquial English usage, *anhoni* might be glossed as the quality of "not gonna happen" (U.S.) or "it's not on" (U.K.).

2. An alternative formulation: "Expect people breaking into song and dance to work out well for the likes of *me?* I'm on the wrong side. Impossible—not gonna happen." The film offers a corollary to this in the "My Name Is Anthony Gonsalves" number, in which Anthony sings of a distinction between rich people, whose hearts are closed, and poor people, who know the magic of romance. To be mapping social class onto representational modalities in this way—with the rich being blinkered by a misguided commitment to realism—implies a certain self-awareness on the part of the filmmakers, who know that it is not the "classes" but the "masses" that will make this movie's fortunes. See the discussions of the film's critical reception and the genesis of the Bollywood format in our introduction.

3. We are reminded of another famous line marking a villain's protest against the reality of the diegesis he is part of: the refrain of "Inconceivable!" voiced by Vizzini, the intellectual kidnapper in *The Princess Bride* (Rob Reiner, 1987).

4. Isn't it curious that the real names are so close to the fake names? In the end, it could be said, the question of who the three truly are is not answered by any names they have given. Or by any names they could give. Is Akbar, for example, really Raju, the name given him at birth? As we've argued in previous chapters, the film's deeper truth is that beneath the designations of sect or state, the three are brothers—brothers by blood.

5. The code that *Amar Akbar Anthony* follows when characters interact with sacred images is well established in Indian cinema. The diegetic worshipper is shown viewing the image frontally and from slightly below. This positioning is reinscribed with a shot from the worshipper's point of view, such that the audience sees, as it were, through the worshipper's eyes; this move cues the audience to experience *darshan* along with the character. But the next shot does not respond in kind with a god's-eye view. What we get is an angled view (and frequently from a lesser height); the camera does not match the deity's eyeline, which would be a kind of hubris or even sacrilege. The organization of *darshan* in the Sai Baba scene follows the pattern shown in the famous devotional film *Jai Santoshi Maa* (Vijay Sharma, 1975). "The camera repeatedly zooms in on Satyavati's face and eyes, then offers a comparable point-of-view zoom shot of the goddess as Satyavati sees her. Finally, it offers a shot-reverse shot from a position just over the goddess's shoulder, thus approximating (though not directly assuming) Santoshi Ma's perspective, and closing the darshanic loop by showing us Satyavati and the other worshipers more or less as She sees them." Philip Lutgendorf, "A 'Made to Satisfaction Goddess': *Jai Santoshi Maa* Revisited, Part Two," *Manushi* 131 (2002): 28. See also Norman Cutler, *Songs of Experience: The Poetics of Tamil Devotion* (Bloomington: Indiana University Press, 1987), 22–27.

6. In theoretical terms, we read this wink not as an interruption of the diegetic illusion—a moment of rupture—but as a moment of suture.

Appendix: Film Synopsis

1. Sidharth Bhatia, *Amar Akbar Anthony: Masala, Madness and Manmohan Desai* (Noida: HarperCollins, 2013), 22–45; Vijay Mishra, *Bollywood Cinema: Temples of Desire* (New York: Routledge, 2001), 157–201. Several different DVDs of *Amar Akbar Anthony* are available on the market. There is considerable variation among them, with discrepancies in picture quality, subtitling, and—most vexingly—amount of footage reproduced; a share of the complaints about the film's alleged lack of sense may be coming from viewers of truncated cuts. This synopsis is mainly based on the version released by Shemaroo, which we have found to be the most complete.

2. The Hindi of the film incorporates a good deal of English and, to a lesser extent, Urdu. Marathi is a distant fourth, surfacing in the film chiefly in words and speech patterns used by Anthony that give his Hindi patois a distinctively slangy, streetwise tone.

3. The Kolis have historically been a fishing community, and a Koliwada is a fishing village that has become absorbed within the city. The Kolis are generally recognized as the area's original inhabitants. The film's Koliwada is described as such in dialogue, but at the visual level there is nothing to mark the space or its inhabitants specifically as Koli. In contemporary Mumbai many Hindu Kolis have made a bid to move beyond the bounds of caste to embrace the sort of ideologized formulation of generically Maratha identity that has transformed the city's politics (along with its name). The transition is not as inviting for Catholic Kolis, who make up an important subset of the community.

4. Is the gun a toy, or is it an actual weapon? The question, as we demonstrate in each brother's chapter, turns out to have implications not only for Amar but for Akbar and Anthony as well.

5. *"Haram ki kamai,"* is a colloquial expression meaning ill-gotten wealth. Bharati uses the idiomatic *haram*—an Islamic term—over a more Hindu formulation like the fruit of bad action.

6. As with the nanny's frock, one implication of this dress code is that they are Christians, like Robert himself—deracinated and, by Bollywood precedent, associated with Bombay's underworld. Among the group can be recognized the actor who plays the Catholic priest whose place is taken by Anthony at the film's climax. There is also another performer who reappears as one of the Muslim thugs who roughs up Akbar on Tayyab Ali's instructions; this figure wears a Pathan hat in this sequence, marking him as a representative of a group long identified as tough guys and enforcers in Bombay lore. The presence of both characters as guests at Robert's party is just plausible within diegesis.

7. Indeed, life in Bollywood: the most famous case of this sort in recent years has involved the bad-boy film star Salman Khan, who initially tried to extract himself from legal trouble by blaming his driver. One person was killed and four others injured when Khan's car ran into a Bandra bakery in 2002; thirteen years later, just before this book went to press, the actor was found guilty of culpable homicide and given a five-year

sentence. Other actors are privately named in connection with similar incidents that are hushed up with money.

8. An anna is a now-defunct unit of currency that used to be worth one-sixteenth of a rupee. Kishanlal is saying something like, "You didn't give them so much as a farthing."

9. *Seth* is an honorific, a title used to address merchants, guild masters, and, generally speaking, rich people—when less rich people wish to emphasize that distinction.

10. Both machines are boxy black Ambassadors, the definitive Indian make of the post-Independence decades and an icon of the License Raj, the era of the planned national economy.

11. The cult of Santoshi Maa, a Hindu goddess unmarked by specific caste or geographical provenance, rose to prominence in this period as a result of the popularity throughout India of a 1975 Hindi film celebrating her power. We take up the case of this distinctively modern goddess in Chapter 4.

12. We also catch sight of two other inscriptions on the other sides of the pedestal, both in Hindi: *dhairya aur shanti se kya haasil nahin kiya jaa sakta* ("What can't be obtained through patience and peace?") and *satya aur ahimsa ek sikke ke do pahlu hain* ("Truth and nonviolence are two sides of the same coin").

13. How and where did he get the bread? For the second time, the Anthony character is marked as impetuously ready to take what he wants, the first time being the episode with Amar's gun.

14. Even an act as commonplace as public urination can be marked in terms of religious affiliation, inasmuch as Islamic norms of hygiene and modesty enjoin a squatting posture on male Muslims.

15. Amar is the only character who retains the name given by his birth parents. Akbar (formerly Raju) and Anthony (name unknown) are renamed by their foster fathers.

16. Here, at the twenty-one-minute mark, is the film's third hit-and-run accident, with the first being Robert's seminal crime and the second the injuring of young Amar. (If the dead body the young Anthony speaks of having found on the street is attributed to another accident, that would make Bharati's the fourth.)

17. The very first word Rishi Kapoor speaks in this film is a blooper. "Neetu!" he cries out in feigned pain, naming his costar and not the character she's playing. The actors were dating at the time and tied the knot three years later.

18. Here the area is called Anthony Nagar. Later, when Amar seeks Anthony in order to track down Robert, the name used is the more Maharashtrian Anthony Wadi.

19. The wheel (*chakar* or *chakra*) gestures to a number of visual motifs, including the *dharmachakra* at the center of the national flag and the spinning wheel emblematic of Gandhian activism and, subsequently, the Congress Party.

20. The number 108 figures auspiciously in much Indic lore, notably in Hindu myth and didactic literature.

21. Most of the writing shown in this scene is in English and Hindi; there is an easily missed Urdu sign by the theater's entrance. Even Akbar's couplet is written in Hindi.

22. The exchange of flowers as a blessing in material form occurs in ritual practice across religious traditions. The piously expressed wish for the success of another is a specific kind of blessing: *shubhkamna,* a word Bharati uses here.

23. Anthony's outfit in this scene features a red leather jacket and, around his neck, an ankh in place of a more conventional cross. As if in compensation, the jacket bears a patch on the left sleeve with the English words "Jesus Loves Me." The patch can be read as a Christianized response to the coolie badge the Bachchan character wore in the same place in *Deewaar* (Yash Chopra, 1975), which bore the Islamic cipher 786; the motif was recycled when Bachchan again played a coolie in Desai's own *Coolie* (1983). In the "Hamko Tumse Ho Gaya Hai Pyar Kya Karein" number, the patch makes a reappearance on Anthony's white jacket, but it has migrated to the right sleeve.

24. "Inspector" as used here is a courtesy title. In distinction to his foster father's rank, Amar's technical position in the Maharashtra Police, as indicated by his uniform and his ID card, is sub-inspector.

25. The residents of this middle-class bungalow comprise Lakshmi and the Grandmother, daughter and mother respectively of a deceased patriarch; the Stepmother, the patriarch's second wife, loudly garbed in a muumuu by contrast with the modest white sari of the Grandmother; and the rogue male Ranjeet, corrupt scion of a fatherless household. This is an example of a failed family; see Chapter 1.

26. Anderson Montgomery Everton "Andy" Roberts, from Antigua, was famed—and feared—in his day as one of cricket's deadliest fast bowlers. For a sense of his reputation in the 1970s, see the documentary *Fire in Babylon* (Stevan Riley, 2010).

27. The mix was typical of neighborhoods like Bandra as they underwent development in the 1970s, and is still encountered nowadays in plenty of places in the suburbs.

28. The British "Guv'nor" conveys some of the same effect, which in this context is mildly facetious.

29. Kishanlal's playful and outlandish-looking outfits can be read as a parody of Robert's already parodic wardrobe. With his frock coat and wool hat, he also appropriates elements of the aristocratic style of dress associated with such icons of the past as Nehru, Jinnah, and—where the movie is concerned—Tayyab Ali. In the 1970s context, Kishanlal's eccentric dress may not have connoted "underworld" so much as "postcolonial politician"—the Tamil film-star-turned-party boss MGR comes to mind, as do leaders from farther afield known for sunglasses and distinctive hats, such as the Zairian dictator Mobutu.

30. Of Anglo-Burmese origin, Helen has built a career in the Bombay industry that has centered on portraying exotic women from outside mainstream Indian society; her cameo here functions in effect as a citation of this extradiegetic persona. See Chapter 4.

31. And no wonder: the interiors were shot at a different church in a different neighborhood—Don Bosco in Matunga.

32. Among this outfit's reference points is the nineteenth-century British statesman Benjamin Disraeli, whose words are also quoted in Anthony's rapid-fire English patter. See Chapter 3.

33. Among the fantastical features of Anthony's dance is some comic business involving a colonial-looking picture of an African drummer. For some thoughts about the meaning of this peculiar image, see Chapter 3.

34. The beach is made familiar in India as a site of romance through American, not Indian, movies (except when they cite the American ones).

35. For those looking for it, this song supplies ample symbolism to the effect that each couple's love has been consummated: Jenny riding on Anthony's boat and horse; the train

that takes Akbar and Salma through a dark tunnel; the rain that soaks Amar and Lakshmi.

36. The buildings' outlines as shown here are different from those seen through the hospital windows. But there is just enough correspondence in the colors and the architectural styles for the idea to be plausible that we are looking at the same buildings from different angles.

37. Cited here is a genre of performance in which *hijras* assemble in front of houses (typically belonging to families celebrating weddings) and sing and dance until someone comes outside to pay them off. The dancing features ribald and carnivalesque lyrics and is ostensibly offered as a blessing. As with gestures of blessing offered by other marginal but ritually potent figures like fakirs and sadhus, the line is easily crossed from blessing to curse.

38. The original proverb is "When master and wife are both agreed / What can the *qazi* do?" (*Miyan bibi raazi / To kya karega qazi?*)

39. The posh-sounding address suggests that Kishanlal dwells alongside film stars in the suburb of Juhu.

40. Perhaps Gracie is the nanny shown taking the one-year-old Jenny in her arms in the prologue sequence—or perhaps she is a Christian nanny Kishanlal hired to take the first woman's place.

41. The placement of the driver's seat on the left in both station wagons indicates a U.S. import. The film makes use of no fewer than four American cars: the two in this scene, a third station wagon in the lead-up to the Sai Baba number, and a cream-colored sedan in which Amar and Anthony ride to the final showdown. All four appear to be Chevrolet Bel Airs.

42. This battle of the station wagons contrasts sharply with the earlier chase, set twenty-two years before, when Kishanlal and Robert's men drove identical black Ambassadors through spaces identifiable as landmarks of the diegetic city—the park with the Gandhi statue, the slum-like Koliwada.

43. This shot does not seem to correspond to any real hospital in the city, although the late colonial-vintage building it portrays is likely in South or Central Bombay.

44. This detail is not an artifact of sloppy screenwriting but another quotation, like Anthony's arm patch, from that important film of two years before, *Deewaar*. Vijay, the character played by Amitabh Bachchan, is humiliated by enemies who tattoo his arm with the legend "My father is a crook." Here we are shown the tattooed father of another Bachchan character who, as it turns out, really is a crook.

45. The space is liberally decorated with European-style art. The Christian imagery becomes more visible in the finale sequence, in which Robert's flight through his own home takes us past a little grotto. Another Catholic prop is a shrine set in the wall that looks identical to the one inside Anthony's bar.

46. A *dargah* is the tomb of a Muslim saint—who may not necessarily be buried at the spot—and, by extension, the complex that grows around it to accommodate visitors to the holy site. See Chapters 2 and 4.

47. *Shakti,* which has been translated here per colloquial usage as "power," is a term with a rich history in Indic religious and philosophical discourses. Even in everyday parlance it connotes a specifically feminine power. At a more technical remove, it is a volatile elemental energy associated with Hindu goddesses, with vitality and fertility, and

with blood. To identify a goddess such as Santoshi Maa as a form of *"shakti"* is at one level a tautology. See Chapter 4.

48. Sai Baba's cross-sectarian appeal reached a sort of critical mass in the Bombay area in the mid-1970s. We unpack this scene from distinct religious perspectives—just who is the agent of divine power here?—in Chapters 2 and 4.

49. Snakes, especially cobras, are prominent in the mythology and iconography of Shiva as well as of the goddess (Parvati/Durga) who appears under certain conditions as his consort. Some Hindu devotees of Sai Baba regard him as an avatar or emanation of Shiva (via the intermediary avatar of Dattatreya, a god worshipped primarily in Maharashtra).

50. This bit part seems to belong to the actor who earlier portrayed another bearer of bad tidings—the police constable who mistakenly informs Bharati that her family has perished in an accident.

51. Kishanlal appears here in his third Teddy Boy ensemble: slate gray this time.

52. Jenny inaccurately recalls the long period of separation as twenty-five years, not twenty-two. Fans noting the discrepancy tend to ascribe it to a blooper on Parveen Babi's part.

53. The Padre's line uses a Perso-Islamic name for the Almighty, Khuda: *"Yeh Khuda ka ghar hai."*

54. A *mujra* is a dance with erotic overtones traditionally performed by courtesans at high-style North Indian weddings, often featured in Hindi movies of the "Muslim social" genre. Compare *Pakeezah* (Kamal Amrohi, 1972), as discussed in Chapter 2.

55. The word used is *begam,* an Urdu title for a married woman of aristocratic status.

56. The musician's outfit of shabby jacket, trousers, and crumpled hat recalls the Tramp persona assumed by the star Raj Kapoor (Rishi's father) in the films of the 1950s—a persona inspired, in turn, by Charlie Chaplin.

57. The driver is recognizable as Hercules, the actor who played Raghu, Anthony's burly antagonist in his first fight scene. Are we to infer that, deprived of his old neighborhood racket, Raghu has signed on in Robert's service?

Bibliography

"*Albert Pinto Ko Gussa Kyoon Aata Hai.*" In *Encyclopaedia of Indian Cinema*, edited by Ashish Rajadhyaksha and Paul Willimen, 444. New Revised Edition. London: Routledge, 1999.

Alter, Joseph S. "Celibacy, Sexuality, and the Transformation of Gender into Nationalism in North India." *Journal of Asian Studies* 53, no. 1 (1994): 45–66.

———. *Gandhi's Body: Sex, Diet, and the Politics of Nationalism*. Philadelphia: University of Pennsylvania Press, 2000.

———. "Indian Clubs and Colonialism: Hindu Masculinity and Muscular Christianity." *Comparative Studies in Society and History* 46, no. 3 (2004): 497–534.

———. *Moral Materialism: Sex and Masculinity in Modern India*. New Delhi: Penguin Books, 2011.

———. "Seminal Truth: A Modern Science of Male Celibacy in North India." *Medical Anthropology Quarterly* 11, no. 3 (1997): 275–298.

———. "Somatic Nationalism: Indian Wrestling and Militant Hinduism." *Modern Asian Studies* 28, no. 3 (1994): 557–588.

Althusser, Louis. "Ideology and Ideological State Apparatuses." In *Lenin and Philosophy and Other Essays*, translated by Ben Brewster, 121–176. London: Monthly Review Press, 1971.

Anand. "Wordspeak: On the Bollywood Beat." *Hindu,* Sunday, March 7, 2004. www.thehindu.com/lr/2004/03/07/stories/2004030700390600.htm.

Anderson, Benedict. *Imagined Communities: Reflections on the Origin and Spread of Nationalism*. London: Verso, 1983.

Ansari, Ameena Kazi. "Hybridity and the Filmic Text: Re-visiting *Chaudhvin ka Chand*." In *Muslim Culture in Indian Cinema*, edited by Jasbir Jain, 161–170. Jaipur, India: Rawat Publications, 2011.

Attri, Rashmi. "Qawwali: A Mode of Representation of Muslim Culture in Bollywood." In *Muslim Culture in Indian Cinema*, edited by Jasbir Jain, 51–62. Jaipur, India: Rawat Publications, 2011.

Babb, Lawrence A. *The Divine Hierarchy: Popular Hinduism in Central India*. New York: Columbia University Press, 1975.

Banerjee, Sikata. *Muscular Nationalism: Gender, Violence, and Nationalism in India and Ireland, 1914–2004*. New York: New York University Press.

Barthes, Roland. *The Pleasure of the Text*. Translated by Richard Miller. New York: Hill and Wang, 1975.

Bauman, Chad. *Christian Identity and Dalit Religion in Hindu India, 1868–1947*. Grand Rapids, MI: William B. Eerdmans, 2008.

———. "Hindu-Christian Conflict in India." *Journal of Asian Studies* 72, no. 3 (2013): 633–653.

Beaster-Jones, Jayson. *Bollywood Sounds: The Cosmopolitan Mediations of Hindi Film Song*. Oxford: Oxford University Press, 2014.

Behl, Aditya, and Simon Weightman, trans. *The Madhumalati*. New York: Oxford University Press, 2001.

Bellamy, Carla. *The Powerful Ephemeral: Everyday Healing in an Ambiguously Islamic Place*. Berkeley: University of California Press, 2011.

Berlant, Lauren. *Cruel Optimism*. Durham, NC: Duke University Press, 2011.

Bhagavad Gita. Edited by Shripad Krishna Belvalkar. Pune: Bhandarkar Oriental Research Institute, 1943.

Bhalla, Alok, ed. *Stories about the Partition of India*. New Delhi: HarperCollins, 1994.

Bhaskar Rao, U. *The Story of Rehabilitation*. Delhi: Department of Rehabilitation, Government of India, 1967.

Bhatia, Sidharth. *Amar Akbar Anthony: Masala, Madness and Manmohan Desai*. Noida, India: HarperCollins, 2013.

Biardeau, Madeleine. "Ancient Brahminism, or Impossible Non-Violence." In *Violence/Non-Violence: Some Hindu Perspectives,* edited by Denis Vidal, Gilles Tarabout, and Éric Meyer, 85–104. Delhi: Manohar Publications, 2003.

Booth, Gregory. *Behind the Curtain: Making Music in Mumbai's Film Studios*. New York: Oxford University Press, 2008.

———. "Religion, Gossip, Narrative Conventions and the Construction of Meaning in Hindi Film Songs." *Popular Music* 19 (2000): 125–145.

Bright, J. S. *Allahabad High Court to Shah Commission*. New Delhi: Deep and Deep, 1979.

Butalia, Urvashi. "Muslims and Hindus, Men and Women: Communal Stereotypes and the Partition of India." In *Women and Right-Wing Movements: Indian Experiences*, edited by Tanka Sarkar and Urvashi Butalia, 58–81. London: Zed Books, 1995.

Caitanyacaritāmṛta of Kṛṣṇadāsa Kavirāja Gosvāmi. Edited by Radhagovinda Natha. 6 vols. 4th ed. Calcutta: Sadhana Prakasani, 1958.

Carstairs, George Morrison. "Hinjra and Jiryan: Two Derivatives of Hindu Attitudes to Sexuality." *British Journal of Medical Psychiatry* 29 (1956): 128–138.

———. *The Twice-Born*. London: Hogarth Press, 1958.

Chakrabarty, Bandana. "Celebrating the Courtesan in Hindi Films: *Umrao Jaan* and *Pakeezah*." In *Muslim Culture in Indian Cinema*, edited by Jasbir Jain, 132–139. Jaipur, India: Rawat Publications, 2011.

Chakravarty, Sumita S. "The National-Heroic Image: Masculinity and Masquerade." In *The Bollywood Reader,* edited by Rajinder Dudrah and Jigna Desai, 84–96. New York: Open University Press, 2008.

——. *National Identity in Indian Popular Cinema, 1947–1987.* Austin: University of Texas Press, 1993.

Chandra, Vikram. *Sacred Games.* New York: Harper Perennial, 2007.

Chatterjee, Gayatri. *Mother India.* London: British Film Institute, 2002.

Chatterjee, Partha. *The Nation and Its Fragments: Colonial and Postcolonial Histories.* Princeton, NJ: Princeton University Press, 1995.

Chattopadhyay, Saratchandra. *Devdas: A Novel.* Translated by Sreejata Guha. Delhi: Penguin, 2002.

Chidester, David. *Savage Systems: Colonialism and Comparative Religion in Southern Africa.* Charlottesville: University of Virginia Press, 1996.

Cohen, Lawrence. "The Second Kidney: Biopolitics beyond Recognition." *Body and Society* 7, no. 2–3 (2001): 9–29.

——. "The Wives of Gaṇeśa." In *Ganesh: Studies of an Asian God,* edited by Robert L. Brown, 115–140. Albany: State University of New York Press, 1991.

"Community News." *Goan Voice Newsletter,* March 4, 2004. www.goanvoice.org.uk /newsletter/2004/Mar/issue1.

Cox, Jeffrey. *Imperial Fault Lines: Christianity and Colonial Power in India, 1818–1940.* Stanford: Stanford University Press, 2002.

Creekmur, Corey. "Chaudhvin Ka Chand." *Philip's Fil-ums: Notes on Indian Popular Cinema.* www.uiowa.edu/indiancinema/chaudhvin-ka-chand. Accessed April 10, 2015.

——. "Remembering, Repeating and Working through *Devdas.*" In *Indian Literature and Popular Cinema: Recasting Classics*, edited by Heidi M. Pauwels, 173–190. London: Routledge, 2007.

Cutler, Norman. *Songs of Experience: The Poetics of Tamil Devotion* (Bloomington: Indiana University Press, 1987).

Dabholkar, Govind R. (Hedmadpant). *Shri Sai Satcharita: The Life and Teachings of Shirdi Sai Baba*, translated by Indira Kher. New Delhi: Sterling Publishers, 1999.

Daiya, Kavita. *Violent Belongings: Partition, Gender, and National Culture in Postcolonial India.* Philadelphia: Temple University Press, 2008.

Das, Veena. "The Mythological Film and Its Framework of Meaning: An Analysis of *Jai Santoshi Ma.*" *India International Centre Quarterly* 8, no. 1 (1980): 43–56.

Dasgupta, Rana. *Capital: A Portrait of Twenty-First-Century Delhi.* Noida, India: Harper-Collins, 2014.

Dasgupta, Susmita. *Amitabh: The Making of a Superstar.* New Delhi: Penguin Global, 2007.

Dempsey, Corinne. *Kerala Christian Sainthood: Collision of Culture and Worldview in South India.* New York: Oxford University Press, 2001.

Devi Mahatmya. Edited and translated by Swami Sivananda. 2nd ed. Tehri-Garhwal, India: Divine Life Society, 1994.

Devji, Faisal. "Gender and the Politics of Space: The Movement for Women's Reform, 1857–1900." In *Forging Identities: Gender, Communities, and the State in India,* edited by Zoya Hasan, 22–37. Delhi: Kali for Women. 1994.

——. *The Impossible Indian: Gandhi and the Temptation of Violence.* London: Hurst, 2012.

Dhavan, Purnima. *When Sparrows Became Hawks: The Making of Khalsa Martial Tradition.* New York: Oxford University Press, 2011.

Doniger, trans. *The Laws of Manu.* New York: Penguin, 1990.

Doniger, Wendy, and Sudhir Kakar, trans. *Kamasutra.* New York: Oxford University Press, 2002.

Du Bois, W. E. B. *The Souls of Black Folk.* Chicago: A. C. McClurg, 1903.

Dudrah, Rajinder. *Bollywood: Sociology Goes to the Movies.* New Delhi: Sage Publications, 2006.

Dudrah, Rajinder, and Jigna Desai, eds. *The Bollywood Reader.* Berkshire, UK: Open University Press, 2008.

Durkheim, Émile. *Suicide: A Study in Sociology.* Edited by George Simpson. Translated by John A. Spaulding and George Simpson. Glencoe, IL: Free Press, 1951.

Dwyer, Rachel. *All You Want Is Money, All You Need Is Love: Sex and Romance in Modern India.* London: Cassell, 2000.

——. *Filming the Gods: Religion and Indian Cinema.* New York: Routledge, 2006.

——. *100 Bollywood Films.* London: British Film Institute, 2008.

Dwyer, Rachel, and Divia Patel. *Cinema India: The Visual Culture of Hindi Film.* New Brunswick, NJ: Rutgers University Press, 2002.

Dwyer, Rachel, and Christopher Pinney, eds. *Pleasure and the Nation: The History, Politics, and Consumption of Public Culture in India.* New Delhi: Oxford University Press, 2001.

Eaton, Richard. *The Rise of Islam and the Bengal Frontier.* Berkeley: University of California Press, 1993.

Egnor, Margaret Trawick. "The Changed Mother or What the Smallpox Goddess Did When There Was No More Smallpox." *Contributions to Asian Studies* 18 (1984): 24–45.

Elison, William. "Sai Baba of Bombay: A Saint, His Icon, and the Urban Geography of *Darshan.*" *History of Religions* 54, no. 2 (2014): 151–187.

Erndl, Kathleen M. *Victory to the Mother: The Hindu Goddess of Northwest India in Myth, Ritual, and Symbol.* New York: Oxford University Press, 1993.

Ervin, Frank R., Roberta M. Palmour, Beverly E. Pearson Murphy, Raymond Prince, and Ronald C. Simons. "The Psychobiology of Trance II: Physiology and Endocrine Correlates." *Transcultural Psychiatric Research Review* 25, no. 4 (1988): 267–284.

Farooqi, Mehr. "'Akbar' Ilahabadi: Satirical Verses and Excerpts from 'Dialogue between Old and New Ways.'" In *Nationalism in the Vernacular: Hindi, Urdu, and the Literature of Indian Freedom,* edited by Shobna Nijhawan, 269–271. Delhi: Permanent Black, 2010.

Faruqi, Shamsur Rahman. "The Power Politics of Culture: Akbar Ilahabadi and the Changing Order of Things." *Fourteenth Zakir Husain Memorial Lecture.* Delhi: Zakir Husain College, 2002.

Fernandes, Naresh. "Remembering Anthony Gonsalves." *India Seminar* 543, 2004. www.india-seminar.com/2004/543/543%20naresh%20fernandes.htm. Accessed February 26, 2014.

——. *Taj Mahal Fox Trot: The Story of Bombay's Jazz Age.* New Delhi: Roli Books, 2011.

Ferrari, Fabrizio. "Old Rituals for New Threats: The Post-Smallpox Career of Sitala, the Cold Mother of Bengal." In *Ritual Matters: Dynamic Dimensions in Practice*, edited by Christiane Brosius and Ute Hüsken, 144–171. New York: Routledge, 2010.

Freed, Stanley A., and Ruth S. Freed. *Hindu Festivals in a North Indian Village*. New York: American Museum of Natural History, 1998.

Frykenberg, Robert Eric. *Christianity in India: From Beginnings to the Present*. New York: Oxford University Press, 2008.

——. *Christians, Cultural Interactions, and India's Religious Traditions*. New York: Routledge, 2002.

Gandhi, Mohandas K. *The Collected Works of Mahatma Gandhi*. 80 vols. Delhi: Publications Division, Ministry of Information and Broadcasting, Government of India, 1958–80.

——. *Harijan*, November 24, 1933.

——. *Hind Swaraj and Other Writings*, edited by Anthony Parel. Centenary Edition. Cambridge: Cambridge University Press, 2009.

Ganti, Tejaswini. *Bollywood: A Guidebook to Popular Indian Cinema*. New York: Routledge, 2004.

——. *Producing Bollywood: Inside the Contemporary Hindi Film Industry*. Durham, NC: Duke University Press, 2012.

Ghose, Sankar. *Mahatma Gandhi*. Bombay: Allied Publishers, 1991.

Ghosh, Bishnupriya. *Global Icons: Apertures to the Popular*. Durham, NC: Duke University Press, 2011.

Gokulsing, K. Moti, and Wimal Dissanayake. *Indian Popular Cinema: A Narrative of Cultural Change*. Stoke on Trent, UK: Trentham Books, 1998.

Gopalan, Lalitha. "Bombay Noir." In *A Companion to Film Noir*, edited by Andrew Spicer and Helen Hanson, 496–511. West Sussex: Blackwell Press, 2013.

——. *Cinema of Interruptions: Action Genres in Contemporary Indian Cinema*. London: British Film Institute, 2002.

Gorer, Geoffrey. "The British National Character in the Twentieth Century." *Annals of the American Academy of Political and Social Sciences* 370 (1967): 74–81.

Guha, Ramachandra. *India After Gandhi: The History of the World's Largest Democracy*. New York: Harper Perennial, 2008.

Habermas, Jürgen. *The Structural Transformation of the Public Sphere*. Cambridge: Polity Press, 1989.

Haham, Connie. *Enchantment of the Mind: Manmohan Desai's Films*. New Delhi: Roli Books, 2006.

Hall, Donald E., ed. *Muscular Christianity: Embodying the Victorian Age*. Cambridge: Cambridge University Press, 1994.

Harman, William. "How the Fearsome Fish-Eyed Queen Mīṇāṭci Became a Perfectly Ordinary Goddess." In *Goddesses Who Rule*, edited by Elisabeth Benard and Beverly Moon, 33–50. New York: Oxford University Press, 2000.

Hawley, John S. "Prologue: The Goddess in India." In *Devī: Goddesses of India*, edited by John S. Hawley and Donna M. Wulff, 1–28. Berkeley: University of California Press, 1996.

Hitchens, Christopher. *The Missionary Position: Mother Teresa in Theory and Practice*. London: Verso, 1995.

Humes, Cynthia Ann. "Vindhyavāsinī: Local Goddess yet Great Goddess." In *Devī: Goddesses of India*, edited by John Stratton Hawley and Donna Marie Wulff, 49–76. Berkeley: University of California Press, 1996.

Husain, Intizar. *A Chronicle of the Peacocks: Stories of Partition, Exile and Lost Memories*. Translated by Alok Bhalla and Vishwamiter Adil. New Delhi: Oxford University Press, 2002.

Husain, Iqbal. "Akbar Allahabadi and National Politics." *Social Scientist* 16, no. 5 (1988): 29–45.

Hutcheon, Linda. *Irony's Edge: The Theory and Politics of Irony*. London: Routledge, 1994.

Jaikumar, Priya. *Cinema at the End of Empire: A Politics of Transition in Britain and India*. Durham, NC: Duke University Press, 2006.

Jain, Pankaj. "From *Padosi* to *My Name Is Khan*: The Portrayal of Hindu-Muslim Relations in South Asian Films." *Visual Anthropology* 24 (2011): 345–363.

Jay-Z. *Decoded*. New York: Spiegel and Grau, 2010.

Joshi, Priya, and Rajinder Dudrah, eds. *Special Issue: The 1970s and Its Legacies in India's Cinemas. South Asian Popular Culture* 10, no. 1 (2012).

Kakar, Sudhir. *Intimate Relations: Exploring Indian Sexuality*. Chicago: University of Chicago Press, 1990.

———. *Shamans, Mystics, and Doctors: A Psychological Inquiry into India and Its Healing Traditions*. Chicago: University of Chicago Press, 1982.

Kavoori, Anandam P., and Aswin Punathambekar, eds. *Global Bollywood*. New York: New York University Press, 2008.

Kazmi, Fareeduddin. "How Angry Is the Angry Young Man? 'Rebellion' in Conventional Hindi Films." In *The Secret Politics of Our Desires: Innocence, Culpability, and Indian Popular Cinema*, edited by Ashis Nandy, 134–156. Delhi: Zed Books, 1998.

———(as Kazmi, Fareed). "Muslim Socials and the Female Protagonist: Seeing a Dominant Discourse at Work." In *Forging Identities: Gender, Communities, and the State in India*, edited by Zoya Hasan, 226–243. Delhi: Kali for Women, 1994.

Keating, H. R. F. *Filmi, Filmi, Inspector Ghote*. Garden City, NY: Doubleday, 1977.

Kesavan, Mukul. "Urdu, Awadh, and the Tawaif: The Islamicate Roots of Hindi Cinema." In *Forging Identities: Gender, Communities, and the State in India*, edited by Zoya Hasan, 244–257. Delhi: Kali for Women, 1994.

Kimmich, Matt. *Offspring Fictions: Salman Rushdie's Family Novels*. Amsterdam: Rodopi, 2008.

Kinsley, David. *Hindu Goddesses: Visions of the Divine Feminine in the Hindu Religious Tradition*. Berkeley: University of California Press, 1987.

———. "Kālī: Blood and Death Out of Place." In *Devī: Goddesses of India*, edited by John S. Hawley and Donna M. Wulff, 77–86. Berkeley: University of California Press, 1996.

Klieman, Arthur S. "Indira's India: Democracy and Crisis Government." *Political Science Quarterly* 96, no. 2 (1981): 241–259.

Kohli, Atul. "Politics of Economic Growth in India, 1980–2005: Part I: The 1980s." *Economic and Political Weekly*. April 1, 2006: 1251–1259.

Kristeva, Julia. "Stabat Mater." In *The Kristeva Reader*, edited by Toril Moi, 160–186. New York: Columbia University Press, 1986.

Kumar, Sanjeev. "Constructing the Nation's Enemy: Hindutva, Popular Culture and the Muslim 'Other' in Bollywood Cinema." *Third World Quarterly* 34 (2013): 458–469.

Ladd, Tony, and James A. Mathisen. *Muscular Christianity: Evangelical Protestants and the Development of American Sports*. Grand Rapids, MI: Baker Books, 1999.

Lal, Vinay. *Deewar*. New Delhi: HarperCollins, 2011.

Larkin, Philip. *High Windows*. New York: Farrar, Straus and Giroux, 1974.

Lilla, Mark. *The Stillborn God*. New York: Vintage Press, 2008.

Luhrmann, Tanya. *The Good Parsi: The Postcolonial Anxieties of an Indian Colonial Elite*. Cambridge, MA: Harvard University Press, 1996.

Lutgendorf, Philip. "A 'Made to Satisfaction Goddess': *Jai Santoshi Maa* Revisited, Part Two." *Manushi* 131 (2002): 24–37.

——. "Amar Akbar Anthony." *Philip's Fil-ums: Notes on Indian Popular Cinema*. www.uiowa.edu/indiancinema/amar-akbar-anthony. Accessed April 8, 2015.

——. "Mard." *Philip's Fil-ums: Notes on Indian Popular Cinema*. www.uiowa.edu/indiancinema/mard. Accessed April 8, 2015.

——. "Ramayana Remix: Two Hindi Film-Songs as Epic Commentary." In *Ramayana in Focus: Visual and Performing Arts of Asia*, edited by Gauri Parimoo Krishnan, 144–154. Singapore: Asian Civilizations Museum, 2010.

——. "A Superhit Goddess: *Jai Santoshi Maa* and Caste Hierarchy in Indian Films, Part One." *Manushi* 131 (2002): 10–16.

Macaulay, Thomas Babington. "Minute by the Hon'ble T. B. Macaulay, Dated the 2nd February 1835." www.columbia.edu/itc/mealac/pritchett/00generallinks/macaulay/txt_minute_education_1835.html. Accessed May 9, 2015.

Mahabharata. Critically edited by V. S. Sukthankar et al. 19 vols. Poona: Bhandarkar Oriental Research Institute, 1927–1959.

Manto, Saadat Hasan. *Bitter Fruit: The Very Best of Saadat Hasan Manto*. Edited and translated by Khalid Hasan. New Delhi: Penguin Books, 2008.

Manusmriti. *Manu's Code of Law: A Critical Edition and Translation of the Mānava-Dharmaśāstra*. Edited by Patrick Olivelle. Oxford: Oxford University Press, 2005.

Marriott, McKim. "The Feast of Love." In *Krishna: Myths, Rites and Attitudes*, edited by Milton Singer, 200–212. Honolulu: East-West Center Press, 1966.

Mayo, Katherine. *Mother India*. New York: Harcourt, Brace, 1927.

Mazumdar, Ranjani. *Bombay Cinema: An Archive of the City*. Minneapolis: University of Minnesota Press, 2007.

——."From Subjectification to Schizophrenia: The 'Angry Man' and the 'Psychotic' Hero of Bombay Cinema." In *Making Meaning in Indian Cinema*, edited by Ravi Vasudevan, 238–264. New Delhi: Oxford University Press, 2000.

McCabe, Bob. *The Rough Guide to Comedy Movies*. London: Rough Guides, 2005.

McKean, Lise. "Bharat Mata and Her Militant Matriots." In *Devī: Goddesses of India*, edited by John S. Hawley and Donna M. Wulff, 250–280. Berkeley: University of California Press, 1996.

Mehta, Suketu. *Maximum City: Bombay Lost and Found*. New York: Vintage, 2005.

Menon, Ritu, and Kamla Bhasin. *Borders and Boundaries: Women in India's Partition*. New Brunswick, NJ: Rutgers University Press, 1998.

Menon, Usha, and Richard A. Shweder. "Power in Its Place: Is the Great Goddess of Hinduism a Feminist?" In *Is the Goddess a Feminist? The Politics of South Asian Goddesses*, edited by Alf Hiltebeitel and Kathleen M. Erndl, 151–165. Sheffield: Sheffield Academic Press, 2000.

Menzies, Robert. "Lucky You; Lucky Me: Revival Based on Women's Ritual Power in vrat kathas." In *Chakra: tidskrift för indiska religioner (tema: medicin och terapi)*, 58–69. Lund: Fööreningen Chakra, 2004.

Minchin, J. G. Cotton. *Our Public Schools: Their Influence on English History; Charter House, Eton, Harrow, Merchant Taylors', Rugby, St. Paul's Westminster, Winchester*. London: Swan Sonnenschein, 1901.

Mines, Diane P. *Fierce Gods: Inequality, Ritual, and the Politics of Dignity in a South Indian Village*. Bloomington: Indiana University Press, 2005.

Mishra, Vijay. *Bollywood Cinema: Temples of Desire*. New York: Routledge, 2001.

Mishra, Vijay, Peter Jeffrey, and Brian Shoesmith. "The Actor as Parallel Text in Bombay Cinema." *Quarterly Review of Film and Video* 11, no. 3 (1989): 49–67.

Moreno, Manuel. "God's Forceful Call: Possession as a Divine Strategy." In *Gods of Flesh, Gods of Stone: The Embodiment of the Divine in South Asia*, edited by Norman Cutler and Joanne Punzo Waghorne, in association with Vasudha Narayanan, 103–122. New York: Columbia University Press, 1996.

Mullane, Diane. "Trends in Consumer Packaging." White paper for Shikantini and Lacroix, November 2009. www.slideshare.net/Jeap18au55/packaging-trends-23163652. Accessed October 31, 2013.

Murray, Susan. "I Think We Need a New Name for It: The Meeting of Documentary and Reality TV." In *Reality TV: Remaking Television Culture*, edited by Susan Murray and Laurie Ouellette, 65–81. New York and London: New York University Press, 2008.

Nandy, Ashis. *The Intimate Enemy: Loss and Recovery of Self under Colonialism*. New Delhi: Oxford University Press, 1983.

———. "Introduction: Indian Popular Cinema as a Slum's Eye View of Politics." In *The Secret Politics of Our Desires: Innocence, Culpability, and Indian Popular Cinema*, edited by Ashis Nandy, 1–18. Delhi: Zed Books, 1998.

———. "Invitation to an Antique Death: The Journey of Pramathesh Barua as the Origin of the Terribly Effeminate, Maudlin, Self-Destructive Heroes of Indian Cinema." In *Pleasure and the Nation: The History, Politics, and Consumption of Public Culture in India*, edited by Rachel Dwyer and Christopher Pinney, 139–160. New Delhi: Oxford University Press, 2000.

———, ed. *The Secret Politics of Our Desires: Innocence, Culpability and Indian Popular Cinema*. Delhi: Zed Books, 1999.

Narayanan, Vasudha. "Diglossic Hinduism: Liberation and Lentils." *Journal of the American Academy of Religion* 68 (2000): 761–780.

Narula, Smita. "'We Have No Orders to Save You': State Participation and Complicity in Communal Violence in Gujarat." *Human Rights Watch* 14, no. 3 (April 30, 2002): 1–68.

Nayar, Kuldip. *Emergency Retold*. New Delhi: Konark Publishers, 2013.

Nizami. *The Story of Layla and Majnun*. Translated and edited by Rudolph Gelpke. New Lebanon, NY: Omega, 2011.

O'Flaherty, Wendy Doniger. *Asceticism and Eroticism in the Mythology of Śiva*. New York: Oxford University Press, 1973.

———. *Hindu Myths: A Sourcebook Translated from the Sanskrit*. London: Penguin Books, 1975.

———. *Tales of Sex and Violence: Folklore, Sacrifice, and Danger in the Jaiminīya Brāhmaṇa*. Chicago: University of Chicago Press, 1985.

Oldenburg, Veena Talwar, ed. *Shaam-e-Awadh: Writings on Lucknow*. Delhi: Penguin, 2007.

Olivelle, Patrick. *The Āśrama System: The History and Hermeneutics of a Religious Institution*. New York: Oxford University Press, 1993.

Padma, Sree. *Vicissitudes of the Goddess: Reconstructions of the Gramadevata in India's Religious Traditions*. New York: Oxford University Press, 2013.

Pain, Charles, with Eleanor Zelliott. "The God Dattatreya and the Datta Temples of Pune." In *The Experience of Hinduism: Essays on Religion in Maharashtra*, edited by Eleanor Zelliot and Maxine Berntsen, 95–108. Albany: State University of New York Press, 1988.

Pearson, Anne Mackenzie. *Because It Gives Me Peace of Mind: Ritual Fasts in the Religious Lives of Hindu Women*. Albany: State University of New York Press, 1996.

Pinckney, Warren R., Jr. "Jazz in India: Perspectives on Historical Development and Musical Acculturation." *Asian Music* 21, no. 1 (1989–1990): 35–77.

Pinto, Jerry. *Helen: The Life and Times of an H-Bomb*. London: Penguin Books, 2006.

Pocock, D. C. "The Evil Eye—Envy and Greed among the Patidar of Central Gujerat." In *The Evil Eye: A Casebook*, edited by Alan Dundes, 201–210. Madison: University of Wisconsin Press, 1992.

Pollock, Sheldon. "Rāmāyaṇa and Political Imagination in India." *Journal of Asian Studies* 52, no. 2 (1993): 261–297.

Prasad, M. Madhava. *Ideology of the Hindi Film: A Historical Reconstruction*. New Delhi: Oxford University Press, 1998.

———. "This Thing Called Bollywood." *Seminar* 525: 2003. www.india-seminar.com /2003/525/525%20madhava%20prasad.htm. Accessed January 21, 2014.

Putney, Clifford. *Muscular Christianity: Manhood and Sports in Protestant America, 1880–1920*. Cambridge: Harvard University Press, 2001.

Raghavendra, M. K. *50 Indian Film Classics*. Noida, India: HarperCollins, 2009.

Rai, Amit. *Untimely Bollywood: Globalization and India's New Media Assemblage*. Durham, NC: Duke University Press, 2009.

Raj, Selva, and Corinne Dempsey, eds. *Popular Christianity in India: Riting between the Lines*. Albany: State University of New York Press, 2002.

Rajadhyaksha, Ashish. "The 'Bollywoodization' of the Indian Cinema: Cultural Nationalism in a Global Arena." *Inter-Asia Cultural Studies* 4, no. 1 (2003): 25–39.

———. "The Epic Melodrama: Themes of Nationality in Indian Cinema." *Journal of Arts and Ideas* 25–26 (1993): 55–70.

———. *Indian Cinema in the Time of Celluloid: From Bollywood to the Emergency*. Bloomington: Indiana University Press, 2009.

Ram, Kalpana. "Bringing the Amman into Presence in Tamil Cinema: Cinema Spectatorship as Sensuous Appreciation." In *Tamil Cinema: The Cultural Politics of India's Other Film Industry*, edited by Selvaraj Velayutham, 44–58. London: Routledge, 2008.

Ramaswamy, Sumathi. *The Goddess and the Nation: Mapping Mother India*. Durham, NC: Duke University Press, 2010.

Ramayana. Critically edited by G. H. Bhatt et al. 7 vols. Baroda: Oriental Institute, University of Baroda, 1960–1975.

Robinson, Rowena. *Christians of India*. New Delhi: Sage Publications, 2003.

———. *Conversion, Continuity, and Change*. New Delhi: Sage Publications, 1998.

Robinson, Rowena, and Sathianathan Clarke, eds. *Religious Conversion in India: Modes, Motivations, and Meanings*. New Delhi: Oxford University Press, 2003.

Rosen, David. "The Volcano and the Cathedral: Muscular Christianity and the Origins of Primal Manliness." In *Muscular Christianity: Embodying the Victorian Age*, edited by Donald E. Hall, 17–44. Cambridge: Cambridge University Press, 1994.

Rushdie, Salman. *Midnight's Children*. New York: Knopf, 1981.

Russell, Ralph. *Hidden in the Lute: An Anthology of Urdu Literature*. Manchester: Carcanet, 1999.

Russell, Ralph, and Khurshidul Islam. "The Satirical Verse of Akbar Ilahabadi." In *The Pursuit of Urdu Literature: A Select History*, edited by Ralph Russell, 129–175. London: Zed Books, 1992.

Said, Edward. *Orientalism*. New York: Pantheon Books, 1978.

Sangari, Kumkum. "Mirabai and the Spiritual Economy of *Bhakti*." Part 1 of 2. *Economic and Political Weekly*, July 7, 1990: 1464–1475.

Sanneh, Lamin. *Translating the Message: The Missionary Impact on Culture*. Maryknoll, NY: Orbis Books, 2008.

Sardar, Ziauddin. "Dilip Kumar Made Me Do It." In *The Secret Politics of Our Desires: Innocence, Culpability, and Indian Popular Cinema*, edited by Ashis Nandy, 19–98. Delhi: Zed Books, 1998.

Sarkar, Bhaskar. *Mourning the Nation: Indian Cinema in the Wake of Partition*. Durham, NC: Duke University Press, 2009.

Sarkar, Sarasi Lal. "A Study of the Psychology of Sexual Abstinence from the Dreams of an Ascetic." *International Journal of Psychoanalysis* 24 (1943): 170–175.

Savarkar, V. D. *Hindutva: Who Is a Hindu?* Bombay: Veer Savarkar Prakashan, 1969 [1923].

Scott, Paul. *Raj Quartet* (4 volumes: *The Jewel in the Crown, The Day of the Scorpion, The Towers of Silence, A Division of the Spoils*). London: Heinemann, 1966–1975.

Sedgwick, Eve. *Between Men: English Literature and Male Homosocial Desire*. New York: Columbia University Press, 1985.

Sen, Colleen Taylor. *Curry: A Global History*. London: Reaktion Books, 2009.

Sen, Sharmila. "Looking for Doubles in the Caribbean." *Massachusetts Review* 45, no. 3 (2004): 241–257.

Shah Commission of Inquiry. *Interim Report II*. New Delhi: Government of India Press, April 26, 1978.

Shulman, David. "Terror of Symbols and Symbols of Terror: Notes on the Myth of Śiva as Sthāṇu." *History of Religions* 26, no. 2 (1986): 101–124.

Sienkiewicz, Henryk. *The Knights of the Cross*. Trans. Jeremiah Curtin. Boston: Little, Brown, 1900.

Simons, Ronald C., Frank R. Ervin, and Raymond H. Prince. "The Psychobiology of Trance I: Training for Thaipusam." *Transcultural Psychiatric Research Review* 25, no. 4 (1988): 239–266.

Siṅgha, Kirapāla. *The Partition of the Punjab*. Patiala: Punjabi University, 1972.

Smith, Brian K. *Reflections on Resemblance, Ritual, and Religion*. Delhi: Motilal Banarasidass, 1998.

Smith, Frederick M. *The Self Possessed: Deity and Spirit Possession in South Asian Literature and Civilization*. New York: Columbia University Press, 2006.

Srinivas, Lakshmi. "The Active Audience: Spectatorship, Social Relations and the Experience of Cinema in India." *Media, Culture and Society* 24 (2002): 155–173.

Srinivasan, Perundevi. "The Creative Modern and the Myths of the Goddess Mariyamman." In *Religion in Literature and Film in South Asia*, edited by Diana Dimitrova, 83–91. New York: Palgrave Macmillan, 2010.

Sumathipala, A., et al. "Culture-Bound Syndromes: The Story of *dhat* Syndrome." *British Journal of Psychiatry* 184 (2004): 200–209.

Tarlo, Emma. *Unsettling Memories: Narratives of the Emergency in Delhi*. Berkeley: University of California Press, 2003.

Taylor, Charles. *A Secular Age*. Cambridge, MA: Harvard University Press, 2007.

Tejpal, Tarun J. *The Story of My Assassins*. New Delhi: HarperCollins, 2010.

Thomas, Rosie. "Indian Cinema: Pleasures and Popularity." *Screen* 26, no. 3–4 (1985): 116–131.

———. "Melodrama and the Negotiation of Morality in Mainstream Hindi Film." In *Consuming Modernity: Public Culture in a South Asian World*, edited by Carol A. Breckenridge, 157–182. Minneapolis: University of Minnesota Press, 1995.

Tiwari, Bulbul. "Teyyam, Bhuta Kola, and Mudiyettu," *Maha Multipedia*. www.maha multipedia.com/forms/6. Accessed April 13, 2015.

Trivedi, Harish. "All Kinds of Hindi: The Evolving Language of Hindi Cinema." In *Fingerprinting Popular Culture: The Mythic and the Iconic in Indian Cinema*, edited by Vinay Lal and Ashis Nandy, 51–86. New Delhi: Oxford University Press, 2006.

Vasudevan, Ravi, ed. *Making Meaning in Indian Cinema*. New Delhi: Oxford University Press, 2000.

———. "The Meanings of 'Bollywood.'" In *Beyond the Boundaries of Bollywood: The Many Forms of Hindi Cinema*, edited by Rachel Dwyer and Jerry Pinto, 3–29. New Delhi: Oxford University Press, 2011.

———. "The Melodramatic Mode and the Commercial Hindi Cinema: Notes on Film History, Narrative and Performance in the 1950s." *Screen* 30, no. 3 (1989): 29–50.

———. *The Melodramatic Public: Film Form and Spectatorship in Indian Cinema*. New York: Palgrave Macmillan, 2011.

Virdi, Jyotika. *The Cinematic ImagiNation: Indian Popular Films as Social History*. New Brunswick, NJ: Rutgers University Press, 2003.

Viswanath, Rupa. *The Pariah Problem: Caste, Religion, and the Social in Modern India*. New York: Columbia University Press, 2014.

Viswanathan, Gauri. *Outside the Fold: Conversion, Modernity, and Belief*. Princeton, NJ: Princeton University Press, 1998.

Weber, Max. *Weber: Political Writings.* Edited by Peter Lassman and Ronald Speirs. Cambridge: Cambridge University Press, 1994.

White, Hayden. *Tropics of Discourse: Essays in Cultural Criticism.* Baltimore: Johns Hopkins University Press, 1986.

Whitehead, Henry. *The Village Gods of South India.* New York: Oxford University Press, 1921.

Wolfe, Thomas. *You Can't Go Home Again.* New York: Harper and Row, 1940.

Woods, Julian F. *Destiny and Human Initiative in the Mahabharata.* Albany: State University of New York Press, 2001.

Yocum, Glenn E. "Comments: The Divine Consort in South India." In *The Divine Consort: Rādhā and the Goddesses of India*, edited by John S. Hawley and Donna M. Wulff, 278–281. Berkeley, CA: Graduate Theological Union, 1985.

Zūlfaqār, G̱hulām Ḥusain, and Akbar Allāhābādī. *Mohandās Karamcand Gāndhī: Lisānul'aṣar kī naẓar meṉ.* Lahore: Sang-i Mīl Pablīkeshanz, 1994.

Filmography

Akbar Amar Anthony. 1978. Dir. Haider Chaudhary.

Albert Pinto Ko Gussa Kyoon Aata Hai. 1980. Dir. Saeed Mirza.

Amar Akbar & Tony. 2015. Dir. Atul Malhotra.

Ankur. 1974. Dir. Shyam Benegal.

Anthony Kaun Hai? 2006. Dir. Raj Kaushal.

Bawarchi. 1972. Dir. Hrishikesh Mukherji.

Bluff Master. 1963. Dir. Manmohan Desai.

Bobby. 1973. Dir. Raj Kapoor.

Chacha Bhatija. 1977. Dir. Manmohan Desai.

Chaudhvin Ka Chand. 1960. Dir. Mohammed Sadiq.

Chhalia. 1960. Dir. Manmohan Desai.

C.I.D. 1956. Dir. Raj Kosla.

Coolie. 1983. Dir. Manmohan Desai.

Dedh Ishqiya. 2014. Dir. Abhishek Chaubey.

Deewaar. 1975. Dir. Yash Chopra.

Desh Premee. 1982. Dir. Manmohan Desai.

Destination: Bombay. 1976. Films Division.

Devdas. 1935. Dir. P. C. Barua. (Filmed in two versions: Bengali and Hindi.)

Devdas. 1955. Dir. Bimal Roy.

Devdas. 2002. Dir. Sanjay Leela Bhansali.

Dharam Veer. 1977. Dir. Manmohan Desai.

Dhola Maru. 1956. Dir. N. R. Acharya.

Dholak. 1951. Dir. Roop K. Shorey.

Dil Se. 1998. Dir. Mani Ratnam.

Fire in Babylon. 2010. Dir. Stevan Riley.

Ganga Jamuna Saraswati. 2012. Dir. Harry Fernandes.

Gangaa Jamunaa Saraswathi. 1988. Dir. Manmohan Desai.

Garam Hawa. 1974. Dir. M. S. Sathyu.

Geraftaar. 1985. Dir. Prayag Raj.

Guide. 1965. Dir. Vijay Anand.

Helen, Queen of the Nautch Girls. 1973. Dir. Anthony Korner.

Hum Kisise Kum Naheen. 1977. Dir. Nasir Husain.

It's a Wonderful Life. 1946. Dir. Frank Capra.

Jai Santoshi Maa. 1975. Dir. Vijay Sharma.

Jallian Wala Bagh. 1977. Dir. Balraj Tah.

John Jaffer Janardhanan. 1982. Dir. I. V. Sasi.

Johnny Gaddaar. 2007. Dir. Sriram Raghavan.

Johny Mera Naam. 1970. Dir. Vijay Anand.

Julie. 1975. Dir. K. S. Sethumadhavan.

Kaagaz Ke Phool. 1959. Dir. Guru Dutt.

Khoon Pasina. 1977. Dir. Rakesh Kumar.

Kismet. 1943. Dir. Gyan Mukherjee.

Kissa Kursi Ka. 1978. Dir. Amrit Nahata.

Kumar Talkies. 2000. Dir. Pankaj Rishi Kumar.

Laila Majnu. 1976. Dir. Harnam Singh Rawail.

Lal Baadshah. 1999. Dir. K. C. Bokadia.

The Lord of the Rings. 2001. Dir. Peter Jackson.

Mahal. 1949. Dir. Kamal Amrohi.

Mard. 1985. Dir. Manmohan Desai.

A Matter of Life and Death. 1946. Dirs. Michael Powell and Emeric Pressburger.

Mera Naam Joker. 1971. Dir. Raj Kapoor.

Mere Mehboob. 1963. Dir. Harnam Singh Rawail.

Mother India. 1957. Dir. Mehboob Khan.

Mughal-e-Azam. 1960. Dir. K. Asif.

Munimji. 1955. Dir. Subodh Mukherji.

Muqaddar Ka Sikandar. 1978. Dir. Prakash Mehra.

My Name Is Anthony Gonsalves. 2008. Dir. Eeshwar Nivas.

Naseeb. 1981. Dir. Manmohan Desai.

Navrang. 1959. Dir. V. Shantaram.

Pakeezah. 1972. Dir. Kamal Amrohi.

Palki. 1967. Dirs. Mahesh Kaul and S. U. Sunny.

Parinda. 1989. Dir. Vidhu Vinod Chopra.

Paris Is Burning. 1991. Dir. Jennie Livingstone.

Parvarish. 1977. Dir. Manmohan Desai.

The Poseidon Adventure. 1972. Dir. Ronald Neame.

The Princess Bride. 1987. Dir. Rob Reiner.

Ram Robert Rahim. 1980. Dir. Vijaya Nirmala.

Rang De Basanti. 2006. Dir. Rakeysh Omprakash Mehra.

Rashomon. 1950. Dir. Akira Kurosawa.

Sadgati. 1981. Dir. Satyajit Ray.

Sahib Bibi Aur Ghulam. 1962. Dir. Guru Dutt.

Salim Langde Pe Mat Ro. 1989. Dir. Saeed Mirza.

Sant Tukaram. 1938. Dirs. V. G. Damle and Sheikh Fattelal.

Sargam. 1979. K. Vishwanath.

Satya. 1998. Dir. Ram Gopal Varma.

Shatranj Ke Khilari. 1977. Dir. Satyajit Ray.

Shiv Shakti. 1952. Dir. Jayant Desai.

Sholay. 1975. Dir. Ramesh Sippy.

Shree 420. 1955. Dir. Raj Kapoor.

Silsila. 1981. Dir. Yash Chopra.

Star Wars. 1977. Dir. George Lucas.

Suhaag. 1979. Dir. Manmohan Desai.

Sujata. 1960. Dir. Bimal Roy.

Toofan. 1989. Dir. Ketan Desai.

Waqt. 1965. Dir. Yash Chopra.

The Wizard of Oz. 1939. Dir. Victor Fleming.

Yaadon Ki Baaraat. 1973. Dir. Nasir Hussain.

Zanjeer. 1973. Dir. Prakash Mehra.

Acknowledgments

In 2006 we three presented a panel on *Amar Akbar Anthony* at the Annual Conference on South Asia in Madison, Wisconsin. Our arguments were met with generosity and enthusiasm, as was the sibling-rivalry format we devised for delivering them. We came away convinced of the film's enduring popularity and power, and encouraged that a sustained inquiry into the meanings of this extraordinary movie would yield a full book. And so our first "vote of thanks" goes to the conference organizers at the University of Wisconsin and to the many colleagues who squeezed into a Madison conference room and shared with us their insights, laughter, and goodwill. We are especially grateful to Philip Lutgendorf, who graciously joined us as the panel discussant, and whose work on Indian cinema, culture, and religion continues to guide us; to our chair, Christopher Pinney, whose aura of brilliance illuminated the proceedings; and to Priya Joshi, who was the first person to urge us to turn our ideas into a book.

Since then, we have been fortunate to receive generous support for pursuing this project. Our thanks to the American Council of Learned Societies, the American Institute of Indian Studies, the Fulbright-Nehru program, and the National Endowment for the Humanities, as well as Smith College and Dartmouth College. Resat Kasaba and the University of Washington's Jackson School of International Studies provided a generous subvention fund for this book's completion.

And we have been more than fortunate in having found such a sage editor in Sharmila Sen. From its inception, she has championed this project with both total seriousness and constant humor. We also want to thank the editorial team at Harvard University Press, especially Heather Hughes. We also benefitted from the editorial help of Edward Wade, Kathryn Moyer, and Jamie Thaman, as well as from the two anonymous readers of our manuscript, whose careful reports helped us bring the book to its final form. We are likewise grateful to the National Film Archive of India (NFAI) and its staff, who have been extraordinarily helpful.

Along the way, we have presented our work at various institutions and received valuable feedback and support from many colleagues. We would like to thank Brandeis University, Carleton College, Duke University, Middlebury College, Smith College, Stanford University, the University of Chicago, the University of Pennsylvania, the University of Vermont, and the University of Washington. Portions of this book were presented at the "Social Work of Bollywood" symposium, organized by Jennifer Dubrow and supported by Kathy Woodward and the Simpson Center for the Humanities at the University of Washington. Our thanks go to Abhishek Agrawal, Jameel Ahmed, Sareeta Amrute, Deepa Banerjee, Shahzad Bashir, Chad Bauman, Shrikant Botre, Arin Brenner, Allison Busch, Bijoyini Chatterjee, Quinn Clark, Lawrence Cohen, Melanie Dean, Wendy Doniger, Anne Feldhaus, Tejaswini Ganti, Thomas Blom Hansen, Katy Hardy, Jack Hawley, Doug Haynes, Arun Himatsingka, Rubaiyat Hossain, Roger Jackson, Sanjay Joshi, Suvir Kaul, Meera Kosambi, Hariharan Krishnan, Srinivas Krishnan, Wendy Lochner, Ania Loomba, Sudhir Mahadevan, Rebecca Manring, William Mazzarella, Sara McClintock, Rachel McDermott, Abigail McGowan, Karline McLain, Sangeeta Mediratta, Lisa Mitchell, C. M. Naim, Sarah J. Neilson, Ignotus X. Niemendal, Northampton Coffee, Laurie Patton, Heidi Pauwels, Andrea Pinkney, Chakravarthi Ram Prasad, Sophia Preza, A. Sean Pue, Priti Ramamurthy, Sumathi Ramaswamy, Rakesh Ranjan, Ram Rawat, Rachel Reuben, Cabeiri Robinson, Bhaskar Sarkar, Adheesh Sathaye, Ira Schepetin, Parna Sengupta, Svati Shah, Gowri Shankar, Imam-bi Sheikh, Danny Silverman, Dhrub Kumar Singh, Harleen Singh, Rakesh Singh, Ajay Sinha, Shana Sippy, Keith Snodgrass, Lakshmi Srinivas, April Strickland, Bulbul Tiwari, Rupa Viswanath, Anand Yang, and Karin Zitzewitz. Any and all errors that remain are of course our own, except for the early scene where Akbar addresses Salma as "Neetu," which is clearly Rishi Kapoor's fault.

A big shout-out to Sidharth Bhatia, author of *Amar Akbar Anthony: Masala, Madness and Manmohan Desai*, who has been unstintingly generous with his knowledge and encouragement, and to Connie Haham, author of the excellent *Enchantment of the Mind: Manmohan Desai's Films*. Francesca Chubb-Confer has also been an expert resource, especially with passages in literary Urdu. Her ideas were crucial in helping us work out the book's conclusion. And this book would simply not have been possible without Laura Desmond. She has been a great friend and conversation partner, offering vital advice and interpretations since the days of the original conference panel. She also made sure our costumes were perfect.

A special word here for our students at our respective institutions. We have each taught the film many times to many students, and their responses and enthusiasm have been invaluable. Thanks also to Hinesh Jethwani and the talented team of artists at Indian Hippy, who gave us a way to visualize our writerly partnership, and to the Smith College Imaging Center for their excellent reproductions.

We thank our families and friends who have supported us along the way: Jurgis Elisonas and Toshiko, Tony, and Yasuko Elison, and Ivonne Pérez; William and Mary Novetzke, Shobha and Sharad Kale, Vidula Kale and Michael Coggins, Minal Kale and Stephan Pierson, and Danielle and Dan Greene; Arline, Barry, Alan, David, and Ida Rotman, and David White and Sally Knight; and Rabindra Goswami, Ramu Pandit, and Hari Paudyal.

We owe special thanks to Gayatri Chatterjee, who played a catalyzing role in our development not only as scholars of Indian cinema but also as friends. It was in Pune in 1998 that we three got to know one another, watching films, exploring the city, and wandering in and out of the continuous *adda* that Gayatri hosted in her apartment. Gayatri's brilliant work on cinema remains a key inspiration to us.

Finally, to our partners—of intellect, life, and love—Lisa Pérez, Sunila S. Kale, and Janna White: Thank you for climbing into the jalopy with us.

Index

Absurdity, 7–8, 83–84, 255n26; film logic and, 9–10

Adoptive fathers, 39–40, 42, 44–47, 50, 67, 147, 261n1, 263n18

Akbar, 21, 28–30, 33–34, 36, 43–45, 62, 65–66, 68, 74–114, 118–119, 132, 136, 140, 154–155, 161–174, 177, 182, 184–186, 188, 203–204, 217, 234–239, 243–245, 251, 260n105, 263n16, 263n19, 264n20, 270n74, 272n10, 273n12, 275n29, 276n39, 279n5, 286n11, 288n25, 295n4, 296n4, 296n6, 298–299n35; Anthony invited to concert of, 215–216; Anthony linking together Amar and, 120; Anthony's marriage advice for, 233; Bharati receiving *sindoor* from, 242; Bharati's blessing of, 216; Bharati's case pled by, 172; Bharati's eyesight restored by, 240–241; Bharati's veil stripped by, 106; Bharati uniting with, 172–173; charisma of, 94; corruption resisted by, 292n53; disguise discarded by, 202, 249–250; disguise of, 82, 246, 248, 273–274n18; double identity of, 83; in finale, 200; as Gandhi's heir, 103; as heart of film, 81; as hero, 9, 33, 74–77, 81, 106–107; *hijras* assisting, 101, 232–233; insightfulness of, 161; *kama* pursued by, 46–47, 49; Mother India view of, 183; multidimensionality of, 75; mystical tropes in musical numbers of, 80–81, 108, 168; name origins of, 78; name proclaimed by, 214, 279n5; neighborhood toughs beating up, 233; nonviolence and, 38, 102–103; poetry and, 80–81, 84–85, 103, 168; Robert knocked out by, 107, 251; Sai Baba praised by, 105, 114, 240; Salma courted by, 48, 92–95, 214, 230–233; Salma rescued by, 106–107, 241–242; stage persona of, 93–94; Sufism and, 108, 214; Tayyab Ali's hypocrisy and, 112–113; Urdu note used by, 78, 247; Urdu spoken by, 78–79; Zabisko tricked by, 246–247

Akbar, Jalaluddin (Mughal emperor), 78, 273n13

Akbar Amar Anthony (1978), 253n2

Akbar Ilahabadi (Syed Akbar Husain), 74, 89, 105, 273n15; double identity of, 83; Gandhi and, 85; history of, 82–83; satire of, 83–84, 111; self-mockery of, 84

Albert, 261n109, 263n15, 284n70; appearance of, 237–238; Robert's antagonistic relationship with, 136–137, 238; Zabisko's plan for Robert and, 238

Albert Pinto Ko Gussa Kyoon Aata Hai (1980), 276n44

Ali, Naushad, 130

Alter, Joseph, 61, 266nn46–48, 267n58

Amar, 9, 21, 29–30, 33–34, 36–73, 74, 76, 102–103, 111–112, 118–120, 136, 147, 154, 174–190, 192, 195, 200, 203, 215, 223, 230, 231, 238, 247–248, 254n5, 260nn103–104, 261n1, 261n106, 263n19, 267n51, 269n72, 270n74, 272n10, 273n18, 276n43, 278n53, 279n5, 280n20, 284–285n70, 286–287n12, 286n11, 287n18, 288n25, 290n42, 296n4, 297n13, 297n18, 297nn15–16, 298–299n35, 298n24, 299n41; Anthony as fictive and real brother of, 222, 224; Anthony disrespected by, 55; Anthony fighting, 221–222; Anthony linking together Akbar and, 120; as all religions in one, 65–66; backstory of, 37; Bharati's goddess possession recognized by, 177–178; biological father disobeyed by, 66–67; body politic and, 56–57; *brahmacarya* code and, 61–62, 69, 267n52; corruption resisted by, 292n53; *dharma* pursued by, 36, 47–50, 56; disguise discarded by, 202, 249–250; divinity protecting, 261n2; fatherhood and, 69–70; in finale, 200; gun burial and sexuality of, 60; gun buried by, 40–41, 60–62, 208; gun unearthing and, 68–71, 112, 243; as hero, 33, 50, 66; Hindi spoken by, 78, 271n4; Hinduism's diverging tendencies in Bharati and, 189–191; Inspector Khanna finding and raising, 38–39, 181–182, 212; Inspector Khanna visited in hospital by, 220; Kishanlal abandoning, 39, 67, 212; Kishanlal imprisoned by, 70; Kishanlal reunited with, 68–71, 243–244; Kishanlal's gun gift to, 41, 208, 262n5, 270n76; Koliwada neighborhood as veil of illusion for, 112; Koliwada neighborhood nostalgia of, 71, 243, 270n80; Lakshmi entrapping, 47–48, 56, 217–218; Lakshmi offered home instead of jail by, 57, 218; morality of, 39, 54, 81; Mother India view of, 183–184; name proclaimed by, 214, 279n5; Rama compared to, 65–67; religion and, 39–40; Robert sought by, 55, 221; secularism and, 39–40, 55; Shiva's self-castration and gun burial of, 62, 64–65; state as religion and, 191;

266n37; state rule and, 54–55; state service and sexuality of, 58–60, 64–65; violence and, 40; wayward woman rehabilitated by, 49, 58–59

Amar Akbar & Tony (2015), 253n2

Amnesia, 71, 91, 177, 289n37, 294n68

Anglo-Indians, 131, 134–138, 140, 282nn41–42, 283n49

"Anhoni Ko Honi Kar De," 81, 107, 110, 119, 199–204, 249, 273–274n18

Ankur (1974), 58

Anthony, 21, 26, 28–29, 33–34, 36, 39–41, 43–44, 56, 60, 62, 65–66, 74, 81, 115–149, 151–161, 177, 182, 184, 203, 217, 231, 234–235, 244, 253n2, 261n106, 263n19, 264n20, 272n10, 273–274n18, 275n28, 278–279n4, 280n21, 284–285n70, 285n3, 295n2, 297nn15–16, 299n41; Akbar and marriage advice of, 233; Akbar's concert invitation to, 215–216; Amar and Akbar linked together by, 120; Amar as fictive and real brother of, 222, 224; Amar disrespecting, 55; Amar fighting, 221–222; as Anthonyville leader, 55, 126, 148, 215; Bachchan's persona mixed with, 122–123; berating himself for drinking, 144–145, 228–229; Bharati abandoning, 161; Bharati blessing, 222; Bharati offered ticket from, 216; Bharati rejected by, 156–157; Bharati reunited with, 286n11; Bharati taken to hospital by, 213–214; breaking fourth wall, 203, 204, 249; Catholic Church as foster mother to, 286n7; character inspiration and background for, 129–130; charity of, 128; childhood abandonment of, 118; Christianity and, 115–116, 143–144; Christianity and naming of, 118–119; conversions of, 149; corruption resisted by, 292n53; disguise discarded by, 202, 249–250; Disraeli impersonation of, 144–146, 148; Easter "rebirth" of, 119, 144, 146, 227–228; English spoken by, 280n28; as Father Anthony, 35, 148, 200, 202, 249; in finale, 200; as hero, 33, 116–117, 119–120, 139, 143–144, 149; Hindi style spoken by, 78–79; Hinduism as true nature of, 126; Hinduism rejected

by, 157; irony and, 115–116, 118, 121,
145–146; Jenny as veil of illusion for,
112, 228; Jenny courted by, 47–48,
226–227, 229; Jenny saved by, 147,
236–237; Jenny's karmic connection
to, 116–118; Jesus and devotion of, 123,
125–126, 128–129; Jesus and donations
of, 124–125; Jesus badge worn by,
298n23; Jesus talked to by, 147; *kama*
pursued by, 46–47, 49; Kishanlal
capturing, 223; Kishanlal reuniting
with, 246; lucky liquor license of,
280n20; as main attraction, 119–120;
middle brothers and, 120; morality of,
125; Mother India view of, 157–159, 166;
as motherless, 154–155; name proclaimed
by, 213; national integration's failure
and, 116; Padre criticizing, 128, 213;
Padre raising, 137, 212; Padre's death
and, 147, 245–246; priest disguise of,
147–148, 248–249; religious outlook
of, 38, 149; Robert pitted against, 140,
224; Robert protected by, 220; Santoshi
Maa as mother to, 154; Santoshi Maa
pendant of Bharati discovered by, 246;
scarecrow disguise of, 146–147, 236;
screen time of, 119; selfhood found by,
148–149; self-invention and, 117, 159;
state rejected by, 125, 158–159, 191;
Tayyab Ali berated by, 233; violence
and, 102–103; Zabisko fighting, 135,
228
Anthony's Country Bar, 28, 215, 221, 231
Anthonyville, 28–29, 38, 128, 147, 159, 220,
221, 261n106, 280n20; Anthony as leader
of, 55, 126, 148, 215; Christianity in,
261n106
Artha (profit), 46, 63, 72
Audiences, 13–14, 20, 22–25, 73, 80, 85,
88–89, 93, 101, 113, 116, 121, 146, 160,
163, 174, 203, 242, 249, 259n79, 259n84,
280n28, 295n5; *Amar Akbar Anthony*'s
mass appeal for, 8–9; Bollywood films'
appeal to, 17–18; as godlike, 203; of
"Parda Hai Parda," 94, 108. *See also*
Mass audiences
Awards, 2, 57–58; of *Amar Akbar Anthony*,
7–8

Azmi, Shabana, 20, 57–58, 217, 259–260n95,
274n20, 292n56

Babi, Parveen, 120, 225, 300n52
Babri Masjid–Ram Janmabhoomi
controversy, 133–134
Baby Sabina, 208
Bachchan, Amitabh, 7, 19, 21–24, 62, 66,
76, 117, 119, 155, 213, 258n75, 261n1,
274n20, 279n12, 284n66, 292n56,
294n67, 298n23, 299n44; Anthony
mixed with persona of, 122–123; critical
reception of, 120; "media assemblage"
and, 122; "My Name Is Anthony
Gonsalves" and notable performance of,
144; politics and, 281n36; privileged
background of, 121; Roy's many films
with, 151; stardom of, 115, 121–122,
278n2, 280n19; versatility of, 121
Bajrang Dal, 138
Bakshi, Anand, 85
Bandra neighborhood, 26, 28–30, 70, 101,
108, 129, 131, 167, 208, 210, 212–213, 215,
227, 232, 243, 260n102, 261n107,
261n109, 296n7, 298n27
Barthes, Roland, 18
Bawarchi (1972), 176
Behl, Aditya, 257n54
Benegal, Shyam, 18, 24, 58
Bhagavad Gita, 195
Bharati (Maa), 5, 27–30, 34, 44, 46, 67, 68,
70, 114, 118, 150–198, 209, 212, 215, 217,
223, 238, 243, 263n13, 270n79, 273n12,
275n28, 277n47, 291n48, 294n68, 296n5,
297n16, 297n22, 300n50; Akbar blessed
by, 216; Akbar pleading case of, 172;
Akbar restoring eyesight of, 240–241;
Akbar's *sindoor* gift for, 242; Akbar
strips veil from, 106; Akbar uniting with,
172–173; Anthony abandoned by, 161;
Anthony blessed by, 222; Anthony
offering ticket to, 216; Anthony rejecting,
156–157; Anthony reunited with, 286n11;
Anthony taking to hospital, 213–214; as
bad mother, 155–156; as beggar, 288n25;
blessings of, 104, 168–169, 176, 216, 222,
241, 288n25; blindness of, 150, 161, 165,

Bharati (Maa) *(continued)*
168–169 181, 195, 217; blood sacrifice
and, 173, 182–183, 194; bloodstain on
forehead of, 172–173, 187, 196–197, 210,
213, 240; City of Illusion and blindness
of, 168; *dharma* mistake of, 164–165;
disease and goddess worship of, 179–180;
divinity of, 176–177, 194–195; domestic
contentment of, 189; escapes from
Robert, 104, 185–186, 239; flower-selling
of, 168–169; goddess possession of,
177–178, 182–183, 187; Haider Ali
helping, 163–164, 211; Hinduism's
diverging tendencies in Amar and,
190–191; homelessness and, 162, 167,
178, 290n41; Kishanlal abandoned by,
181, 210; Kishanlal reuniting with,
187–188, 251; modernity and, 189–190;
as Mother India, 43, 158–161, 166–168,
293n66; name origins of, 158; as
nation-state allegory, 157–161; as
parasite, 156; punishment of, 46, 181,
210; recognition for, 196; redemption
of, 240–241; Robert threatening, 27,
104, 185, 239; Sai Baba and, 27, 104, 161,
170–173, 185–188, 240; salvation for, 170;
Santoshi Maa pendant of, 153–155, 176,
181, 185, 208, 223, 239, 246, 277n47;
saris of, 163, 166, 189, 213, 216, 287n18;
as sinner, 164; sons protected from
blindness by, 195; submission and,
171–174, 189; suffering of, 152, 174, 176;
suicide note of, 37–38, 156–157, 162–163,
176, 210, 212, 263n13, 286n11, 291–292n48;
tuberculosis and, 37, 155, 162, 164–165,
179–181, 292n49; voice of, 197–198; as
widow, 163–164, 176
Bharatiya Janata Party (BJP), 57, 138
Bhatia, Sidharth, 73, 166, 207, 253n3,
258n72, 278n53, 296n1
Bijli, 30, 99, 100–101, 106, 232, 241,
287n16
Biological fathers, 40, 117, 149, 160,
286–287n12; Amar disobeying, 66–67;
broken families and, 44–45; distrusting,
45; punishment of, 46
Biomorality, of Gandhi, 60–61
Blind men and elephant fable, 5–6, 254n9

Blindness, 51, 150, 162, 166, 169, 172, 178,
183, 187, 217, 239, 292n49; of Bharati,
150, 161, 165, 168–169, 181, 195, 217; of
Bharati in City of Illusion, 168; Bharati
protecting sons from, 195; as challenge,
165; Mother India protecting nation
from, 195; possession and, 180–181;
as symbolic epidemic, 161
Blood sacrifice, 147, 173, 178, 182–183,
193–194, 294n67
Bluff Master (1963), 72
Bobby (1973), 77, 132, 271n1
Body politic, 56–57
Bollywood films, 2, 57–58, 96, 133, 139,
150, 151, 212, 255n27, 256n49, 258n75,
261n108, 269n69, 271n3, 274n20,
292n53, 295n2, 296nn6–7; class in, 17;
formula of, 17; hallmarks of, 16–17; Islam
in, 273n17; *mahurat* in, 276n38; *masala*
films as foundation of, 15; mass audience
appeal of, 17–18; romance in, 150;
running times of, 272n11; terminology
history of, 15–16
Bombay, 2, 7–9, 12–17, 20, 58, 70, 71, 79,
81, 87, 90, 96–98, 101, 103, 105, 109, 120,
124, 125, 127–130, 136, 140, 175, 179, 185,
187, 204, 207–209, 212, 216, 217, 219, 238,
247, 254n4, 260n105, 260nn100–103,
261n107, 272n6, 276n37, 276n44,
276nn40–41, 280n25, 281n31, 281n35,
292n53, 296n6, 298n30, 299n43,
300n48; as allegory, 25–31; as City of
Illusion, 168; as fantasy, 110–111; forest
mythology and, 27, 31; geography of
time and, 25–26, 30–31, 166–167; holy
places in, 129, 185; Islam in, 86; location
shooting in, 26, 261; modernity and, 90,
98, 110, 167–168, 185, 195; name change
of, 35; Portuguese Catholics shaping
history of, 130–131; sea mythology and,
26; suburbs of, 25–28, 31, 109, 111,
166–167, 189–190
Borivali neighborhood, 26, 28, 31, 167, 212,
244, 260n102
Borivali Park (Sanjay Gandhi National
Park), 27–28, 98, 181, 210, 225, 276n37
Bose, Subhas Chandra, 193–194
Brahmacarya code, 61–62, 63, 69, 267n52

British sportsmanship, Gandhi's pacifism compared to, 268n61

Broken families: adoptive fathers and, 45; biological fathers and, 44–45; in *Chhalia,* 50; India and Pakistan Partition metaphor of, 42–43; punishment of, 46

Buddhism, 127, 254n9, 280n20, 280n24, 288n27

Burman, R. D., 130

Butalia, Urvashi, 54, 265n33, 265n35

Car chase locations, 27, 103, 235, 260n103

Celibacy, 154; *brahmacarya* code and, 61–62, 69, 267n52; *dharma* and, 266–267n48; Gandhi and, 60–61; night emissions and, 267–268n58. *See also* Sexuality

Central Jail, 30–31, 208

Central Recovery Operation, 53, 58, 265n32

Chacha Bhatija (1977), 7, 12

Chattopadhyay, Bankim Chandra, 158

Chaudhvin Ka Chand (1960), 87–88, 95, 274n23, 274–275n25, 275n30

Chesterton, G. K., 150

Chhalia (1960), 32–33, 59, 66, 264n22, 264n25, 264n28, 264–265n29; *Amar Akbar Anthony*'s similarities to, 54; broken families in, 50; framework of virtue in, 52–53; Partition and repatriation of women in, 53–54; Partition's unjust world in, 52; story of, 50–52

Chopra, Yash, 21, 151, 258n75, 269n69, 285n1, 298n23

Christianity, 2, 4, 13, 34, 66, 123, 145, 157, 160, 257n54, 280nn24–25, 281n36, 282n38, 285n71; *Amar Akbar Anthony* protested by, 125; Anglo Christians, 134–135, 137; Anthony and, 115–116, 143–144; in Anthonyville, 261n106; *Bobby* and, 132; cinematic representation of, 131–133; colonialism and, 127, 141–142; Confirmation in, 118; conversion critiques of, 137–139; Desai on English and, 129; as Hinduism's opposite, 142; in India, 126–128, 133–135, 283n54; Indian Christians, 134–135, 138–139; Indian national flag and, 133–134; India's demographics of, 280n25; *Julie* and, 131–132; masculinity in, 62, 142; missionaries and, 127, 141–142; muscular, 62; naming of Anthony and, 118–119; as neutral, 133–134; "othering" of, 134; personalized, 129; personal law for, 135, 137; Robert as stereotype of, 135; romance and, 230; "ten percent" rule in, 124; as villain, 139–140; Western clothes and, 284n60, 296n6

C.I.D. (1956), 294n68

Class, 4, 51, 72, 88, 92, 98, 109, 121, 122, 124, 129, 132, 160, 176, 177, 207, 209, 229, 230, 255n25, 264n20, 268n61, 276n44, 280n27, 298n25; in Bollywood films, 17; Desai on, 20–21; poverty, 111; realism and, 9; romance and, 295n2; theaters and, 1–2

Cobras, 22, 186, 236, 240, 292n55, 300n49

Cohen, Lawrence, 294n67

Colonialism, 24, 26, 29, 30, 77, 82–84, 87–88, 111, 131, 133–134, 143–144, 146, 148, 158, 167, 189, 193, 219, 225, 245, 268n59, 278n1, 284n68; Christianity and, 127, 141–142; missionaries and, 127, 141–142; psychic internalization of ("intimate enemy"), 141; Robert as remnant of, 140, 184; selfhood and, 142

Confirmation, in Catholicism, 118

Congress Party, 1, 51, 105, 108, 277nn50–51, 297n19

Conversion, 103, 127, 137–140, 146, 149, 159, 283n51, 285n71

Coolie (1983), 19, 259n90, 294n68, 298n23

Critics, 10, 18, 32, 53, 138, 151, 177, 255n25, 255n27; *Amar Akbar Anthony* reactions of, 3–4, 6–8, 254n4; Bachchan's reception by, 120; contrasting expectations of, 7; *masala* film metaphors used by, 13–14; of Urdu literature, 84

Daṇḍa. See Rod

Darshan, 289n30, 295n5

Dasgupta, Rana, 115, 260n99

Dasgupta, Susmita, 122

Decoy, 45; Robert held at gunpoint by,
    226; Robert kidnapping, 225; sacrifice
    of, 160, 284n70; *shakti* of, 159–160
Dedh Ishqiya (2014), 275n26
Deewaar (1975), 151, 155, 269n69,
    285nn1–2, 285n4, 298n23, 299n44
Desai, Manmohan, 2, 7, 8, 10, 13-14, 31–34,
    36, 50, 66, 85, 101, 103, 105, 110, 115, 122,
    128-130, 133, 177, 194, 199, 253n3,
    256n32, 256n49, 258n71-72, 259n84,
    259n92, 260n96, 261–262n3, 264n22,
    271n85, 275n33, 278n53, 285n1, 292n56,
    294n68, 298n23; Benegal on social
    messages and, 18, 24; blockbuster
    success of, 8, 73; children as audience
    of, 259n84; on Christianity and English,
    129; on class, 20–21; criticism of, 6;
    crowd-pleasing techniques of, 13; death
    of, 73; escapism and, 18–20; fantasy of,
    20; flops of, 73; on *Garam Hawa,* 266n40;
    Khetwadi neighborhood nostalgia of,
    71–72; kinship emotion used by, 259n79;
    Kishanlal's suffering compared to, 72–73;
    on Krishna, 73; "lost and found" genre
    work of, 11–12, 21; mood manipulation in
    work of, 22, 259n90; morality in films of,
    23–25, 54–55; mythological tropes
    borrowed by, 2; narrative recycling of,
    21–22; politics and, 281n36; on Rafi's
    comeback, 96–97; on realism, 20; social
    messages in films of, 18–19, 24–25
Desh Premee (1982), 36
Destination: Bombay (1976), 276n37
Devdas (1935, 1955, 2002), 77, 87, 271n3
Devi, 178, 197; Shiva and, 172, 187–189,
    191-192, 197
Devi (1960), 291n46
Devi Mahatmya, 197, 295n74
Dharam Veer (1977), 7, 10, 12, 260n96
Dharma (duty), 37, 46, 53, 55, 56, 63, 66, 72,
    102, 112, 163, 210, 254n5, 269n68, 297n19;
    Amar pursuing, 36, 47–50, 56; Bharati's
    mistake of, 164–165; celibacy and, 266n48
Dil Se (1998), 79, 272n6
Disease, 32, 178, 182; goddess worship
    and, 45, 179–180, 291n44
Disraeli, Benjamin, 144–146, 148, 284n67,
    298n32

Divinity, 34, 62, 153, 170, 289n30, 292n56;
    Amar protected by, 261n2; of Bharati,
    176–177, 194–195; gender and, 290n42;
    Hinduism and recognition of, 175–176
    (see also *Shakti*); mass audiences
    accepting, 177
Diwali, 173, 188, 240
Doniger, Wendy, 266n48, 269n65, 269n69,
    288n20
Du Bois, W. E. B., 278n54
Durga, 22, 178, 180, 300n49
Dutt, Guru, 77, 87, 95, 271n3, 274–275n25
Duty. See *Dharma*
Dwyer, Rachel, 4, 254n4, 254n7, 256n48,
    257n55, 266n42, 271n2
Dyer, Reginald, 23–24, 259n95

Easter, 29, 47, 117, 119, 124, 132–133,
    144–146, 148, 226–228
Egnor, Margaret Trawick, 180, 287n18
Elison, William, 277n48, 288n29
Emergency, 1, 25, 36, 42, 255n19, 256n32,
    275n35, 277n51, 279n7; state corruption
    during, 124, 280n23; state sterilizations
    during, 42, 59, 63, 266n45
Emerson, Ralph Waldo, 150
English, 8, 16, 24, 35, 76–79, 100, 120, 123,
    127, 136, 144, 145, 160, 200, 212, 215, 217,
    220, 227, 228, 232, 237, 244, 254n9,
    277n51, 284n69, 291n45, 295n1, 296n2,
    297n21, 298n23, 298n32; alienation from
    "masses" of speakers of, 255n25; Anthony
    speaking, 280n28; Christianity and, 129
Escapism, 18–20
Essentials of Hindutva, The (Savarkar),
    138–139, 284n55, 284n59

Familial disintegration. *See* Broken families
Family values and the state, 58–59, 67
Fantasy, 16, 19–25, 92, 110–111, 116, 270n80,
    272n10
Faruqi, Shamsur Rahman, 84, 273n15
Fathers, 12, 24, 28, 30, 37–43, 47, 48, 50, 51,
    54, 60, 64, 65, 68–78, 89, 91, 93, 94, 98,
    99, 101, 103, 105–107, 112, 113, 116, 117,
    119, 125, 131, 132, 137, 140, 148, 149,

152–154, 156, 159, 160, 176, 190, 210,
212–217, 225, 230–232, 241–249, 259n94,
260n104, 261n1, 261n111, 262n10,
262nn7–8, 263n12, 263nn16–18, 270n76,
274n19, 275n29, 278n3, 282n41,
284–285n70, 286–287n12, 286n11,
297n15, 298nn24–25, 299n44, 300n56;
adoptive, 45–46, 147; biological, 44–46,
66–67. *See also* Kishanlal; Robert
Filmfare, 6–8, 12; awards, 7
Film genres, 7, 17, 256n29; "lost and
found," 10–12, 21; *masala* films, 2, 13–15,
22; "multi-starrer," 10–11, 139; "social,"
10, 12–13. *See also* Muslim social genre
Filmi (style), 32, 62, 96, 256n39, 261n13,
274n23
Filmi, Filmi, Inspector Ghote (Keating),
15–16, 257n51
Film noir, 281n35
Fire in Babylon (2010), 298n26
Fourth wall, breaking, 203–204

Gandhi, Indira, 1, 24, 43, 58, 105, 215,
266n43, 277nn50–51
Gandhi, Mohandas K., 36, 39–40, 43, 62,
105, 116, 122, 128, 142, 159, 169, 193–194,
211–212, 254n5, 260n96, 266n46,
273n16, 276n45, 288n26, 297n19; Akbar
as heir to, 103; Akbar Ilahabadi and, 85;
biomorality of, 60–61; British sportsmanship compared to pacifism of,
268n61; celibacy and, 60–61; on
conversion over coercion, 103; Gandhi-
anism, 35; Kishanlal compared to, 38;
nonviolence of, 37–38 268n62, 277n46;
statue of, 27, 37–40, 43, 67, 103, 159,
210–212, 299n42
Gangaa Jamunaa Saraswathi (1988), 23,
73, 285n1
Ganga Jamuna Saraswati (2012), 259n92
Ganti, Tejaswini, 16, 254n4
Garam Hawa (1973), 58, 266n40
Gender, 2, 33, 34, 47, 49, 53, 92, 95, 101,
133, 141, 142, 161, 166, 178, 180, 190, 192,
195, 232, 264n23, 267n49, 268n61,
272n6, 272n9, 274n22, 276n42, 285n71;
divinity and, 290n42

Geography of time, Bombay and, 25–26,
30–31, 166–167
Geraftaar (1985), 261n1
Goan Catholic musicians, 33, 130, 281n32
Goddesses, 54, 151–155, 158, 159, 175, 181,
184–186, 189–191, 197–198, 208, 210, 218,
277n47, 285n5, 286n6, 289–290n38,
290n40, 290n43, 290nn45–46, 292n49,
292n51, 292n55, 293n61, 293n66,
294nn72–73, 295n5, 297n11, 299–300n47,
300n49; Bharati's possession of,
177–178, 182–183, 187; blood sacrifice
and, 182–183; disease and worship of,
45, 179–180, 291n44; domesticating, 192;
Hinduism qualities of, 176–177, 188;
localized, 61, 293n59; modernity and,
192; Mother India's persona as, 193–194;
restoring primacy of, 192–193, 196;
teams of, 180; volatility and danger of,
178–179
Gonsalves, Anthony Prabhu, 130, 281n31
Grandmother, of Lakshmi, 35, 48, 56–58,
90, 163, 218, 298n25
Great Gama, 135, 282nn43–44
Guide (1965), 280n28, 281n35
Guns, 36–37, 55, 63, 112, 160, 223, 235,
243, 261n2, 296n4, 297n13; Amar and
unearthing of, 68–71; Amar burying,
40–41, 60–62, 208; Amar's sexuality and
burial of, 60; as childhood and poverty
representation, 70–71; of Decoy pointed
at Robert, 226; Inspector Khanna
wounded by, 42; Kishanlal and, 41–42;
of Kishanlal given to Amar, 262n5,
270n76; Kishanlal shooting at Robert
with, 209; *Mahabharata*'s Rod compared
to, 64; morality and, 41–42; as phallic,
60; Robert shooting Inspector Khanna
with, 219; Robert shooting Kishanlal
with, 219; Shiva's self-castration and
Amar burying, 62, 64–65

Haham, Connie, 259n90, 260n96,
261–262n3, 266n40
Haider Ali, 28, 39, 103, 154, 163–164, 182,
211, 241, 244, 246–248, 273n12, 274n19,
292n56

"Hamko Tumse Ho Gaya Hai Pyar Kya Karein," 26, 28, 81, 97–98, 229–231, 275n31, 276n37, 298n23

Helen, 159–160, 225, 287n13, 287n16, 298n30

Helen, Queen of the Nautch Girls (1973), 287n13

Hercules, 215, 251, 300n57

Heroes, 9, 10, 17, 21, 24, 33, 43, 74, 76–78, 85, 88–90, 92, 94, 99, 101, 102, 108, 109, 112, 113, 116–118, 121–125, 129, 130, 137, 146–148, 154, 158, 183, 194, 201–204, 215, 220, 221, 223, 228, 241, 259n94, 271n3, 272n6, 277n46, 279n12, 282n38, 282n45; Akbar as, 9, 33, 74–77, 81, 106–107; Amar as, 33, 50, 66; Anthony as, 33, 116–117, 119–120, 139, 143–144, 149; each chapter as hero's tale, 5, 33; unity of all, 43, 199–200

Heroic romance, 257n54

Hijras, 47, 101–102, 112–113, 299n37; Akbar assisted by, 101, 232–233

Hindi, 19, 24, 34, 43, 100, 102, 110, 129, 136, 150, 158, 168, 180, 200–202, 217, 232, 237, 271n3, 274n20, 280n28, 284n59, 286–287n12, 288n24, 288n27, 289n32, 290n40, 296n2, 297n12, 297n21; Amar speaking, 78, 271n4; Anthony's style of, 78–79; in Bollywood films, 16; Robert speaking, 136, 185; translating, 35

Hinduism/Hindus, 2, 4, 9, 13, 17, 19, 26, 31–34, 36, 39, 44, 46–50, 58–62, 66, 77–79, 96, 100, 102–104, 116, 118, 119, 131, 133, 134, 137–140, 144, 149, 142, 151–154; 157–160, 163–164, 168–170, 172, 174–178, 183–192, 196, 198, 208, 211, 257n54, 264n28, 279n6, 280n24, 282n38, 283n49, 290n41; abduction of women in, 265n35; Amar and Bharati as diverging tendencies within, 190–191; Anthony rejecting, 157; as Anthony's true nature, 126; Bombay's holy places for, 185; *Chhalia* and virtue in, 52–53; Christianity as opposite of, 142; goddess qualities in, 176–177, 188; Indian Christians and, 138–139; maintenance in, 292n56; masculinity in, 142; possession in, 177–178; recognition of

divinity in, 175–176; romance and, 230; Sai Baba absorbed in, 186–187; two camps of, 191; Village Hinduism, 178, 192–193; widows in, 163–164. *See also* Muscular Hinduism

Hindutva, 57, 58, 138, 273n17, 284n58

Hitchens, Christopher, 137–138

Holi festival, 19, 258n75, 259n92

Homelessness, 57, 106, 162–164, 167, 168, 178, 179, 188, 290n41

Homeopathy, 31–32

Hum Kisise Kum Naheen (1977), 272n8

Hussain, Nazir, 90, 212

Ilahabadi, Akbar. *See* Akbar Ilahabadi

Imprisonment, 1, 37, 40, 59, 64, 67, 70, 153, 187, 208, 220, 223, 237, 238, 239, 261n109, 261n3, 262n5, 263n15, 270n79; state and, 159

India Act of 1858, 144

Indian Christians, 13, 26, 29, 31–34, 47, 62, 66, 103, 115, 126, 127, 129, 130–133, 134–135, 138–146, 149, 212

Inspector Khanna, 40–42, 47, 49, 55, 67, 91, 154, 214, 217, 251, 261n1, 284–285n70; Amar found and raised by, 38–39, 181–182, 212; Amar visiting hospital bed of, 220; gun wound of, 42; Robert firing gun at, 219

Intimate Enemy, The: Loss and Recovery of Self under Colonialism (Nandy), 141–142, 278n1, 284n64

"Intimate enemy," 34, 53, 115, 142–144, 148–149

Iqbal, Muhammad, 84

Irony, 7, 34, 36, 61, 125, 127, 258n68; Anthony and, 115–116, 118, 121, 125, 127, 133, 145–146; film logic of morality compared to, 10; in "My Name Is Anthony Gonsalves," 121; in postmodern Indian cinema, 18

Islam, 2, 13, 30, 34, 66, 77, 78, 80, 81, 84, 93, 96, 103, 104, 108, 133, 134, 139, 163, 169, 172–173, 216, 233, 240, 257n54, 273n13, 275n29, 277n48, 280nn24–25, 282n38, 296n5, 298n23, 300n53; in Bollywood films, 273n17; in Bombay,

86; maintenance in, 292n56; public urination and, 297n14; romance and, 230–231; submission and, 174; veil of stereotypes of, 113. *See also* Muslim social genre; Muslim subplot

It's a Wonderful Life (1946), 165

Jainism, 254n9, 280nn24–25
Jai Santoshi Maa (1975), 152–153, 164, 175–176, 285n5, 289n34, 289n38, 295n5
Jallian Wala Bagh (1977), 259–260n95
Jallianwala Bagh massacre, 24, 259n95
Jay-Z, 262n10
Jeevan, 10, 136, 208, 237
Jenny, 26, 28, 29, 103, 107, 136, 137, 143, 159, 231, 238, 246–249, 263nn12–14, 263nn17–18, 264n20, 275n31, 277n47, 278–279n4, 278n3, 283n49, 284n70, 298n35, 299n40; Anthony saving, 147, 236–237; Anthony's courtship of, 47–48, 226–227, 229; Anthony's karmic connection to, 116–118; cobra attacking, 236, 292n55, 300n49; Kishanlal explains loss of sons to, 225; Kishanlal kidnapping, from Robert, 43–45, 219; Kishanlal told of wedding news of, 244–245; Robert refused by, 45; Robert stalking, 224–225; Salma diagnosing pregnancy of, 250; *shakti* lacking in, 160–161; as veil of illusion to Anthony, 112, 228; wedding dress tailored for, 244; winners and losers configured around, 143; Zabisko bringing Robert to, 234; Zabisko meets, 226; Zabisko refused by, 200–201; Zabisko tying up, 234–236
Jesus, 38, 105, 152, 154, 159, 169, 170, 203, 212, 213, 220, 285n3; Anthony's badge of, 298n23; Anthony's devotion to, 123, 125–126, 128–129; Anthony's donations to, 123–126, 128; Anthony talking to, 147; in India, 127; Padre's death juxtaposed with bleeding of, 245, 263n18, 284n70; Santoshi Maa teaming up with, 154
John Jaffer Janardhanan (1982), 253n2
Johnny Gaddaar (2007), 281n35
Johny Mera Naam (1970), 281n35

Juhu neighborhood, 28, 261n109, 299n39
Julie (1975), 131–132

Kaagaz Ke Phool (1959), 271n3
Kali, 151, 153, 178–179, 188, 194
Kama (pleasure), 46–47, 49, 63, 72
Kapoor, Kamal, 91, 212
Kapoor, Prithviraj, 78
Kapoor, Raj, 51, 76–78, 132, 146, 271n1, 300n56
Kapoor, Rishi, 81, 87, 93, 108, 132, 214, 272n8, 277n46, 277n52, 278n53, 278n56, 297n17; cinema family heritage of, 76–77; physical features of, 77
Kapoor, Shammi, 72
Kapoor, Shashi, 151
Karna, 279n12
Keating, H. R. F., 15–16, 257n52
Khan, Kader, 85, 276n41
Khan, Mehboob, 285n4, 292n51
Khan, Salman, 296n7
Khan, Shah Rukh, 79, 133–134, 271n3
Khan, Syed Ahmad, 89
Khanna, Vinod, 57–58, 62, 76, 214, 259–260n95, 292n56
Khetwadi neighborhood, 20, 71–73, 101, 129, 276n41
Khoon Pasina (1977), 285n1
Kinsley, David, 288n22, 293n61
Kishanlal, 26–30, 37–46, 67–73, 103–4, 107, 112, 116–120, 136–137, 140, 143, 147, 149, 153–156, 160, 162, 167, 176, 184, 185, 189, 190, 192, 203, 208, 211, 223, 225, 234, 238, 261n111, 262–263n11, 263n15, 263n18, 263nn12–13, 266n37, 270n74, 270nn77–79, 277n47, 278–279n4, 278n3, 283nn48, 286–287n12, 286n11, 291–292n48, 292n54, 297n8, 299n42, 299nn39–40, 300n51; Amar abandoned by, 39, 67, 212; Amar gun gift from, 262n5, 270n76; Amar imprisoning, 70; Amar reuniting with, 68–71, 243–244; Anthony escaping capture of, 223; Anthony reuniting with, 246; Bharati abandoning, 181; Bharati reuniting with, 187–189, 251; children forgetting, 44; Desai's suffering compared to, 72–73;

Kishanlal *(continued)*
  family reunification request of, 67–68;
  Gandhi compared to, 38; guns and,
  41–42; Jenny listens to story of lost sons
  of, 225; Jenny's wedding news told to,
  244–245; Jenny taken from Robert by,
  43–45, 219; Koliwada neighborhood
  nostalgia of, 71, 243, 270n80; outlandish
  outfits of, 298n29; release from jail, 208;
  Robert chasing, 103–104, 209–210,
  235–237; Robert firing gun at, 219;
  Robert shot by, 209; Robert sought by,
  221; Robert's promise with, 209;
  Robert's similarities to, 262n11, 283n49;
  Robert trading identities with, 43;
  Robert working for, 218–220; Salma
  attempting to revive, 239; secularism
  practiced by, 137
Kismet (1943), 130, 293n66
Kissa Kursi Ka (1975), 58, 266n39
Kolis, 29, 70, 127, 167, 296n3
Koliwada neighborhood, 29–30, 68, 70, 72,
  111, 127, 179, 188, 208, 299n42; Amar
  and Kishanlal's nostalgia for, 71, 243,
  270n80; fishing and, 296n3; unchanging
  poverty in, 167; as veil of illusion, 112
Krishna, 73, 176, 195, 258n75
Kumar, Ashok, 89, 91
Kumar, Dilip, 77
Kumar, Kishore, 97, 275n35, 284n66
Kumar, Rajendra, 77, 89–90, 95
Kumari, Meena, 91, 95, 274–275n25, 274n24
Kumar Talkies (2000), 253n1
Kurosawa, Akira, 4

Laila Majnu (1976), 272n8, 278n56
Lakshmi, 29, 45, 50, 54, 65, 140, 160, 163,
  185, 192, 217–218, 231, 245, 249, 250,
  261n109, 267n52, 298–299n35, 298n25;
  Amar entrapped by, 47–48, 56, 217–218;
  Amar offering home instead of jail to, 57,
  218; domestication of, 230; grandmother
  of, 48, 56–58, 218; Ranjeet manhandling, 247–248; rehabilitation of, 58–59;
  rough background of, 48; stepmother of,
  45, 48, 56–57, 218, 261n109, 287n14,
  298n25; as wayward woman, 49, 58–59

Lakshmi (Hindu goddess), 151, 153, 192
Lal Baadshah (1999), 285n1
Layla and Majnun, The Story of (Nizami),
  277n46
Lord of the Rings, The (2001), 20
"Lost and found" genre, 10–12, 21–23, 130,
  259n79
Lucknow, 86–92, 99, 101, 105, 107, 109–110,
  260n105, 274n21
Lutgendorf, Philip, 4, 24, 66, 269n72,
  285n5, 289n34

Maa. *See* Bharati
Maai-baap, 56, 223, 286–287n12
Maara-maari, 102
Madhumati, 99, 232, 287n16
Mahabharata, 2, 21, 73, 158, 188,
  269nn65–68 ,291n47, 292n50; Amar
  compared to Rama in, 65–67; Karna in,
  279n12; Rod in, 63–64, 269n68; Shiva's
  self-castration in, 62–65
Mahal (1949), 130
Mahurat (inaugural shot), 276n38
Mard (1985), 22–24, 73, 260n96, 285n1
Mariamma, 180
Masala films, 10, 18, 23, 75, 102, 121, 122,
  254n4, 256n49, 259n92, 274n20; artistry
  in, 22; Bollywood film foundations in,
  15; critics beginning to use metaphor of,
  13–14; elements of, 2; genre emergence
  of, 14–15; goal of, 14
Masculinity, 49, 62, 141–144, 230,
  266-267n48, 268n59
Mass audiences, 1, 4, 10, 12, 13, 21, 50, 61,
  81, 121, 122, 166, 183, 255n25, 255n27,
  288n26, 292n51, 295n2; *Amar Akbar
  Anthony*'s appeal to, 8–9; Bollywood
  films' appeal to, 17–18; divinity and, 177;
  English-speakers' alienation from,
  255n25. *See also* Audiences
Master Bittu, 208
Master Ravi, 208
Master Tito, 208
Matter of Life and Death, A (1946), 165
Maya (cosmic illusion), 168, 170, 278n55
Mera Naam Joker (1971), 76, 271n1
Mere Mehboob (1963), 87–89, 95, 110

Midnight's Children (Rushdie), 42–43, 262n7

Mira, 278n55

Mishra, Vijay, 3, 207, 254n5, 279n9, 281n36, 283n46

Missionaries, colonialism and, 127, 141–142

Morality, 2, 267–268n58; of Amar, 39, 54, 81; of Anthony, 125; in Desai's films, 23–25, 54–55; film logic of irony compared to, 10; Gandhi and biomorality, 60–61; guns and, 41–42; state and, 59

Moreno, Manuel, 179, 290–291n43

Mother India, 4, 34, 286n10, 288n28; Akbar's view of, 183; Amar's view of, 183–184; Anthony's view of, 157–159, 166; Bharati as, 43, 158–161, 166–168, 293n66; as goddess persona, 193–194; modernity and, 168, 188–190, 192; nationalist concept of, 158; nation protected from blindness by, 195; recognition for, 196; revival of, 184; *shakti* of, 161

Mother India (1957), 285n4, 292n51

Mothers, 5, 9, 12, 33, 34, 44, 46, 51, 56, 67, 69–73, 88, 90, 91, 106, 114, 118, 123, 128, 129, 162, 166–167, 169, 175, 177–184, 187–191, 194–198, 212–217, 222–224, 241–243, 250, 254n5, 259n94, 262n7, 263n19, 273n12, 275n28, 279n12, 281n36, 286–287n12, 286n7, 286n11, 289n38, 291n45, 292n55, 294n67, 294n69, 298n25; Anthony without, 154–155; Bharati as bad, 155–156; grown men crying out for, 150; as nation-state allegory, 157–161; Roy playing, 151; Santoshi Maa as, 152–154; satisfaction of, 152–153; suffering of, 151–152, 174, 176; as villains, 157; Virgin Mary as, 152. *See also* Bharati

Mount Mary church, 29, 212, 226, 244

Mughal-e-Azam (1960), 78, 113, 264n22

Mukesh, 97

Mukri, 98, 216

Mulchand, 247

"Multi-starrer" genre, 10–11, 17, 139, 292n92

Mumbai. *See* Bombay

Munimji (1955), 294n67

Muqaddar Ka Sikandar (1978), 285n1

Muscular Christianity, 62, 268n60

Muscular Hinduism, 34, 36, 62

Musical numbers, 17, 75, 103, 272–273n11; dream-as-reality in, 80; elite vocalists for, 95; in Muslim social genre, 92; mystical tropes in, 80–81, 108, 113–114, 168; poetry and, 79; running times of, 272–273n11; time and, 79–80, 195; truth and, 110; unpredictability of, 201

Muslim Quarter, 28, 30, 106, 110, 114, 241, 260n105, 261n110, 276n40, 277n51, 293n58; history and, 86; production design of, 100–101

Muslim social genre, 30, 74, 77, 80, 96, 102, 108, 131, 274–275n25, 275n26, 300n54; *Chaudhvin Ka Chand* in, 87–88; features of, 75; Lucknow and, 86–92, 101, 109–110; *Mere Mehboob* in, 88–89, 95; musical numbers in, 92; origins of, 86–92; *Pakeezah* in, 91–92, 95–96; *Palki* in, 90–91, 95, 107, 113; voyeurism and, 99

Muslim subplot, 75, 113, 114, 231–233, 287n16; Akbar's courtship of Salma in, 92–95; "Hamko Tumse Ho Gaya Hai Pyar Kya Karein" and, 97–98; history and, 77; origins of, 86–92; parody and, 75, 109; resolution of, 106–107; third act of, 104. *See also* Akbar

My Name Is Anthony Gonsalves, 278n2

"My Name Is Anthony Gonsalves," 81, 112, 116, 118, 227–228, 274–275n18, 280n28, 295n2; Bachchan's performance of, 144; irony in, 121; popularity of, 129

Mystical tropes, in musical numbers, 80–81, 108, 113–114, 168

Nadira, 218, 287n14

Naming, 128, 202; of Anthony in Christianity, 118–119; familial aspiration and, 263n19

Nanavati Hospital, 28, 128, 213–214, 237

Nandy, Ashis, 77, 115, 141–143, 148, 284nn64–65

Narayanan, Vasudha, 191, 291n45

Narrative recycling, 2, 54, 259n92; of
  Desai, 21–24
Naseeb (1981), 21–22, 66, 281n36
National integration, 4, 31, 61, 281n36;
  Anthony and failure of, 116; exchange of
  blood for, 294n67; nonviolence and, 102;
  religion and, 12–13; secular ideology
  and, 105; unity in, 201
Navrang (1959), 278n56
Nayar, Kuldip, 124, 280n23
Night emissions, 61, 267n58
Nonviolence, 28, 40; Akbar and, 38,
  102–103, 107, 292n53; of Gandhi,
  37–38, 210, 297n12; national integration
  and, 102

O'Flaherty, Wendy Doniger. *See* Doniger,
  Wendy
Originality, *Amar Akbar Anthony*'s lack of,
  2, 7

Padre, 29, 35, 38, 90, 123, 124, 126, 129,
  148, 154, 156, 160, 182, 227, 285n3,
  286n7, 286n11, 300n53; Anthony
  criticized by, 128, 213; Anthony raised
  by, 137, 212; death of, 119, 125, 147,
  245–246, 263n18, 284–285n70;
  forgiveness of, 131; Jesus bleeding
  juxtaposed with death of, 245, 263n18,
  284–285n70; wedding excitement of,
  244
Pakeezah (1972), 87, 91–92, 95–96, 98, 104,
  274n24, 274–275n25, 300n54
Pakistan, 42–43, 53, 54, 84, 253n2,
  264–265n29, 269–270n72, 282n44
Palki (1967), 87, 90–91, 95, 104, 107, 110,
  113, 275n30, 294n68
Parda. See Veil
"Parda Hai Parda," 29, 46–47, 74, 81, 93,
  97, 102, 113, 114, 255n16, 275n27, 279n5;
  audiences of, 94, 108; compulsion of,
  94–95; performance synopsis of,
  216–217; precedents for, 95; Sufi
  symbolism in, 216
Parinda (1989), 269n69
Paris Is Burning (1991), 276n42

Parody, 22–24, 34, 36, 98, 145, 184,
  283n49, 287n16, 298n29; Muslim
  subplot and, 75, 77, 87, 109
Partition, 4, 36, 50, 57, 58, 59, 254n5,
  264n23, 265nn 32–33, 266n40,
  282n44; broken families metaphor of,
  41–43, 107, 150; *Chhalia* and unjust
  world of, 52; repatriation of women
  after, 53–54; sexual aggression and,
  269n69
Parvarish (1977), 256n32, 292n56
Pedro, 29–30, 140, 247, 249–250
Pleasure. See *Kama*
Poetry, 74, 82, 86–91, 95, 110, 203; Akbar
  and, 80–81, 84–85, 103, 105, 168; of
  Akbar Ilahabadi, 82–85, 273n15; musical
  numbers and, 79; Urdu and, 79
Politics, 13, 24, 33, 47, 56, 60, 97, 103, 116,
  125, 138, 150, 269n69, 278–279n4,
  280n23, 282n38, 283n54, 284n58,
  296n3; of Bachchan and Desai, 281n36
Postcoloniality, 23, 34, 78, 84, 134, 140,
  145, 184
Postmodernism, 18, 33
Portuguese Catholics, 130–131, 283n46
Poseidon Adventure, The (1972), 255n27
Possession, 175, 179, 191, 287n18, 289n37,
  289–290n38, 290–291n43, 291n47; of
  Bharati by goddess, 177–178, 182–183,
  187; blindness and, 180–181; in
  Hinduism, 177–178
Poverty, 24, 37, 38, 69, 90, 111, 114, 212,
  266n43; class of, 111; guns representing
  childhood and, 70–71; Koliwada
  neighborhood unchanging in, 167
Pran, 10, 89, 132, 208, 264n24, 294n67
Prasad, M. Madhava, 17
Princess Bride, The (1987), 295n3
Profit. See *Artha*
Prologue, 6, 37, 103, 123, 128, 156, 208–212,
  254n5, 283n48, 299n40
Protima Devi, 90, 218

Qawwali music, 29, 38, 80, 90, 93–94, 96,
  98, 104, 105, 108, 113, 169, 171–172, 214,
  216–217, 230, 239, 240, 264n20, 272n8,
  275n28, 279n5

Rafi, Mohamed, 35, 81, 95, 104, 108, 110, 113, 114, 214, 255n16, 276n36, 278n56; Desai on comeback of, 96–97; popularity of, 96

Raghavendra, M. K., 14, 18, 254n4

Raghu, 140, 215, 222, 300n57

Rama, 36, 52–54, 56, 133–134, 188, 265n36; Amar compared to, 65–67

Ramaswamy, Sumathi, 193–194, 286n10, 292n51

Ramayana, 21, 36, 188, 264n27, 265nn35–36

Ramlila, 52–53

Ram Robert Rahim (1980), 253n2

Rang De Basanti (2006), 282n38, 294n68

Ranjeet, 27, 48–49, 56, 104, 140, 160, 185, 217–218, 226, 237, 239, 240, 245, 247–251, 279n5, 284n70, 298n25

Rashomon (1950), 4

Ratnam, Mani, 79, 272n6

Ray, Satyajit, 19, 87, 258n72, 274n20, 291n46

Realism, 9, 20, 32, 110, 201, 202–204, 295n2

Reality television, 255n15

Rehman, 87, 90, 95, 264n24, 274–275n25, 275n30

Rehman, A. R., 130

Rehman, Waheeda, 88, 90, 95, 275n30, 294n68

Religion, 2, 21, 33, 36, 39, 76, 92, 118, 123, 126, 127, 131–134, 137, 144, 169, 189–191, 207, 223, 263n12, 273n13, 280n24, 280n27, 285n71, 292n52, 294n67; Amar and, 39–40; Amar as all religions in one, 65–66; Anthony's outlook on, 38, 149; choice and, 139; India's freedom of, 125; national integration and, 12–13; Robert's hybridity of, 135–136; state as, 55, 191, 266n37; unity of all, 202–203, 248. *See also* Christianity; Hinduism; Islam

Repatriation, 52–54, 139, 159, 162

Robert, 26, 27, 29, 37–41, 46, 55, 63–67, 70, 72, 73, 86, 103, 116, 129, 144, 147, 148, 153, 156, 160, 167, 181, 187, 190, 193, 199, 201, 202, 222, 223, 227, 240, 243, 245–250, 261n109, 263nn13–15, 263nn17–18, 270n79, 276n40, 277n47, 278–279n4, 280n21, 281n35, 284n70,

285n3, 292n54, 296n6, 297n16, 297n18, 299n42, 299n45, 300n57; Akbar punching, 107; Albert's antagonistic relationship with, 136–137, 238, 287n15; Amar looking for, 221; Anthony pitted against, 140, 224; Anthony protecting, 220; Bharati escaping from, 104, 185–186, 239; Bharati threatened by, 239; as Christian stereotype, 135; as colonial remnant, 140, 184; Decoy holding gun to, 226; Decoy kidnapped by, 225; henchmen of, 139–140; hybridity of, 135–136; Inspector Khanna shot by, 219; in jail, 251; Jenny refusing, 45; Jenny stalked by, 224–225; Jenny taken by Kishanlal from, 43–45, 219; Kishanlal as boss to, 218–220; Kishanlal chased by, 103–104, 209–210, 235–237; Kishanlal firing gun at, 209; Kishanlal searching for, 221; Kishanlal shot by gun of, 219; Kishanlal's promise with, 209; Kishanlal's similarities to, 262–263n11, 283n49, 298n29; Kishanlal trading identities with, 43; luxurious Westernized lifestyle of, 208; mansion of, 29, 237, 283n48; masculinity lacking in, 142–143; Santoshi Maa pendant of Bharati held by, 239; *shakti* and, 184–185; as "team leader," 139–140; Zabisko bringing Jenny to, 234; Zabisko's plan for Albert and, 238

Rod *(daṇḍa),* 63–64, 69–70, 269n68, 270n76

Romance, 14, 22, 30, 85, 92, 98, 101, 108, 117, 121, 150, 217, 253n1, 271n1, 277n46, 298n34; Christianity and, 230; class and, 295n2; heroic, 257n54; Hinduism and, 230; Islam and, 230–231; three models of, 228–231

Roy, Nirupa, 10, 22–23, 177, 208, 286n6, 294n67; Bachchan's many films with, 151; charisma of, 152; mother characters played by, 151

Rushdie, Salman, 42–43, 262n7

Sadgati (1981), 274n20

Sahib Bibi Aur Ghulam (1962), 274–275n25

Sai Baba, of Shirdi, 104, 203, 300n48;
Akbar praising, 105, 114, 240; Bharati
and, 161, 170–173, 185–187, 196–197;
Hinduism absorbing, 186–187, 196,
293n57, 294n72, 300n49; iconography
of, 186–187, 277n50; practice of
following, 169–170; representations of,
170; secularism and, 187; teachings of,
169, 277n48, 289n30
Sai Baba shrine, 22, 27–28, 104–105, 169–173,
175, 186–189, 240, 292n55, 294n73
Said, Edward, 141
St. Thomas's Church, 29, 212, 244
Salim Langde Pe Mat Ro (1989), 276n44
Salma, 9, 28, 30, 44–47, 75, 97, 99, 101, 102,
104, 108, 109, 161, 168, 203, 216, 217,
247–249, 260n104, 263n16, 264n20,
275n29, 275n31, 298–299n35; Akbar
rescuing, 106–107, 241–242; Akbar's
courtship of, 48, 92–95, 214, 230–233;
attire of, 230; Jenny diagnosed as
pregnant by, 250; Kishanlal operated
on by, 239; veil as accessory for, 98
Saṃsāra, 288n27
Sanjay Gandhi National Park. *See* Borivali
Park
Sanskrit, 35, 64, 78, 138, 158, 179, 191, 210,
271n4, 274n13, 280n28, 288n27, 290n41,
293n61
Santoshi Maa, 105, 155, 158, 161, 171, 175,
181, 192, 193, 285n5, 295n5, 297n11,
299–300n47; Bharati's pendant of,
153–154, 176, 185, 208, 210, 223, 239,
246, 277n47, 283n48; Jesus teaming up
with, 154; as mother figure for Anthony,
154; origins of, 152
Sant Tukaram (1938), 176
Sargam (1979), 277n52
Satya (1998), 269n69
Savarkar, V. D., 138–140, 142, 284n59
Secularism, 3, 4, 12, 13, 31–33, 35, 58, 103, 125,
133; Amar and, 39–40, 55; of Kishanlal,
137; national integration ideology of,
105; resilience of, 254n5; Sai Baba and,
187; unity in, 201; violence and, 40
Selfhood: Anthony finding, 148–149;
colonialism and, 142; Indian predicament of, 141

Sexuality: of Amar and gun burial, 60; of
Amar in service to state, 58–60, 64–65.
See also Celibacy; Romance
Shakti (divine feminine power), 153, 180,
182–184, 187, 192, 193, 195, 198, 277n47,
283n48, 287n16, 290n40, 299–300n47,
299n47; of Decoy, 159–160; heat
manifestation of, 196–197; Jenny lacking,
160–161; of Mother India, 161; Robert
attempting to hold, 185
Sharma, Pyarelal, 130
Shatranj Ke Khilari (1977), 87, 274n20
"Shirdi Wale Sai Baba," 74, 81, 85, 104,
113–114, 161, 169–173, 186, 240–241,
275n28
Shitala Mata, 180, 291n44
Shiva, 36, 73, 196, 269n70, 292n55, 293n57,
294nn72–73, 300n49; Devi and, 178,
187–188, 190, 192; iconography of, 172,
186; self-castration of, 62–65
Shivraj, 211
Shiv Shakti (1952), 286n6
Sholay (1975), 10, 258n75
Shree 420 (1955), 146
Shukla, K. K., 22, 259n79
Shulman, David, 63
Sibling rivalry, 4–5, 33, 136–137, 269–270n72
Sikhism, 32, 51–53, 65–66, 133, 248,
264–266n29, 280nn24–25, 282n38
Silsila (1981), 258n75
Sindoor, 35, 44, 163, 187, 242
Singh, Neetu, 93, 214, 292n56
Smallpox, 180, 291nn 44–46
Smith, Frederick M., 177
"Social" genre, 10, 12–13. *See also* Muslim
social genre
Sportsmanship, 62; Gandhi's pacifism
compared to British, 268n61
Star Wars (1977), 20
State, 3–4, 30, 33, 34, 36–40, 47, 53–54, 78,
83, 87, 102, 105, 116, 121, 124, 137, 149,
166, 188–191, 254n5, 257n55, 263n19,
264–265n29, 264n29, 271n4, 276n43,
280n20, 282n38, 295n4; Amar and rule
of, 54–55; Amar's sexuality and service
to, 58–60, 64–65; Anthony rejecting,
125–126, 158–159, 191; Bharati as allegory
for, 157–161; body politic and, 56;

Emergency and corruption of, 124, 280n23; Emergency and sterilizations by, 41–42, 59, 63, 266n45; family values and, 58–59, 66–67; imprisonment and, 159; morality and, 59; mothers as allegory for, 157–161; as religion, 55, 191; as veil, 84

Stepmother, of Lakshmi, 45, 48–49, 56–57, 185, 218, 261n109, 287n14, 298n25

Sterilizations, by state during Emergency, 41–42, 59, 63, 266n45

Story of Layla and Majnun, The. See *Layla and Majnun, The Story of*

Submission, 107, 114, 193, 251; Bharati and, 170–174, 190; Islam and, 174

Sufism/Sufis, 80, 92, 104–105, 108, 110, 112, 169–174, 186–187, 214, 216, 240, 254n9, 257n54, 275n26, 277n46, 277n48, 288n27, 294n68

Suhaag (1979), 285n1

Suicide note, of Bharati, 37–38, 156–157, 162–163, 176, 210, 212, 263n13, 286n11, 291–292n48

Sujata (1960), 294n67

Takhallus, 82, 85, 89, 202, 274–275n25

Tarlo, Emma, 59

Tayyab Ali, 9, 28–30, 45, 47, 75, 86, 98–102, 106–107, 112–113, 216, 230–234, 241, 242, 261n111, 275n29, 287n16, 296n6, 298n29

"Tayyab Ali Pyar Ka Dushman," 47, 81, 101–102, 112–113, 231–232, 260n105, 277n51

"Ten percent" rule, in Christianity, 124

Theaters, 7, 29, 58, 93, 94, 108, 216, 253n1, 259n92, 272n6, 297n21; class and, 1–2

Thomas, Rosie, 22–23, 157, 255n18, 259n94

"Three-in-oneness," 4, 65, 248

Time: geography of, 25–26, 30–31, 166–167; migration across, 260n99; musical numbers and, 79–80

Title sequence, 81, 118, 183–184, 214–215, 232, 250, 260n103

Tiwari, Bulbul, 291n47

Toofan (1989), 73

Trains, 48, 53, 89, 91, 92, 95, 98, 110, 230–231, 264–265n29, 298n35

Trivarga, 46, 63

Trudeau, Pierre, 58

Tuberculosis, 37, 69, 72, 155, 162, 164–165, 179–181, 208, 292n49

Unity, 4, 195; exchange of blood for, 294n67; of heroes, 199–200; in national integration, 201; of religions, 169, 202–203; in secularism, 201

Urdu, 75, 80, 82, 84, 85, 93–95, 97, 100, 105, 110, 111, 129, 164, 202, 204, 214, 216, 232, 271n4, 273n15, 274–275n25, 297n21; Akbar speaking, 78–79; Akbar writing note in, 247; Lucknow and, 86–92; poetry and, 79; *takhallus* in, 82, 89; theatrical use of, 272n6; translating, 35

"Vande Mataram," 158

Veils, 47, 85, 88–95, 101, 107–108, 111, 168–170, 172, 216–217, 230, 275nn 27–28, 278n54, 279n5; Akbar seeing Tayyab Ali through illusory, 112–113; Anthony seeing Jenny through illusory, 112, 228; of Bharati stripped by Akbar, 106; cinema screen as, 109; of Islamic stereotypes, 113; Koliwada neighborhood through illusory, 112; love as, 112; musical numbers rupturing illusory, 113–114; as Salma's accessory, 98; state as, 84. *See also* "Parda Hai Parda"

Village Hinduism, 178, 192–193

Vimlet, Hotel Raviraj, 420

Violence, 37, 50, 63, 64, 81, 138, 160, 220; Amar and, 40; Anthony's use of, 102–103; in muscular Hinduism, 36; secularism and, 40

Virdi, Jyotika, 3–4, 257n55

Virgin Mary, 152, 154, 161, 285n3

Voyeurism, Muslim social genre and, 99

Vrat (vow), 152, 176, 184, 289n34

Walker, Johnny, 87–90

Waqt (1965), 21

Weber, Max, 40, 55, 262n4
Widows, 43, 154, 176, 218; homelessness and, 163–164
Wizard of Oz, The (1939), 110
Wolfe, Thomas, 73

Yaadon Ki Baaraat (1973), 21
"Yeh Sach Hai Koi Kahani Nahin," 81, 114, 184, 194, 214–215
Yocum, Glenn, 178–179, 290n42
Yusuf, 226

Zabisko, 23, 31, 112, 136, 139, 143, 190, 227, 229, 237, 244, 245, 247, 249–251, 284n70; Akbar tricking, 246; Albert's imprisonment by, 238, 261n109; Anthony fighting, 135, 228; as groom, 248; Jenny brought to Robert by, 234; Jenny meets, 226; Jenny refusing, 200–202; Jenny tied up by, 234–236; sadism and costume of, 287n15
Zanjeer (1973), 261n1, 281n35, 294n67
Zbyszko, Stanislaus, 135, 282n43, 282n45